## DATE DUE

| | |
|---|---|
| | |
| | |
| | |
| | |
| | |
| | |
| | |
| | |
| | |
| | |
| | |
| | |
| | |
| | |

# A HISTORY OF
# *Weber County*

# A HISTORY OF *Weber County*


Richard C. Roberts
Richard W. Sadler



1997
Utah State Historical Society
Weber County Commission

ISBN 0-913738-14-X
Library of Congress Catalog Card Number 96-60679
Map by Automated Geographic Reference Center—State of Utah
Printed in the United States of America

Utah State Historical Society
300 Rio Grande
Salt Lake City, Utah 84101-1182

*Contents*

# *Preface*

On 31 January 1850 the first counties in Utah Territory were established, with Weber County formed first, followed by Great Salt Lake County, Utah County, San Pete County, Tuilla (Tooele) County, and Little Salt Lake County. Weber County was established with a huge territory stretching from the Rocky Mountains to the Sierra Nevada. Over time the county was reduced in size, but it remained very important to the state in terms of its population, its economy, and its influence. Ogden, the county seat, became the "Junction City" for the transcontinental railroad lines in 1869, and the railroad changed Ogden, Weber County, and Utah Territory. Ogden had become the first permanent settlement in the future state when it was founded by fur trapper Miles Goodyear in 1845. The county was formed around Ogden, with the city gaining much of the population and the outlying areas remaining rural. Following World War II, the towns and villages of the county began to grow, and, by 1995, the population of the county was estimated to be 175,000. The economy of the county became more diversified over the last four decades of the twentieth century.

Weber County is more than the land, the people, and the climate. It is an entity that is larger than the combination of all of its parts. The history of the county is a history of pioneers—past and present—who worked to develop the resources found along the banks of the Weber and Ogden rivers and in the hillsides above. It is a history of triumph and failure. It is a history of individuals, families, and communities facing difficulties and challenges and working to make life better for themselves, their children, and their neighbors.

Writing the history of this county has been a community effort, and we have been helped throughout the process by numerous individuals. Weber County commissioners Joe Richie and Joan Hellstrom have championed this project and helped us with advice and support from the very beginning; and their colleague commissioners Spencer Stokes, Bruce Anderson, Randall Williford, and Glen Burton have encouraged and helped us. David Wilson, an attorney with the Weber County Attorney's Office, has been an ongoing advocate for the project and has made our task easier through his intercession.

The staff of the Weber County Library, particularly Fran Zedney, was helpful to us. Lynnda Wangsgard, Weber County Library Director, was most generous with her time and resources, sharing much interest in the project. University librarians John Sillito and Robert Parsons were of great help. JoAnn Reynolds, Beth Taylor, Julie Jenkins, Vicki Smith, Jennifer Judd, and Susie McCreary have assisted at all stages with the technical production of the manuscript. Ben Tueller and James Barnhill of the Weber County Agricultural Extension Service were generous with their time and archival resources.

A number of Weber County residents have assisted us with their time and expertise; they include Clix Swaner, Mark Stuart, Carol Charlesworth, Emma Wilson, Ron Smout, Brian Taylor, Howard Widdison, O. Scott Wayment, Lynn Singleton, Shanna Edwards, Arvil and Ida Mae Hipwell, Donald R. Carpenter, Marilyn Yoshida, Catherine Conklin, John Conklin, and Emma Russell. Brooke S. Arkush, Thomas R. Burton, David Wilson, and Dean Hurst read parts of the manuscript and advised us of needed changes, and Thomas Alexander and Stan Layton gave us invaluable assistance with their critiques of the manuscript. Kent Powell and Craig Fuller have been true colleagues in this process; they assisted us during numerous phases of the project, from the beginning through publication. Richard Firmage, our copy editor, has made this volume better because of his efforts. We take responsibility for any errors in the book.

We express gratitude to our wives, Colleen Roberts and Claudia Sadler, and to our families for their patience with us and assistance to us throughout the project. This history is dedicated to the pioneers of Weber County—past, present, and future.

# *General Introduction*

When Utah was granted statehood on 4 January 1896, twenty-seven counties comprised the nation's new forty-fifth state. Subsequently two counties, Duchesne in 1914 and Daggett in 1917, were created. These twenty-nine counties have been the stage on which much of the history of Utah has been played.

Recognizing the importance of Utah's counties, the Utah State Legislature established in 1991 a Centennial History Project to write and publish county histories as part of Utah's statehood centennial commemoration. The Division of State History was given the assignment to administer the project. The county commissioners, or their designees, were responsible for selecting the author or authors for their individual histories, and funds were provided by the state legislature to cover most research and writing costs as well as to provide each public school and library with a copy of each history. Writers worked under general guidelines provided by the Division of State History and in cooperation with county history committees. The counties also established a Utah Centennial County History Council to help develop policies for distribution of state-appropriated funds and plans for publication.

Each volume in the series reflects the scholarship and interpretation of the individual author. The general guidelines provided by the Utah State Legislature included coverage of five broad themes encompassing the economic, religious, educational, social, and political history of the county. Authors were encouraged to cover a vast period of time stretching from geologic and prehistoric times to the present. Since Utah's statehood centennial celebration falls just four years before the arrival of the twenty-first century, authors were encouraged to give particular attention to the history of their respective counties during the twentieth century.

Still, each history is at best a brief synopsis of what has transpired within the political boundaries of each county. No history can do justice to every theme or event or individual that is part of an area's past. Readers are asked to consider these volumes as an introduction to the history of the county, for it is expected that other researchers and writers will extend beyond the limits of time, space, and detail imposed on this volume to add to the wealth of knowledge about the county and its people. In understanding the history of our counties, we come to understand better the history of our state, our nation, our world, and ourselves.

In addition to the authors, local history committee members, and county commissioners, who deserve praise for their outstanding efforts and important contributions, special recognition is given to Joseph Francis, chairman of the Morgan County Historical Society, for his role in conceiving the idea of the centennial county history project and for his energetic efforts in working with the Utah State Legislature and State of Utah officials to make the project a reality. Mr. Francis is proof that one person does make a difference.

ALLAN KENT POWELL
CRAIG FULLER
GENERAL EDITORS

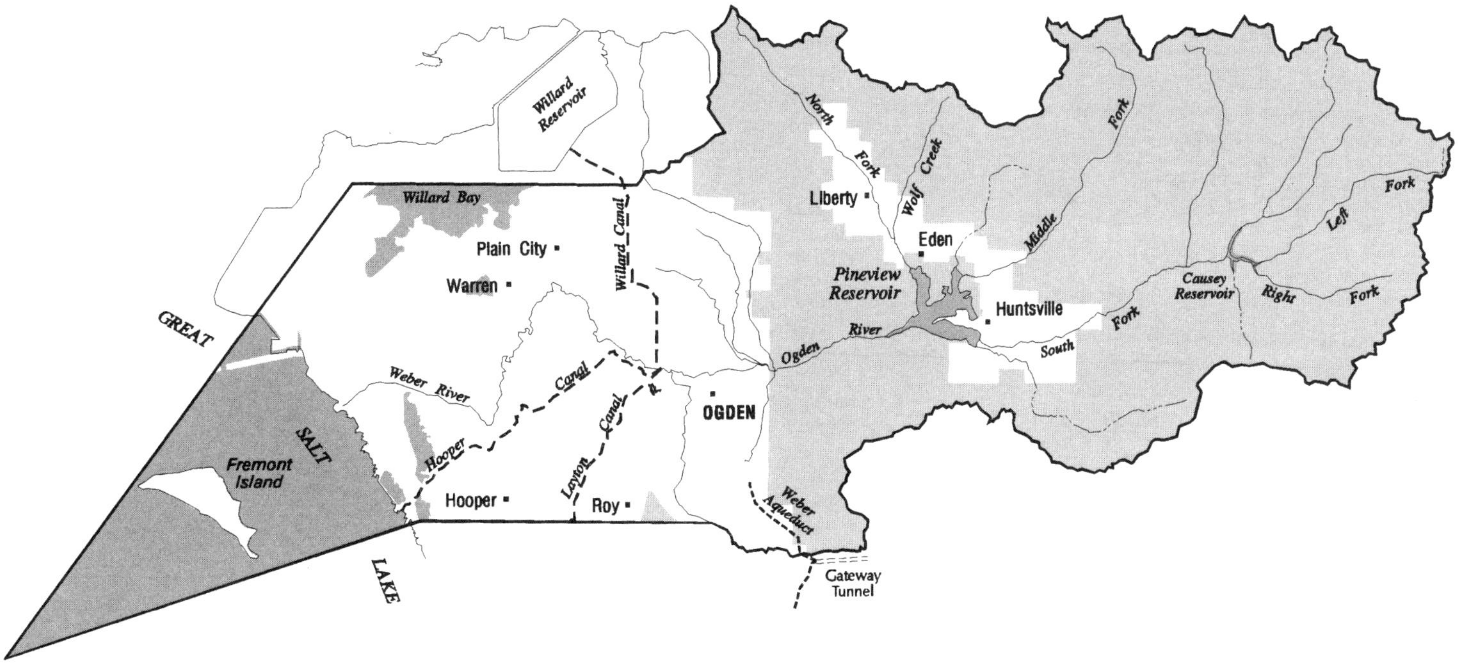


# WEBER COUNTY

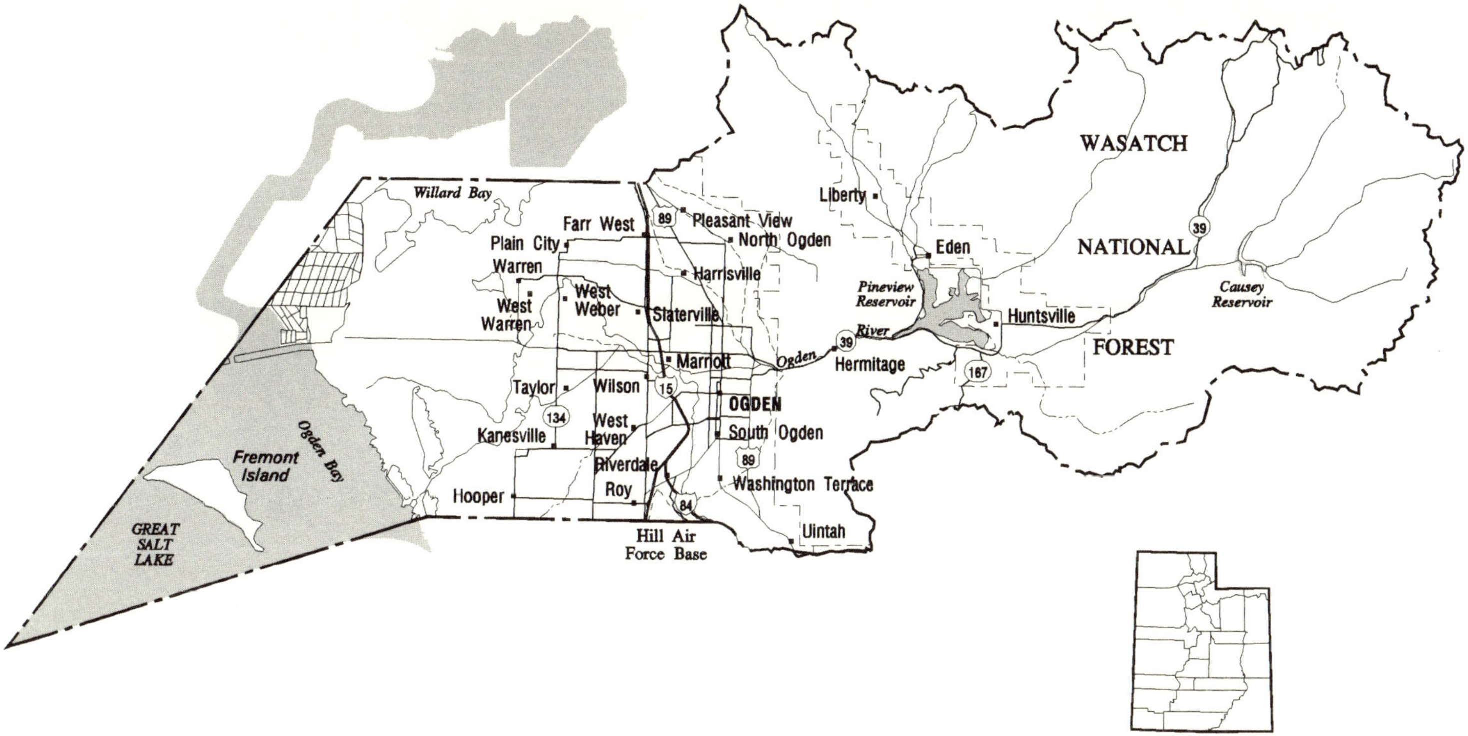


# WEBER COUNTY

INDEX MAP

1

# WEBER COUNTY TO 1847

1846 was indeed a "year of decision" as described by Ogden-born historian Bernard DeVoto. The Smithsonian Institution was founded by Congress and Francis Parkman, a twenty-three-year-old Harvard student, began to travel west on the Oregon Trail and write his monumental history of the westward movement. More than 2,700 travelers journeyed west on the Oregon and California trails that year. John A. Roebling revolutionized bridge engineering by using twisted wire cables to support a suspension bridge over the Monongahela River in Pennsylvania. Violence was widespread in the country and included the Mormons being driven from their settlements in Illinois westward into Iowa, where they established temporary settlements at places like Mount Pisgah and Garden Grove as well as along the Missouri River at Council Bluffs. The first recorded baseball game was played at Elysian Field in Hoboken, New Jersey, between the New York Nine and the Knickerbockers. The New York Nine won 23–1.

In 1846 James K. Polk was nearly halfway through his only term as president of the United States, and he was pushing for expansion to both Oregon and Texas on the theme of Manifest Destiny—that it was the nation's destiny to control the continent. During that same year, the Oregon question with Great Britain was settled peacefully, with the United States acquiring all of the Oregon Territory west of the Rocky Mountains and northward from the 42nd parallel to the 49th parallel. Texas had been annexed to the United States in 1845 and controversy related to the Texas-Mexico border erupted into the Mexican War in May 1846. This generally popular war in the United States ended early in 1848 with the Treaty of Guadalupe Hidalgo which granted to the United States the Mexican Cession, which included the current states of California, Nevada, and Utah, as well as large parts of Arizona, New Mexico, Colorado, and Wyoming.

During the nearly two years of the Mexican War, overland pioneers were not deterred by what might be construed as the dangers of war. In fact, if anything, it appears that the war helped to stimulate travel from the Missouri River Valley to Oregon and California. Some 4,450 overlanders traveled to Oregon and California in 1847, and an additional 2,200 traveled to Utah during that same year. In 1848, 1,700 emigrants traveled to the west coast while 2,400 traveled to Utah. By the end of 1848 there were about 4,600 settlers who had begun to establish homes in the vicinity of the Great Salt Lake Valley. The large majority of them were Mormons who had traveled the Platte River route from the Mormon settlements along the Missouri River. The discovery of gold in California on 24 January 1848 brought about one of the largest migrations experienced in the United States. Thousands of fortune seekers traveled to California expecting to get rich in quick fashion.

## *The Creation of Weber County*

The issue of providing a government for the western territories was pushed to the forefront with the settlement of the Great Basin by the Mormons and the myriad of gold rush camps which blossomed in California. The Mormons in the Great Basin decided to petition the United States Congress in 1849 for the establishment of what they called the State of Deseret. The proposed State of Deseret, with its headquarters in Great Salt Lake City, included all of the present states of Utah and Nevada as well as large parts of Arizona, Colorado, and

New Mexico, small portions of Oregon and Idaho, and much of southern California, including San Diego as a seaport. Deseret, as proposed, was larger than the then massive state of Texas. Although the Congress of the United States did not act favorably on the proposal from the Mormons, the actual government for the Mormons and other settlers in the Great Basin was that of the provisional State of Deseret from 12 March 1849 until 1851.[1]

The Congress of the United States acted on the western territorial questions in 1850 by passing in rather slow fashion the pieces of the Compromise of 1850. Slavery was a major thread running through all of the compromise measures. California was admitted to the Union as a free state. The New Mexico and Utah territories were created, and slavery was not prohibited by Congress in those two territories but rather was left to be decided by the settlers. This new political doctrine for dealing with slavery was entitled "popular sovereignty." The territory of Utah included within its boundaries all of the current state of Utah, much of Nevada, and small parts of Colorado and Wyoming. The territory of Utah was whittled down over the next several years, with the largest slice going to Nevada Territory in 1861. Utah would be governed as a territory from 1850 until statehood was granted in 1896.

The constitution of the State of Deseret which was written and locally accepted in 1849 claimed that it involved the "inhabitants of that portion of Upper California lying east of the Sierra Nevada Mountains." The government of Deseret included a governor, a general assembly which consisted of a senate and a house of representatives, and a judiciary. Members of the legislature convened for their first regular session in December 1849 in Heber C. Kimball's school. Hosea Stout noted in his diary for 3 and 4 December 1849 that he had received a notification to meet with the House of Representatives on the next Saturday (8 December) and did not know by what process he had become a representative. Historian Juanita Brooks writes that he was chosen by the Mormon church's leadership called the Council of Fifty, and she quotes Benjamin F. Johnson, who said that "this council did continue and become the legislature of the state of Deseret."[2]

One of the first spheres of business to be deliberated by the legislators was the establishment of counties. On 31 January 1850 "An Ordinance Providing For The Location Of Counties And Precincts Therein Names, &c" was passed by the legislative assembly. Included in the act was the following:

> Sec. 1. Be it ordained by the General Assembly of the State of Deseret, that all of that portion of country known as Weber Valley, and extending as far south as Stony Creek, and west to the Great Salt Lake, shall be called Weber County.
>
> Sec. 2. The County seat of said County shall be located at Ogden City.
>
> Sec. 3. The County of Weber shall be divided into three Precincts, as follows:—The City Precinct shall include all of the country lying in said County, between Ogden River and Sandy Creek, all north of Ogden shall be called Ogden Precinct and all south of the second Creek in said County, Sandy Precinct.[3]

The act also established Great Salt Lake County, Utah County, San Pete County, Tuilla (Tooele) County, and Little Salt Lake County.

These initial six counties were established in a fashion to begin local government within some semblance of geographical areas covered by counties. The counties were essentially based upon a major settlement or settlements, which was the case of Ogden and Weber County. Little Salt Lake County would later be renamed Iron County. The outer boundaries of the counties were not particularly outlined except when they adjoined another county.

The dividing line between Weber and Salt Lake counties was Stony Creek, which apparently was one of the creeks running from the Wasatch Mountains westward through what is today Davis County. The three precincts of Weber County as noted by the ordinance were generally laid out in relationship to the mountains, the Great Salt Lake, and streams which flowed east to west from the Wasatch Mountains to the lake. The Ogden Precinct was the area of the county located north of the Ogden River. The City Precinct included the area south of the Ogden River to the creek south of the Weber river, which was named Sandy Creek. It appears that Sandy Creek is today's Kays Creek, which runs through a number of sand hills. All of the land between Sandy Creek and Stoney Creek became the third precinct of the county and was named the Sandy Precinct of Weber County. This precinct would stretch today through much of Davis County. Although some of the boundaries of Weber County were drawn rather specifically by this ordinance of 1850, the northern boundary was not mentioned or designated in any fashion, but was rather everything north of the Ogden River.

The legislature of the State of Deseret met until the end of 1850 when the authority was passed to the Utah Territorial Legislature. In early 1851 the legislature of the newly established territory of Utah first met. The territorial legislature incorporated all acts adopted by the government of the State of Deseret into the laws of the territory of Utah. By the order of organization in the ordinance passed in January 1850, Weber County was the first county to be established in the territory.

The assembly of the State of Deseret had met throughout 1850. On 5 October1850 the assembly met in joint session and authorized the organization of Davis County by the marshal of the state. By 1852 the boundaries of Weber County were drawn as follows:

> Sec. 1. Boundary of Weber County: Be it enacted by the Governor and Legislative Assembly of the Territory of Utah, that all that portion of the Territory bounded north by Oregon, east by the meridian, passing through a point where the Weber River enters a kanyon about four miles below the ford on Emigration road, south by the parallel of latitude, through the junction of the county road and the head waters of Rocky Creek, being about two miles south of the mouth of Weber River Kanyon, and west by California,—is hereby included within the limits of Weber County.[4]

The boundaries of Weber County were much better defined by this act, and the county became immense. The 42nd parallel, the southern boundary of the Oregon Territory (the current southern boundary of Oregon and Idaho), became the northern boundary of Weber County and was also the northern boundary of Utah Territory. The western boundary of Utah Territory was the Sierra Nevada in California, which also became the western boundary of Weber County. The county also acquired new territory to the east, with the county boundary being set where the Weber River "enters a kanyon about four miles below the ford on Emigration road." Emigration road was the name of the pioneer road through Echo Canyon which ended in Salt Lake City. This road crossed the Weber River in the vicinity of Henefer, and four miles down the river, north and west of Henefer, was the eastern point of the Weber County boundary. The boundary ran north to the 42nd parallel from this point, which is about where the Weber River enters a high and narrow canyon carved out of rough red sandstone. The southern boundary of the county ran through a point at "the junction of the county road and the head waters of Rocky Creek, being about two miles south of the mouth of Weber River Kanyon." This spot can be located today by taking U.S. Highway 89 south from Ogden to two miles south of the Weber River, where the north fork of Kay's Creek crosses the road (approximately the eastern terminus of Utah Highway 193). This was the southern point through which a line drawn east to west created the southern boundary of Weber County. This line extended west to California. Weber County at this point included all of its present area, but it also included most of present-day Morgan, Box Elder, and Cache counties as well as a large slice of northern Nevada and northern Davis County. With its 1850 boundaries, Weber County rivaled some small states in size. Had Weber County retained the 1850 boundaries, it would border the states of California, Oregon, and Idaho. But that was not to be. In 1861 Nevada Territory was created; and three years later, in 1864, Nevada became a state—in part to ensure the reelection of Abraham Lincoln, the Republican president.

Weber County was whittled down in other ways as the territorial legislature of Utah created other counties in response to increased settlement. In 1855 the territorial legislature passed an act which in part said,

> That all that portion of Weber county south of a line running down the center of the main channel of the Weber river to a point due north of the north-west corner of Kington's fort, then due west to the Great Salt Lake, be, and is hereby attached to Davis County.[5]

This boundary change gave to Davis County the land south of the middle of the Weber River to the site of Kington Fort. If present Adams Avenue in Ogden were extended south today to the river and across it, it would run into the site of Kington Fort in South Weber.

With the continued immigration to Utah and the settlement of the territory during the last half of the 1850s, it became necessary to form new towns and villages and new counties like Box Elder and Cache. In 1862, with the Civil War raging, the Utah Territorial Legislature again adjusted the boundaries of Weber County:

> All that portion of the Territory, bounded on the south by Davis County, west by the eastern shore of Great Salt Lake, north by a line drawn due east from a point in said shore to the Hot Springs by the Territorial road north of Ogden City, thence by the summit of the Spur range, terminating at said Hot Springs, to its intersections with the summit of the Wasatch mountains, east by the summit of said mountains passing around the head waters of Ogden river, is hereby made and named Weber County.[6]

The western boundary of the county now became the eastern shore of the Great Salt Lake. The northern boundary of the county began on a line running from the lakeshore east to the hot springs just west of present-day Pleasant View. With the hot springs as an axis point, the mountains of the county now became an integral part of the county's boundary. The boundary jumped to the summit of the mountains running east and north from the hot springs—the spur range which included Ben Lomond and then continued eastward to include all of the tributaries of the Ogden River. The Ogden and Weber rivers, which would provide the lifeblood for the county, continued to be an important part of its boundaries.

In 1866 Weber County lost a piece of land that became part of Morgan County. The 1866 law stated that the land between "the dividing ridge between Ogden Hole and Weber Valley" was to be pruned from Weber County to become part of Morgan County. The dividing ridge between Ogden Valley and Morgan Valley became the county dividing line, and the Weber River in Morgan Valley ceased being that line.

In 1880 a most interesting change took place in the boundaries of Weber County. This change gave Weber County a wedge-shaped portion of the Great Salt Lake. The 1880 law noted that the new Weber boundary in the lake would begin at the northwest corner of Davis County, which was about in the middle of the lake, and would run in a northeasterly direction to a point due west of the hot springs near the territorial road north of Ogden City. This also now added Fremont Island to the county.

In 1898, two years after Utah became a state, the legislature of the state codified the boundaries of counties which had been in a state of gradual change over the past half century. The boundaries of Weber County were generally left unchanged by this 1898 enactment.[7]

## *The Land, Water, and Climate*

Present-day Weber County is made up of several distinct physiographic areas. Anyone who has lived in the county or has visited the county for a period of time remembers the distinct nature of these physiographic areas—the lake, the mountains, the mountain valleys, and the sloping plain running from the mountains to the lake—during all seasons of the year. Fremont Island and its adjoining wedge of the Great Salt Lake occupy the westernmost part of the county. The most populated section of the county is a rather level plain which slopes westward from the Wasatch Mountains to the Lake. This undulating piece of the eastern Great Basin varies between ten and fifteen miles in width from east to west from the mountains to the lake. This area has ready access to water and became the first area of the county to be settled both for towns and agriculture.

The Wasatch Mountains rise majestically, bisecting the county and running from north to south. The Wasatch and the other mountains to the east which form the boundaries of the Ogden River watershed are spectacular to view in every season of the year. Major peaks and their heights in feet include: Willard Peak (9,764), Ben Lomond (9,717), Mt. Ogden (9,575), Lewis Peak (8,031), Black Mountain (8,187), James Peak (9,422), and Monte Cristo (9,148). The part of the county located east of the Wasatch range are back valleys of the Wasatch, in particular Ogden Valley. This portion of the county is bounded by Cache, Rich, and Morgan counties.

Two river systems dominate and give life to Weber County—the Ogden and the Weber. Both are named for nineteenth-century fur trappers who walked their banks seeking beaver and other animal pelts. The Ogden River was named after the famous British trapper Peter Skene Ogden, a brigade leader of two legendary fur companies—the North West Company and the Hudson's Bay Company. The Ogden River drains the easternmost portion of the county with streams that flow into its north, south, and middle forks. These forks come together today in Pineview Reservoir. The Ogden River has cut a picturesque canyon through the Wasatch Mountains. Today, homes dot Ogden Canyon, and those residents seek the river and its canyon beauty and coolness. As the Ogden River enters the flat and open plain of the Great Basin, it meanders through Ogden City before discharging its water into the Weber River west of the city.[8]

The Weber River and the county were named for the American fur trapper John Henry Weber, friend and employee of William Henry Ashley. The Weber River has its source north of Bald Mountain, high in the Uinta Mountains of eastern Utah. Its headwaters include some fifty-nine natural lakes and between 80 and 100 ponds of less than two acres in area. As the river begins, it flows north and west through Summit and Morgan counties and then scratches its way through the Wasatch Mountains. As the Weber River claws its way through the Wasatch, spectacular views such as the one at Devils Gate are available. Leaving the canyon which bears its name, the Weber winds it way west and then north to join with the Ogden River. The Weber eventually enters the Great Salt Lake near Hooper after making a big bend and turning to the west. The artistic beauty of Weber and Ogden canyons has long been drawn, painted, publicized, and photographed.

The Weber River with all of its tributaries including the Ogden River produces an annual volume of 505,187 acre-feet of water. Weber County and its environs would not be able to survive with their current needs and demands without the lifegiving waters of the Weber River drainage system. Before being dammed and controlled, the Weber and the Ogden were often ferocious at floodstage. Over the past century, dams and reservoirs have harnessed the river water for current use. Reservoirs of major consequence to Weber County include Pineview, with a capacity of 110,000 acre-feet of water; Causey, with a capacity of 6,900 acre-feet of water; and Willard Bay, with a capacity of 193,000 acre-feet. All of the streams of Weber County drain into the Great Salt Lake and the Great Basin. Physiographically, about half of Weber County lies within the Great Basin and about half of it lies within the Rocky Mountain physiographic province.

Mountain, rivers, and climate have played a major role in the settlement of Weber County. The climate of the county is affected by its inland position in relationship to the Pacific Ocean, its latitude (distance from the equator), its altitude above sea level, and its proximity to the Great Salt Lake. Much of the western half of Weber County experiences a climate which has hot summers with little rainfall. This type of climate is located in a narrow band which runs along the Wasatch Front from the Idaho border to Mt. Nebo. Winters are cold and summers are hot. The average July temperature for Ogden is 76 degrees, Fahrenheit, while the average January temperature is 28 degrees. Yearly average rainfall in Ogden is 16.08 inches. The Wasatch Mountains serve as a barrier to moisture-laden clouds approaching from the west, causing the clouds as they rise to drop much of their moisture in the form of rain or snow.[9]

The climate of the eastern half of the county (Wasatch Mountains and eastward) is designated by geographers as undifferentiated highlands. Eastern Weber County shares a similar climate with Cache, Morgan, Summit, and Wasatch counties. Characteristics of this climate include often severely cold winters and cool summers with a generally humid precipitation pattern.

Precipitation falls in the form of rain and snow, with March and April normally being the wettest months of the year and July, August, and September being the driest months. Precipitation varies, with amounts generally becoming higher as one moves from west to east. Fremont Island averages between 8 and 12 inches of precipitation while the area from Hooper and Warren eastward to within two miles of the Wasatch Mountains receives between 12 and 16 inches. The Wasatch foothills receive between 16 and 20 inches while the Wasatch peaks and mountains surrounding the Ogden River drainage may receive between 30 and 50 inches. Ogden Valley annually receives between 16 and 25 inches of precipitation. Average annual snowfall amounts vary in the county, with the Powder Mountain region receiving between 150 and 200 inches of snow. The Wasatch Front generally receives between 20 and 40 inches of snow; but the Ogden Valley receives between 40 and 100 inches of snow.

Fremont Island is considered a steppe climatic region—a zone which lies between Utah's deserts and the higher mountain regions. About 40 percent of Utah is classified as steppe land. About half of Weber County—that part west of the Wasatch Mountains—is below 5,000 feet elevation above sea level, with the eastern half of the county being above 5,000 feet.

The observable geologic record of the county stretches back more than 570 million years. For much of the earliest time periods (from 570 to 208 million years ago, the Cambrian to the Jurassic periods), Weber County along with much of the rest of Utah was largely under water. Utah's oldest observable rocks can be found in Farmington Canyon. They are metamorphic in nature and are some 3 billion years old. From the Jurassic period onward (208 million years ago) northwestern Utah was uplifted and folded by immense geologic forces. In the middle of the Tertiary period (about 35 million years ago) much volcanic activity took place, some of which is still evident in Weber Canyon west of Mountain Green.[10]

The Wasatch Mountains have been in existence as we know them for some 20 million years. The Wasatch Range is about 200 miles in length and has been shaped to a great extent by faulting. Pressures have pulled the earth's crust apart, weakening it, and the Wasatch Mountains were an upraised and eastward-tilted faultblock which was thrust upward while the valley floors dropped. Weber County is crossed by four fault lines, or breaks in the underlying rock structure: the Wasatch, the Cache Valley, the Willard, and the Charleston-Nebo. Earth movements along faults are termed earthquakes, and during the 125-year period from 1853 to 1978, Weber County experienced three earthquakes with a magnitude measured on the Richter Scale of 4.3 or above. All three of these quakes were centered in the vicinity of Ogden. The strongest of these, which measured over 5.6 on the scale, occurred in 1914.

One of the dominant features of Weber County today is the Great Salt Lake. This salty inland sea can trace its roots to Lake Bonneville, which covered much of western Utah as well as small portions of Idaho and Nevada. Lake Bonneville existed during the latter portion of the Pleistocene epoch and first appeared about 30,000 years ago. Shorelines visible today along mountain benches in the county were formed during the growth or receding of Lake Bonneville. The highest shoreline left by Lake Bonneville was the Bonneville shoreline (5,090 feet above sea level), formed about 16,000 to 14,500 years ago. This shoreline was formed before the lake burst through an outlet near present Red Rock Pass in southeastern Idaho, flooding into the Snake River Basin. As the lake drained, other levels were formed; they include the Provo (about 300 feet below the Bonneville level), the Stansbury (about 400 feet below the Provo level), and the Gilbert, below the Stansbury level. A number of lake terraces are visible within Weber County. At its greatest extent, when it cut the Bonneville shoreline, Lake Bonneville was 346 miles long, 145 miles wide, occupied some 20,000 square miles, and was about 1,000 feet deep. The western half of Weber County, the broad plain sloping to the Great Salt Lake, was formed in part as the bottom of Lake Bonneville.

About 10,000 years ago, Lake Bonneville receded to the Gilbert level, which is about from thirty to ninety feet higher than the current lake level. At this time there was a widespread area of glaciation in North America, and the glacier from Little Cottonwood Canyon extended into the remnant of Lake Bonneville. The lake continued to shrink as time passed; it is thought that the climate also became warmer and drier. The deposits left by Lake Bonneville have been of great significance to the Wasatch Front. Sand and gravel deposits as well as the materials that make up the soils of the valley floors were in part formed by Lake Bonneville. Ogden Valley and Morgan Valley were both bays of Lake Bonneville, and the Great Salt Lake, Utah Lake, and Sevier Lake are all remnants of the ancient lake.

Today's Great Salt Lake is a terminal lake fed by three major rivers—the Bear, the Weber, and the Jordan. The lake is divided among five counties, with Box Elder County having the largest piece—about half of the lake. Davis County has the next largest section of the lake, including Antelope Island; and Tooele County has the third largest piece of the lake. Weber County with its wedge-shaped piece of the lake has the fourth largest area, and Salt Lake

County has a small portion of the lake located at the southeast corner of the lake and the northwest corner of that county. The level of the lake is in a constant state of change. Generally, the lake will rise and fall between six and eighteen inches per year. Tiny brine shrimp inhabit the lake and are harvested commercially. The Great Salt Lake covers about 1,500 square miles and has a maximum depth of about thirty-four feet. It is seventy-five miles long (north to south) and fifty miles wide (east to west).

The lake attracts large varieties of waterfowl, particularly into its major bird refuge areas—Farmington Bay, Ogden Bay, Locomotive Springs, and the Bear River Bird Refuge. At these four areas, freshwater marshes are separated from the saltwater of the lake by dikes. The salinity of the lake varies from season to season and from place to place. The bays where fresh water enters the lake have the lowest salt content, while the large northwest arm of the lake has the highest content. In general, the lake is about the same salinity as the Dead Sea—about eight times as salty as seawater. Sodium chloride makes up about four-fifths of the solids dissolved in the lake's water.

Water from the lake was used by early settlers and explorers as brine, particularly for preserving meat. Efforts have been made without much success to grow fish, oysters, and other wildlife where the streams enter the lake. In the nineteenth century, efforts were made to grow oysters near the mouth of the Weber River; but this proved to be a total failure. An effort to raise eels at the mouth of the Jordan River proved equally unsuccessful. With the passage of time, salts from the lake have become an important natural resource. Production of minerals extracted from the lake is a multimillion dollar business.

The Great Salt Lake has on occasion served as a barrier to transportation and communication and it also impacts the climate of the region and tourism to the area. Storms passing over the lake may pick up moisture from the lake, dropping it along the storm track as the air masses are pushed up to cross the mountains. "Lake effect" storms have been known to drop excessive amounts of precipitation on the Wasatch Mountains. The level of the lake has varied as much as twenty feet over the past 150 years. In 1873 the lake reached a high level of 4,211.6 feet above sea level; however, in 1987 the highest level measured for the lake came when the lake reached a height of 4,211.85 feet. At that time, pumps were installed to drain the lake into the west desert. In 1963, the lake reached a historic low level of 4,191.35 feet.

Another natural feature which has been important to Weber County is the two hot springs within its boundaries. The hot springs of Weber County were valued by the Shoshoni Indians for what seemed to be their rejuvenative and health-giving qualities. At the mouth of Ogden Canyon is a spring which has been visited by Indians and residents of Ogden. Rainbow Gardens was constructed to make use of its waters. The temperature of the Ogden Canyon hot spring is measured at 57 degrees centigrade. The other county hot spring, located near the Weber County-Box Elder County line, has been called the Utah Hot Springs. The temperature of this spring is 58.5 degrees centigrade. The location of this spring has been noted particularly because the boundaries of the county have been drawn using it as a marking point since 1862.[11]

## *Native Americans*

Archaeologists suggest that human occupation of the area began about 10500 B.P. (before present) and was related to the ebbing of freshwater Lake Bonneville before it became increasingly saline as the Great Salt Lake. At about 10300 B.P. the lake stood at about the Gilbert Shoreline (4,250 to 4,300 feet) and was shrinking. By about 9750 B.P. the lake stood at about 4,235 feet. The bulk of archaeological evidence indicates that human populations first occupied northern Utah during terminal Pleistocene and early Holocene times (ca. 11,000–9,000 B.P.). Most prehistoric Great Basin native groups were part of the Western Archaic Tradition, an aboriginal lifeway characterized by a broad spectrum hunting-and-gathering economy, highly nomadic camp groups consisting of between six and thirty individuals related by ties of blood and marriage, lack of domesticated plants and animals, and production of a diverse lithic (rock) tool assemblage. The prehistoric cultural chronology of Utah includes the Early Archaic period (8000–2000 B.C.). Life for most was nomadic. Grinding stones were used for preparation of seeds for food. Baskets, spears, darts, and woven cloth were also used by these early peoples.

There is evidence of long-term prehistoric trade with Pacific Coast peoples mostly in the form of marine shell beads and ornaments; early marine shell beads in the eastern Great Basin date from about 5150 B.C.

The Weber and Ogden rivers and their confluence with the Great Salt Lake provided extensive riparian and marshland ecozones for these early inhabitants. These lush wetland settings allowed many Wasatch Front groups to lead a more sedentary lifeway than those natives who occupied more arid areas such as the Great Salt Lake Desert. Both saltwater and freshwater marshes were formed and periodically changed with the lake level. In large measure, the human culture of this era was devoted to hunting and gathering, with some modifications depending on where in the Great Basin these people generally were located.[12] Virtually all plant and animal life was put to use during this period. Rabbits, skunks, porcupines, coyotes, bobcats, birds, deer, elk, antelope, and bison were all used as sources of food and tools. Roots and bulbs including the sego lily as well as grass and other seeds were eaten. The pinyon nut was widely used. Crickets and grasshoppers often were the objects of group hunts during which thousands of insects were driven into ditches lined with dry grass which was then set afire. The roasted insects were gathered and then eaten whole or ground into a meal. Waterfowl were accessible in the marshy areas surrounding the Great Salt Lake.

For the past 2,000 years it appears that the climate of this region and the level of the lake has been quite similar to that which has been experienced during recent historic times. Beginning sometime around A.D. 400, many native groups of this area became marginally involved in agricultural activities and became more sedentary than their Archaic predecessors. This more complex society has been termed the Great Salt Lake Fremont Culture. Hundreds of Fremont Culture sites have been identified in the eastern Great Salt Lake wetlands area. Hunting, gathering, and some raising of corn, squash, and beans seem to have been the basic lifestyle of this culture. Near Warren in Weber County where several sites have been excavated, the excavation yield included corn, bison bones, and "bushels of fish bone." Sites near Willard and on the lower Bear River also have been excavated by archaeologists with important findings.[13]

By about A.D. 1300, archaeologists have noted a distinct transition from the more complex Fremont Culture to the arrival of more nomadic and aggressive Numic speakers. In Utah these hunter-gatherers consisted of the Western Shoshoni, Ute, and Southern Paiute Indians. Anthropologists use the term "Numic" to refer to one of the four representatives of the Uto-Aztecan language stock in western North America. With the exception of the Comanche, all Numic languages are associated with the Great Basin culture area. It is believed that these newcomers either drove out or absorbed the Fremont people in the region. Recent archeological explorations have added much to our previous knowledge of the prehistoric inhabitants of Weber County and northern Utah.[14]

A group of the Western Shoshoni people was largely the sole Native American inhabitants of the Weber County area from about A.D. 1300 through the mid-1800s. The Shoshoni homeland was occupied by numerous Western, Northern, and Eastern Shoshoni groups and included the Snake River country, the Great Basin, and much of present-day Wyoming west of the Rockies. Throughout this area the Shoshonis intermingled with other tribes and groups including Utes, Crows, Blackfeet, Nez Perces, Flatheads, Arapahos, Comanches, Bannocks, and Cheyennes. The Shoshoni people were divided into seven groups: the Eastern Shoshoni, led by the famous Chief Washakie, ranged through much of the Green River Valley west of South Pass; the Fort Hall Shoshoni were centered on the fur-trading post (Fort Hall) on the Snake River; the Lemhi Shoshoni were centered in the Salmon River country and the Beaverhead area of western Montana; the Boise and Bruneau Shoshoni ranged the area west of Salmon Falls on the Snake River to Fort Boise; the Northwestern Shoshoni occupied the valleys of present-day northern Utah, including Weber County; the Goshutes were a Shoshoni-speaking people who lived in the area of Tooele Valley and the Deep Creek Mountains; and the Western Shoshoni occupied the area of eastern Nevada along the Humboldt River west to Winnemucca. Neighbors to the Western Shoshonis were the Northern Paiutes who occupied the area from Winnemucca west to Pyramid Lake and Walker Lake. The Snake Indians were a group within the Northern Shoshoni, and the

Bannocks were Northern Paiute speakers who lived with the Northern Shoshoni after acquiring the horse.

At the beginning of the nineteenth century, all of the Shoshoni groups had a combined total of about 17,000 people. Brigham Madsen describes in some detail the relationships among the groups.

> Although the various Shoshoni groups spoke a similar language, visited with other Shoshoni in friendly exchange, occasionally hunted together, and rarely went to war with each other, they, nevertheless, were quite aware and jealous of the lands they claimed, and they understood the cultural differences between various tribes. From the Eastern Shoshoni and the Fort Hall Shoshoni and Bannock, who were considered the aristocrats of all the Shoshoni because of their large herds of horses, their easy mobility, and their proclivity to war with other Indians, there was a perceptible gradation to a more precarious existence for the Shoshoni in the western regions of the Shoshoni nation (or to a less "noble" Indian in the eyes of ethnocentric whites). While the eastern tribes lived on buffalo meat, their western cousins ate whatever could be found in desolate desert areas. Nevertheless, before the coming of the white man, all the Shoshoni lived rather well. Buffalo were available in Idaho and northern Utah areas, salmon and trout thronged the streams, and camas roots abundantly covered the prairies. In western Utah and throughout Nevada, grass seeds for flour, pinon nuts, and small game provided plentiful food. Emigrants along the trails and Mormon farmers in the Great Basin quickly destroyed what had once been a mostly comfortable existence.[15]

In 1863 when the Treaty of Box Elder was signed following the battle at Bear River in which hundreds of Indians were brutally killed, the Northwestern Shoshoni numbered about 1,500 people. The ten bands of the Northwestern Shoshoni at that time were led by chiefs Pocatello, Toomontso, Sanpitch, Towowitz, Yahnoway, Weerahsoop, Pahragoosahd, Tahkuetoonah, Omrshee, and Sagwitch. They occupied much of northern Utah including the eastern shores of the Great Salt Lake and the Promontory Range, and the Weber, Ogden, Cache, Bear Lake, and Malad valleys. The Northwestern Shoshoni incorporated aspects of the lifestyles of both their eastern and western kinsmen. Their horse herds were not as large as those of their northern and eastern relations. Their food-gathering practices included traveling to Wyoming for buffalo; gathering seeds, insects, and berries in the Great Basin; digging roots; hunting animals including birds, rabbits, deer, antelope, mountain sheep, skunks, raccoons, squirrels, beaver, otter, ducks, geese, mice, and rats; and fishing the mountain streams. A comfortable summer living was found in the mountain valleys, and the rivers flowing into the Great Salt Lake provided areas for adequate winter survival for both the Indians and their horses.[16]

Trading played an important part in survival as well as in enhancing lifestyles. Animal skins and furs, dogs, knives, pottery, pine nuts, native paints, colored shells, beads, buffalo robes, blankets, horses, and Indian slaves were among the goods exchanged. Native tools included bow and arrows, flint knives, digging sticks, seed beaters, gathering baskets, and grinding stones. Groups often participated together in rabbit, insect, and antelope drives. The Utes who occupied central and eastern Utah often came in contact with the Northwestern Shoshoni.

As the lands of the Northwestern Shoshoni began to be invaded—first by fur traders, followed by explorers, overlanders, and Mormon settlers—the lifestyle of the Indians was changed forever. Iron cooking implements and firearms perhaps improved the lifestyle of the Shoshoni; however, diseases such as cholera, smallpox, and measles laid a devastating hand on Native American groups. Indian food sources such as grasses and big game became the victims of the encroaching white civilization. Along the Wasatch Front where small herds of buffalo had roamed for centuries, most had disappeared by 1840.

Weber County, the Great Basin, and the Wasatch Mountains were among some of the last areas penetrated by Europeans and Americans. In 1776 Franciscan friars Antonio Domínguez and Silvestre Velez de Escalante first led a group into the region. Their cartographer, Don Bernardo Miera y Pacheco, mapped what he knew and made up the rest, including rivers that flowed across the Great Basin to the Pacific Ocean. Miera's "Rio de San Buenaventura" is one such river that explorers and overlanders subsequently tried to locate for nearly three-quarters of a century. This Spanish party ventured as far north as the valley of Utah Lake.

## *The Fur Trade*

Fur trappers were the first whites to explore, map, and capitalize on northern Utah. Weber County and the Weber River owe their names and much of their early exploration to fur trappers. The Lewis and Clark expedition of 1804–1806 stimulated the American fur trade up the Missouri River and on to the Pacific Northwest. John Jacob Astor briefly established the beginnings of an empire at Astoria in present-day Oregon with his Pacific Fur Company; but this was short-lived, as the War of 1812 forced the sale of this enterprise to the British. Returning Astorians under the leadership of Robert Stuart discovered South Pass across the Continental Divide in present Wyoming in 1813 as they made their way to St. Louis, but this discovery was little known until Jedediah Smith made the effective rediscovery of the pass in 1824. Scores and eventually hundreds then began to use it. It appears that neither the American Astorians nor the British Hudson's Bay trappers and North West Company trappers ventured into northern Utah prior to 1820.

The British had moved into the Oregon Country earlier than any of their competitors, and in 1821 the Hudson's Bay Company eliminated much of its competition by absorbing its earlier bitter rival, the North West Company. Headquarters for the Hudson's Bay Company was Fort Vancouver on the north bank of the Columbia River (across the river from present-day Portland). It was from this headquarters that orders were issued to Peter Skene Ogden for his Snake River expeditions which would convey him into Utah and into the Great Basin.

International agreements affected the Rocky Mountains and northern Utah even though Native Americans and fur trappers were not often bothered by decisions made in far-distant cities by individuals who knew little of their areas. In 1818, after much discussion, Great Britain and the United States took several giant steps toward solving the ownership questions of the Pacific Northwest and also in eliminating two other rivals from competition in the area—Russia and Spain. The Convention of 1818 which was signed by Great

Britain and the United States established the northern border of the Louisiana Purchase at the 49th parallel westward to the Rocky Mountains and stated that the Oregon Country (essentially the country from the Rockies to the Pacific Ocean) would be jointly occupied by Great Britain and the United States. A year later, in 1819, the United States and Spain signed the Adams-Onis Treaty, which set the southern and western boundary of the Louisiana Purchase, ceded Florida to the United States, and set the 42nd parallel as the northern boundary of Spanish territory from the Pacific Ocean eastward to the Louisiana Territory. The 42nd parallel is and always has been the northern boundary of Utah, but there were many in the decades of the 1820s, 1830s, and 1840s who considered northern Utah to be part of the Oregon country. The Oregon question was solved in 1846 when the United States and Great Britain agreed to divide the Oregon Country at the 49th parallel.

Furs, particularly beaver skins, had been sought by Europeans since their arrival in the New World. Beaver pelts were the most important raw material of the Rocky Mountain trapping system and until 1834 the most valuable product of the fur trade of the Trans-Mississippi West.[17] The most important part of the beaver pelt was its fibrous underhair which was used to make felted beaver hats. Two events which serve to define the fur trade in the Rocky Mountains are the Lewis and Clark Expedition (1804–1806) and the Mexican War (1846–48), with the trade being most intense in northern Utah during the 1820s. An important change which took place in the trade as it moved to the Rocky Mountains was the shift from base camps of fur trading posts and forts to a system utilizing mountain men who would live in the mountains year around.

The invention of the "mountain man," or someone who would stay in the mountains all year, was not necessarily new, but it was improved upon by William Ashley and Andrew Henry. As the early French explorers of Canada pushed westward and became engaged in the fur trade, a new breed of men sprang up who were called the *coureurs de bois,* which was defined as the "wood runners" or the "bushrangers." These men lived in the woods with the Indians and were usually tied to Indian tribes by marriage and adoption. It is perhaps from this very effective French example that Ashley and Henry took their idea for their fur trappers who would become mountain men. In early 1822 Ashley and Henry advertised in several Missouri newspapers for individuals to join them in their new Rocky Mountain Fur Company:

> To Enterprising Young Men
>
> The subscriber wishes to engage ONE HUNDRED MEN, to ascend the river Missouri to its source, there to be employed for one, two or three years—For particulars, enquire of Major Andrew Henry, near the lead mines, in the County of Washington, (who will ascend with and command the party) or to the subscriber at St. Louis, Feb. 13
>
> Wm. H. Ashley[18]

Ashley and Henry introduced several major changes in the fur trade including depending on their men rather than Indians to trap the furs and paying their men on the basis of commission. The men hired under these terms were often called "Ashley's men" and included many who would become legendary for their exploits in the mountains: Jedediah Smith, William and Milton Sublette, John H. Weber, Thomas Fitzpatrick, Jim Bridger, Hugh Glass, James Clyman, and David Jackson, among others. After spending 1822 and 1823 trying to penetrate the Rocky Mountains via the Missouri River and experiencing many Indian difficulties, particularly with the Arikaras (also known as the Rees), Ashley and Henry decided to move overland to the rich fur country of the Rockies. In the spring of 1824, Jedediah Smith made the effective discovery of South Pass and opened the country west of the Rockies to Ashley's enterprising young men.

The race for the Rocky Mountain beaver was on. Each beaver trap weighed five pounds and was usually attached to a length of chain which was used to secure the trap after it was set. The end of a small stick was dipped in the musk or castor taken from the beaver's sex glands, and the other end of the stick was pushed under the water in the jaws of the trap. As the beaver swam past the baited stick, it lifted its nose to smell and, as its hind legs were lowered, they were caught in the trap. Furs were prime only in the cold season of the year, the time when most trapping was done. This meant much wading in cold streams by trappers, who usually placed between five and ten traps a day. The traps were usually positioned about dusk and raised in the gray light of dawn. Since the trappers were usually dressed in buckskins which would become dry and brittle after being soaked in water, trappers would often go naked into the streams to set and retrieve their traps. The beaver were usually skinned on the spot, with only the castor glands, the tail, and the fur taken to camp, where the pelt would be stretched on a hoop made by bending a willow in a circle and tying it tightly. The pelt was scraped with a sharp knife or an axe blade to clean it. It would dry rapidly and would be resistant to insects. The beaver fed on the bark of such trees as aspen, cottonwood, willow, birch, and alder. Although beaver meat might be used as food by the mountain men, the beaver tail was roasted before the fire and was eaten as a delicacy.

The years 1824 and 1825 opened up Weber County to the fur trade from three directions—St. Louis, Fort Vancouver, and Taos—by three trappers: John Henry Weber, Peter Skene Ogden, and Etienne Provost. For the next two decades, fur trappers would be major players in exploring, trapping, and mapping the future county.

John Henry Weber was born in Denmark in 1779. He spent some of his early years at sea before arriving in the United States in the years just prior to the War of 1812. Weber found his way to what would become the state of Missouri and became engaged in lead mining. In 1822 he answered Ashley's and Henry's advertisement to become a fur trapper in the American West. Weber became one of the trusted leaders of the fur company. He spent 1822 and 1823 trapping rivers and streams flowing into the upper Missouri River, and in 1824 Weber and his men followed Smith across South Pass. He had from twenty-five to fifty men under his charge, and by the fall of 1824 Weber and his men had trapped the Bear River and Bear Lake area. They spent the winter of 1824–25 in Cache Valley, and during this season Jim Bridger made his famous discovery of the Great Salt Lake. As the spring of 1825 approached, Weber and his men moved to trap the streams flowing west from the Wasatch Mountains. They most likely traveled the Bear River to the Great Salt Lake and began to trap the lower Bear, Ogden, and Weber rivers. From this time onward, the

Weber River was named for Weber, Rocky Mountain Fur Company trapper and leader. By May 1825, Weber and his men had moved up the Weber River and camped near Mountain Green, where the famous confrontation would take place between Rocky Mountain fur men and Peter Skene Ogden and his Hudson's Bay men.[19]

Peter Skene Ogden was born in Quebec in 1790 and by his teenage years had decided to become involved in the fur trade. Ogden gained employment with the North West Fur Company in 1810 as a trapper and trader and worked for that company until 1821 when it was absorbed by the Hudson's Bay Company. After he made a series of appeals, Ogden was allowed to become associated with the Hudson's Bay Company and he made his home at Spokane House in the Oregon territory. It was from this base that Ogden would conduct six Snake River country expeditions which would make him one of the West's most significant explorers.

Ogden's 1824–25 expedition was of major significance to Ogden and to Weber County. Both Ogden and his chief clerk William Kittson kept detailed daily journals during this expedition which recounted their trapping successes and their encounters with Americans. These journals contain the earliest descriptions of northern Utah. The Snake River expedition of 1824–25 included fifty-eight men equipped with sixty-one guns, 268 horses, 352 traps, an interpreter of the Piegan language, thirty women, and thirty-five children. The women were Indian wives of trappers. The party was to live off of the land, using deer, elk, buffalo, and beaver as chief sources of food and consuming their horses if all else failed.

This expedition began on 20 December 1824 at the Hudson's Bay Flathead Post, located northwest of Missoula, Montana. During the first four months of 1825, Ogden and his party trapped along the Gibbon River and the Salmon River, reaching the Snake River on 6 April near the site of present-day Blackfoot, Idaho. During April the party continued to trap southward, reaching the Bear River on 26 April (near Alexander, Idaho). The Hudson's Bay party continued south on the Bear River, entering present-day Utah early in May. From 2 May until 10 May the Ogden party trapped the Cache Valley from the area of Preston south to the Blacksmith Fork River, including the Cub River. In doing this, they were trapping in what was then called Willow Valley but by 1826 would be named Cache Valley by Rocky Mountain Fur Company trappers. Cache Valley had been the wintering spot for John H. Weber and his men; to avoid them, Ogden continued to travel south and on 16 May 1825 crossed over the divide into Ogden Valley and Weber County.

William Kittson described the route from Cache Valley into Ogden Valley as a "rugged road." Ogden Valley he described as a "hole," which he defined as a "place surrounded by lofty mountains and hills."[20] Ogden's Snake River brigade spent nearly a week—from 16 until 21 May—in what he named New Valley and which has since been renamed Ogden Valley. They initially trapped the north fork of the Ogden River and then moved on to trap the middle fork and the south fork. Ogden's Hole, as it came to be called, was described as being about fifty miles in circumference. Kittson recorded with accuracy the number of beaver trapped each day from the branches of the Ogden River. After six days of trapping Ogden's hole, the British party had trapped 563 beaver. Both the British and the Americans often trapped as many beaver as possible, having no concern about trapping the beaver into extinction. Each group of trappers seemed to want to practice a "scorched earth" trapping policy aimed at discouraging others from trapping near them. Ogden, Kittson, and their party knew that the Ogden River flowed westward into the Great Salt Lake, but they did not venture down Ogden Canyon far enough to see the lake or do much trapping because beaver were so numerous in the valley and because they also had knowledge that the Americans had gone along that route.

In his journal, Ogden noted the beauty of the valley and also the competition he was involved in with the Americans:

> Wednesday [May] 18th.—As all the Traps in Camp were Set last night we did not raise Camp & our expectations as usual most Sanguine, but the Water Constantly rising at night & falling in the day is not in our favour we had however nearly 100 Traps snapp'd to take 109 Beaver one nights Setting, three of the Trappers did not Come in it is to be regretted that this Spot is not ten times as large I presume the Americans intended returning this way but they will be as we were on Bear River taken in they ought to keep at home

> not infringe on their neighbours territories—one trap again lost by chain.[21]

It is obvious that Ogden and his party were very successful trapping in Ogden Valley and that they had not been as successful on the Bear River in Cache Valley where the Americans had spent the winter. It is also clear that it was Ogden's intention to trap all the beaver he could to discourage the Americans, since he felt they were encroaching on British territory (Oregon) and should be taught a lesson to stay in their own territory. Such a territorial issue would cease being theoretical and become a major conflict within the next week.

At this point, it is evident that while Ogden and his brigade were the first in Ogden Valley and were trapping with great success, the John H. Weber group of mountain men were trapping the front streams of the Wasatch in the vicinity of present-day Ogden, and that they both came upon the Weber River near Mountain Green at about the same time. Weber's men traveled up the river and Ogden's men traveled south over what is today Trapper's Loop. Kittson suggested that they were entering the borders of the "Utas" where most of the Indians were thought to be Christians and had been influenced by the Spanish to wear crosses made of brass and silver on their necks.

It is important at this point to introduce Etienne Provost, who spent so much time in the fur trade that he was called the "Man of the Mountains."[22] Provost was born in Chambly, Quebec, in 1785 and began his trapping career in 1815 as a member of the Chouteau-DeMun party exploring the upper reaches of the Platte and Arkansas rivers. In 1822, following Mexican independence from Spain, Provost traveled to New Mexico and formed a partnership with Michael (Francois) Leclerc to trap in the Rocky Mountains. By 1824 Provost had trapped the Green River below the Uinta Mountains and had moved westward into the Great Basin. On either the lower Provo River or on the Jordan River, Provost and his company of trappers were attacked by a band of Snake Indians and fifteen trappers were killed. Provost and three or four others barely escaped.[23]

Some historians credit Provost with the discovery of the Great Salt Lake in the autumn of 1824, thinking he traveled there from the vicinity of Utah Lake. Others suggest that Jim Bridger discovered the lake sometime during the late fall or winter of 1824–25 traveling down the Bear River. It is also possible that Hudson's Bay trappers working with Donald McKenzie and Michel Bourdon first observed the lake while they were trapping the upper Snake River, the Bear River, and perhaps as far east as the Green River Basin in the years from 1818 to 1822. From all accounts, however, it seems most likely that the group that first spent extended time along the east shore of the lake was John H. Weber's group of mountain men who were involved in trapping in Weber County during the spring of 1825.

Following the nearly complete massacre of his men, Provost and his three or four remaining trappers spent the winter of 1824–25 in the Uinta Basin. By the spring of 1825, Provost and his party were trapping down the Weber River; on 23 May they came upon Peter Skene Ogden's company near present Mountain Green. The stage was set, with three distinct companies of trappers converging on the Mountain Green area. Ogden and his men had just crossed the Trapper's Loop pass, while Provost and his men had traveled down the Weber River. John H. Weber and his men had traveled up the Weber from the west side of the Wasatch Mountains, and they were joined at this time by Jedediah Smith and six others including William Sublette who also had traveled up the Weber. The events of 23 May 1825 were recorded by Ogden and Kittson. Early in the morning, Provost visited Ogden's camp with a party of fifteen men, described as "Canadians and Spainards." This confrontation between opposing fur groups may have been more substantial were it not for a more serious encounter which took place late in the afternoon. At that time, a party of thirty-nine men marched on Ogden's camp. This assailing group included twenty-five Americans who were flying the American flag and fourteen deserters from Ogden's Hudson's Bay brigade. The group had come from the Weber camp and was headed by one of Weber's trappers, Johnson Gardner. The men marched to within 100 yards of Ogden's camp and informed all in Ogden's camp that they were encroaching on United States territory and that the Weber camp would pay top dollar for any beaver that had been trapped. The amount offered was $3.50 a pound for beaver skins, and Ogden later noted that this was eight times as much as he could pay for the pelts.[24] The initiative of the Americans and their new comrades was aimed at destroying Ogden's efforts by having more of his men desert with their furs and forcing Ogden to leave the area, which they claimed for the United States.

While all of this was happening, it appears that Weber and Smith determined to stay in their camp and digest the reports brought to them by their men. Following his early morning appearance, Provost also was not active in this episode. During the evening and night of 23 May, Ogden and his men kept "Strick watch." On the morning of 24 May, Johnson Gardner again visited Ogden's tent and bullied him by asking why he was on American soil and stealing American beaver. Gardner noted that they were in a land of liberty and that all of Ogden's engaged men were free to sell their furs to whomever they pleased. Ogden replied that the country where they were currently camping was in dispute between their two countries and that until his government asked him to leave he was determined to stay and trap and do the best possible. During the day, twelve more of Ogden's trappers deserted and moved to the camp of the Americans. Ogden called the place of this confrontation and desertion "Deserter's Point." As the day passed, several more altercations between individuals and groups took place; by evening the Americans had moved their camp about a half mile from Ogden's camp. The Hudson's Bay men set a double watch for the night. On 25 May, Ogden ordered his camp to prepare to move. Just as they were ready to leave the area, the Americans arrived again and persuaded three more to desert. By this time Ogden was angry and discouraged, as he confided to his diary following his rapid exit that day northward into Ogden Valley:

> Here I am now with only 20 Trappers Surrounded on all Sides by enemies & our expectations and hopes blasted for returns this year, to remain in this quarter any longer it would merely be to trap Beaver for the Americans for I Seriously apprehend there are Still more of the Trappers who would Willingly join them indeed the tempting offers made them independent the low price they Sell their goods are too great for them to resist.[25]

Johnson Gardner and his men had not been bashful in any sense as they harassed Ogden and his men. Gardner had threatened Ogden by saying, "You will See us shortly not only in the Columbia but at the

Flat Heads & Cottanies we are determined you Shall no longer remain in our Territory."

This confrontation on the Weber River was a wake-up call for all concerned. The British realized that they now had very real competition in the fur trade, and the Americans and those trapping out of Taos realized that although treaties might be decided in far off places, might and money could change the course of the fur trade in the mountains.

Ogden and his shrunken brigade continued to flee northward out of the range of the Americans. On 29 May three more men deserted, and during the previous ten days Ogden had lost more than 700 beaver skins. By the time Ogden and his men ended their journey at Fort Nez Perce in November 1825, it was clear that the Americans were a fur trapping force to be reckoned with.

Although he was discouraged with this, his first Snake River expedition, and its results, Ogden had left an imprint on northern Utah and Weber County—his name is affixed to a city that he never visited; his diary which illuminated his visits to the area remained unpublished until 1952. During the next five years, 1825 to 1830, Ogden conducted five more expeditions to explore the West looking for possible fur-trapping sites. During his fifth expedition, in 1828–29, he again ventured into northern Utah. He entered Utah from the west after following the Humboldt River east. By late December 1828 he had skirted the Great Salt Lake to the north and trapped in northern Utah along the Malad River and the Bear River, venturing into Cache and Ogden valleys. Here his men began to eat antelope and buffalo, happy to abandon the horseflesh they had been eating along the Humboldt.

An incident occurred during this expedition in Ogden Valley which noted mountain man Joe Meek later recounted. In the spring of 1829, the Hudson's Bay party under Ogden found themselves again facing American fur trappers, this time in the area of Ogden's Hole—Ogden Valley. The Americans were led by Thomas Fitzpatrick, who determined to procure some of Ogden's furs by inviting Ogden's Indians to bargain with him. He underlined his friendliness by opening several kegs of liquor. As the hours progressed, feelings of hostility grew. Some of Ogden's horses were stampeded into the

Americans' camp. One was a pack horse loaded with furs and another had a saddle on it with a baby tied to the saddle. It was Ogden's child, and his Indian wife immediately took action. She ran after the horse and the baby, right into the American camp. She quickly mounted the horse and then spied the Hudson's Bay Company pack horse loaded with furs. She grasped the halter of the pack horse and led it out of the hostile camp. Some American trappers felt the furs were theirs by a piece of luck and urged their comrades to shoot the fleeing woman; others suggested she was a brave woman and should be left alone. While they briefly debated the issue, she rode to safety with her baby and the pack horse loaded with furs.[26] Ogden and his party trapped in excess of 4,000 beaver on this expedition.

Following the May 1825 confrontation with Ogden, John H. Weber, Jedediah Smith, and their men traveled up the Weber River to Chalk Creek and then up Chalk Creek and to the east to Henry's Fork. One of Ashley's important innovations of the fur trade was the summer rendezvous where his men would converge and trade the furs they had gathered all year for supplies and goods that he had conveyed from St. Louis. The first of these summer get-togethers was held on Henry's Fork near the confluence of Burnt Fork and Birch Creek. The rendezvous was a key to Ashley's success. With it, he was not dependent upon trade with the Indians; rather, he relied on his men who had spent the previous year in the mountains to trap the pelts. At the rendezvous, Weber, Smith, and the other mountain men were able to trade their furs for needed goods and luxuries including coffee, lead, beads, sugar, knives, tobacco, gunpowder, salt, rifles, blankets, traps, fishhooks, scissors, buttons, and liquor. By early July, Ashley had dispensed his goods, packed his furs, and departed for St. Louis, while the trappers and Indians made plans for their trapping ventures for the next year. Summer rendezvous were held from 1825 to 1840. The 1826 rendezvous was held on the Cub River in Cache Valley while the 1827 and 1828 rendezvous were held on Bear Lake (then called Sweet Lake). The proximity of these summer gatherings to Weber County suggests that the area of northern Utah was trapped extensively during those years.

During the autumn of 1825, Weber and his men trapped along the Bear River and planned to spend the winter again in Cache Valley along the Bear River. As the winter came, however, and the running water began to freeze, snow began to pile high in Cache Valley. Some reported depths as high as eight feet. It became such a harsh winter that Weber and his party as well as other trappers decided to move nearer to the Great Salt Lake. Areas near the lake were generally free from deep snow, and the trappers divided into two camps with one party under Weber wintering near the mouth of the Weber River and the other party under William Sublette or Jedediah Smith camping near the mouth of the Bear River. There were buffalo in the vicinity for food, and the climate near the lake was much more conducive to horses surviving the winter. There were as many as one hundred trappers who spent this winter along the Weber and Bear rivers as well as 800 to 1,000 Indians in 200 lodges. Jim Beckwourth later described this winter encampment and ongoing interchange with Snake and other Indians. Winter was a time for enjoying good food, friends, and avoiding as much as possible the freezing weather. Shortly after the party with which Beckwourth was staying had settled in for the winter on the Weber River, a group of Bannock Indians stole about eighty horses, and a party of forty of the trappers followed their trail on foot. After a pursuit of five days, they found a Bannock village with a number of their horses scattered in with others. The trappers divided into two groups: Thomas Fitzpatrick and his men were to charge the Indians while Jim Bridger and his men would stampede the horses. A pitched battle ensued and the trappers recovered more than their share of horses. As they returned to their winter camp on the Weber River, they were "greeted with the liveliest demonstrations."[27]

As the spring of 1826 approached and the trappers began to divide into groups for the spring trapping, it was decided that a reconnaissance of the Great Salt Lake with particular emphasis on beaver streams would be helpful. James Clyman volunteered for the venture, and he was joined by Louis Vasquez, Moses "Black" Harris, and Henry Fraeb. They spent some time constructing bull boats, which were made by bending and fastening willows or birches into the shape of a large basket. The willows were then covered with "green" buffalo skins which were sewn tightly. The seams and skins were sealed with melted tallow. It is probable that the men began their journey near the mouth of the Weber River. In twenty-four days they paddled and poled their way around the entire lake; and, in doing so, they determined that the lake was desolate of beaver and also that it had no outlet. These trappers were the first to circumnavigate the lake; yet, even after they did, rumors of hidden whirlpools and a river running from the lake to the Pacific continued to linger.

For the next two decades the fur trade was continued, with some emphasis being paid on occasion to the area of northern Utah. Ashley sold his Rocky Mountain Fur Company to Jedediah Smith, William Sublette, and David Jackson in 1826, and they in turn sold the company to Jim Bridger, Milton Sublette, Thomas Fitzpatrick, Henry Fraeb, and Jean Baptiste Gervais in 1830. The American Fur Company began to expand its operations into the Rocky Mountains, and the establishment of Fort Hall on the Snake River near the confluence of the Portneuf River in 1834 by Nathaniel Wyeth led to further interest in trapping the area of northern Utah. In 1837 Fort Hall was purchased by the Hudson's Bay Company, which operated it until 1855.

In 1826 and 1827 Jedediah Smith made one of the most significant explorations of the American West. He began in the summer of 1826, following the yearly rendezvous held near Cove in Cache Valley on the Cub River, where he and his two partners purchased the fur company from Ashley. Smith and his small party of trappers who were exploring for beaver country journeyed south through Cache Valley and across the Weber River. They blazed the overland route to California through Utah and southern Nevada. After traveling northward in California, Smith and two of his men (Silas Gobel and Robert Evans) made a very difficult crossing of the Sierra Nevada in May 1827, becoming the first white men to do so. Difficulties continued as they crossed Nevada and entered Utah near the Deep Creek Mountains. They journeyed through Skull Valley and around the south and east shores of the Great Salt Lake. As Smith first viewed the lake on this return journey, he described it with great feeling in his diary:

> Those who may chance to read this at a distance from the scene may perhaps be surprised that the sight of this lake surrounded by

> a wilderness of More than 2000 miles diameter excited in me those feelings known to the traveler who, after long and perilous journying comes again in view of his home. But so it was with me for I had traveled so much in the vicinity of the Salt Lake that it had become my home of the wilderness.[28]

For Smith, Weber, Bridger, and other trappers, the area of the lower Weber and Bear rivers adjacent to the lake was looked upon as their home away from home. Smith and his two companions arrived just in time for the 1827 rendezvous at Bear Lake. John H. Weber may have left the mountains for good in 1826 or he may have left following the 1827 Bear Lake rendezvous. At any rate, his name was firmly attached to the Weber River. In 1826 Daniel Potts called it the Weber and, a year later, Jedediah Smith called it by the same name. Osborne Russell recorded it as the "Weaver" River, probably hearing the name often but uncertain of how it should have been spelled.[29]

Two other fur trappers had major roles in the area of Weber County over the following two decades—Osborne Russell and Miles Goodyear. Osborne Russell came west in 1834 as a member of Nathaniel Wyeth's fur expedition. Russell assisted Wyeth in building Fort Hall that same year. From 1835 until the fall of 1842, Russell was engaged in the fur trade, largely as an independent trapper, with his headquarters remaining at Fort Hall even though the fort became a part of the Hudson's Bay empire in 1837. During his years in the trade, Russell ranged throughout the northern Rockies. In 1840, 1841, and 1842 he ventured into northern Utah and Weber County and he later recorded his views and his exploits in this country in his journal. In the Wasatch Mountains east of the Great Salt Lake he stalked and shot elk, deer, and mountain sheep and he trapped beaver in the valley. On one occasion a wolverine stole a mountain sheep he had shot. He described the country in great detail; and he also described Christmas Day in 1840, which he spent on the lower Weber River:

> Decr. 25th It was agreed on by the party to prepare a Christmas dinner but I shall first endeavor to describe the party and then the dinner. I have already said the man who was the proprietor of the lodge in which I staid was a French man with a flat head wife and

> one child the inmates of the next lodge was a half breed Iowa a Nez percey wife and two children his wifes brother and another half breed next lodge was a half breed Cree his wife a Nez percey 2 children and a Snake Indian the inmates of the 3d lodge was a half breed Snake his wife (a Nez percey and two children). The remainder was 15 lodges of Snake Indians Three of the party spoke english but very broken therefore that language was made but little use of as I was familiar with the Canadian French and Indian tongue. About 1 oclk we sat down to dinner in the lodge where I staid which was the most spacious being about 36 ft. in circumference at the base with a fire built in the center around this sat on clean Epishemores all who claimed kin to the white man (or to use their own expression all that were gens d'esprit) with their legs crossed in true turkish style—and now for the dinner The first dish that came on was a large tin pan 18 inches in diameter rounding full of Stewed Elk meat The next dish was similar to the first heaped up with boiled Deer meat (or as the whites would call it Venison a term not used in the Mountains) The 3d and 4th dishes were equal in size to the first containing a boiled flour pudding prepared with dried fruit accompanied by 4 quarts of sauce made of the juice of sour berries and sugar Then came the cakes followed by about six gallons of strong Coffee already sweetened with tin cups and pans to drink out of large chips or pieces of Bark Supplying the place of plates. on being ready the butcher knives were drawn and the eating commenced at the word given by the landlady as all dinners are accompanied with conversation this was not deficient in that respect The principal topic which was discussed was the political affairs of the Rocky Mountains.[30]

Following dinner, the tobacco pipes were filled and lit, followed by a "frolic shooting at a mark" which occupied the remainder of Christmas Day. Russell and his comrades not only enjoyed a cordial fellowship along the Weber River but also enjoyed the location and its congenial winter climate. Other fur trappers including Miles Goodyear would seek the area for a temporary or even a more permanent home.

## *Explorers and Overlanders*

As the 1840s advanced, Americans became particularly interested in acquiring much or most of the West for the United States. This concept of "Manifest Destiny" was stimulated by government explorers, particularly John C. Frémont. Frémont was a noted explorer, soldier, and politician who conducted five major explorations of the American West during the 1840s and 1850s. Frémont was an officer in the U.S. Army Corps of Topographical Engineers and often included in his expedition noted mountain men guides such as Thomas Fitzpatrick and Kit Carson as well as a tall, red-faced and blond-haired German named Charles Preuss, who became his topographer and mapmaker. Frémont married Jessie Benton, daughter of Senator Thomas Hart Benton of Missouri. Both played major roles in advancing Frémont's career.

Frémont's 1842 expedition to the Rocky Mountains promoted South Pass as an emigrant route west. His second expedition of 1843 and 1844 established him as a preeminent explorer. With Thomas Fitzpatrick and Kit Carson to guide him and Preuss to make the maps, Frémont's initial effort was to locate an emigrant route across northern Colorado. It was not successful. The expedition then traveled west along the Oregon Trail and passed by Fort Bridger. They continued on the trail, following the Bear River to Soda Springs, and then decided to leave the emigrant trail and follow the Bear River to the Great Salt Lake. As the expedition traveled down the Bear River through Cache Valley, Frémont noted the decline in the buffalo population and also described his efforts to trade for food with the Snakes and the Shoshones he encountered.

Tobacco and other trade goods were exchanged, usually for edible roots. As they neared the lake, Frémont and Basil Lajeunesse inflated their eighteen-foot-long India-rubber boat and floated down a portion of the Bear River which they described as being from sixty to one hundred yards "broad." On the lower Bear River, Frémont encountered several families of "Root Diggers":

> . . . [they] were encamped among the rushes on the shore and appeared very busy about several weirs or nets which had been rudely made of canes and rushes for the purpose of catching fish. . . . They had the usual very large heads, remarkable among the Digger tribe, with matted hair, and were almost entirely naked; looking very poor and miserable, as if their lives had been spent in the rushes where they were, beyond which they seemed to have

> very little knowledge of anything. From the few words we could comprehend, their language was that of the Snake Indians.[31]

Rather than follow the Bear River to its mouth, Frémont and his men left the lower Bear River and traveled south between the lake and the mountains, entering Weber County at the hot springs, which Frémont took time to scientifically analyze and describe. From the hot springs, Frémont turned south and west toward the lake and camped on "a comparatively well timbered stream called Weber's fork." He described the Weber River as being about 100 to 150 feet wide, "with high banks, and very clear pure water, without the slightest indication of salt." On the morning of 6 September 1843 the expedition continued west toward the "butte" (Little Mountain). As they approached the shore of the lake near Little Mountain, Frémont described their grand view of the panorama of the lake.[32]

Frémont and his men spent the week of 6 through 12 September exploring and investigating western Weber County. They camped the evening of 6 September near the lake in a grove of cottonwoods on the Weber River. The next day was spent preparing their India-rubber boat for a journey on the lake and investigating their surroundings. Frémont noted that the cottonwood trees along the river had large leaves and were sixty feet in height. The sunsets they experienced were brilliant, with golden orange and green colors. Frogs sang into the night and the evenings and nights were enlivened by numerous waterfowl. The 1842 expedition had used an India-rubber raft which had sewn seams, but the 1843–44 India-rubber boat had only pasted seams and Frémont and his men were worried about its seaworthiness. For this reconnaissance of western Weber County, Frémont used his usual scientific instruments: a sextant, telescope, spyglass, thermometer, and barometer. He had calculated the altitude of the Great Salt Lake above sea level to be 4,200 feet, and as the men camped on the Weber River they measured the water to be generally eight or ten feet deep. During the week, food for the party consisted of ducks, geese, seagulls, yampah roots, kamas roots, and coffee, among other things. The expedition was running low on food and had even eaten skunk meat in the recent past.

The day of 8 September was spent floating the boat down the

river to the lakeshore, where they camped; and on 9 September the party dragged the boat through shallow water making a "very disagreeable smell" as the lake mud was disturbed and they sank up to their knees at every step. After about a mile of dragging, deeper water was reached and they began to paddle to the nearest island—Fremont Island. They were uncertain of what they might find either on the islands or in the lake, and they had discussed whirlpools and other possible dangers. When they were about halfway to the island, the boat began to leak air, and it soon required the constant use of the bellows to keep the boat afloat. Upon reaching the shore of the island, the boat was lifted from the water with care to avoid further puncture problems. Along the shore were found large quantities of the dried bodies of insects. These piles of insects measured from seven to twelve inches in depth and from ten to twenty feet in length. Frémont commented that this would make excellent food for Indians but was generally repugnant to all others.

An extensive exploration of the island was undertaken, with Frémont noting that the island was twelve to thirteen miles in circumference and yet was basically only a rocky outcrop protruding out of the lake. Frémont and Preuss climbed to the highest point on the island, which was some 800 feet above the water, and conducted a telescopic survey of the lake and its surroundings. They drew a map of the lake from this single vantage point, and Frémont accidentally left the brass cover to his spyglass on the summit of the island. While Frémont and Preuss were engaged in mapping the lake, Kit Carson and others in the party engaged themselves in ascending the "mountain and under a shelving rock, cut a large cross which is there to this day."[33]

After a day of exploration hoping for more fertile and exotic findings, Frémont named the island "Disappointment Island." In 1850 Captain Howard Stansbury renamed the island in honor of Frémont. The night of 9 September was spent on the island "in perfect security," with no worries of a surprise attack, with a large driftwood fire, lodges made out of driftwood for sleeping, and all listening to the "roar of an ocean surf."

The next day dawned with a storm brewing and the lake dark and agitated. Frémont and his men took to their boat and began to row for the mainland, and it took all of their efforts to make headway against the blowing wind and the waves of the lake. The boat was continually filling with water from the waves, which kept some busy bailing while others rowed for their lives. Eventually they reached shallow water, which they celebrated with a loud shout. As they beached their boat, they found they were about nine miles from their camp on the Weber River, and Charles Preuss set off to get their horses to carry their boat and equipment back to camp. September 11 was spent in making further observations of the area, including boiling five gallons of lake water, which yielded fourteen pints of a very fine-grained white salt. Frémont described the general area as being well-timbered along the streams and rivers and of "tolerably good sandy soil." This report, which was written in the field, was later edited with his wife Jessie's help and printed in 1845. It was read by the Mormons in Nauvoo with great interest as they looked for a home in the West. Part of the report specifically described in detail the area of Weber County and the environs of the Bear River as it flowed through present-day Box Elder and Cache counties.

After their exploration of the lake, the Frémont expedition moved northward up the Bear and Malad rivers to Fort Hall and eventually west to California. Frémont returned to the area of Utah as he returned to the east from California in 1844. In 1845, during his third expedition to the West, he visited Utah Lake, the Great Salt Lake, and rode on horseback onto Antelope Island before he departed across the salt desert for California. His 1843–44 expedition was his most important not only for his survey of northern Utah and the Great Salt Lake but also for his reconnaissance of the Great Basin, the Sierra Nevada, and California. It was during this expedition that he recognized and described the Great Basin as having no outlet to the sea. His journal and descriptions of northern Utah were instrumental in influencing the Mormons to settle in the area within two years of the publication of the report. Within Weber County, Fremont Island and Fremont High School are two of many things named for John C. Frémont, who made the first scientific observations of Weber County.

Frémont's explorations were contemporary with the last years of the fur trade and he depended substantially on seasoned trappers to guide him on his expeditions. Miles Goodyear broke into the fur trade during its decline, but Goodyear's establishment of Fort Buenaventura on the Weber River gave Ogden and Weber County the distinction of being the oldest continuously settled areas in the state of Utah. Goodyear was born in New England in 1817, and in 1836 he traveled west on the Oregon Trail to Fort Hall in the company of Marcus and Narcissa Whitman and other missionaries. For the next decade, Goodyear, who was a slight, red-headed young man, became well educated in the ways of the mountain man. As a free trapper, unattached to any company, he trapped and traded out of Fort Hall, Fort Bridger, and Fort Winty in the Uinta Basin. As the fur trade began to decline, Goodyear became proficient as a trader of all kinds of goods, particularly horses. He enjoyed company and was fond of the summer rendezvous held by and for the mountain men and their Native American friends.

As was the custom with most mountain men, in 1839 Goodyear married an Indian bride named Pomona. She was a member of the Ute tribe, and their relationship was beneficial to his trapping and trading activities. Miles and Pomona became the parents of two children—William Miles Goodyear and Mary Eliza Goodyear. Goodyear became more aware that the fur trade was in decline and that in order to survive he would have to be more versatile than being just a trapper. He began thinking of establishing a fort—a place to trade for furs and a way station for overland emigrants—as early as 1840 and certainly by 1844. He had experienced first-hand the social and economic benefits of forts as well as their problems.

During the summer of 1845, Goodyear traveled east to Independence, Missouri, to purchase trade goods for what he described as a "half way house" for emigrants in the Rocky Mountains.[34] For Goodyear, his fort was to serve as a way station for emigrants to trade used up and tired animals for fresh ones; to trade for furs, particularly with Indians; and to cultivate the immediate area around the fort to grow fresh vegetables and corn which could be sold to overland emigrants. In 1845 none of the then-existing overland stations provided freshly grown produce, wheat, and corn. Goodyear's proposed establishment would be unique, but it would need to be located at an altitude and with a climate that would be compatible to farming as well as in a location that would adjoin the overland trails.

Goodyear located a site on the Weber River as the spot for his new fort and way station. This site was on a large westward bend of the Weber River, approximately two miles south of its confluence with the Ogden River and approximately a quarter mile west of the present end of Ogden's 28th Street. Goodyear had no doubt located the site much earlier, and had probably even camped at it on numerous occasions. In 1845 he obtained goods in Missouri for trading purposes, and he then spent much of the summer of 1846 at Fort Bridger, trading with overland emigrants. During the late summer and fall of 1846, Goodyear, his wife and children, and a friend, a Captain Wells, formerly of the British Army, carried out the construction of what Goodyear named Fort Buenaventura.[35]

Goodyear's Fort Buenaventura was likely named for the mythical western river which was drawn on many early maps and supposedly flowed from the Rocky Mountains into San Francisco Bay. There may have been others, both mountain men and Indians, who helped with the construction of the fort. By the end of 1846, a stockade made of cottonwood logs from along the river set upright in the ground enclosed about one-half acre. Three log cabins occupied three corners of the fort, and sheds, corrals, and a garden were also located within the enclosure. Earlier log structures had housed mountain men and trading activities in Utah, particularly in the Uinta Basin, but Fort Buenaventura proved to be the first to be continuously occupied as a settlement from that time until the present. Additional corrals adjoined the outside of the stockade to accommodate Goodyear's forty horses, ninety Spanish goats, eighty head of cattle, as well as numerous sheep.[36]

About seventy-five yards southwest of Goodyear's fort rose a large sand knoll, from the top of which it was possible to view the surrounding area as well as to observe approaching emigrant trains from Weber Canyon to the southeast or from the Bear River Valley to the north. The Great Salt Lake was approximately ten miles to the west, and to the east the Wasatch Mountains rose majestically.

By the late autumn of 1846, Goodyear was ready to leave his newly constructed fort in the care of Captain Wells, his wife and children, some Indian retainers, and some of his mountain men friends who wished to winter there while he traveled to California to sell the deer- and elk skins which he had procured in his trade with the Indians. He arrived in Los Angeles early in 1847 and sold his trade goods, acquiring a herd of about 100 horses. With his horses, he then traveled north, spent some time at Sutter's Fort, and then traveled east over the Sierras and along the Humboldt trail route toward his home. His intentions were to make a profit by selling his horses to emigrants traveling overland in 1847. To do this, after he reached Fort Buenaventura, he drove his horses eastward up Weber Canyon to intercept the main Oregon and California trails in western Wyoming.

On 10 July 1847 Goodyear and his fellow travelers and horse drivers encountered the initial group of Mormon pioneers near the Bear River crossing on Sulphur Creek about eight miles southeast of present Evanston. The Mormons had heard of Goodyear and his farm and fort from Jim Bridger and others. Much of that Saturday evening of 10 July was spent with the Mormons questioning Goodyear about the Salt Lake Valley. Orson Pratt, Wilford Woodruff, George A. Smith, and William Clayton all recorded their encounter with Goodyear, although Clayton was a bit more skeptical than the rest as he noted:

> After camping Mr. Miles Good[year] came into camp. He is the man who is making a farm in the Bear River valley. He says it is yet 75 miles to his place, although we are now within two miles of Bear River. His report of the valley is more favorable than some we have heard, but we have an idea he is anxious to have us make a road to his place through selfish motives.[37]

The Mormons were following the wagon road established by California emigrants (including the ill-fated Donner-Reed party) the previous year on the advice of Lansford Hastings, and they asked Goodyear about the route for the next several miles because they had a question concerning the better of two forks on the immediate trail between the Bear River and Cache Cave. Goodyear gave them some advice, which the majority agreed to follow. An erroneous story has grown from Goodyear's encounter with the Mormons which suggests that he guided Orrin Porter Rockwell and others down much of the Weber River, hoping they would make that their route to the Salt

Lake Valley.[38] Goodyear did not take Rockwell down the Weber River, nor did he make any effort to have the Mormons take the Weber River route to the Great Salt Lake Valley and to his fort. The Mormons had already determined they were taking Hastings's route, which would take them through East and Emigration canyons. Following his discussions with the Mormons on the evening of 10 July, Goodyear left the next morning to herd his horses down the Bear River, as the Oregon immigration was earlier than usual and he wished to trade as many horses as possible to emigrants. The Mormons also left that morning and continued on their route to their new home, Great Salt Lake City.

During the next five months, a series of events took place which changed the course of history for Weber County in a dramatic fashion. Goodyear spent much of the summer and fall trading, and in September 1847, as he passed through the new Mormon city, he purchased a cat which had crossed the plains with the Mormons as a present for his wife and children. In November, Goodyear's brother Andrew arrived at Fort Buenaventura to visit and become reacquainted. From July through November, a number of Mormons visited Fort Buenaventura inspecting the garden and the livestock as well as the general vicinity. The fifteen-square-yard garden at Fort Buenaventura grown during 1847 was primarily the work of Captain Wells, who carried the water by bucket from the Weber River to irrigate the beans, cabbages, radishes, Spanish and American corn, and carrots (which grew to one foot in length).[39] Wells lived at the fort for about one year before departing late in the summer of 1847. The Mormons were concerned about survival in the Great Basin. Jim Bridger had questioned the feasibility of growing corn in the northern Great Basin because of the coolness of the nights; but it was growing at Goodyear's fort, and the Mormons were undeniably heartened.

As Brigham Young left the Salt Lake Valley on 26 August, the government for the Mormon colony became the Mormon High Council. The conditions of the new settlement did not meet the expectations of all of its inhabitants and some talked of going to California or returning to the east. In early October, William Weeks, Hazen Kimball, William Gardner, and a man named Babcock and their families and teams traveled north to Goodyear's settlement. The High Council did not like this group leaving and requested by letter that they return. As the marshal for the High Council negotiated with the dissenters near the Weber River, they noted that they "did not like so much bondage" and they directed their comments to him by use of "harsh remarks."[40]

Events and circumstances by early autumn began to suggest that Fort Buenaventura might change ownership. By the end of October, Mormon leaders felt that the Goodyear fort might be a haven for dissenters, and they also looked upon the area along the lower Weber River as a proven agricultural district. For a mountain man and trader who was used to remoteness and the solitary life, Goodyear was beginning to feel that civilization was too close. Some 2,200 emigrants had arrived in the Salt Lake Valley from July through October 1847. On 9 November, Henry G. Sherwood reported to the High Council that Brigham Young had advised him to make efforts to buy Goodyear's property for $2,000. A committee composed of Ira Eldredge, Daniel Spencer, and Henry G. Sherwood made efforts to procure the needed funds, but they reported on 11 November that they were unsuccessful. On 16 November, Goodyear arrived in the Mormon settlement, and over the next ten days negotiations were conducted for the sale of Fort Buenaventura, with both parties being very interested in the success of the discussions.

Well-intended negotiations were made possible in part because of the return of Captain James Brown. Brown, who had served in the Mexican War as a member of the Mormon Battalion, had arrived in the Salt Lake Valley following the new Mormon Trail on 29 July with about 140 battalion members who had spent the previous winter in Pueblo because of sickness. His group was augmented by an additional 100 Mormons who had begun their journey in Mississippi. Shortly after his arrival in the Salt Lake Valley, Brown left for California to collect back pay for battalion members. He collected "five thousand dollars in Spanish doubloons"[41] at Monterey for the service of battalion members and returned the money to Utah via a difficult journey over the Humboldt route. In Great Salt Lake City on 25 November 1847 the transaction was completed, with Goodyear receiving $1,950 in gold for his fort and what Goodyear described as his "Mexican grant" which "commenced at the mouth of Weber Canyon and followed the base of the mountains north to the hot springs; thence west to the Salt Lake; then south along the shore to a point opposite Weber Canyon thence east to the beginning."[42]

To complete the bargain, Goodyear also threw in with his "land grant" his cattle, goats, sheep, and the cat which he purchased two months earlier. He retained his horses and pelts for trading purposes. Although Goodyear claimed he had a Mexican or Spanish land grant, this claim probably had little to back it up. However, the Mormons were mainly interested in physically securing the fort area, the proven agricultural property, and the animals; and through their agent James Brown the deal was consummated. The land purchase measured about fourteen miles north to south by fifteen miles east to west, and encompassed more than 210 square miles. Thus, the purchase price in this land deal for more than half of Weber County was about nine dollars a square mile.

The Mormon migration of 1847 was part of a much larger movement of settlers westward. Initially the interest of most had been in Oregon; but, in 1841, thirty-four overlanders had cut across the northwestern portion of Utah heading directly for California. In 1845, 5,397 emigrants traveled west to Oregon and California; and this number increased to 8,097 in 1846. In 1847, Utah was added as a place of destination, as 14,747 traveled west. In 1846, Lansford Hastings was able to persuade four groups of overlanders to follow his suggested cutoff route to California. This route proved to extend the travel time rather than to decrease it, however. The first three of these groups traveled down Weber Canyon and around the south end of the Great Salt Lake as they blazed a new trail toward California and as Miles Goodyear was building his fort on the lower Weber River. Nine men were included in the first overland group—the Bryant-Russell party—to travel down Weber Canyon. They traveled by horse and mule and were guided by James Hudspeth. Edwin Bryant gained much of his writing experience as a journalist in Kentucky, and his journal is a well-written account detailing this journey. On 26 July 1846 Bryant and his group traveled through lower Morgan Valley and then through a very difficult and narrow part of lower Weber Canyon before exiting the mountains. This is the current section of Weber Canyon between Uintah and Mountain Green, although the canyon has been "straightened" over the past half-century for automobile traffic. This part of the canyon came to be called Devil's Gate.[43]

Bryant described the canyon and the emigrants' passage:

> Entering between the walls of the mountains forming the canon, after laborious exertions for several hours, we passed through it without any serious accident. The canon is four or five miles through, and we were compelled, as heretofore, to climb along the side of the precipitous mountains, frequently passing under, and sometimes scaling, immense overhanging masses and projections of rock. To be thus safely enlarged from this natural prison-house, locked at every point, was an agreeable, if not an important event in the history of our journey.[44]

The group camped near the mouth of the canyon and Bryant made some further observations on the landscape, noting that the plain or valley of the lake seemed fertile as the river wound through the countryside to the north. One of the party had taken "with his hook about a dozen salmon-trout, from eight to eighteen inches in length," with the largest weighing four or five pounds. The party lingered at their camping spot near the mouth of the canyon the next day as they all successfully fished using insects resembling crickets for bait. They also spent part of the day gathering serviceberries to eat.

The Harlan-Young party was the first to take wagons down Weber Canyon, and they were guided by Lansford Hastings. The leaders of the party were George W. Harlan and Samuel C. Young, and as they traveled west from Fort Bridger to cross the Great Basin they had forty wagons in their company. They had a most exacting and arduous time through lower Weber Canyon and Devil's Gate. At least one wagon and team was lost in the chasm.

Following close on the heels of the Harlan-Young group was a group of Swiss and German overlanders. One of them, Heinrich Lienhard, kept an excellent journal, and because of that the party has been identified by his name. The Lienhard party was about half the size of the Harlan-Young group, with about twenty wagons. As they approached Devil's Gate, Lienhard wrote:

> On August 6 we ventured upon this furious passage, up to this point decidedly the wildest we had encountered, if not the most dangerous. We devoted the entire forenoon and until full one o'clock in the afternoon to the task of getting our four wagons through. In places we unhitched from the wagon all the oxen except the wheel-yoke, then we strained at both hind wheels, one drove, and the rest steadied the wagon; we then slid rapidly down into the foaming water, hitched the loose oxen again to the wagon and took it directly down the foaming riverbed full of great boulders, on account of which the wagon quickly lurched from one side to the other; now we had to turn the wheels by the spokes, then again hold back with all the strength we had, lest it sweep upon a low lying rock and smash itself to pieces. In going back for each wagon we had to be very careful lest we lose our footing on the slippery rocks under the water and ourselves be swept down the rapid, foaming torrent.[45]

Lienhard noted that by this point in his westward journey he had worn out three pairs of boots and one of shoes and would from that point onward need to make his own footwear. He also commented shortly after leaving the mouth of Weber River Canyon as he gazed upon the beautiful landscape that the soil was rich and deep black and that he felt the area was so beautiful that had it been inhabited he would have remained and established his home.

The Donner-Reed party was the next group to follow the Hasting's route west, but they received instructions from Hastings that the Weber River canyon was too difficult for wagon travel and instead pioneered a new route across the Wasatch Mountains up East Canyon, over Big Mountain, and down Emigration Canyon. This newly blazed Donner-Reed route was the one which the Mormons followed the next year into the Salt Lake Valley.

A final government exploration of the area of northern Utah took place under the direction of Captain Howard Stansbury of the Corps of Topographical Engineers between August 1849 and August 1850. Stansbury and his surveying party explored and mapped around the Great Salt Lake and Utah Lake and as far east as Fort Laramie. Their findings influenced later western travel, including stagecoach and railroad routes. Stansbury's exploration group was made up of eighteen men including his second in command, Lt. John W. Gunnison. Their major tasks included identifying new and better routes west from Fort Laramie and exploring and mapping the environs of the Great Salt Lake. On 27 August 1849 Stansbury described in detail Ogden Valley and Ogden Canyon as he approached them down the south fork of the Ogden River.

> After passing through this kanyon the ridges separate & you come upon a most lovely broad open valley somewhat in the shape of a half moon about 15 miles in length & from 5 to 7 in width, bounded on all sides especially on the South & West by lofty hills & rocky mountains upon which the snow was lying in patches in many places. The valley is very rich & level. Ogdens creek running at the base of the mountains on the left for rather more than half the length of the valley when it breaks thro the range dividing Ogdens hole from S. Lake Valley, by a kanyon which is almost impassable for even pack mules. Springs break out from the hills on the right & facilities for irrigation are very great. A fine branch rising at the north end of the valley in a ridge separating Ogdens hole from Cache valley, washes the base of the ridge between the former & S.L. Valley & joins Ogdens Creek just before it enters the kanyon after passing thro which it discharges its waters into Weber river. Numerous beautiful little streams of bright clear running water are to be met with in abundance. Rather more than half way between the Kanyon of Ogdens Creek & the North end of the Valley, a pass is to be found by which a crossing of the mountain into the Salt Lake valley can be obtained.[46]

For the next year, Stansbury and his men spent much of their time exploring the Great Salt Lake and in doing so spent some of their time camped in and passing through Weber County. Their daily diaries describe life and the landscape in the region in good detail. On 6 April 1850 they began their reconnaissance of Fremont Island. Stansbury observed that the Mormons called it Castle Island while noting that Frémont had named it Disappointment Island. Stansbury reported in his journal, "I deemed it but due, however, to the first adventurous explorer of this distant region to name it after him who first set foot upon its shores, and have therefore called it Fremont Island."[47] Stansbury described the island as being fourteen miles in circumference, with neither timber nor water upon it. The sides of the island were covered with luxuriant grass as well as great quantities of wild onion, wild parsnip, and sego lily. He noted that the sego lily had a small bulbous root about the size of a walnut that was very palatable and nutritious and was often used by the Indians as food. Near the summit of the island, the sage grew to an extraordinary size—eight feet high and six to eight inches in diameter.

Stansbury's accurate description of the island did little to excite individuals to homestead its shores, however. As he finished his explorations and reported them to Congress, Weber County was created in northern Utah. The 1840s had seen many changes in the area—moving from the fur trade to a permanent fort established by Miles Goodyear, to overlanders and explorers, and finally to Goodyear selling his Fort Buenaventura to the Mormons.

## ENDNOTES

1. Dale L. Morgan, *The State of Deseret* (Salt Lake City: Utah State Historical Society, 1940).

2. Juanita Brooks, ed., *On the Mormon Frontier: The Diary of Hosea Stout* 2 vols. (Salt Lake City: University of Utah Press, 1964), 358–59.

3. Historical Records Survey, *Preliminary Inventory of the County Archives of Utah, No. 29, Weber County* (Ogden: Utah Historical Records Survey Project, 1940), 180.

4. Ibid., 149

5. Ibid.

6. Ibid.

7. Ibid., 149–50.

8. Richard W. Sadler and Richard C. Roberts, *The Weber River Basin: Grass Roots Democracy and Water Development* (Logan: Utah State University Press, 1994).

9. Deon Greer, ed., *Atlas of Utah* (Provo: Brigham Young University Press, 1981), 16–19.

10. See Lehi F. Hintze, *Geologic History of Utah* (Provo: Brigham Young University Department of Geology, 1988); and William Lee Stokes, *Geology of Utah* (Salt Lake City: Utah Museum of Natural History, 1988).

11. Stokes, *Geology of Utah,* 14–15.

12. Jesse D. Jennings, "Early Man in Utah," *Utah Historical Quarterly* 28 (January 1960): 3–28.

13. See Steven R. Simms, with Mark E. Stuart, Sheila Beckstead, Eva Jensen, and Suzanne Sarver, *Archaeological Reconnaissance in the Lower Bear River Marshes, Utah,* Utah State University Contributions to Anthropology, Number 13 (May 1991), 12. See also C. Melvin Aikens, *Excavations at Snake Rock Village and the Bear River No. 2 Site,* University of Utah Anthropological Papers no, 87, 1966, Salt Lake City; Neil M. Judd, "Notes on Certain Prehistoric Habitations in Western Utah," in *Proceedings of the 19th International Congress of Americanists,* 1917, Washington, D.C.; and Neil M. Judd, "Archaeological Observations North of the Rio Colorado," *Bureau of American Ethnology Bulletin* 82, 1926, Washington, D.C.

14. William B. Fawcett and Steven R. Simms, *Archaeological Test Excavations in the Great Salt Lake Wetlands and Associated Analyses, Weber and Box Elder Counties, Utah,* Utah State University Contributions to Anthropology, Number 14 (1993).

15. Brigham D. Madsen, *The Shoshoni Frontier and the Bear River Massacre* (Salt Lake City: University of Utah Press, 1985), 12.

16. See Madsen, *The Shoshoni Frontier;* and Catherine S. Fowler and Don D. Fowler, "Notes on the History of the Southern Paiutes and Western Shoshonis," *Utah Historical Quarterly* 39 (Spring 1971): 95–113.

17. David J. Wishart, *The Fur Trade of the American West, 1807–1840* (Lincoln: University of Nebraska Press, 1992), 27.

18. Richard M. Clokey, *William H. Ashley* (Norman: University of Oklahoma Press, 1990), 67.

19. Wishart, *The Fur Trade of the American West,* 121–48. See also Dale L. Morgan, *Jedediah Smith and the Opening of the West* (Lincoln: University of Nebraska Press, 1953).

20. David E. Miller, ed., "William Kittson's Journal Covering Peter Skene Ogden's 1824–1825 Snake Country Expedition," *Utah Historical Quarterly* 22 (1954): 135.

21. David E. Miller, ed., "Peter Skene Ogden's Journal of His Expedition to Utah, 1825," *Utah Historical Quarterly* 20 (1952): 178.

22. LeRoy R. Hafen, "Etienne Provost," in Hafen, *Trappers of the Far West* (Lincoln: University of Nebraska, 1983), 1.

23. Milton R. Hunter, ed., *Beneath Ben Lomond's Peak* (Salt Lake City: Publishers Press, 1966), 14–15. Hunter in *Beneath Ben Lomond's Peak* locates this surprise attack on the lower Weber River. Virtually all historians of the fur trade dispute this fact and place it on either the lower Provo or the Jordan River near Utah Lake.

24. Miller, ed., "Peter Skene Ogden's Journal," 181.

25. Ibid., 184–85.

26. Stanley Vestal, *Joe Meek, the Merry Mountain Man* (Lincoln:

University of Nebraska, 1966), 83–84; Ted Warner, "Peter Skene Ogden," in Hafen, *Mountain Men and Fur Traders of the Far West* (Lincoln: University of Nebraska Press, 1982), 134; LeRoy R. Hafen, *Broken Hand: The Life of Thomas Fitzpatrick, Mountain Man, Guide and Indian Agent* (Lincoln: University of Nebraska Press, 1981), 92.

27. Hafen, *Broken Hand*, 59–60.

28. Morgan, *Jedediah Smith*, 213–14.

29. *Preliminary Inventory, Weber County;* Dale L. Morgan, *The West of William H. Ashley* (Denver: Old West Publishing Company), 1964, 149; Aubrey L. Haines, *Journal of a Trapper* (Lincoln: University of Nebraska Press, 1970), 114.

30. Haines, *Journal of a Trapper*, 114–15.

31. John C. Frémont, *The Exploring Expedition to the Rocky Mountains* (Washington, D.C.: Smithsonian Institution Press, 1988), 148.

32. Ibid., 151.

33. Milo Milton Quaife, ed., *Kit Carson's Autobiography* (Lincoln: University of Nebraska Press, 1966), 76.

34. Dale L. Morgan, "Miles Goodyear and the Founding of Ogden," *Utah Historical Quarterly* 21 (1953): 208–9.

35. Edwin Bryant, *What I Saw in California* (Lincoln: University of Nebraska Press, 1985), 119–20. Bryant described Captain Wells in his journal: "July 3, 1846 . . . We were joined today by Capt. Welles and Mr. McClary, the first a mountain-trapper, intending to accompany us as far as Fort Bridger, and the last an emigrant bound for California. Capt. Welles, as he informed us and as I was informed by others, had once held a commission in the British army. He was in the battles of Waterloo and New Orleans. He was a man of about sixty, vigorous and athletic, and his manners, address, and general intelligence, although clothed in the rude buckskin costume of the wilderness, confirmed the statements in regard to him, made by himself and others."

36. Wayne L. Venable, "Miles Goodyear," M.A. thesis, University of Utah, 1966, 99.

37. George D. Smith, ed., *An Intimate Chronicle: The Journals of William Clayton* (Salt Lake City: Signature Books in association with Smith Research Associates, 1991), 355; Elden J. Watson, *The Orson Pratt Journals* (Salt Lake City: Elden J. Watson, 1975), 442–43. Orson Pratt noted on 10 July 1847: "I discovered a smoke some two miles from our encampment, which I expected arose from some small Indian encampment. I informed some of our men and they immediately went to discover who they were; they found them to be a small party from the Bay of St. Francisco, on their way home to the States. They were accompanied by Mr. Miles Goodyear, a

mountaineer, as far as this point, where Mr. Goodyear learning from us that the Oregon emigration was earlier than usual, and that they, instead of coming by way of Bridger's had taken a more northern route, concluded to go down the Bear River, and intersect them for the purpose of trade. Mr. G. informed us that he had just established himself near the Salt Lake, between the mouths of Weber's Fork and Bear River; that he had been to the Bay of St. Francisco on business & just returned with this company following the Hastings new route; that those left in charge at the lake had succeeded in making a small garden which was doing well by being watered."

38. Charles Kelly and Maurice L. Howe, *Miles Goodyear, First Citizen of Utah* (Salt Lake City: Western Printing Company, 1937), 73–75.

39. Morgan, "Miles Goodyear and the Founding of Ogden," 315.

40. Journal History of the Church of Jesus Christ of Latter-day Saints. 6, 7, 11, 24 October, and 3 November 1847, LDS Church Historian's Office, Salt Lake City.

41. Will Bagley, *Frontiersman: Abner Blackburn's Narrative* (Salt Lake City: University of Utah Press, 1992), 111.

42. Kelly and Howe, *Miles Goodyear,* 90.

43. J. Roderic Korns, "West From Fort Bridger, The Pioneering of the Immigrant Trails Across Utah, 1846–1850," *Utah Historical Quarterly* 18 (1951): 132.

44. Bryant, *What I Saw in California,* 156–157.

45. Korns, "West From Fort Bridger," 132–33.

46. Brigham D. Madsen, ed., *Exploring the Great Salt Lake, The Stansbury Expedition of 1849–50* (Salt Lake City: University of Utah, 1989), 149–50.

47. Ibid., 327.

2

# THE SETTLEMENT OF WEBER COUNTY, 1847–1869

With the arrival of the Mormon pioneers in 1847, a process of settlement and change started which has had a continuous effect on the area of Weber County to the present. The Mormon emigrants who were led to the Great Basin by Brigham Young were organized into functional groups which took their religious and social directions from the hierarchy of the Mormon church, the Quorum of Twelve Apostles with Young as its president. For the first two decades of the Mormon settlement in Utah, governmental operations were very theocratic in nature, as many Mormons looked forward to the establishment of the Kingdom of God on earth. The entire area of the Great Basin remained ostensibly under Mexican control until the end of the Mexican War in 1848, although little control from Mexico was ever exerted over the area.

On 22 August 1847 before returning east to Winter Quarters to aid in the migration of other Mormons to Salt Lake, Brigham Young recommended to the community in Salt Lake City that a president be appointed to preside over the settlement in his absence and that other officials be chosen to help to govern the new community. From that recommendation John Smith (uncle to murdered church founder Joseph Smith) was chosen as president along with a high council and a marshall for Great Salt Lake City.[1] On 3 October 1847, in a church conference, these nominations were ratified. The high council government was the ruling authority in the Salt Lake region from 3 October 1847 and this government authorized James Brown to purchase Fort Buenaventura in the Weber River area in November 1847. While at Council Bluffs, Young was sustained as the president of the Church of Jesus Christ of Latter-day Saints and he returned to Salt Lake on 20 September 1848.

On 9 December 1848 Young changed the main body of civil government to a general council (sometimes called the General Assembly) which assumed law-making powers for the community. A judiciary was provided through the local bishops' courts, from which appeals could be made to the church high councils. The police power functions were carried out by the militia (known as the Nauvoo Legion) and appointed law enforcement officers. Tithes and offerings made to the church provided the revenues to run the system. This general council government continued, under Brigham Young's guidance, to make decisions and laws until it was replaced by the provisional State of Deseret in March 1849.

### *Early Government*

The general council government divided the city of Salt Lake into nineteen ecclesiastical wards on 14 February 1849, and on 16 February created additional wards in the valley outside the city and organized three wards north of Salt Lake: "first, all north of the City so far as to include Sessions Settlement [Bountiful]; second, the country between Sessions' and the settlements on the Weber River; third, the Brown Settlement. (Ogden.)" These early governments passed laws related to the pressing needs of the community, including regulation of land, water, and timber resources.

The State of Deseret constitution was drafted in February 1849. The Constitution was adopted on 10 March, and on 12 March officials of the new government were elected and appointed. This first election was proclaimed as a "general election," with 624 votes being polled. The ticket presented only one slate of candidates, and apparently all votes were cast for them. The election made Brigham Young governor and elected several others to official positions.

In addition, magistrates were elected to the nineteen political wards of the city and also for the six outlying precincts, of which the Weber River Precinct was one. James Brown was elected as magistrate of the new civil Weber River Precinct on 12 March 1849 and was ordained bishop of the Weber River ecclesiastical ward on 25 March 1849.

Political changes came quickly. This government stayed in power until 26 March 1851, when the State of Deseret was formally dissolved. Although the leaders of Utah had spent much of this period petitioning Congress for approval of the State of Deseret, their efforts failed in part because of the size of their proposed state and also because members of Congress had reservations about the Mormon religion and its shadow political government. The State of Deseret proposal became a part of the larger national discussion and ended up being a portion of the Compromise of 1850 in which Utah Territory was organized under the congressional territorial system.

This territorial bill was passed by Congress and became effective when President Millard Fillmore signed it on 9 September 1850. Even though the State of Deseret was never officially approved, it operated as the government of Utah for two years before the territory was organized. In this period, laws were passed which fixed boundaries and established officials and duties of county government. One of the first acts passed was a law of 9 January 1850 which organized the judiciary of the proposed state of Deseret and had several sections relating to county officers.

In "An Ordinance, to provide for the Organization of the Judiciary of the State of Deseret," approved on 16 January 1850, numerous sections outlined the various judicial officers and their functions for the counties. The ordinance provided for county prosecuting attorneys, county courts (made up of one chief justice and two associate justices), clerks of the county courts, county sheriffs and deputies, justices of the peace and constables in the precincts, and a coroner.[2] In an ordinance passed a year later, the county court's titles of members were changed to probate judge and selectmen, and, as the governing body of the county, the courts were given civil and criminal jurisdictions as well as administrative duties. Such a fusion of judicial functions with executive and legislative functions was noteworthy, for the county governing body was technically an arm of the legislature, not an arm of the judicial system. This administrative power was something that was not paralleled until recent times, when regulatory commissions and agencies of state and national governments have been created.[3]

On 15 January 1850 "An Ordinance providing for State and County Commissioners, On Roads" was passed. The ordinance allowed county courts "power to appoint one or more Commissioners, whenever they deem it necessary, to locate all County roads within the limit of said County, whose term of office shall be two years. . . . " On 1 February 1850 "An Ordinance, Authorizing the Location of State Roads, &c." approved a state road, "eight rods in width, be located from Ogden, the County seat of Weber County, south, passing the Temple Block, in Great Salt Lake City, and terminating at the Town of Provo, the County Seat in Utah County."[4] Increased travel and the spread of communities had led to this ordinance. On 2 March 1850 the office of county recorder was created.

In "An Ordinance, Providing for the Location of Counties and Precincts Therein Named, &c.," approved 31 January 1850, six counties were created by the State of Deseret—Weber County, Great Salt Lake County, Utah County, San Pete County, Tooele County, and Little Salt Lake County. Ogden City was designated as the county seat of Weber County, and Ogden City was incorporated eleven months later on 6 February 1851.[5] The boundaries of Weber County changed in the period between 1850 and 1898 as previously noted. The legislature of the Territory of Utah, by a joint resolution passed on 4 October 1851, legalized the acts of the earlier governments.

## *Early Settlement*

In August 1847 Jesse Little took an exploring expedition to Fort Hall in Idaho to see what the nature of the land to the north was like. Wilford Woodruff reported that

> the messengers Bring a Glorious report of the cash valley & the Country between us & there, that [there] is rich soil & well watered

> & well calculated for farming purposes Also bear river valley for stock grazing. . . . [The expedition] Called at Miles Goodyiers place. Had about 30 yards picketed in A small garding Corn and vegitation doing well.[6]

After the purchase of Miles Goodyear's fort in November 1847, Captain James Brown sent his two sons, Alexander and Jesse, to take possession of the property on 12 January 1848. Two months later, on 6 March 1848, Brown moved his family, accompanied by the families of Henry C. Shelton, Louis B. Meyers, and George W. Thurkill, into the fort region on the Weber River. A few days later, the families of Robert Crow, Rueben Henry, Artemus Sprague, Daniel Burch, William Stewart, Mrs. Ruth Stewart, and Urban Van Stewart followed to the new settlement. The Brown family occupied Goodyear's fort and the other settlers built homesteads along the Weber River to the south and as distant as Mound Fort, two miles to the north beyond the Ogden River.

After the purchase of Goodyear's fort, Captain James Brown had been appointed bishop over the ward area designated as Brown's Settlement Ward or the Weber River Ward in 1849 by Brigham Young and the ruling council in Salt Lake, and he was also elected to be the civil leader of the Weber River Precinct. Early in 1850 the Brown family abandoned the old Fort Buenaventura of Miles Goodyear and relocated on higher ground near present 29th Street and west of Wall Avenue because of flooding of the Buenaventura settlement by the Weber River. This new fort consisted of about a block of houses built in the fort plan. Besides the Brown family, the new fort drew several other families to this more southern location.[7] At that same time James Brown also moved one of the original Goodyear cabins to the Tabernacle Square near present Grant Avenue and 22nd Street where some of his family lived. That same building was moved several times through the years, but presently stands near where Brown had once placed it on Tabernacle Square.[8]

The Weber River site of Fort Buenaventura was the first of the Mormon settlements in Weber County; but, during a visit to the Weber River community in September 1849 by Brigham Young and other Mormon leaders, including Heber C. Kimball, Jedediah M.

Grant, and Thomas Bullock, it was decided where the city of Ogden should be located. Thomas Bullock wrote on 2 September 1849:

> after spending a comfortable night in Brownsville, President Brigham Young and party spent a pleasant day visiting about in and near the settlement. They turned up Ogden's Fork going as far as the mouth of the canyon where the hills rise very abruptly. There we were regaled with plenty of mountain trout, and then went into the Goodyear's farm which had not been irrigated this year, but it looked tolerably well. After chatting for some time we again made preparations to travel and return to Brown's at 11:45 A.M. The sky was very hazy and dull and at times we could scarcely see the top of the mountains, but the air was warm. Ogden's Fork is about a rod wide and 18 inches deep, the water being soft and clear and the banks of the river lined with willows, rose bushes and small trees. Ezra Chase said that the land was very productive in grain. A short distance below he said, it will yield a hundred bushels of crickets to the acre and 50 bushels of mosquitoes.[9]

On the next day, 3 September, Young gave James Brown permission to build toll bridges across the Weber and Ogden rivers. Young, Kimball, Grant, Bullock, and others climbed to the top of the sand hill near Brown's Fort and spent an hour discussing how the town of Ogden should be laid out. It was decided that the town should be laid out on the south side of Ogden's Fork at the point of bench land in order that the waters from the Weber River and Ogden's Fork could be taken out for irrigation and other purposes.

Shortly after the visit of Brigham Young and his party to Weber County, the general conference of the Mormon church voted on 7 October 1849 to lay out a city "in the district known as Brownsville, some forty miles to the north of Salt Lake."[10] In 1850 Lorin Farr, who was one of the settlers in Salt Lake, was selected by Brigham Young because of his pioneering experience, leadership ability, and long-time acquaintance with Young to go to Ogden and take charge of affairs there. Farr moved to Ogden on 12 January 1850; but, instead of remaining at Captain Brown's Fort, he went north of the Ogden River to the flat land just below the mountains and close to the Ogden River. He purchased a piece of land and occupied a cabin which had been built on the land by his father-in-law Ezra Chase, who had moved there in 1848. This became the site of Farr's Fort, which was built in 1850 because of Indian threats. Farr's Fort was located one and a half miles northwest of the mouth of Ogden Canyon and about a block north of the Ogden River, which is the south side of 1051 East Canyon Road. The protective walls of the fort drew several families besides the Farrs to take up residence there.[11]

On 26 January 1851 the Weber County area was reorganized by the Mormon church into a broader ecclesiastical district as the Weber Stake of Zion. Ecclesiastical jurisdiction was placed more in line with the secular county boundaries, and this was an effort to break up any schism that had "grown up between some of the members living about the South [Brown's] and North [Farr's] forts." On this date Lorin Farr was made the first president of the Weber Stake, replacing James Brown as the ecclesiastical leader; and by this time Farr was also mayor of Ogden City. This organizational meeting was conducted by Brigham Young, and was held at the South Fort, which was Brown's new fort. Charles R. Dana and David B. Dille were chosen as Farr's counselors. The following were chosen as high councilors: Joseph Lake, George Pitkin, Lemuel McCory, Daniel Birch [Burch], Joseph Grover, William Earl, David Moore, Edward Bunker, Phillip Garner, Samuel Stickney, Horace Rawson, and Joseph Lish. Bryant W. Nowling was selected as clerk.[12]

At this same time two ecclesiastical wards were created within the Weber Stake—the South Ward and the North Ward. Isaac Clark became the bishop of the South Ward, with James Browning and James Brown as his counselors; and Erastus Bingham became the bishop of the North Ward with Charles Hubbard and Stephen Perry as counselors.[13]

Lorin Farr and his family played an important and busy role in the Ogden community, and Farr accumulated over the years an extensive estate to support his large families from six plural wives. He held approximately 400 acres of land, widely scattered along the Ogden River, and city lots with six homes for his families at 21st Street and Washington Boulevard. On these various farms he kept forty to one hundred head of cattle, ten to thirty head of horses, and about 300 sheep, as well as many hogs and chickens. Besides the farms, Farr developed a sawmill, a gristmill, a woolen mill, a store, and other miscellaneous enterprises.[14]

The presence of church control initially made civil government somewhat superfluous, since practically all the people were Mormons and their ecclesiastical government managed much of their lives. The selection of civil officers and the beginnings of Weber County government did not take place until the election of 4 August 1851, with the following results: Isaac Clark as chief justice of the county court; Erastus Bingham as associate justice; Daniel Birch (Burch) as associate justice; Francillo Durfey (Durfee) as justice of the peace; Edward Bunker as justice of the peace; Benjamin F. Cummings as sheriff; Sandford Bingham as constable; Clifton Browning as constable; and Joseph Grover as road commissioner. David Moore was appointed by territorial governor Brigham Young as county recorder and David Dille was appointed as county clerk. The chief justice and the associate justices of the county were the governing body of the county.

In an election held on 2 August 1852, Erastus Bingham, Lewis Hardy, and Jonathan S. Wells were elected selectmen, the new title for the justices. The county selectmen, designated together as the county court, were the governing body of the county during the territorial period. Under the Utah State Constitution of 1896, county governments were restructured into a county commission format. At that time, the title of the governing officials was changed from selectmen to county commissioners.

The incorporation of Weber County preceded the Ogden City incorporation, and Weber County functioned to organize and serve the larger geographical area. Ogden City, as county seat, was the center of political and economic control. In many ways the county was closely related to Ogden, and in the early days much of county life was dominated by Ogden. Much of the early history of the area involved the interplay between the county government and the county seat, and over time there were struggles to define the roles of each. Cooperation was evident in June 1852 when the Weber County Court approved loans to Ogden to construct a canal to carry water to the city; and, even though through the years there were disagreements between the county and Ogden City, there were also times of cooperation.

After an incident in which an Indian leader was killed in 1850 at Five Mile Creek in Harrisville as well as a general uprising of the Indians in the Walker War in central Utah in 1853, the Indian threat led Brigham Young to order Utah communities to "fort up" as a protective action. In response to that admonition, several other forts were constructed or partially constructed in Weber County. The forts included Goodyear's original fort on the Weber River, Farr's Fort (at Mill Creek, near present-day 12th Street and Monroe Avenue), Brown's Fort (located near 29th Street and Pacific Avenue), Mound Fort (located between 9th Street and 12th Street and west of Washington Boulevard to the bluff at 250 East), Bingham's Fort (located on both sides of 2nd Street and mainly west of Wall Avenue), Fort Ogden (located between 21st Street and 28th Street and between Wall Avenue and Madison Avenue), North Ogden Fort (located in the vicinity of 2700 North and 500 East), Uintah Fort (located west of the mouth of Weber Canyon on the Weber River—now in Davis County), Kington Fort (located at approximately 475 East and 6650 South in South Weber, which is now in Davis County), and Huntsville Fort (in the upper valley of the Ogden River).[15]

Three of these forts would be added to Ogden City proper—Bingham's Fort, Mound Fort, and Farr's Fort. Bingham's Fort was a community that took its water from Mill Creek and transported the water through what later was called the Lynne Ditch to the area of 2nd Street west of Washington Boulevard. The name of Bingham's Fort came from the fort's first leader, Erastus Bingham, who came to Weber County in 1850 and first settled in a more central area of Ogden City. In 1853 he moved to the northern end of the city to establish his fort. Bingham's son-in-law, Isaac Newton Goodale, was also instrumental in building the fort and digging the three-mile Lynne Ditch that brought water to the fort. The fort was a wood-frame structure, interwoven with willows and filled in and covered with mud and adobe. It had dimensions of 120 rods by 60 rods, with gates on the east and west walls. The east wall of the fort was approximately 110 feet east of Wall Avenue and the west wall was 1,870 feet west of Wall Avenue.[16]

The Mound Fort settlement started in 1848 when a few settlers moved to the vicinity north of the Ogden River where a prominent mound was a major land feature. Here Indian groups frequently camped. During threatening times with the Indians in 1854 a fort was constructed which was named Mound Fort. It enclosed the district from the present 12th Street to 9th Street, and from the west side of the state road (present Washington Boulevard) to the west face of the mound at 250 East. The west slope of the mound was very steep, and with a small amount of work it was cut to make a precipitous face about ten feet high. To strengthen the west side, a breastwork approximately three feet high was erected along the top of the mound. A mud wall nine feet high, three feet wide at the base, and sixteen inches wide at the top was built around the other three sides of the enclosure. David Moore was the leader at this fort, and about ten or twelve other families joined his family there.[17]

The Barker and Malan families had farms in the Mound Fort area. The Malan family presents an example of how some pioneer families moved to different areas of the county as communities developed. The Malan family first homesteaded in the river-bottom area at 12th Street and later moved to develop the bench land at 24th Street and Monroe Avenue, where they found rattlesnakes around their cabins. By 1894 they had moved to the Knob Hill area of east Capital Street and at the same time acquired the Malan's Heights land which ran from the base of the mountains to Malan's Peak. In less than half a century they had moved across the developing areas of Ogden City.

After a severe flood in the spring of 1850, Brigham Young, Heber C. Kimball, and Orson Hyde visited Lorin Farr in August 1850 and carried out the business of laying out a city on the site designated during the earlier visit. The south limits of the city were defined as a line going east from Brown's Fort (at 29th Street and Pacific Avenue) to the mountains; and the north limits ran from the mountains west to the southwest of Farr's Fort (at Mill Creek and Monroe Avenue) and jogged to the north to 12th Street (south of Mound Fort); this included the territory between the forks of the Weber and Ogden rivers. This gave the town a most beautiful setting, with several creeks and two major rivers for water. Young's party set the corner stake and gave a detailed plan for a modern city of wide streets.[18]

During 1850 Mayor Farr engaged William M. Lemon to survey

portions of the county adjacent to the plat of Ogden City. Shortly after commencing the work, however, Lemon died. William M. Dame continued the work, and Jesse W. Fox completed it. Farm land was divided into blocks half a mile wide by one mile in length, with streets running north and south every mile and east and west every half mile. Each farm contained twenty acres and fronted the streets running east and west. The survey covered an area approximately six miles square.[19]

The newly surveyed region outside of Ogden City was divided into districts. The first district to the north of the Ogden River and Ogden City was called the Bingham Fort district (Lynne). It occupied land on both sides of present 2nd Street. The second district north and west was called Slaterville. Extending northward from this district to the mountains and westward to Utah Hot Springs was an extensive district about nine miles in length called North Ogden. When Ogden City was first organized, it included most of the North Ogden district; but, when these new districts were created, Ogden's boundary line was moved to two miles north of the Ogden River and excluded North Ogden. Other districts were Marriott, Pleasant View, Harrisville, Farr West, West Weber (including Taylor) on the Ogden River domain, and Uintah and Burch Creek in the Weber River area.

Settlers, as they arrived, could take up a city lot, which provided space for a house and garden, while those who wanted more land could also get a larger piece of land in the outlying areas. Many of these early settlers lived on a city lot and worked a farm in the county. Brigham Young counselled the leaders not to settle in the country but to "move on to the city lots, build good houses, school houses, meeting houses, and other public buildings, fence their gardens and plant out fruit trees, that Ogden might be a permanent city and suitable headquarters for the northern country."[20]

On 6 February 1851 the territorial legislature incorporated Ogden City, and on 23 October 1851 the first election was held, resulting in the election of Lorin Farr as mayor of Ogden, a position he held for twenty-two years.

Matthew William Dalton claimed to have built the first house within the surveyed Ogden townsite. In 1851 he built a log house on the southeast corner of Grant Avenue and 24th Street. Dalton arrived in Ogden on 5 September 1850, a few days after Brigham Young had visited and laid out the city. Dalton described the area:

> Now on my arrival at the place now called, Ogden, but then part of the wilderness, I saw a few scattered families, of people, who for protection lived in a fort on the outskirts, of what is now the platted part of the City. The afternoon I came in, the surveyors were running the first lines of the City, and began staking off some of the lots. It was a barren looking wilderness, in places, covered with "sage Brush" and "bunch grass." . . . Upon inquiry, I found the prices of provisions very high. Flour was One Dollar per pound. One hundred pounds of flour would purchase a fine horse! I began at once to look for work, and fortunately made the acquaintance of a man named David Moore; who being in need of a man, engaged me to work for him at a wage of Two Dollars per day and board. I got busy at once, and did my first work, the afternoon I came in. This consisted in cutting and hauling a load of Box Elder trees, from the Weber River bottoms.[21]

Dalton's house was a two-room log house, and he fenced the three city lots he acquired and plowed and planted a garden in what would become the heart of the city. He also farmed twenty acres of land north of the Weber River, where he harvested 33 bushels of wheat to the acre.

William Lang built one of the first houses on a surveyed lot in Ogden at the corner of 27th Street and Washington Boulevard. It was built of ax-hewn cottonwood logs taken from the banks of the Ogden and Weber rivers. It had a roof of dirt and the doors hung on wooden hinges and were fastened by wooden latches. Isaac Clark built the first adobe home in Ogden; it was located at 2386 Washington Boulevard which also served as the first post office and first meeting place for the county court. Isaac Clark was the first postmaster and the first Weber County Chief Justice.

In December 1854 Mormon leader Wilford Woodruff visited the Weber County settlements and described them in his extensive diary. He described East Weber (Uintah) as having some thirty-five families and a school. Woodruff reported that Ogden "is a flourishing place containing some 150 families," and that the Ogden city wall, which was just in the beginning phase of construction, would enclose one mile square and was to be built of earth eight feet high, three feet wide at the bottom and eighteen inches at the top. Ogden had two stores and two schools with about 120 students. The residents of the city had raised 10,000 bushels of wheat during the past season. As Woodruff continued his journey, he described Bingham's Fort and North Ogden. Bingham's Fort had 732 residents and North Ogden had forty-seven families. The North Ogden families had raised 16,000 bushels of wheat in 1854. Both communities had begun schools, and the early winter weather was cold.[22]

In 1855 the English traveler William Chandless described the flourishing settlements on the Weber River. After spending a night with the Captain James Brown family, Chandless commented on Ogden city:

> Ogden City was a specimen of the settlements in Utah on the model of Salt Lake; precisely a mile square, part on the bench, part in the valley-bottom, enclosed by an earthen wall, and laid out in "blocks;" a large portion was still unoccupied, but dobie-houses were fast springing up. In the middle of the place was a school-house, also used as a church, and its door plastered over with parochial notices; near it were two small stores—few settlements have as many, and what people want they must get direct from "the city," as best they can. The roads, except on the "bench," were a miserable alternation of mud and water, and if not frozen over, hardly passable for a foot traveller; there was little cleanliness or neatness about them. Several small mountain burns ran through the place, and to the north lay a small, deep, sluggish river, closed in by kinnikinnik, and crossed by a substantial wooden bridge; to this a list of tolls were affixed, but as far as I could see they were never exacted. Cattle on all sides straggle about, picking up what they can find, and at night return, or are driven within the walls; the cultivated land is necessarily more or less distant, but danger gathers the inhabitants and their stock to a single place."[23]

The U.S. Census of 1850 noted that Weber County had 687 males and 454 females—a total of 1,141—living within its jurisdiction. This census did not record any Native Americans, nor did it make any reference to any other ethnic group. Virtually all of the some 200 family heads reported that they were farmers or stock growers. Other occupations reported in the census included 155 students and a varied assortment of carpenters, masons, wheelwrights, wagonmakers, tinners, chairmakers, a draper, a stonecutter, tailors, coopers, shoemakers, merchants, saddlers, a potter, cabinet makers, a machinist, a woodcarver, a soapmaker, a dairyman, a baker, a butcher, a dentist, schoolteachers, an engineer, an artist, a printer, sailors, soldiers, and a peddler. A chimneysweep listed himself as a gardener.

## *The Development of Water Resources*

The development of water resources was a major concern in the settlement process. Water use typically progressed from simple diversions of major streams through brush and rock diversions turning the water into lateral ditches constructed by settlers to irrigate land adjacent to the streams. As time went on, with more population available to do the work, it was possible to cooperatively construct more complex water systems which allowed the lands farther away laterally and on the higher benches to be developed. This is the pattern in Weber County water development, which the Weber Canal, the Ogden Canal, the Hooper Canal, Wilson Canal, North Ogden Canal, the Mill Creek Canal, the Lynne Ditch, Marriott Ditch, and others, verify.[24]

Virtually every community in the county was sited because of the availability of water or the potential of water being brought to it. Without water, communities could not survive. The first systematic irrigation, after the experience at Goodyear's Fort, was taken out of Canfield Creek, a stream that came out of Waterfall Canyon and entered Ogden near present 32nd Street and Harrison Boulevard. It flowed to the Weber River, traversing the land near 29th Street and Madison and Jefferson avenues. It was at this spot on Canfield Creek that Jesse and Alexander Brown in the spring of 1848 plowed the first furrows in Weber County to prepare it for planting with a plow made of iron from wagon wheels by the blacksmith Artemus Sprague. They then put a dam in the stream and turned water on to the crops which had been planted on land above the Weber River level. The water irrigated five acres of wheat, a patch of corn, and some turnips, cabbage, potatoes, and a few watermelons grown from seeds brought from California by Captain James Brown. This plowing occurred on 1 June

1848. Later, the Weber Canal completed in June 1858 brought water to this area.

Other families settled within the city and diverted water from the Ogden River to bring water to their farms. Many of these ditches and some areas were named after the families that developed the farmlands. The Chase Ditch, developed by Ezra Chase, took water out of the Ogden River in 1849 for the area north of the river; and the Moore Ditch completed in the same year delivered water to the Mound Fort area. Lorin Farr utilized the Moore diversion in part to get the water to his gristmill. Farr's diversion was known later as Mill Creek, and it became the main source of water to the communities on the lower northern side of the Ogden River. This stream still provides most of the irrigation water for those communities.

Other ditches were named after local citizens—Enoch Farr's Ditch, the Stone Ditch (named for Amos P. Stone), and the Tracy-Shaw Ditch (named after Moses Tracy and Ambrose Shaw). In 1851 Jeffrey Dinsdale took water out of the Ogden River near the west end of the present Ogden municipal stadium and farmed an area between the Ogden River and south of 17th Street that became known as Hell's Half Acre.

The Shupe-Middleton Ditch (named after John W. Shupe and Charles A. Middleton) was dug in 1854 and watered their farms south of the Ogden River and east of the Weber River. Charles Zeimer and John Broom dug a canal in 1854, known as the Zeimer-Broom Canal, which went from Mill Creek to an area on the north side of lower 12th Street called Broom's Bench. Much of this area is now within the Defense Depot Ogden boundaries. After residents of Weber County were forced to move from the county because of the threatened invasion of Colonel Albert Sidney Johnston's federal troops in 1858, many who returned from the areas of refuge to the south in Utah County settled on Broom's Bench. This area also had been known as Tracy's Bench after earlier settler Moses Tracy. After the return, Charles Zeimer and John Broom were prominent in the community. They established farms on the bench which were watered by the canal. This area was known for Charles Zeimer's orchard that was west of Butler's Lane, one of the main thoroughfares on the bench. Broom's Bench was also known for the excellent watermelons, cantaloupes, and varieties of orchard fruits that were grown there.

The development of the water supply was essential to community development. Settlers had to devote a considerable amount of time and effort to bring the precious commodity on a continual basis to water crops and provide water for households. Each member of the community was required to contribute a certain amount of money or labor to build and maintain the system.

The first major irrigation enterprises were the Weber Canal and the Ogden Bench Canal. The Weber Canal was completed in 1852 when a seven-mile canal was dug from the Weber River near Riverdale to irrigate the lower part of Ogden. The Weber County Court at its first meeting on 24 April 1852 ordered that two-thirds of the county revenue for the year should be loaned to Ogden City for the construction of the canal.

Isaac N. Goodale recorded that he spent 88 days in helping to construct the Ogden Bench Canal. In his journal, he recorded his experiences. Goodale was chosen as a director of the Ogden Bench Canal Company, and on 5 September he went to "run out Ogdon canal." This was the beginning of the construction of the Ogden Bench Canal, which ran from the mouth of Ogden Canyon (at present-day Rainbow Gardens) along the south side of the canyon and entered the bench north of 20th Street between Jackson and Van Buren avenues. The canal slanted southwesterly from 22nd towards 32nd Street and Liberty Avenue where it terminated—at a distance of two miles. The canal was approximately six to eight feet wide and eighteen inches deep and was dug by shovels. At the head of the canal, the water was diverted out of the Ogden River and was conducted by a wooden flume for a short distance before flowing into the open ditch. Goodale recorded the many days that he had spent on the construction of the canal. He did a variety of jobs such as getting wood out of the canyon for making flumes and headgates, digging on the canal, "giving out jobs" on the canal, and "giving out lots on the Ogden canal." The canal was opened in May 1856, or, as Goodale recorded on 16 May, "was on the canal goot [got] the water out this day." The water opened up a large portion of settlement on the Ogden bench. The original cost of the canal was $22,000; but it was an investment that lasted until 1945 when it was replaced by the Pine View water system.[25]

Under the direction of I. N. Goodale, the Lynne Ditch was dug from Mill Creek, the ditch extending for three miles. The same mill-stream was tapped in the same year (1856) by a mile-long canal to the Marriott region. Irrigation commenced in East Weber (Uintah) at the mouth of Weber Canyon in 1851 when a small stream called Spring Creek was tapped.

These streams of water, the lifeblood of the communities, served other purposes than to make the fields green. The canals also operated waterwheels which ran lathes, sugar mills, and other commercial enterprises; they supplied drinking water, even though at times it was so "black with mud that hours were required for this mud to settle in pails; and often they were found convenient when the need of a bath was felt."[26]

In 1880 Joseph Stanford recorded that the following canals had been established in the county:

| | | | |
|---|---|---|---|
| North Ogden | 15 miles | cost | $30,000 |
| West Weber | 10 " | " | $25,000 |
| Hooperville | 30 " | " | $60,000 |
| Harrisville | 10 " | " | $20,000 |
| Plain City | 20 " | " | $40,000 |
| Marriott and Lynne | 15 " | " | $30,000 |
| Ogden Valley | 20 " | " | $35,000 |
| Ogden Weber | 10 " | " | $30,000 |
| Totals | 130 miles | cost | $270,000[27] |

As was common in Weber County communities, the settlers of West Weber cooperatively dug canals and smaller ditches, each man receiving shares of water according to the amount of work rendered. West Weber experienced frequent flooding and washouts by the Weber River. In 1859 a canal was dug that put water on the land by 1860. This canal was dug by shovel and was completed after much difficulty. The eight miles of ditch had to be dug by hand over sun-baked plains and through sagebrush hollows and mounds of sand. In 1860–61 it cost the settlers of West Weber $2,500 to irrigate ten small farms.

Maintaining the canal was a matter of constant attention. In the first year, the canal broke because of a lack of slope to carry the water, which caused the water to back up and put pressure on the banks. In 1862 an unusually high spring run-off destroyed the dams and most of the canals and ditches in the system. Problems were dealt with by the communities by the forming of local water districts. In this case of the lower Weber River, the organization of the West Weber Irrigation District, the Hooper City Irrigation Company, and the Wilson Irrigation District provided organizations that took action to counter some of these recurring problems of controlling the water. The development of water in West Weber was difficult and fraught with many problems, and from 1859 to 1880 about $75,000 was expended to complete the water system.[28] The low farmlands along the Weber River had been a constant test of the community effort to make successful use of the water.

### *Communities Established in the County*

Settlements in Weber County developed from the communities of Brown's Fort, Farr's Fort, Mound Fort, and Bingham's Fort along the Weber and Ogden rivers. Communities that located along the lands of the Weber River in the upper part of the valley were Uintah (at first called East Weber and Easton) in 1850, and Riverdale (in early days called Stringtown, Thompson, and Union) in 1850. On the lower part of the Weber, communities included Slaterville (1850), West Weber (known also as Weston and Alma) in 1851—later abandoned and then resettled in 1859, Taylor (1851), Farr West (known in early days as West Harrisville) in 1851, West Warren (also known as Blossom or Reese) in 1853, Wilson (1853), Plain City (1859), Hooper (1867), Kanesville (1868), Warren (1872), and Roy (1899).

Communities along the Ogden River water system included Marriott (1849), Harrisville (1850), North Ogden (1850), and Pleasant View (1851) on the lower Ogden River. Eden (1859), Huntsville (1860), and Liberty (1892) were established in the upper valley of the Ogden River.

These communities grew and created their own governments, following the general pattern of progression from early settlement by a few pioneer families organized as a branch of the Mormon church to a secular government. Through the years, many became incorporated cities; others remained unincorporated communities under Weber County jurisdiction.

One of the early developments on the Ogden river, as the settlements began to push out from the center, was the community of Marriott, located northwest of Ogden and west of the Farr's Fort District. It was first occupied in the winter of 1849–50 by William Rowe, a non-Mormon who built a log cabin near the forks of the Ogden and Weber rivers; after being accused of stealing, he fled to California. In 1850 Moses Tracy built a double log cabin near the forks of the Ogden and Weber rivers. Other settlers also located there, but the region was considered "somewhat unattractive," because it was heavily timbered by box elder, cottonwood, brush, and willows. Wolves, bears, and coyotes roamed in this heavy growth and ravaged the livestock pastured in the area. A large Indian encampment in this place also made the settlers uneasy.

Moses Tracy is credited with making the first irrigation ditch in the confluence area; but settlement was slow. In 1855 John Marriott settled in a dugout farther east, near where the crossroads of the center of the later town was established. Marriott dug a larger ditch from the Ogden River. He cleared the land of brush, erected the first log house, which later was extended with adobe walls, and became the first permanent settler, after whom the settlement was named. Others who joined the Marriotts included the families of Thomas Joyce, William Gill, William Beckington, Henry Reeder, Robert Hewitt, and Simon F. Halverson.

North Ogden, which for several years was mistakenly called Ogden's Hole, was first settled in 1850 when Jonathan Campbell, his nephew Samuel Campbell, and John Riddle moved on to the land. They came into the area as two separate parties and perhaps did not even meet during the fall and winter of 1850. The Campbells first set up tents to live in. Jonathan Campbell stayed on as a permanent settler and was one of the first to plant crops, set out an orchard, and grow fruit. John Riddle and his son Isaac came a little later than the Campbells to winter in North Ogden with a herd of 200 cattle from the Ogden settlement. The Riddles stayed in North Ogden during the winter and returned the cattle to Ogden during the spring of 1851.

The Campbells and Riddles were forced to leave shortly after by hostile Indians; but on 4 March 1851 they returned with several other settlers including Thomas Dunn, Lemuel Mallory, Benjamin Cazier, Newton D. Hall, Newman G. Blodgett, Franklin G. Clifford, Enoch Burns, Solomon Campbell, David Garner, Noah Brimhall, and their families.

They erected their shelters—which ranged from tents, dugouts, and log cabins to later adobe and brick homes. They set about clearing the land of the large sagebrush, or "Mormon Hickory," as it was called, and preparing the land for crops. The early settlers stayed on land in the eastern part of the valley near where the fort was later built. Later settlers spread out towards the west. The community cleared one large field, fenced it with poles and willow lattice, and planted potatoes, vegetables, wheat, and other grains. Isaac Riddle stated in his journal that "this was our first experience with irrigation and our first crops raised in Utah were good."[29]

The community was at first a part of the ecclesiastical North Ward of Weber Stake; but in 1852 it was made a separate branch, with Thomas Dunn as presiding elder. The next year, Brigham Young visited the branch and organized it into a ward, with Thomas Dunn as bishop and Ira Rice and Edwin Austin as counselors and Robert Montgomery as clerk. Under this leadership the functions of the community were carried out, including the building of a rock fort in 1854 as a protection from Indian threats and a communal effort to bring water to the farms.

In 1851–52 Newman Blodgett and some assistants marked the town site into blocks and streets. The streets were laid out in four-acre blocks with eight one-half acre lots, and water was brought to the settlement from the surrounding streams including Rice Creek, Cold Water Creek, North Ogden Canyon, and Randall Springs. In 1856 a large canal was dug from the Ogden River, near the mouth of the canyon, to North Ogden. This project required virtually all the local manpower plus the efforts of one woman (Mrs. John Cardon—probably Anne Regula Furrer Cardon) to complete the arduous task.

Pleasant View was first part of North Ogden. In 1852 William Bailey Lake, Thomas Dunn, John Mower, and Simeon Cragun settled in the western part of North Ogden, which was called at different times West District, Hot Springs District, String Town, or simply Out West. Eventually the area took the name of Pleasant View because of its location on the bench overlooking the Great Salt Lake Valley.[30]

Harrisville, located about six miles northwest of Ogden City, was first settled in the spring of 1850 by Urban Stewart. He built a log cabin on the south side of Four Mile Creek (about 300 yards southwest of the present Harrisville LDS Ward meetinghouse). He was unable to continue living in the area, however, because of an incident on 16 September 1850 in which he killed Chief Terikee, a Snake Indian chief. The ensuing Indian reaction forced Stewart to leave the area and forced the surrounding communities to take precautionary measures against the Indians, including building forts for protection.

In the spring of 1851, other settlers moved from Ogden and Farr's Fort to Harrisville. At that time, Martin H. Harris, after whom the community was named, erected a house on the west side of Four Mile Creek and sowed ten acres of grain. A poor harvest led him to move to higher ground to farm the next year. Others followed to the more fertile ground in 1851. They included James Lake, David Jenkins, Pleasant Green Taylor, Luman Shurtliff, and Dudley Chase.

The western portion of Harrisville, comprising the area lying north of Slaterville to the Box Elder-Weber County line at the Hot Springs, organized into the community of Farr West, named in honor of Lorin Farr and Chauncey W. West. The first settler, Joseph Taylor, came in 1853; later settlers included Ezra Chase, his son Dudley Chase, and Hugh McClellan. Although separation of the school and other activities came earlier, it was 1890 before the official incorporation of the town of Farr West was recorded. Water from a canal dug from the Ogden River, completed in 1858, and some local springs and wells allowed this area to develop prosperous farms.

The experience of Luman Shurtliff in the Harrisville region is typical of development in the western part of the county. In November 1851 Shurtliff moved to Harrisville and established a forty-acre farm, raising apples, grapes, "seed locus," and "coffy nuts." He also raised cattle, wheat, and corn. Shurtliff wrote that it was difficult to maintain a fenced area because of the poor quality of box elder poles available, so he created a fence. His method was to dig a "ditch three feet deep and three feet wide throw the earth all in a bank on the inside then stick up stakes in that bank three or four feet high then weave in willows thick to the top of the stakes." These ditches became the boundary lines for the property sections as well as the means to carry water to the crops.

In 1852 Shurtliff recorded:

> This spring we had much trouble in making water ditches or sects [sections] not having any experience in such work we built a levy and made it to [too] small and we could not get enough water through it without raising it so high that Lewis or I had to stay by it and watch it while the other water our grain and sect would break once or twice a day and it would take sometimes half a day to mend it thus we worked night and day to water our crop.'[31]

Shurtliff's comments indicated some of the on-going problems of early-day irrigation maintenance. A large amount of time and effort was necessary to keep the canals in service and in getting the water to the farms and crops as needed. Shurtliff relates the difficulty of digging the ditches and the struggle to survive. He concluded, "I worked verry hard untill I fineshed my ditch." He was "verry thankfull" that several neighbors and church members had helped him with his ditch and farm. Shurtliff's life in Weber County over a period of thirty years illustrates that the problems of farming in early Weber County were continual. Through the years, many settlers would not be able to find economic success on their small farms.

Another community that developed along the Ogden River was Slaterville, located six miles northwest of the center of Ogden. Alexander Kelley was the first settler there in the fall of 1850; he built a log cabin with a dirt roof. In the spring of 1851, Stephen Perry and his family built a log cabin about forty rods southeast of Kelley's house. This cabin was constructed on the bank of the north channel of Mill Creek. In 1853 Richard Slater, after whom the town was named, moved his family there.[32]

The abundance of water which produced grass and meadows for pasture lands had induced the first settlers to locate on the spot. As population grew, more land was put into production and more water was brought from Mill Creek and the Ogden River through the South Slaterville Ditch and the Warren Canal. One of the common occurrences that the farmers in this area had to contend with was flooding of the Ogden River. Because of flooding, especially in 1863, the high waters inundated the land and forced many families to leave their farms and houses and locate on higher ground. Crops were ruined and other employment had to be found. Some families gathered sagebrush and sold it on the streets of Ogden as firewood to obtain flour or other provisions to survive.

In 1850 two communities—Riverdale and Uintah—were organized along the Weber River. Riverdale had its first settler in the spring of 1850 when James Graham claimed a large tract of land on the west side of the Weber River. Riverdale spread out along the river, running from 33rd Street in Ogden south to the bend of the Weber River as it turns north. In recent times, Riverdale has realized most of its growth along the "Old Territorial Road" line that goes from the bend in the river up the hill to Roy. In the early days the region was principally known as a sheep-herding ground. In 1853 Daniel Burch built a flour mill on the east side of the Weber River. In 1858 John Taylor acquired the mill, which is usually referred to as Taylor's Mill. Burch also added a sawmill at the site. Burch developed a part of the Weber Canal, which was approved and funded by the Weber County Court in 1852 to be continued into Ogden and eventually to the Ogden River. The Riverdale area had rich soil that became very productive for "good crops of hay, potatoes, vegetables, fruits, berries, and later, sugar beets."[33]

Farther up the Weber River was Uintah, located in the steep-sided valley west of where the Weber River breaks out of the Wasatch Mountain Range. The area had been a site of Indian camps. This is also the area that the trapper Osborne Russell recorded traveling and passing through as "a narrow defile which led us thro the mountain into the valley on the East borders of the lake."[34] The first settlers of Uintah in 1850 were John M. Bybee, Lewis Hardy, Joseph Kingsbury, Daniel Smith, Henry Beckstead, Joseph Hardy, John W. Winward, and John L. Smith.

Uintah was considered that part of the country lying between the Weber River on the south and the hill, or bluff, on the north. The west part of this area was settled first. John M Bybee built his cabin approximately 800 feet east of Cook's Point. At a later time, a fort was constructed in the west part which was named Fort Kington, after Thomas Kington.

After the settlements of 1850, communities continued to inch their way out from the hub of Ogden. In 1851 Pleasant View and Farr West were settled as breakaways from North Ogden and Harrisville; West Weber organized as a community in 1851, with Taylor forming out of its suburbs. West Weber is situated on the south side of the "big bend" of the Weber River. Early in 1851 (some say 1850) Oliver Bybee and William Middleton erected a log cabin in West Weber which was used as a "herdsman's house." This cabin was located on the riverbank in a grove of box elder trees. The first settlers brought their cattle there to graze during the summers and did not stay in the cabin during the winter. The first permanent settlers arrived in 1857 when John Martin came to stay. Two years later, other families took up farms after purchasing land from Captain James Brown at five dollars per acre.

The land was mainly a herd ground, but in 1851 William Middleton and his son Charles plowed a few acres and planted them with corn, wheat, and vegetables; but the crop failed for lack of water. In 1859 Archibald McFarland dug a canal from one of the sloughs bordering the river and was able to irrigate part of his land. This was the first irrigation ditch dug in this area west of the Weber River.

Other communities established in the West Weber area during the same time period were Taylor in 1851, West Warren in 1853, Wilson in 1853, and Plain City in 1859. Taylor was first settled in 1851 as the "West Field," located southwest of the West Weber community. It gradually assumed its own identity and on 14 March 1909 it became separate as the Taylor LDS Ward. Early settlers included the families of James Jardine, James F. Hunter, Samuel F. Walker, Charles Buck, William McGee, George Welch, William Hadley, Peter Mattson, Isaac Isaacson, Andrew Anderson, Peter Peterson, Jacob Nielson, and William Purrington. The settlement's name is controversial. One account says it derived its name from Samuel F. Walker, a leading citizen after whom it was being considered to be named but who did not want the community named after him. Instead, the name came from his profession as the first tailor in the settlement. Although this account is well known, it does not sound as likely as other accounts which say the town was named after Mormon apostle John Taylor, who owned the gristmill in nearby Riverdale, or that it was named after the Taylorsville School District, which included this area in its jurisdiction.[35]

Taylor was a farming community. Some of the first crops grown were grain, alfalfa, sugar cane, and potatoes. In later years sugar beets, tomatoes, and peas became the main crops. The main fruits grown in early years were apples, peaches, and wild plums; in later years, pears, plums, apricots, and grapes. Kitchen gardens included peas, beans, rhubarb, berries, and native currants. The community brought the water for their gardens from the south branch of the Weber Canal.

One aspect of Taylor history relates to the building of a bridge over the Weber River. In 1870 the railroad built a bridge for tracks spanning the river, and in conjunction with it they also constructed a pedestrian bridge. In 1879 Weber County constructed a wooden vehicle bridge across the river on 24th Street alongside the railroad bridge. Settlers could then take their produce to Ogden markets without going around by way of the Riverdale bridge or trying to cross the river at the McFarland ford.

Wilson was another community along the Weber River; it is located directly west of Ogden City on the west side of the Weber River along the route from Ogden to West Weber. It is also known as Wilson Lane. Farming and dairying were its main industries. The community started in 1853 when John Staker purchased land about a half mile east of where the LDS Wilson meetinghouse was located. That fall, Staker raised grain on the land; the next spring, brothers George C., Lewis D., Bradley B., and Barlow B. Wilson purchased land just east of the Staker farm. The Wilson brothers engaged in farming and built the first bridge across the river. It was from the Wilsons that the community took its name. On 16 July 1882 the community was organized into an ecclesiastical ward and on 7 July 1884 incorporated as a city. In 1860 John Staker and the Wilson Brothers dug an irrigation ditch known as the Wilson Ditch that brought water out of the Weber River near the 24th Street railroad bridge. In 1879 a new canal was dug that watered some 4,000 acres of farmland in Wilson, Kanesville, and Hooper.

Plain City deviated somewhat from the pattern of communities moving out from the Ogden hub. Most of its settlers came directly from another area without first having settled in Ogden or Weber County. Located ten miles northwest of Ogden and four miles east of the Great Salt Lake, it was quite remote from the earlier settlements. Most of the first inhabitants came from Lehi with an exploring party in 1858. The main settlement group was made up of Daniel Collet, Joseph Skeen, his son William, Thomas Fryer, William W. Raymond, John Spiers, Joseph Robinson, John Folker, Joseph Folkman, Jesse Folkman, Ezekiel Hopkins, David Francis, Robert Maw, and John Carver. A year later, others came, including William Van Dyke, Daniel James, Henry Newman, John Draney, Jonathan Moyes, and William Geddes.

The search for an area with water led them to Plain City. After exploring the region thoroughly, including the Hot Springs to the northeast, the party selected the site for the proposed settlement before returning to Lehi for their families. They liked the flat sagebrush plain and gave it the name of Plain City. Before returning for their families, they made a preliminary survey for a canal, selected their farms and lots, and cleaned out some of the springs on the west side of their proposed settlement.

In March 1859 the settlers moved on to the land. The town was laid out in square blocks, each block containing five acres and divided into four lots. A block in the center of the town was designated as the "Public Square," and on it were the church house, the schoolhouse, and other public buildings. It essentially followed the Mormon pattern of city building. The first city plat at Plain City was three blocks wide and six blocks long. A large field one mile square was laid out east of town and was later enclosed with a willow fence. It was called the "Big Field," and each family was given a city lot and twenty acres of land in the Big Field.

After some dispute with the town of Marriott over water out of a common canal, the people of Plain City solved the problem by digging a ten-mile canal from the Ogden River. They later connected to the Weber River in 1873, giving them enough water for their farms, except in dry years. This problem was finally solved in 1932 when water was delivered from the Echo Dam, to which the Plain City

Irrigation Company had subscribed. With more water available crops of corn, squash, potatoes, wheat, sugar cane, small fruits, and later apples, pears, apricots, plums, grapes, melons, and tomatoes were grown. Plain City also was known for its asparagus and strawberries. In 1859 a Mr. Rollett, a French settler, brought asparagus seed from France, and there soon developed a market for the product in the town and in Ogden. Strawberry plants were imported in 1861 when Edwin Dix brought the first plant from Salt Lake City; the parent plant of this start had reportedly been brought from California to Utah by Pony Express. Over the years strawberries became a major export item.[36]

Associated with Plain City development were the areas to the west which became the Warren and West Warren communities. The boundaries of this area are Plain City and West Weber on the east, the Weber River on the south, and the Great Salt Lake on the west. West Warren is on a peninsula that extends into the Great Salt Lake. In 1996 West Warren became the Reese Township. The area is farming land located on the delta of the Weber River where silt from the canyons and mountain slopes has been deposited, forming rich alluvial soil.

In early times the area was referred to as the Salt Creek district of Plain City. "It received that name from the fact that it is traversed by three distinct overflow channels of the Weber River, and at the time of the settlement there, the Great Salt Lake was at a much higher level than at present. In the summer time the lake waters would flow back through these channels, leaving a heavy deposit of salt which enterprising citizens collected to further develop the salt industry."[37] The first settlers came into the area in 1872, but it was in 1896 that it took the name of Warren, the name derived from Lewis Warren Shurtliff, who was a longtime stake president of the Weber Stake of the Church of Jesus Christ of Latter-day Saints.

The region was a farming area, with alfalfa, grain, sugar beets, onions, tomatoes, and potatoes as the major crops. A large amount of acreage was also devoted to grazing land, with a significant number of small dairy herds being grazed there. Because of frequent flooding, the surface of the land was very rough. There were no tracts of any considerable size that did not require leveling, which was done with much effort. Over the years, the land has been leveled out and small and large farms now exist. Like other Weber County towns, the supply of water for irrigation purposes was a vital factor in the economic prosperity of the community. Warren took water from Four Mile Creek and later developed larger supplies from the Weber River and from the Echo Reservoir by buying stock in the latter project. As a result, in later years the entire district of Warren and West Warren has been quite amply supplied with irrigation water. With this increase, supplemented by artesian wells for culinary use, the community was able to accommodate a larger number of farms and families.

Two other communities in Weber County on the lower Weber River are Hooper and Roy. Hooper was the farthest extension of settlement in the southwestern part of Weber County. In fact, the community is divided by the county line—the northern section is in Weber County and the southern section is in Davis County. The community lies three miles east of the Great Salt Lake, the last community before the mouth of the river empties into the Great Salt Lake, and it is twelve miles on a direct line from Weber Canyon.

At first, Hooper was a herd ground, with Muskrat Springs being the main water source. William H. Hooper grazed his cattle from Clearfield to the Weber River. In 1854 Hooper built an adobe house for the herdsmen that was the beginning of the settlement. This house was located near Hale's Bend about one and one-half miles southwest of the Hooper LDS meetinghouse. In 1863 James Hale moved to Hooper. Hale lived on the shore of the Great Salt Lake about one and one-half miles southwest of the herd house. He made his living by gathering salt from the sloughs to sell in the region. At first, water blown into the sloughs from the lake provided the salt. Later, water was pumped into the sloughs from the lake and Hale's Bend became the place where the water was boiled and evaporated to process salt for sale.

In 1867 and 1868 more settlers moved in. In the spring of 1867 William Baker built a log house about a quarter of a mile north of the Hooper herd house. Other settlers were Peter Lowe, Gilbert Belnap, Thomas Read, William Garner, John Everett, Alexander and James Lowe, Thomas Hull, W. E. and Edwin Parker, Edwin Stone, W.

E. Baker, Charles Parker, George Davis, Harry Stone, Levi Hammond, John Thompson, Levi Cox, Thomas Smith, James Henry, Arvil Atwood, and their families. William Hooper moved his cattle to Skull Valley to make room for the new settlers. Soon after these families arrived, surveyor Jesse W. Fox was brought from Salt Lake to lay out the townsite. A quarter-section of land owned by Franklin D. Richards was divided into blocks. Lots sold for five dollars each. The farming land was laid out in one-half mile blocks with streets running parallel. Each block was divided into twenty acre lots by Charles Hardy. In 1858 the settlement was called Hooperville after William Hooper; it later was changed to Hooper.

Hyrum Belnap described the area in 1868. As a young man he was placed on a horse at the head of the Hooper ditch and was told to follow it to the settlement. He later wrote:

> I was placed on this ill-fated animal and taken to the Hooper ditch, head of which began where the present Sugar Factory is built, and told to follow the same until I reached the end, where I would see a covered wagon, which was to be our future home. I first beheld the Buttermilk Lake, covering 40 acres or more, between Taylor and Kanesville, next the Pete Terry Spring, now called Hadlock Springs, On the east side of what is now called Hooper, I recall the round Hooper pond, about 200 by 300 feet, on the northwest side of which was a cold fresh water spring, from which later we obtained our drinking water and supply for the family use and laundry. There was not a growing tree or willow after leaving Weber River, only some flags and rushes in Musk Rat Spring. Just as the sun was setting, I observed a small dugout, on the top of which was standing an Indian girl. This was the home of Thomas Hull, the father of your townsman Will Hull. The shadows of the sun reflected over the wide spreading plain or vast prairie, and I saw two houses looking like tall trees or objects about two miles south, which were the only signs of a residence as far as the eye could reach. I finally reached the end of the ditch, which had never yet been filled with water. There was the wagon box, about ten and one-half feet long with a cover over it, where the family slept with our heads to the ends and our feet overlapping each other. I lay near the opening at the end. Soon all were sound asleep, but I looked out and listened to the howling wolves. They came closer

> and closer to the wagon until the dog drove them away a short distance, then they in turn would drive her back. This pleasant music continued until the wee hours of the night.[38]

Springs and wells at first provided water to the community; but by the spring of 1869 a 7.5-mile canal brought water sufficient to plant crops of sugar cane and corn. John Thompson and Thomas Smith set out the first orchards. In 1875 the canal was extended another ten miles to Syracuse in Davis County at a cost of $75,432.53 up to that time. In 1926 the Hooper City Irrigation Company invested in the Echo Dam project, and in 1934 water was delivered from this dam to meet the needs of the community.[39]

The settlement of the community of Roy was the last major community in Weber County in the lower Weber River area. Early settlement began there between 1870 and 1873 when several families moved there to take up claims of land. The first settlers were William E. Baker, Justin Grover, Henry Fields, Edward Bell, Samuel Fowler, Richard Jones, and others who homesteaded eighty acres each. The area was not known as Roy then, and it was described as a

> forbidden, forsaken, piece of land without a name or settler. The acreage was mostly blowing sand covered with sandburrs, prickly pears, rabbit brush, sage brush and bisquit root. It had its inhabitants, but they were not human. It provided a habitat for snakes, lizards, coyotes and even a wolf or two, but worst of all there was no water and no trees. One thing in its favor was that Indians left it alone; it was too barren for them to bother.[40]

In the first year, settlers homesteaded at least six months of the year to satisfy the requirements of the homestead laws. In 1874 William E. Baker established the first permanent home; other settlers followed and the community was known by several names—Central City, Sandridge, Lake View, The Basin. Finally, when residents applied for a post office, it took the name of Roy, after a son of Reverend David Peebles who had recently died. Peebles had drafted a letter to the post office department trying to get the office established and told post office officials of the problem of finding a name for the office. The post office officials preferred the short name Roy, and thereby officially named the town on 25 May 1894.

During the first few years of settlement, farmers concentrated on growing wheat because they did not have enough water to irrigate their land. The settlers were forced at first to haul their water for culinary purposes from Muskrat Springs in Hooper, some three miles northwest. Later William E. Baker dug a fifty-foot well and secured good drinking water. This was the only well between Ogden and Kaysville at the time. It supplied sufficient water for the families of Roy to drink, but they were still obliged to water their livestock at the Hooper Springs. Roy did not have sufficient water for its farms until the development of the Davis-Weber Canal in 1883 and East Canyon Reservoir in 1896.

The settlement of the upper region of the Ogden River, or Ogden Valley as it was called, came later in time than that of the lower parts of the Ogden and Weber rivers. This area included the communities of Eden, established in 1859; Huntsville, in 1860; and Liberty, in 1892. This valley had been trapped in 1825 and written about by Peter Skene Ogden in his journal. It was after his expedition that the valley was called Ogden's Hole because of the mountains that enclosed it. In 1849 Captain Howard Stansbury traversed the valley and described it extensively in his exploration notes as a broad, green, beautiful valley covered with grass.[41]

In 1848 Brigham Young sent Thomas Abbott and others from Farmington to explore Ogden Valley; in 1854 Young sent another party under the direction of David Moore and Charles Middleton from Ogden to report on the region. Both expeditions found it difficult to get into the valley through either North Ogden pass or the narrow Ogden Canyon, and because of the difficult access the valley remained somewhat isolated from the lower Weber area.

As various reports began to disseminate about the area, there developed an interest in the valley as a grazing pasture for livestock. In September 1856 William Middleton, his son Charles F., Alvin West, and Alfred Borum took a herd of cattle from Ogden through North Ogden pass into the valley. This was the first herd of cattle that grazed there, and after this time the area was used as a summer herd ground. For several years after 1856, Ogden's Hole was used by the livestock owners of Weber County as a grazing ground.

In the beginning, the area served as a summer range only, and a few small cabins were built for summer occupancy. The first cabin was built by Erastus Bingham and Joseph Hardy in 1857 near a little spring near the middle fork of the Ogden River about one and a half miles east of the present center of Eden near Geertson Canyon. In 1860 Captain Jefferson Hunt and his sons Joseph, Hyrum, and Marshall, along with Joseph Wood, Nathan Coffin, and Coffin's mother, Abigail, went into the valley with the intention of making a permanent settlement. Others followed, and seven families made up the settling group. These settlers located in the riverbottoms of what is now the south end of Huntsville. The hill on the bench to the north protected them from the winter winds, and the area was first called Hawkins Grove, with the southern part named Winter's Grove. The valley remained quite isolated, however, until a road in Ogden Canyon was completed in 1860. With better communication with the outside, the population grew and developed into the communities of Eden, Huntsville, and Liberty.

In the fall of 1860 temporary log houses were built at Huntsville in fort style, with all the houses facing the center. After a rather severe winter, in the spring the snow began to melt and the creek overflowed its banks. The meadow became marshy, and Jefferson Hunt moved his colony onto the bench to avoid the swampy conditions. It is suggested that Joseph Wood built the first house there in the spring of 1861. During that year, David Jenkins and a surveying party laid out a base line starting at Moffet's Spring (now covered by Pine View Reservoir) and running east and west along what became the state road through town. The ground on the north and south sides of the road was fenced as two big fields. The town was also surveyed into nine blocks of about six acres in a block, and each block was divided into eight lots. The families then moved into the new town and took up the lots. Water for the community was supplied from the south fork of the Ogden River by a ditch which originated about two miles upstream.

With improvements being made, more people came into the valley. By 1870 the population had grown to over 1,000 people, with 200 families who earned their livelihood on approximately 1,700 acres of tillable land, with barley, oats, potatoes, grasses and hay being the main crops and with hundreds of other acreage for pasture land. In

1871 it became necessary to enlarge the townsite. Joseph A. West resurveyed the townsite with new lines which created so many problems that the survey was rejected, and in 1872 a new survey was done by the United States surveying engineer, with David Jenkins aiding him. In that same year, the Mountain Canal was constructed, bringing water from South Fork one mile above the earlier ditch. This new water supply allowed the community to take on additional population.[42]

Eden is in the area between the north and the middle forks of the Ogden River. The first settlers came into the valley with the first herders, and in 1859 Joseph Grover and John Riddle settled on the north fork at a point about three miles northwest of the future town of Eden. Other families traveled over North Ogden Pass to settle there. The town was surveyed by either Washington Jenkins or David Jenkins. The surveyor was impressed with the beauty of the site and remarked, "We shall call it Eden after the famous Biblical times." Water for Eden was provided from Wolf Creek and later by a canal from the north fork of the Ogden River.[43]

The settlement of Liberty was a part of the valley development. The town is located in the north end of the valley. The name "Mountain Dell" was considered, but when John Freeman remarked that cattle belonging to Weber County residents had full liberty and bothered the early settlers after they had taken up farms in the valley, Freeman is reported to have said, "This is sure one place where the people take full liberty"; and apparently because he had some difficulty with the law in his own life, he added, "This is where I got my liberty too." From this incident the name stuck.

The first settlers were Dan and Ammon Campbell, who came in 1859 and remained in the north end of the valley. Others soon followed, including John Riddle, John Freeman, James Fisher, Charles Card, and a Mr. Murray. John Riddle is believed to have erected the first house in the Liberty town area on the south bank of Spring Creek. Most of the early settlers had access to individual springs for their water supply.[44]

These communities engaged primarily in farming alfalfa, grain, and vegetables; in raising cattle and sheep, dairy animals, and poultry; and in the lumber business. The rich pasture lands and the heavy stands of timber made this upper Ogden River valley a very prosperous and productive area as time passed.

### *Hard Times at First*

Even devoting all their time to agriculture, the first settlers struggled to survive. Food was very scarce in Utah the first winter of 1847–48. Long before spring arrived, the food supply brought from Winter Quarters was nearly gone. The location, nearly 1,000 miles from the closest supply towns of the east, made it virtually impossible for the colonists to replenish their needs. During the winter they had to resort to putting people on rations and hoped that an early spring would bring relief. Some help came when James Brown sent a group of men to Fort Hall, 160 miles to the north, to get 200 pounds of flour for the settlement; but the main food supply for Weber County during the first winter was the dairy products obtained from the cows purchased from Miles Goodyear and others that Brown had accumulated. This herd provided the colony with milk, butter, and cheese, some of which was taken to the settlers in Salt Lake City.

In the spring of 1848 the Browns plowed a considerable tract of land, planting wheat and corn. The tally for the harvest of 1848 was one hundred bushels of wheat, seventy-five bushels of corn, some cabbages, potatoes, watermelons, and a good crop of turnips. That first planting resulted in a good return; and even though frost, drought, and crickets ravaged the crops in other areas, the Weber County residents were delighted with their first harvest.

Food was hard to come by for many of the early years. Pauline Combe Malan recalled that when her family arrived in Ogden they found

> Zion a desert, but with patient industry, perseverance and God's blessing, we have noticed it gradually transformed from a forbidding desert to a fruitful and most desirable land to dwell on. As we came in the year of the grass-hopper war, bread stuff was very scarce and a hard winter followed. We suffered much hunger and cold. In the spring of '56 we subsisted mostly on weeds and bran. Fish were quite prolific in the Ogden River, so father made traps with willow twigs to catch fish. In the fall we gleaned our bread

> stuff. We thrashed and separated the wheat from the chaff by hand.[45]

In 1858 Nancy Naomi Tracy had complained that "Winter was approaching and my children were destitute of clothing and I had but very little to feed them, so I scarcely knew what to do."[46]

With foodstuffs so scarce in early years, it was necessary to share among the colony; and there are numerous stories of that sharing. Outsiders got different treatment, however, depending of what they had to trade or how they related to the community. On 27 August 1849 Captain Howard Stansbury, on a mission for the United States government to explore the Great Salt Lake area, was looked upon with some suspicion by the Mormon community, and he recorded rather brusk treatment. He said that the settlement was "an extensive assemblage of log buildings, picketed, stockaded, and surrounded by out-buildings and cattle yards, the whole affording evidence of comfort and abundance far greater than I had expected to see in so new a settlement." Yet, his reception and the hospitality was cold:

> Upon requesting food and lodgeing for the night, we were told to our great surprise, that we could not be accommodated, nor would the occupants sell us so much as an egg or a cup of milk, so that we were obliged to remount our horses; and we bivouacked under some willows, within a hundred yards of this inhospitable dwelling [Brown's Fort], turning our animals loose, and guarding them all night, lest, in search of food, they should damage the crops of this surly Nabal. From a neighboring plantation we procured what we needed; otherwise we should have been obliged to go supperless to bed.[47]

Gold seekers on their way to California earlier in the summer had received better treatment from the Mormons at the Brownsville community; possibly because they had items to trade that the community needed and they did not pose a perceived threat to the community. Brigham Young had condemned going to the gold fields to try to strike it rich; instead, he admonished that the people should "stay at home, build houses, and make their fields green," which most of the settlers of Weber County did.

## *Early Commerce and Industry*

There were some rudimentary businesses in the early years of the county, but it was 1863 before anything substantial was begun. The first store was opened by a Mr. DeVorsen who operated a business in a one-room log building in 1850–51 at Farr's Fort. DeVorsen exchanged merchandise for horses and cattle; and, when he acquired a sufficient herd, he drove them to California.

By the winter of 1855–56 "several" mercantile houses were said to be operating at Bingham's Fort. The trade there was largely in hides of cows, horses, oxen, or wildlife. In the spring of 1860, Richard Ballantyne brought merchandise to Ogden and opened a general store on the northwest corner of Washington and 24th Street. Up until 1863 most of the trading was carried out at the church tithing office, but after that time several new businesses were established. Among the early businessmen were Jonathan Browning, James Horrocks, Chauncey W. West, Arthur Stayner, William Pidcock, Samuel Horrocks, William Jennings, David H. Peery, Lester Herrick, Charles Woodmansee, and Lorin Farr—all of whom were local people. N. R. Ranchoff, a Jewish merchant, opened a business with Henry Tribe as manager. Fred J. Kiesel came to town in 1866 with a load of goods which was sold to C. Coy, Job Pingree, Richard White, "Old man Baker" Riter, Robert Wilson, and others who organized an Ogden cooperative store that was a forerunner to the ZCMI (Zion's Cooperative Mercantile Institution) of a later date. Kiesel returned to Ogden in 1867 with a larger and more permanent business operation.

Early stores were mainly general merchandise stores; but within a short time a greater variety of stores was established, and some even manufactured the items they sold. In 1851 Mathew William Dalton began making furniture in his shop at 24th and Grant Avenue during the winter months while he was not occupied with farm work. He made a good quality of furniture which was described as sturdy pioneer furniture, suitable for pioneer times. He made cane- and leather-bottomed chairs, rockers, bedsteads, and other pieces. He found a ready market in Weber County and Salt Lake City, and he hired several other people to assist him. In 1853 he expanded into pottery making, which also enjoyed a good market. Dalton was rec-

Washington Boulevard and 25th Street in Ogden during the 1890s. Buildings from left to right are the Broom Hotel, the spire of Saint Joseph's Church, the Gordon Academy, the Reed Hotel, the Orpheum Theater, and the City Council Building on Municipal Square. (Utah State Historical Society)

ognized as the "first furniture maker in Ogden City."[48] In 1862 Peter A. Boyle began making and selling furniture, spinning wheels, and sole pegs. In 1864 Samuel S. Tucker made and sold furniture from his store at 25th Street and Kiesel Avenue. James Gale, Thomas S. Harrison, and E. Stratford and sons also participated in the furniture business.

Confectionery stores had an early start in Ogden. Possibly the first was opened by John Jost in 1863 on Washington Boulevard between 25th and 26th streets. It featured homemade candy, pastries, and pies. Other early confectioners in the city were David H. and Albertine Petersen Stephens, who built an adobe store at 268 25th Street and in 1869 established an ice cream parlor there. In the summers it was a profitable business, with eight tables seating six people each; home-made ice cream and a piece of hot yellow cake were served for fifteen cents. Albertine Stephens also made and sold fancy leather gloves from this store.[49]

Many of the early industries before the coming of the railroad in 1869 were mills to process timber into lumber, grist into flour, sugar cane into molasses, and wool into textiles. In the early summer of 1850 Lorin Farr built the first sawmill, and in the fall of 1850 he used the lumber from his mill to construct the first gristmill on a stream he had diverted out of the Ogden River at what now is 1251 Canyon Road. The stream not only provided power for Farr's Mill but was an important water source for the area north of the Ogden River. This mill operated until 1862, at which time Lorin Farr erected a new mill at 1950 Washington Boulevard. This mill operated until 1897 although being destroyed twice by fires. It changed hands twice and was known at various times as the "Ogden Mills" and the "Advance Roller Mills." It was later used as a macaroni factory and a potato-chip factory.

In 1850 Daniel Burch established a sawmill on the Weber River, and in 1854 he erected a gristmill at the same location. Burch ran the mill until 1858 when he sold it to John Taylor, apostle of the Mormon church, and it still stands at the Riverdale location, although it has not operated for several years. Another flour mill was operated after 1854 in North Ogden on Cold Water Creek by Newman G. Blodgett and James Barker. Chauncey West built the "Weber Mill" for grist at 1440 Washington Boulevard in 1866. It was a two-story building with a lower floor of rock and a second floor of adobe. It was powered by a huge waterwheel driven by the water of Mill Creek. This mill was purchased by David H. Peery in 1872 and was known after that as "Peery's Mill." Other early mills included the Huntsville Mill in Huntsville, built in 1862; the Boyington Mill in Slaterville, built in 1864; the Naisbitt Mill in Hooper, built in the 1860s; and the Arave Mill in Hooper, built in the 1860s.

Molasses milling was another early enterprise in the county. The first molasses mill was built in 1851 by George Hill and was operated by Captain James Brown. It was located on the south side of 24th Street, on the east bank of the Weber River. Here sugar cane was processed into molasses. James Brown, the first Mormon settler of the county, was killed when the sleeve of his shirt was caught in a cog of mill machinery at the molasses mill and he was dragged into the wheel and was fatally injured. He died on 30 September 1863 In 1851

Francis M. and Noah Shurtliff operated a molasses mill in Harrisville; and in 1852 Amos Pease Stone established a mill at 1328 Washington Boulevard. John Cardon, Peter Boyle, and James McIntyre also had mills. The largest molasses mill in Weber County was operated by David Moore on the brow of the hill at 25th Street and Washington Boulevard where the Raddison Hotel stands today. This mill operated after 1859. Moore later moved his mill to Washington Boulevard between 13th and 14th streets, and moved it again to Grant Avenue.

Blacksmithing was an important business which provided all kinds of services including shoeing horses, making and fixing wagon wheels, and other metal forging. Iron was scarce, and much of it was obtained from emigrants passing through the area or by scavenging along the emigrant trails to find abandoned materials. Artemus (some sources say Ithamar) Sprague is credited with doing the first blacksmithing in Weber County when he made a plow for James Brown's sons in the spring of 1850 for the planting of the first crops. The census of 1850 listed twenty-two blacksmiths, but not all of them were working at the trade at the time. Among the earliest to run shops were William N. Fife and George Douglas, who worked at 25th Street and Washington Boulevard, Asael Farley, William Pearce, Armsted Moffatt, and Amos Pease Stone, who used one of Goodyear's cabins as a shop for a period of time. Winthrop Farley had a shop on the northeast corner of 24th Street and Adams Avenue in 1850.

Jonathan Browning was a blacksmith and a master mechanic who learned his trade in Tennessee and Illinois. In 1852 he came to Ogden and set up a shop on the east side of Washington Boulevard between 24th and 25th streets. He sharpened plows, shoed horses, set wagon tires, and repaired guns, and he also made some of the first nails, fire tongs, fire shovels, pokers, horseshoes, hoes, shovels, and grubbing hoes used in Weber County. In addition, he developed the first iron-roller molasses mill made in Ogden. John Isaac Hart, Charles McGary, and John Nicholas were also known for the many farm implements that they made in their shops. In 1865 Christian Schade opened the first blacksmith shop in Huntsville.

Photography was introduced in the county by a Mr. Vaughn, who established the first practice of the trade in Ogden in 1862 or 1863.

He conducted his business out of a covered wagon drawn by a team of mules. He used painted scenery as a backdrop and posed his subjects by putting their heads in a brace to keep them steady while the photograph was taken. Vaughn sold his business in 1867 to James Otha Stephens, who built a shop between 24th and 25th streets on Washington Boulevard. Other photographers who captured portraits of early Weber County residents and scenery were J. Pasevitch, Albert J. Hoffman, Adams Brothers, J. Smith, William Lowe, Smith and Careswell, H. Drewery, a Mr. Carpenter, Newcombe Brothers, Sooey and LaRoche, and H. H. Thomas.

John Frost in 1849 was the first to operate a "Job Wagon," using a team of horses to hire out to haul coal, sand, gravel, lumber, brick, move furniture, or do other hauling work. Michael Beus manufactured charcoal in Weber County in 1856. Charcoal was produced in Uintah for several years in the 1850s and 1860s. Leather goods were in demand in early years; as a result, several tanneries were operated in the county. One of the first was established at the corner of 24th Street and Grant Avenue by Chauncey West and Francis A. Hammond. Jonathan Browning built a tannery on the Weber Canal east of Washington Boulevard near 25th Street. William Roylance, Sr., had a tannery in North Ogden and Sidney Stevens also operated a tannery there. Jonathan Browning and Sidney Stevens also made shoes and boots from their leather. Edwin Bingham made shoes for men and women in the early 1860s.

Many families kept a few sheep which were used for meat and wool. The equipment for home production of wool was brought by the pioneers—cards, spinning wheels, and looms. At first, much of the wool was processed at home. Early wool producers in the county included Sarah Stewart Hill and John Gibson. John Gibson came to Ogden in 1860 and, using a loom he brought with him, he did a considerable amount of weaving for the community. Susan Buel Wilcox Wright is claimed to be the first to weave a carpet from wool in 1849. In 1863 John Cardon built the first carding mill, and in 1867 Philip Pugsley, William C. Neal, and Lorin Farr joined with Alfred Randall, who had been sent from Salt Lake by Brigham Young, to organize the "Ogden Woolen Mills." They constructed a three-story stone building to accommodate the machinery for the woolen mill. The factory was located at the "Old Mill Site" at 1251 Canyon Road and cost $60,000 to construct. Through the years the mill produced woolen broadcloth, woolen blankets, and men's and women's wearing apparel. In 1912 it became a mattress factory and in 1940 it was purchased by Harmon W. Perry and operated for several years as a restaurant and dancing club known as the "Old Mill Inn" before it fell into disuse. The property was later developed into condominiums.

There were early attempts to produce cotton, flax, and silk in Weber County, but the lack of suitable climate or the labor-intensive requirements of the processes soon led to abandonment of the industries. Roxanan Ive Jones, Mrs. Gilbert Belnap, and Sarah Jane Taylor in Harrisville each grew some cotton and made thread or some cloth and some clothing from it; but cotton growing in Weber County was nothing more than a novelty because the climate was not suitable to make it profitable. Flax production was tried unsuccessfully by Gilbert Belnap and John Everett in Ogden and by Peter Johnson in Eden. There was talk of making silk in the late 1860s, and in the 1870s there were attempts to promote that industry; but it too was no more than a novelty in the impact it had on Weber County industry.

## *County Roads*

Roads were a community concern, and in the early days of the county there was a constant problem of providing adequate means to get about the county for purposes of commercial and social intercourse. Early roads usually followed common trails established by animals or by earlier Indians and trappers as they made their way to various parts of the county. As the towns spread throughout the valley, the first pioneer roads made from settlement to settlement were constructed on the easiest grades and the roads were crooked and rough. Later, however, roads were established in the communities based on survey lines laid out when the communities were first settled and along the surveyed section lines. The roads then were made straighter and more manageable.

Before the days of macadam roads, in rainy weather the dusty streets were transformed into quagmires which "gave Ogden the reputation of having the muddiest streets in Utah." In the downtown business district there were plank walks in front of some of the stores and saloons, and from 24th Street and what is now Wall Avenue, a wide boardwalk ran southwest for about a quarter of a mile to the old wooden structure which served as the Union Depot.[50] William Chandless had described the county roads as "the best and most plausible, . . . the county is laid out for miles by roads intersecting at right angles, and which of these to choose, as you successively come to them is puzzling." James Bonwick, a visitor to Ogden in the winter of 1871–72, said that one of the complaints of a newly arrived gentile (non-Mormon) population was that the Latter-day Saints were devoting territorial returns to their missionary enterprises instead of making decent roads. But the Mormons might reply "that the western Americans were so accustomed to unmade streets and corduroy plank causeways elsewhere, as to be able to put up with no worse in Utah."[51]

Early roads were authorized by the General Council of the provisional State of Deseret. The "Ordinance providing for State and County Commissioner, On Roads," passed on 15 January 1850, allowed the county courts power to appoint one or more commissioners to "locate all County roads within the limit of said County." Another bill in February 1850 provided for a road from Ogden to Provo. Under this and later authorization by the territorial government, the Weber County Court and Ogden city governments carried the responsibility of managing the program of road administration on county roads; and, for long periods of time, especially from 1870 until statehood was achieved in 1896, the county assumed complete jurisdiction over local territorial road matters. In 1852 a territorial law provided for a poll tax in support of highway and road construction that placed a "one day of ten hours of labor requirement upon the roads or highways annually from every able-bodied male over eighteen years of age, or the payment of $1.50 in lieu, with the additional requirement that supervisors may require teamwork from those having teams allowing the same ratio for the use of teams as for labor."[52] Through this means most county roads were constructed.

The Ogden City Council also dealt with the road question within the city's boundaries. For instance, in April 1851 the council set the tolls that could be charged on bridges across the Weber and Ogden rivers. These were bridges approved by the State of Deseret to enhance traffic along the territorial road from Ogden to Provo. The toll fixed was "from three to five dollars for one wagon drawn by four animals, all succeeding animals twenty five cents per head. Sheep and hogs twelve and a half cents per head. Men in company with said wagons free." Pack animals were one dollar each, and "all men living South and coming to Ogden Mills shall be free." The Ogden bridge keepers could only charge two to three dollars per wagon.[53]

From time to time, the council approved new roads to be constructed. For instance, in November 1852 the council approved a bill to make a road through Ogden Hole (North Ogden) Canyon; on 18 February 1854 it approved a poll tax of three days on each person in Ogden City and a road tax of $1,000 be assessed the inhabitants of Ogden City for the purpose of making a road on each side of the Ogden River; on 3 June 1854 it approved an ordinance to "open the first street north of Mill Creek." On 28 March 1856 a petition for the first east-west street south of the city was read and instructions to make roads four rods wide were approved. On 2 May 1856 a bill provided for setting out shade trees and establishing sidewalks along the roadway. On 28 February 1857 a bill was passed which probably only could have happened in early Utah; the bill granted the Mormon bishops of their respective ecclesiastical wards power to collect and expend the road and poll tax "in the improvement of roads and streets in their respective wards. And with power to raise as much tax for that purpose as the people of those wards may think proper."[54]

Important in understanding the early development of Weber County was the building of the road up Ogden Canyon. This was initially constructed as a private toll road. In 1857 Lorin Farr, Isaac Newton Goodale, and others staked out and surveyed the Ogden Canyon road; they did not start construction on it until September 1858, however. The road was finished and opened to the first travelers on 19 November 1860. Tollgate keepers collected fares at the mouth of the canyon on the north side of the river by controlling a gate which "swung on a heavy wooden framework and completely blocked the road." Toll charges ranged from 25 cents to $1.50, depending on whether the vehicle was lightly or heavily loaded, or the person was walking or on horseback. Toll charges were $1.00 for a loaded wagon, 50 cents for an unloaded wagon, and 25 cents for horsemen. Payment was made with money or various produce. In 1865 the Ogden Canyon Road Company was incorporated and continued to operate the road as a toll road until February 1882 when it was sold to Weber County and became a public road.

## *The County Militia and Native Americans*

The establishment of a militia force was an important development in early Weber County. When Lorin Farr arrived in Ogden in 1850, one of his duties was to organize a unit of the militia, which he did in February. The first company of militia in Weber County was part of the territorial militia, the Nauvoo Legion. Cyrus C. Canfield, who had served as a senior lieutenant in the Mormon Battalion, was elected captain, and Francillo Durfey (Francis Durfee), another battalion soldier, was elected first lieutenant. In 1851 a regiment of the Nauvoo Legion was organized in Weber County, with Cyrus Canfield elected as colonel and B. W. Nolan as adjutant. There were two companies organized in the regiment, with David Moore designated as major of cavalry and B. F. Cummings as captain of Company A (infantry) and J. C. Thompson captain of Company B (cavalry).

On 11 April 1857 Lieutenant-General Daniel H. Wells, commander of the Nauvoo Legion, in a published general order, created military districts throughout the territory. The Weber Military District, including Weber and Summit counties, was to be organized by David Moore. The muster rolls indicate that by 1857 Weber County had a large militia force, consisting of the 5th Regiment of Infantry, which was all in Weber County, and part of the 6th Regiment, which was part in Weber County and part in Box Elder County. The regiments were made up of one battery of artillery, a squadron of cavalry, and several companies of infantry. The infantry companies were organized into seven battalions in the following configuration of battalions and commanders: lst Battalion, Major Benjamin F. Cummings; 2nd Battalion, Major James Fife; 3rd Battalion, Major Lorenzo Clark; 4th Battalion, Major Isaac Allred; 5th Battalion, Major Erastus Bingham; 6th Battalion, Joseph Taylor; and 7th Battalion, Major Lyman A Shurtliff. Major David Moore was in command of the cavalry squadron and Chauncey W. West was the colonel in charge of the 5th Regiment.[55]

The units of the Nauvoo Legion (the Mormon militia formed in Illinois) had continued their training since the entry of the Mormons into the Salt Lake Valley. Brigham Young stressed the need for the people of Zion to be cautious and ordered the militia to continue its training. Training and participating in parades and celebrations occupied much of the activity of the militia in this early period. An account describing elements of the Nauvoo Legion in the Weber Military District in 1866 stated that there were 960 men organized into twelve companies in the district, and that regimental, company, and platoon drills were held on Ogden Tabernacle Square "every Saturday until November, from 10 A.M. to 4 P.M. Three days drill and parade with camp and garrison duty, with the Box Elder County Regiment, at Camp Weber, on the Weber-Box Elder County line" was considered the annual training.[56]

Charles Middleton, a member of the Weber County militia since 1852 and at the time a member of a light horse brigade, listed his equipment as "one horse, one bridle and saddle, no rifle, one pound of powder and four pounds of lead." Militia members apparently provided their own weapons.[57]

The Weber County Militia drilled in public and participated in public demonstrations and ceremonies. The stated purposes of the militia were to "preserve the peace and to repel Indian depredations." Relations with the Indians in Weber County were good for the most part, and the community tried to keep peace with the Indians who were in the area first and continued to use the area as camping and wintering grounds. Several journals of the early settlers give accounts of the relations with the Indians in Weber County. For the most part, peace was kept. Most journal accounts record that the native peoples were usually hard-pressed for food, and would beg for food from the local settlers. Most difficulties were settled by providing the supplies when demanded. Mormon communities actually made conscious efforts to help the Indian people in a paternalistic manner, and in some cases Mormons took destitute Indian children into their homes and raised them as part of their family. Despite this, Mormons effectively displaced the Indians from the land, thus causing the predicament of the Native Americans. Weber County residents Lewis Shurtliff, B. F. Cummings, David Moore, Charles F. Middleton, and Gilbert Belnap were all part of a proselyting effort on the Salmon River in Idaho known as the Fort Lemhi Mission, which lasted from 1855 to 1858. This mission had as its major thrust the goals of converting Indians to Mormonism and bettering Indian relations.

A Weber County incident in September 1850 required the calling of the armed militia into action. On 16 September, Urban Stewart, who had established a farm on Four Mile Creek (now known as Harrisville), claimed that he heard someone in his cornfield and went out to try to drive the intruders out. He ordered them to leave; but, getting no apparent results, he fired at random into the direction of the noise. His shots hit and killed Terikee, the chief of a band of Shoshoni Indians. Terikee had the reputation of being a "friendly" Indian. In fact, he had earlier in the day paid his respects to Lorin Farr and his family in Ogden. He was on his way to his camp, which was located near Stewart's farm, while the rest of his band continued north to do some hunting and to return to their Idaho camp. Wrote one historian: "It was afterwards the prevailing opinion of the settlers that Terikee was not in Stewart's corn with any intent to steal, but to drive out his ponies which had got into the unfenced corn."[58]

Realizing the seriousness of what had happened, Stewart went to the home of David Moore, who chastised Stewart not only for killing Chief Terikee but for provoking a situation that would certainly bring the whole Indian band against the community. Stewart continued to try to find some help and went to Lorin Farr's home in the early morning hours. Stewart received another rebuke there, brought on by the fear that there would certainly be an attack on the settlement. It was decided that Urban Stewart should leave the settlement, so that he would not be killed. Indian justice was considered to be retributive and arbitrary, and Stewart stood little chance to explain his error in the killing of Terikee. Lorin Farr directed ten or twelve militia men to proceed to the area around the Hot Springs to the north and gather cattle that belonged to the settlement. David Moore went to Brown's Fort and informed that settlement of the impending trouble. After consultations, the leaders of the settlements decided to send

David Moore to Salt Lake to inform Governor Brigham Young of what had transpired in Weber County. Moore was also to inform the militia in Davis County of what had happened.

There was another band of Indians camped on the Weber River that also had to be dealt with. This was a band of Indians sometimes referred to as "Weber Utes," who were actually Shoshoni Indians led by Chief Little Soldier. This band had become enraged by the killing of Terikee and threatened to burn the settlement and kill the settlers unless Stewart was given up to appease the vengeance of the Indian bands. Before leaving on his mission to Salt Lake to inform Governor Young of the trouble, Major Moore went to the camp of Little Soldier to negotiate a settlement. He was met at first with a "passionate show of hostility." Little Soldier fired his rifle near Moore's head and his warriors shouted and expressed their anger. Moore was able to calm them by convincing them that the settlers were also upset with the killing of Terikee. The Indians wanted Stewart to be delivered to them, but Moore convinced them that Stewart had fled and no one knew where he was. Little Soldier agreed that his men would not attack the Weber settlements and that they would wait for word from Young as to how the problem could be resolved.

Scarcely had Moore departed for Salt Lake when word was received that Terikee's band had returned from the north and attacked the men who had been sent out to gather in the cattle. One man had been killed in that raid—a Mr. Campbell—who worked as a mechanic at Farr's mill and who had intended to move on to California as soon as he had means to do so. As soon as the death of Campbell was reported, Lorin Farr sent another dispatch to Salt Lake with Daniel Burch. Burch arrived in Salt Lake two hours after Moore, and, with his report of the Indian attack, it was decided to send a contingent of 150 Salt Lake militiamen to Weber County under the command of General Horace S. Eldredge. This group was well armed and was accompanied by baggage wagons which would allow them to conduct a vigorous campaign. The force arrived at Brown's Fort early in the morning of 18 September. It was decided that Eldredge's mounted force would continue north to overtake the Indians and try to reach a settlement with them. A show of force in this matter might impress the Indians into making some kind of peace agreement.

The Indians, having learned of the approach of troops, had recovered the body of their chief and made a quick retreat to the north. The troops pursued them to Box Elder Creek; Eldredge then sent a reconnoitering party nearly to the Bear River, a distance of about forty miles from Ogden. But the Indians had put a great distance between them and their pursuers, and it was decided to return the militia to Ogden. A meeting of the leaders decided that the response of such a large force had seemed to settle the Terikee incident, and the matter was dropped. A resolution such as this might leave some questions in the minds of a modern reader, but frontier justice was many times not as thorough or complete as is present-day justice.

In July 1851 the Weber County militia was called out when a band of Indians stole seven head of horses. Sixteen militiamen led by David Moore and Francillo Durfey pursued the thieves and overtook the Indian camp, but the horses had been driven on ahead. The militia force tried to get the Indians to go with them to recover the horses, but one Indian refused to go and drew a knife in a menacing way. He reportedly "pitched into the men right and left, when one of the men stopped his mad career with a musket ball." After this incident, the company felt it was useless to continue the hunt for the horses and returned back to Ogden.

One final incident with the Indians and the militia in Weber County happened in 1854 after a visit of Brigham Young. This was at the time of the larger Walker War, and there was much uneasiness about the Indians and attacks on the communities. In fact, part of Brigham Young's purpose in coming to Weber County was to make some agreement with the local Indians and to encourage the settlers to take precautions to protect themselves, including the building of forts around the communities. After distributing some presents to the Indians, Brigham Young proposed to the Shoshoni group gathered with Chief Catalos at a Weber River camp that it would be good for them to settle down like the white man, and learn of him to cultivate the land. The Indians reportedly felt good about the meeting.

Matters seemed to be under control; but in November 1854 orders came from Salt Lake to disarm Chief Little Soldier and his band of Indians, and distribute the Indians among the families in

Weber County where the people were best able to feed and clothe them for the winter and set them to work. Major Moore, James Brown, and other militiamen visited the Indian camp and persuaded them to come to Ogden, which they did; but they refused to give up their arms. The Indians made a camp near Mound Fort on the Ogden River. A day later, when the whites visited the camp, they found the Indians very hostile when the proposal was made that they be distributed among the whites for the winter. A squad of armed white men persuaded them, however. Sullenly and reluctantly the Indians marched back to Ogden. Under these circumstances the weapons were gathered from the Indians. After an aborted attempt to rally all the other Indians in the area against the taking of their arms, a larger force of militiamen were assembled, and under those conditions the weapons were taken.

The settlements of the Mormons occupied increasing amounts of Indian land. The militia continued to make efforts to keep the peace and to keep threats from Indian attacks at a minimum. By the arrival of the railroad, difficulties with Indians were a thing of the past in Weber County, as the Indians had been in large part pushed out of or to the fringes of the county.

In 1857, during the so-called Utah War, the Weber County militia were called into another kind of service. Brigham Young concluded that the 2,500-man army sent by U.S. President James Buchanan and led by Colonel Albert Sidney Johnston to the territory was to drive the Mormons once again from their homes. Young was determined that they would not to be driven out without a fight. As a result, Nauvoo Legion units throughout the region were ordered to prepare to do battle, and the communities in the northern part of the territory were ordered to abandon their homes and move south, leaving guards behind prepared to burn their communities and destroy their supplies and crops if Johnston's Army attempted to take over the region.

Weber County was an area that was deeply affected by this policy. Lorin Farr, Colonel Chauncey W. West, Adjutant F. A. Brown, Captain James Brown, Aaron Farr, and other families from Ogden, including the Ogden City Band and the Ogden Martial Band, were in attendance at the tenth anniversary celebration of the Mormon arrival in Salt Lake Valley that was being held in Big Cottonwood Canyon when word was received that the U.S. Army was on its way to Utah to put down the alleged Mormon rebellion. Church leaders decided that they would stand and fight. The Ogden contingent started back to Ogden on 27 July, and the "group went as a procession, more funeral-like than holiday participants."[59]

Throughout Utah Territory, the Nauvoo Legion was mustered for armed conflict. Among the units summoned for action were the units from Ogden under the command of Colonel Chauncey W. West. On 19 October 1857 the Ogden troops were sent north to reconnoiter into Cache Valley and beyond to the Bear River to check out rumors that part of Johnston's Army had gone north to enter the Salt Lake Valley through the Bear River Valley. Finding no enemy in that area, the Ogden troops returned to Weber County by way of Malad Valley and Brigham City, arriving home on 2 November. A few days after returning from the Bear River, the Weber County troops were ordered to Echo Canyon to block Johnston's Army from coming down that route. Joining with other Nauvoo Legion units, they "engaged in drills" while watching the movements of federal troops until 3 December 1857. Some of the men remained at the Echo Canyon fortifications throughout the winter, but most of the troops returned home at that time. Destruction of supplies by guerrila members of the Nauvoo Legion and the coming of winter forced Johnston and his troops to go into winter camp at Camp Scott in western Wyoming.[60]

In the spring of 1858, Brigham Young decided to abandon or threaten to abandon the northern Utah settlements instead of fighting. Lorin Farr, the religious and governmental leader, and Colonel Chauncey West, religious and military leader, led the Weber County residents to the south and made an encampment near Payson. They had piled what goods they could in their wagons and left their homes and farms in the hands of three companies of ten men each, under the command of Colonel David Moore, with "instructions to burn the houses and crops if worst came to worst and the Saints definitely must seek a new homeland."[61] By 1 May 1858 Lorin Farr reported that

> nearly all of Weber county were down on the Provo bottoms which we had before selected. Some made their quarters in wagons, tents and wickiups, built of long canes and flags. In many places the cane houses had the appearance of villages. Here on these bottoms the bulk of the Weber County people located themselves for two months.[62]

In June 1858 the Mormons and the United States government worked out their differences and the "war" was brought to an end. The move back to Weber County was begun on 2 July 1858. It took some people only a few days to return home to their farms and crops, which for the most part had matured well through the summer. There were others, however, who had no crops or matters to press them, and they took several weeks to come back. In addition, there were some people who had met the Weber County residents and had been impressed with what they had heard about the county, and they followed the Weber County people home. Plain City was settled in this fashion.

The effect of the Utah War changed Utah and Weber County considerably. It would never be the same again. With the coming of the federal troops, the peace and serenity of the isolated Mormon community was gone. Influences from the outside would gradually affect the daily life. With the army came new government appointments, including new governor Alfred Cumming, and adjustments needed to be made. Outsiders brought money to invest in the area; new businesses challenged older businesses. Ogden ceased being a small frontier town. There was a new vigorous heartbeat in the pioneer settlement. The population of Ogden City in 1860 was 1,464 people—323 more than the total population of the entire county ten years earlier, and home builders continued to regard it as a choice place to settle. During the 1860s, Ogden began to look forward toward rapid growth in commerce and industry.

## ENDNOTES

1. Howard Egan, *Pioneering the West* (Richmond, UT: Howard Egan Estate, 1917), 126–27; Dale L. Morgan, *The State of Deseret* (Salt Lake City: Utah State Historical Society, 1940), 9–10; Journal History of the Church of Jesus Christ of Latter-day Saints, 6 and 9 September 1847, LDS Church

Historians Office. Nominated was John Smith, president, with liberty to select his own counselors; but Charles C. Rich and John Young were suggested. Nominated for the LDS High Council were Henry G. Sherwood, Thomas Grover, Levi Jackman, John Murdock, Daniel Spencer, Stephen Abbott, Ira Eldredge, Edison Whipple, Shadrach Roundy, John Vance, Willard Snow, and Abraham O. Smoot.

2. Morgan, *The State of Deseret,* 134–38.

3. Ibid., 46–47.

4. Ibid., 142–46.

5. Ibid., 182–83.

6. Scott G. Kenney, ed., *Wilford Woodruff's Journal: 1833–1898* (Midvale, Utah: Signature Books, 1983), 3:156.

7. Elwood I. Barker, "Pioneer Forts in Ogden, Utah: 1848–1855: Brown's, Farr's, Bingham's, Mound Fort," Weber County Library, Ogden, Utah. Those living at Brown's Fort first included Captain James Brown and his wives Abigail Woods Brown, Mary Black Brown, and Esther Rapier Brown, and his sons James, Moroni, Alexander, Jessee, John, Daniel, William, and Frank, and their families. Others living there later included David B. Dille, James Greene Browning, Chauncey Hadlocke, Lemuel G. Lewis, David Lewis, James P. Stow, and William Critchlow. Living out from the fort were George and Richard Hill, Datus Ensign, and Gilbert Belnap.

8. Hunter, *Beneath Ben Lomond's Peak,* 580–83. This original Goodyear cabin was again moved in 1857 to 1440 Washington Boulevard by Amos P. Stone, who used it as a blacksmith shop. In 1866 it was moved to 1842 Washington Boulevard to make room for the new Phoenix Mills. In 1896 Stone's daughter, Mrs. Minerva Shaw, moved the building to her residence at 1265 Washington Boulevard. It stayed there until 1916, when it was moved to a lot at the rear of the fire station at Washington Boulevard and 9th Street. On 8 November 1926 Mrs. Shaw presented the building to the Daughters of Utah Pioneers of Weber County, and two years later it was moved to the museum site at 22nd and Grant Avenue, where it remains.

9. Thomas Bullock, "Notes," in Journal History, 2 and 3 September 1849.

10. *The Latter-day Saints' Millennial Star,* 1 May 1850, 12:134.

11. Barker, "Pioneer Forts." Those who first lived in the Farr Fort in early days were the families of Lorin Farr, Ezra Chase, John Shaw, Charles Hubbard, David Moore, Clinton Bronson, William Shaw, Charles Dana, Amos Andrews, Myrtillo Shaw, Merlin Jones, Francillo Durfee, George and Frederick Barker, Asael Rice, Newton Hall, Joseph Grover, William Strong, Jonathan Campbell, John Campbell, John Riddle, Robert Berrett, and Franklin Clifford.

12. Journal History, 26 January 1851.

13. T. Earl Pardoe, *Lorin Farr, Pioneer* (Provo: Brigham Young University Press, 1953), 124–25; Andrew Jenson, comp., *Church Chronology: A Record of Important Events Pertaining to the History of the Church of Jesus Christ of Latter-day Saints* (Salt Lake City: Deseret News Press, 1899), 2nd ed., 42.

14. John Farr, *My Yesterdays* (Salt Lake City: Granite Publishing Company, 1957), 20–21, 26; Pardoe, *Lorin Farr, Pioneer,* 134.

15. See Gordon Jones, *Pioneer Forts in Ogden, Utah* (Ogden: Gordon Jones, 1996).

16. Jones, *Pioneer Forts;* Hunter, *Beneath Ben Lomond's Peak,* 86–90; Barker, "Pioneer Forts." In Bingham's Fort lived the families of Noah and George Brimhall, Joseph Taylor, Eb Richardson, Mr. Beebe, William Elmer, Orvil Child, William Dixon, Levi Murdock, P. B. Taylor, Luman Shurtliff, Haskel Shurtliff, Widow Green, William Strong, Martin Harris, a Mr. Corbett, a Mr. Kelly, a Mrs. Baker, Thomas Foy, a Mr. Bergdall, Matt Field, Orson Drake, Joe Hardy, John Lord, Isaac Clark, Stephen Parry, Lewis Hardy, John Knight, Sam Eggleston, John Etherington, Moses Tracy, John Leavitt, John Hart, Davis Bartholomew, Thomas Wilson, Widow Burke, three Bingham families (including Bishop Erastus Bingham), Henry Grow, Warren G. Child, David Sargant, Charley Elmer, Sam Gates, Peter Jones, Warren Child, J. Schaeffer, John Schaeffer, Joseph Schaeffer, Alex Brown, Newell Drake, Widow Langlois, Jim Gardner, Thomas Richardson, and Newton Goodale.

17. Hunter, *Beneath Ben Lomond's Peak,* 85–86; Barker, "Pioneer Forts"; David Moore, *Compiled Writings of David Moore* (Provo: Brigham Young University Library, 1962), 67, 71. Families first living in Mound Fort were those of David Moore, George and Frederick Barker, and Robert Porter in October 1849, joined in November by Isaac Clark, John Thompson, Phillip Garner, and other families—making a small settlement of about ten or twelve families.

18. Pardoe, *Lorin Farr,* 118–19; Dale L. Morgan, ed., *History of Ogden* (Ogden: Ogden City Commission, 1940), 21; *Deseret News,* 7 September 1850.

19. Edward W. Tullidge, *Tullidge's Histories: Containing the History of All the Northern, Eastern, and Western Counties of Utah, also the Counties of Southern Idaho* (Salt Lake City: Juvenile Instructor Press, 1889), 24.

20. *Deseret News,* vol. I, 95; Journal History of the Church, 28 August 1850.

21. Fred J. Holton, *Matthew William Dalton: A Biography* (Brigham City: n.p., 1917), 33.

22. *Deseret News,* vol. 4, 157. See also Kenney, *Wilford Woodruff's Journal: 1833–1898,* 4:291–93.

23. William Chandless, *A Visit to Salt Lake* (New York: AMS Press, 1972), 228–33; Morgan, *A History of Ogden,* 33–34.

24. Richard W. Sadler and Richard C. Roberts, *Weber River Basin: Grass Roots Democracy and Water Development* (Logan: Utah State University Press, 1994), chap. 2.

25. Isaac Newton Goodale, "Journal:1850–1857," typed copy by Elden J. and Anne S. Watson, 1981, 91–115; Electa Goodale and Martha Goodale Buswell, "Isaac Newton Goodale;" Irving W. Jones and Emma Anderson Jones, "The Ogden Bench Canal;" Gordon Jones, interview, 5 September 1982, Ogden, Utah, by Richard Roberts; Raymond E. Wardleigh, interview, 5 September1982, Ogden, Utah, by Richard Roberts.

26. Morgan, *A History of Ogden,* 29; Sadler and Roberts, *The Weber River Basin,* 30–31

27. Joseph Stanford, *Ogden City and Weber County: A Historical Sketch* (n.p.,n.d.), 33.

28. Leila C. Heslop, comp., *History of the West Weber Relief Society, 1868–1968* (n.p., n.d.), 96–101, 103; Arvil C. Hipwell and Ida Mae Deem Hipwell, comps., *The Big Bend of the Weber River: History of West Weber, 1859–1976* (Ogden: Empire Printing Company, 1976), 403–6; Hunter, *Beneath Ben Lomond's Peak,* 198–202.

29. Hunter, *Beneath Ben Lomond's Peak,* 175–79; Edward Tullidge, "History of Weber County," *Tullidge's Quarterly Magazine* 2 (July 1883): 74–75; John Q. Blaylock, "History of North Ogden: An Economic and Social Study," M.A. thesis, University of Utah, 1922, 1–3; Leonard H. Judkins, "Two Decades in North Ogden," paper, 1928, Utah State Agricultural College, 17–18.

30. Floyd and Clara Woodfield, comps., *A History of North Ogden: Beginnings to 1985* (Ogden: Empire Printing, 1986), 13; *Inventory of the County Archives of Utah: Weber County,* 27.

31. Luman Andros Shurtliff, *His Personal History, 1807–1884* (Salt Lake City: Litho grafics, n.d.), 93–94.

32. Andrew Jenson, *Encyclopedic History of the Church of Jesus Christ of Latter-day Saints* (Salt Lake City: Deseret News Publishing Co., 1941), 798; *Inventory of County Archives, Weber County,* 11; Jerome Wheeler, *History of Slaterville* (n.p., n.d.), 1–12; Norman F. Bingham, Lillian B. Belnap and Lester S. Scoville, comps., *Sketch of the Life of Erastus Bingham and Family: Utah Pioneers of 1847* (n.p., n.d.), 30–31, 35; Tullidge, *Tullidge's Quarterly Magazine of Utah* 2 (1883): 632–34.

33. *Inventory of the County Archives, Weber County,* 10; Hunter, *Beneath*

*Ben Lomond's Peak,* 161–62, 164; Ogden City Council Minutes, Record Book A, 9–10, 18–19.

34. Osborne Russell, *Journal of a Trapper* (Lincoln: University of Nebraska Press, 1965), 113–15.

35. Hunter, *Beneath Ben Lomond's Peak,* 206; Emma Anderson, Marian Berrett, and Rosalie Clark, comps., *A Brief History of Taylor in Story and Pictures: About 1822–1975* (n.p., n.d.), 1–5, copy in Family History Library, Ogden, Utah; Jenson, *Encyclopedic History of the Church,* 862; *Inventory of County Archives, Weber County,* 27.

36. Jenson, *Encyclopedic History of the Church,* 659–60; Hunter, *Beneath Ben Lomond's Peak,* 211–14, 217–18; Lyman and Dorothy Cook, eds., *History of Plain City: March 17th 1859 to Present* (n.p., n.d.), 1–2; 5–8, copy in Family History Library, Ogden, Utah; Tullidge, *Tullidge's Quarterly Magazine* 2 (1883): 53–58; Tullidge, *Tullidge's Histories,* 51–52.

37. Hunter, *Beneath Ben Lomond's Peak,* 23.

38. Hyrum Belnap, "Early Reminiscences of Hooper, Utah," manuscript taken by dictation and typed by Flora Belnap, in authors' possession.

39. Roger and Kay Rawson, *A Bicentennial History: Hooper-Kanesville,* (n.p., 1976); Arvil C. and Ida Mae Deem Hipwell, *The Big Bend of the River: History of West Weber, 1859–1976,* 403–5; John M. Belnap, *History of Hooper, Utah: Land of Beautiful Sunsets,* 37–43; John D. Hooper, *Memoirs and Life of John D. Hooper,* 16.

40. Emma Russell, *Footprints of Roy: 1873–1979* (Roy, Utah: Emma Russell, 1979), 9.

41. Brigham D. Madsen, ed., *Exploring the Great Salt Lake, The Stansbury Expedition of 1849–50* (Salt Lake City: University of Utah Press, 1989), 148–53.

42. LaVerna B. Newey, *Remember My Valley* (Salt Lake City: Hawkes Publishing Company, 1977), 51–52, 258–59; Hunter, *Beneath Ben Lomond's Peak,* 242–45; "Huntsville Ward Dedicatory Services: Short History of Huntsville," 3 May 1859, copy located in Family History Library, Ogden, Utah; Andrew Jenson, comp., *Homecoming Week* (Huntsville, Utah, 1917), 5–21, 29.

43. Newey, *Remember My Valley,* 32–34; 72–73; 258–59; Hunter, *Beneath Ben Lomond's Peak,* 253–58; Melba and Ron Colvin, *Over 100 Years in Eden: History of Eden Ward, Ogden Utah, 1877–1977,* copy located in Family History Library, Ogden, Utah.

44. Newey, *Remember My Valley,* 34–35, 258; Mary Chard McKee, *Early History of Liberty and the People* (n.p., n.d.), copy located in Family History Library, Ogden, Utah; Parley J. Clark, *History of Liberty* (n.p., n.d.), copy located in Family History Library, Ogden, Utah.

45. Emily and Madeline Malan Farley, "A Brief History of Pauline Combe Malan," in James Barker Knighton, Lisa Knighton Delap, and J. Malan Heslop, *Malan Book of Remembrance: John Daniel Malan* (n.p., 1992), 48.

46. Nancy Naomi Tracy, "A Sketch of the Life of Nancy Naomi Tracy" (n.p., n.d.), 16–17, copy located in Family History Library, Ogden, Utah.

47. Howard Stansbury, *An Expedition to the Valley of the Great Salt Lake of Utah* (London: Sampson Low, Son, and Co. 1852), 83–84.

48. Holton, *Matthew William Dalton,* 34–35, 38–39, 44.

49. Hunter, *Beneath Ben Lomond's Peak,* 409; "Biography of David Henderson Stephens" and "Biography of Albertine Petersen," genealogical file in possession of authors.

50. Morgan, *A History of Ogden,* 33, 49, 50.

51. James Bonwick, *The Mormons and the Silver Mines* (London: n.p., 1872), 22–25.

52. Ezra C. Knowlton, *History of Highway Development in Utah* (n.p., n.d.), 21, 53.

53. Minutes of City Council, Ogden City, 1851–1869, 1.

54. Ibid., 14, 22, 25, 46, 47, 57.

55. Hamilton Gardner, *History of the 222nd Field Artillery* (Salt Lake City: Adjutant General of Utah, n.d.), 183–84, copy in possession of authors.

56. Charles F. Middleton, Journal, LDS Church Historian's Office; *Deseret News,* 28 September 1850; *Ogden Standard,* 4 April 1917, 5.

57. Henry J. Middleton, "The Life of Charles Franklin Middleton: A Man and His Times," M.A. thesis: Utah State University, 1965, 12.

58. Andrew Jenson, "The Building of Utah and Her Neighbors," in a scrapbook of a series of Jenson's writing in the Weber County Library, items 98 and 99. See also David Moore, *Compiled Writings of David Moore,* 8–11; and Pardoe, *Lorin Farr, Pioneer,* 112–18.

59. Pardoe, *Lorin Farr, Pioneer,* 154–56.

60. Kate Carter, ed., "Military Life in the West," in *Heart Throbs of the West,* vol. II, 10–11; Pardoe, *Lorin Farr, Pioneer,* 164; Morgan, *A History of Ogden,* 38–39; Shurtleff, *His Personal History,* 104–7.

61. Morgan, *A History of Ogden,* 39.

62. Pardoe, *Lorin Farr, Pioneer,* 159–70.

3

# Railroads and Growth, 1869–1889

By 1869 Weber County had experienced more than two decades of colonization and settlement by the Mormons, but the area was still an agricultural and rural county of small villages and towns dependant particularly on the water from the Weber and Ogden rivers. The county's population of 1,141 in 1850 and 1,807 in 1860 increased to 7,358 in 1870, and much of this tremendous growth was tied to the coming of the railroad. By 1880 the county had 12,344 people; this multiplied to 22,273 in 1890. Ogden, the major city and county seat, was similarly affected by the railroad. In 1860 Ogden's population stood at 1,463 people, an increase of only a few hundred over that listed for 1852. In 1860 the majority of the county's population resided in Ogden, with only 344 living elsewhere in the county. By 1870 Ogden's population jumped to 3,127; in 1880 it was listed at 6,069; and by 1890 it had reached 12,889. Ogden had become the "junction city" of the Union and Central Pacific railroads and had grown in population, commerce, and diversity.

## *The Railroads*

Discussions of a transcontinental railroad had permeated American society during the decades of the 1840s and 1850s. In July 1862 President Abraham Lincoln signed the Pacific Railroad Act into law, and, as the Civil War threatened to tear the nation apart, the railroads were begun from Omaha and Sacramento to bind the nation together with iron rails. As late as 1868, many, including Brigham Young, felt that the rails for the transcontinental route should be laid south of the Great Salt Lake, with Salt Lake City rather than Ogden on the route. Grenville Dodge, the chief engineer of the Union Pacific, labored to promote the route around the north end of the Great Salt Lake, however, and he was successful in his efforts.

Late winter snows delayed the arrival of the railroad into Weber County until March 1869. On 8 March 1869 the Union Pacific track was completed to Ogden and a massive celebration was held. A grandstand was erected near the bottom of Fourth Street (later renamed 24th Street) and the community celebrated the arrival of the railroad with prayers, speeches, band music, artillery firing, railroad whistles, and the cheering of the crowd. Ogden mayor Lorin Farr presided over the ceremony and Mormon church apostle and Ogden community leader Franklin D. Richards delivered the address welcoming the railroad to the territory and the county. In his speech, Richards noted that the railroad would permit "the world's greatest men—of wisdom, science and intellect to visit . . . our mountain homes and to form a true estimate of our character and position."[1] The arrival of the Union Pacific locomotive *Black Hawk* with military brass band music under the direction of Captain William Pugh symbolized that a giant step into the future was being taken—Ogden and Weber County would never be the same after the arrival of the railroads. Weber County Mormons had quietly pushed and cheered for the northern route, which took the trains through their county.

Brigham Young contracted with the Union Pacific (UP) to provide grading and other work between Echo Canyon and the terminus of the line. Young's contract for about $1 million provided work to between 500 and 600 Mormon men from northern Utah villages in 1868 and 1869. Many of these came from Weber County. Work for the UP in Weber Canyon included tunnelling, blasting, laying track, and stone work building bridge abutments. Lorin Farr, Ezra T. Benson, and Chauncey West as partners contracted with the Central Pacific Railroad for similar work, and they employed Aaron F. Farr as the superintendent of their operations. West and the two Farrs all resided in Weber County. They employed some three dozen northern Utah subcontractors to work on the project along with dozens of other men.

The building and completion of the transcontinental railroad was accomplished by a series of compromises, including the routes. An 1866 act of Congress stated that the two railroads would be allowed to build until they met. This meeting point was not agreed upon until the Union Pacific had surveyed some 225 miles of roadbed across the Great Basin as far west as the Humboldt region and the Central Pacific crews, which were largely Chinese, were working their roadway to the vicinity of Echo City in Weber Canyon. On 10 April 1869 Congress set the junction point for the two rails at Promontory Summit, and a month later, on 10 May 1869, the last spike was driven.

The Promontory celebration included the two railroad presidents—Thomas Durant of the Union Pacific and Leland Stanford of the Central Pacific—driving the final spikes. The driving of the final golden spike was accompanied by other ceremonial spikes including one made of California gold, one of Nevada silver, and an Arizona spike made of iron, silver, and gold. All were driven into a highly polished railroad tie made of California laurel on which a silver plate bearing a dedicatory inscription had been placed. Bishop John Sharp represented Brigham Young at the Promontory celebration, while Weber County was represented by Ogden mayor Lorin Farr, General Chauncy W. West of the Nauvoo Legion, Mormon apostle Franklin D. Richards, county probate judge, and T.B.H. Stenhouse, who was preparing to publish Ogden's first newspaper, the transplanted Salt Lake *Daily Telegraph.* Stenhouse's paper was only briefly published in Ogden in 1869; Weber County's first newspaper with a lasting impact was Franklin D. Richards's *Ogden Junction,* which was first issued in January 1870.

Champagne and wine flowed freely at the celebration, as the first transcontinental railroad in the world was finished. The first train from Omaha to Sacramento began its journey westward from Omaha on 12 May 1869. The daily passenger train between Sacramento and Omaha was known as the Atlantic Express eastbound and the Pacific Express westbound. Passengers could complete the 3,167-mile Sacramento to New York trip in seven days.

As the Union Pacific advanced westward from Omaha, it had spawned some rough towns. Bear River City, located just east of the Utah border, Wahsatch, Echo City, Uintah (or Easton), Ogden, and Corinne all became in part typical railroad boom towns. As the railroad advanced westward, violence and crime moved with it. Bear River City was governed by a vigilance committee and included several hundred tents, wagons, and shanties, many selling whiskey, others gambling and dance houses. At Wahsatch located just inside Utah Territory, Union Pacific paymaster O. C. Smith recorded in his diary, 29 June 1869, "There was a man shot and hung at Wasatch tonight, Reason given, He is a Dammed Nigger."[2] Violence and prejudice ran sometimes uncontrolled.

In its earliest days, Uintah was also called Easton, and this village near the mouth of Weber Canyon served as a jump-off place for Salt Lake City passengers, who left the railroad for a stagecoach to complete their journey to the capital city of the Latter-day Saints. The Uintah stop was the departing point for Salt Lake City until January 1870 when the Utah Central Railroad was completed. John Jaques viewed Uintah as he was departing the territory for Great Britain as a Mormon missionary, and it seemed to him that every building was either a grog shop, a gambling den, or what might be loosely termed a restaurant.[3]

Before the completion of the Utah Central, ore from mining operations in Salt Lake County was loaded at Uintah on trains to be shipped to smelters. The Walker brothers were the first to use the railroad for transporting ore, as they hauled a carload of copper ore by wagon from Bingham Canyon to Uintah and then by rail to Baltimore, Maryland. In July 1869 the Woodhull brothers, owners of the Monitor and Magnet mines in the Little Cottonwood Mining District, shipped ten tons of silver ore from Uintah to San Francisco.

With the completion of the railroad, the decision as to which

One of the engines used on the Utah Central Railroad between Ogden and Salt Lake City after 1870. (Union Pacific Railroad)

spot near Promontory would be the junction site of the two railroads was pushed to the front. Ogden citizens and the Mormons in general prodded the decision in Ogden's favor, but other places in contention from east to west included Evanston, Uintah, Taylor's Switch, Harrisville, Bonneville, Corinne, and Promontory. Of all these, it was Corinne that gave Ogden its greatest competition. Corinne did not die after the completion of the railroads but instead continued to grow in population. For nearly a decade, until 1878, Corinne battled with Ogden to become the commercial center of the transcontinental railroad. The Utah territorial legislature approved a charter for Corinne on 18 February 1870, and for the next several years Corinne dominated the freighting business from the railroad to Montana and Idaho mining towns. The "Burg on the Bear," as Corinne became known, included among its businesses freighting, wholesale and retail liquor dealers, cigar and tobacco dealers, billiard table facilities, banking houses, job wagons, ice cream and soda fountains, breweries, livery stables, auctioneers, and Chinese work houses. The struggle between Ogden and Corinne for commercial and political dominance was a reflection of similar struggles in Utah over the next several decades between Mormons and non-Mormons. These struggles included matters of politics, mining, commerce, religion, education, and polygamy. Sometimes the conflicts were on individual issues; at other times many factors were woven together as they became contests between local ideologies and national standards.

The railroad continued to change northern Utah. Some have suggested that before the railroad, drunkenness and crime were almost unknown in Ogden. Brigham City had great difficulty in supplying hotel rooms for the new railroad travelers. Corinne, which was laid out on the Bear River near the junction point for the Union Pacific and Central Pacific at Promontory Summit, was considered the most "hell on wheels" town in the territory. Mormons referred to it as the "headquarters for libertines." J. H. Beadle, one of its first citizens, described it in the following fashion:

> It was a gay community. Nineteen saloons paid license for three months. Two dance-houses amused the elegant leisure of the evening hours, and the supply of "sports" was fully equal to the requirements of a railroad town. . . . At one time, the town contained eighty "nymphs du pave," popularly known in Mountain English as "soiled doves." Being the last railroad town it enjoyed "flush times" during the closing weeks of building the Pacific Railway. The junction of the Union and Central was then at Promontory, twenty-eight miles west, and Corinne was the retiring place for rest and recreation of all employees. Yet is was withal a quiet and rather orderly place. Sunday was generally observed; most of the men went hunting or fishing, and the "girls" had a dance or got drunk.[4]

The social character of the previously Mormon landscape was changed greatly by the railroad, and Corinne seemed to many to be the embodiment of the worst of the East being visited upon the territory. A *Deseret News* reporter commented, "God Almighty have mercy on the people of Ogden, if the carcass of Corinne is to be disemboweled in their streets!"[5] And, within a few years, many residents of Corinne did become part of Ogden and Weber County.

One of the first moves in the political chess match to make

Ogden and Weber County the junction of the railroads came on 17 May 1869. Brigham Young, as president of the Utah Central Railroad, broke ground in Ogden for the building of the Utah Central to connect Ogden with Salt Lake City. The groundbreaking took place near the Weber River west of Ogden and included in the official party were George Q. Cannon, Joseph A. Young, Daniel H. Wells, David F. Kimball, Christopher Layton, Bryant Stringham, Isaac Groo, David O. Calder, George A. Smith, John Sharp, William Jennings, Feramorz Little, and J. T. Little. These were men of church position and commerce in Weber, Davis, and Salt Lake counties. The first rails were laid for the new railroad in Ogden on 22 September 1869, and the line was completed on 10 January 1870. At the celebration held on that day in Salt Lake City, Brigham Young drove the final iron spike made with native Utah iron with a steel mallet made of Utah iron. The mallet was engraved with a beehive and the phrase "Holiness to the Lord."

Passenger service on the Utah Central from Ogden to Salt Lake City began on 10 January 1870, and the service was enhanced by a policy of the Union Pacific which allowed its passengers to make side trips from Ogden to Salt Lake City without any addition to their fares. In order to make travel as smooth as possible from Ogden to Salt Lake City, the Utah Central constructed a depot north and east of the Union Pacific Depot in Ogden, and backed its passenger trains down the track to the Union Pacific station. In this fashion the service to Salt Lake City was made more convenient and Ogden became the junction site for routes south.

The next move toward eliminating Corinne from contention as the junction site came in August 1871 when the Utah Northern Railroad was organized. The strategy behind this new rail line was to have it monopolize the trade between the Union Pacific and the Idaho and Montana markets and shift the trade away from Corinne. The Utah Northern was built with narrow-gauge track and the groundbreaking ceremony was held in Brigham City on 26 August 1871. The line from Brigham City to Logan was completed by 31 January 1873, and the line from Brigham City to Ogden was completed on 5 February 1874. A line was also constructed to Corinne from Brigham City and finished on 9 June 1873. The continued railroad development provided jobs for Weber County residents. In April 1878 John W. Young, president and superintendent of the Utah Northern, sold the line to Jay Gould and Sidney Dillon; nine months later they resold the line to the Union Pacific. In 1884 the newly renamed Utah and Northern Railway Company was connected with the Northern Pacific Railroad at Garrison, Montana. Ogden and the Utah and Northern became the major connecting point between the Union Pacific and the northern transcontinental railroad.

There were other events which underlined Ogden's role as the junction city. On 10 November 1869, Union Pacific sold to Central Pacific over forty-eight miles of its transcontinental track from Ogden to Promontory. Until December 1869, Promontory was used as the transfer point for passengers and freight; but in that month those transactions were moved to Ogden. With this action, Ogden was accepted as the junction city by the railroad companies.

A maneuver by Brigham Young all but guaranteed Ogden's position as the junction. As early as January 1869, Young began to acquire property in west Ogden for a railroad depot and shops. Young purchased 131 acres of land during the five-year period from 1869 to 1874. On 6 October 1874, Young deeded 131 acres to the Union Pacific and Central Pacific companies with the proviso that "this grant of land herein described is made on the express consideration on condition that the said Union Pacific and Central Railroad Companies, will make the City of Ogden and the land herein granted the permanent Junction of the two roads."[6]

The Ogden City Council made efforts to secure the junction position for Ogden including gaining an appropriation from the city on 30 May 1874 which was to be used to secure Ogden as the junction city. With the construction of the Utah Northern, the last nail was driven into the coffin for Corinne. The *Salt Lake Independent* reported in 1878 that "Corinne is one of the things of the past. It will in another year be simply a way station on the Central Pacific Railroad." Alexander Toponce, western freighter and traveler, chronicled the demise of Corinne in 1878, noting that many of its buildings were in a state of disrepair, that people lived in houses rent free, and that stores and dwellings were vacant. Many of Corinne's citizens moved to Ogden and strengthened the business foundation of Weber

County. Later, in 1904, the Lucin Cutoff was built by laying rails across the two northern arms of the Great Salt Lake. This new route shortened the transcontinental trip, and, with the new route, Brigham City, Corinne, and Promontory were no longer on the cross-country route.

For a century following the driving of the golden spike, the railroads were a mainstay in the economy of Weber County. Ogden's claim as the junction city joined with its position as the county seat of Weber County. Ogden served as the junction for the Union Pacific, the Southern Pacific (which took over the Central Pacific in 1885), the Denver and Rio Grande Western, the Oregon Short Line (which was the new name given to the Utah Northern in 1887), the Utah Idaho Central (which began as the Ogden, Logan, and Idaho Railroad), and the electrified interurban Salt Lake and Ogden railroad (1905), which became the Bamberger Electric Railroad in 1917. Ogden referred to itself and was referred to as the "Junction City" in directories, advertisements, tourist guides, and chamber of commerce brochures. The *Ogden Junction* which was published for a decade after 1869 helped to reinforce the idea. Ogden became the gateway to Utah and much of the West for travelers and immigrants as well as a center of commerce, trade, and finance. The first impressions of the territory often were gained at Ogden. As Ogden and Weber County grew, there were many who felt that it would surpass Salt Lake City as the leading metropolis of the territory.

With the arrival of the railroad, Ogden became more of a city and less of a village. On 19 December1870, the Ogden City Council adopted names to be used for city streets commencing on the east side of the city and moving west: East, Green, Pearl, Smith, Spring, Main (later Washington), Young, Franklin, and Wall. The council designated the east-west running streets as First to Tenth streets (later 21st to 30th streets).[7]

Travel guides listed Ogden in a prominent position in their publications. Crofutt's *New Overland Tourist and Pacific Coast Guide* for 1878–79 noted that Ogden was the junction of the Union and Central Pacific railroads and that the distance from Omaha to Ogden was 1,032 miles and from Ogden to San Francisco was 882 miles. Croffut's reported that all passengers, baggage, mail, and express would change cars at Ogden, and that passengers who were changing trains would have ample time to eat "a good square meal—price $1.00." The citizens of Ogden were described as being "mostly Mormon," and public improvements were said to be under their supervision. Ogden was recommended as a "poor place for carpet-baggers."

A two-story wooden clapboard building served as the city railroad depot for two decades, from 1869 to 1889. The depot was painted red, and it provided a ticket office, waiting rooms, baggage office, and freight facilities. The area around the depot was described as a slough, and for passenger convenience a boardwalk was constructed in 1869 from the depot slanting northeast toward the bottom of Fourth Street. Hotel and eating facilities sprang up in the vicinity of the depot to service outbound, inbound, and layover travelers. The Union Depot Hotel advertised that "all trains stop at this house for meals."

Two presidents of the United States took advantage of the newly built railroad and visited the West, including Weber County, during their terms of office. In 1875 President Ulysses S. Grant, his wife, Julia, and governmental officials were welcomed to Ogden. Grant stood on the rear platform of a Pullman car and the Ogden throng welcomed him by waving hats and handkerchiefs while the Ogden brass band played "Hail to the Chief." Grant responded by removing his hat and bowing to the crowd. After spending a short time in Ogden, Grant and his party (which included by this time a number of Mormon officials including Brigham Young) traveled to Salt Lake City on the Utah Central. Five years later, in September 1880, President Rutherford B. Hayes visited the territory. Hayes and his party were greeted at the Ogden station by a large crowd and the city brass band. Hayes made a few remarks to the crowd before departing for Salt Lake City on the Utah Central.

In April 1876 Emperor Dom Pedro II of Brazil traveled west on the Union Pacific. As the train carrying the emperor and his party traveled down Echo and Weber canyons, Dom Pedro stood on the rear platform and was impressed by the route of the railroad through the canyons. As they passed by Devil's Gate, Dom Pedro remarked to

J. J. O'Kelly that "this country seems to have been made purposely by God for Railways. Who [else] could have cut out those canyons."[8]

As the railroad changed Ogden to a junction city, much of the rest of the county remained agricultural in nature. As time passed, many workers, wanting to stay close to the land, worked two jobs—for the railroad and farming their own land. Prior to the arrival of the railroad, imports to the entire territory seldom exceeded 12,000 tons, which were hauled overland by wagon; but, by 1871, 80,000 tons of imports arrived in the territory via the railroad. By 1880 this figure reached 125,000 tons. About half of the cargo imported to the territory in the 1870s was related to mining. Other imported goods included merchandise, building materials, lumber, railroad materials, and produce.

Passenger service increased along with freight service, and by 1878 three transcontinental passenger trains a day were stopping in Ogden. Fares from New York City to San Francisco in 1869 were set at $150 for first-class accommodations, with a $70 charge for lesser accommodations, which were often used by emigrants. All first-class passenger trains were accompanied by "Pullman's Palace drawing room and sleeping cars." Timetables indicated several daily arrivals and departures on the Utah Central as well as a daily run on the Utah Northern.

By 1910 the Utah Central, the Oregon Short Line, the Southern Pacific, the Denver and Rio Grande, the San Pedro, Los Angeles and Salt Lake, and the Union Pacific were all routing both passengers and freight through Ogden. In that year, railroad payrolls pumped about $4 million into the local economy. The Southern Pacific was the area's leading employer, with about 1,000 residents in its workforce, and it accounted for about one-quarter of the total payroll. By 1913, seventy passenger trains passed through Ogden on a daily basis. Ogden had changed rapidly with the railroad; but the rest of the county changed much more slowly.

## *Commercial Growth*

The first hotels in Ogden were built in anticipation of the railroad. During 1868, the White House (later called the Junction House) was built on the southeast corner of 25th and Washington. The two-story White House was built from adobe bricks and painted white. The Union Depot Hotel was built in 1869, and a year later the Keeney House was completed. The City Hotel and the Beardsley Hotel were both completed during the 1870s. The City Hotel, owned by J.A. Owens, was a two-story frame building located on Grant Avenue between 24th and 25th. James Bonwick, an English traveler who visited Ogden in 1871, noted that the hotels seemed "uncommonly well supported."

One description of the impact of the railroad on Ogden's society suggested that

> At train time it was an interesting sight to watch the makeup of the railroad passengers, amongst whom one would see blue-coated, brass-buttoned officers and soldiers of the United State Army; mining men; prospectors; longhaired buckskin-dressed mountaineers and trappers; red blanketed Indians from the Indian country north, west, and south; Chinamen of the old primitive time wearing the bamboo, top-like hat. Added to these were well-dressed, well-to-do travelers from the eastern cities going to California and quite aristocratic-looking English, French, Dutch, and Germans traveling by way of San Francisco and the Pacific to China, Japan, New Zealand, or Australia.[9]

Much of the building in Ogden's downtown area was done with native lumber, and Ogden, like many other nineteenth-century cities, was subject to fires which might rage out of control. At about 3 A.M. on 5 August 1873 a fire broke out on the west side of Ogden's Main Street (later Washington). It started in the store of Higginbotham & Company and soon spread to the adjoining buildings and threatened much of Main Street. In order to save store goods, workers quickly carried them into the street. Higgonbotham & Company lost their building and all of their merchandise, and several buildings including Robert Wilson's saloon and bowling alley and the building occupied by the Thomas Jones tailor shop were torn down to stop the spread of the fire to both the north and the south. In all, nine stores were destroyed including part of the ZCMI building. The fire was fought with hoses and buckets, and inspections after the fire suggested that it had begun with the spontaneous combustion of phosphorous.

Building in the downtown area continued to be the most rapid in the county. Construction of the Broom Hotel, located on the northwest corner of 25th and Washington, was begun in 1882, and this Ogden landmark opened for business on 15 January 1883. The initial construction costs for the hotel were $70,000, with an additional $25,000 expended for furnishings. The hotel included a large second-floor dining room (fifty-two by twenty-eight feet), and thirty-four elegant parlors with bay windows located on the same floor. There were thirty-five third-floor rooms, and the suites were all equipped with "bathrooms and conveniences modern to the time." The main floor included the offices of the hotel, a tonsorial establishment, a laundry, the hotel kitchens, bath houses, a billiard hall, and reception rooms.

John Broom, who built the magnificent hotel, was born in England, where he converted to the Mormon church. Broom arrived in Ogden in 1851 and experimented in a variety of businesses. He once sold a wagonload of molasses and dairy supplies to a detachment of U.S. troops and, while leaving their camp, happened to notice the charred remains of an army wagon train. He loaded his wagon with old iron tires, spindles, and other iron parts, and he later traded his iron goods to gunsmith Jonathan Browning for the lot which would later became the site of his hotel. His other business dealings included investments in sugar developments and a gold-mining venture.

In order to serve overland travelers and those going to the Montana mines, in 1862 Charles Mathews built the Prairie House in Harrisville. The adobes for this structure were made from clay in the Harrisville vicinity. The Prairie House became a noted tavern and way station, serving both beer and whiskey to travelers and locals. In 1875 the Halfway House was built in Harrisville by the Burnett family, and they furnished overnight accommodations as well as selling candy, soft drinks, and whiskey.

### *Water Development*

As the county grew in population, additional water resources were needed. Canals and irrigation ditches had been dug during the pioneer period, carrying water from the Ogden and Weber rivers.

Irrigation had begun in the county in 1848, and by the coming of the railroad there were twelve major water diversions from the Ogden River used to deliver water to outlying areas of the county. The seven-mile-long Weber Canal, begun in 1852, continued to deliver water. It was fourteen feet wide and five feet deep and left the Weber River in Riverdale at Daniel Burch's gristmill, flowing generally north and east. It was dug below the brow of the hill and below Adams Avenue, and it flowed north to 19th Street and then west and back into the river. The usefulness of the Weber Canal was matched by the Ogden Bench Canal, which had been constructed during 1855 and 1856 and carried water south and west from the Ogden River. Many of the early waterpipes in Ogden which carried water to homes and businesses were made of wood hollowed out in the center and were in continual need of repair. Ditches and canals often were deepened and lengthened as water needs expanded.

In 1880 the Ogden Water Company was incorporated, with 1,500 shares of stock sold to investors, and the city purchased 50 percent of the stock. A holding reservoir was constructed on upper 24th Street about 200 feet above the city proper, and water from the Ogden River as well as from Strong and Waterfall canyon creeks was piped to the reservoir to be held for city use. When the new reservoir was full, it held a ten-month supply of water. In 1883 the city water supply serviced 250 customers, including the Central Pacific Railroad, the Utah Central Railroad, and the Denver and Rio Grande Railroad. In 1889 the Ogden City Council passed a $100,000 bond to pay off the debts of the city, construct a city hall, build a sewer system, and extend the waterworks. In 1890 Ogden sold its water system and water properties to the Bear Lake and River Water Works Company; however, in 1910 the city purchased the water system back from the company.[10]

### *Fremont Island*

Fremont Island, which sits in the western corner of Weber County in the Great Salt Lake, was named for John C. Frémont in 1850 by another significant government explorer, Howard Stansbury. The island was visited by both Frémont and Stansbury as they explored and mapped the Great Basin. The island is about thirteen miles in circumference and is about five miles long and two miles wide at its widest point. The highest point of the island is about 800 feet above the surface of the lake. Mormon explorers under the direction of Albert Carrington visited the island in the spring of 1848 in their boat the *Mud Hen* and named the island Castle Island. Henry W. Miller, a resident of Farmington, described the island and how it began to be used as an area for sheep in his diary:

> In the spring of 1859 I went to the Island known as Fremont Island in the Great Salt Lake and explored it, accompanied by my brother Daniel and Quincey Knowlton. I built a boat and after we had sheared our sheep we took them to the island. There were about 153 head. It was said that there had never been any stock on the Island before we took our sheep there. This island is about 25 miles from Farmington and about six miles north of Antelope Island where the Church had some stock. This Fremont Island is opposite the mouth of the Weber river. After we had taken our sheep on the island, it became known locally as Miller's Island. It proved a good place for sheep, it being about four miles from the mainland and no wild beast on it to destroy the sheep. The herd increased very fast in number and needed no herder to take care of it. We used to visit the Island every few weeks to clean the spring and at times of lambing, shearing, and marketing we spent days on the island at a time.[11]

Fremont Island was an ideal place to raise sheep. There were springs on the island, there were no natural predators, and the sheep could be left for periods of time without a herder. Vegetation included grasses, wild daisies, prickly pear cacti, and sagebrush, some of it "as big around as a man's waist and taller than a man on horseback." The largest sage was found on the north side of the island. Snakes, mice, birds, insects, and lizards comprised the wildlife of the island. Snakes were abundant and included the blow snake and the whip snake. Some blow snakes reached a length of five or six feet and the whip snakes traveled with their heads in the air and could move faster than a man could run. The Miller brothers used the island for sheep for nearly three decades, from 1859 until 1886.

In 1862 a bizarre episode came to an end on Fremont Island. John Baptiste was the Salt Lake City cemetery gravedigger and, although he was born in Europe, he had previously spent some time in the Australian gold fields. The discovery was made at the Salt Lake cemetery that after corpses were buried, Baptiste dug them up and robbed them of clothing and jewelry. An investigation revealed that he had robbed more than 300 graves and his home was filled with personal effects taken from the dead bodies. Salt Lake City residents were angry and some suggested Baptiste should be lynched; but he was tried and sentenced to exile on Fremont Island. Baptiste was taken from the jail in Salt Lake City to Antelope Island by wagon and team, which entered the lake near Syracuse and followed the Antelope bar in the lake to the island. From Antelope Island, Baptiste was transported to Fremont Island by Henry and Dan Miller in the boat they used to travel back and forth to the island and to carry sheep. Baptiste was left marooned on the island with the Miller's sheep. The graverobber lived in the shanty the Miller brothers had erected to house them while they cared for and sheared their sheep. He used their supplies and sheep to his advantage. The Millers visited the island about every three weeks; at their first visit, Baptiste seemed to be doing well, surviving on their provisions. Three weeks later, he was nowhere to be seen. They surmised he had killed a heifer, used the skin of the animal to make rawhide thongs, disassembled the wooden shanty, and constructed a raft to make his escape from the island. Some have suggested he escaped cleanly; others believe he was drowned in the lake trying to escape. The final chapter of the story of the marooned graverobber on Fremont Island remains a mystery.

For a five-year period from 1886 to 1891 the Wenner family lived on Fremont Island. Judge Uriah J. Wenner of Salt Lake City and his wife Kate decided to move to the island in 1886 because of Judge Wenner's declining health. The Wenners had moved to Salt Lake City in 1880 for Uriah to practice law; and in 1882 he was appointed a probate judge. Wenner contracted tuberculosis and was advised by his doctors that he needed complete rest and fresh air. In 1886 the Wenners and their two small children, George and Blanche, moved to the island, where they began to homestead with the help of two hired men and a hired girl. They first constructed a wooden home they named the Hut and then a two-story rock house. For five years they lived on Fremont Island, receiving their mail and supplies by boat. Their days were filled with exploring, swimming, caring for their pets, observing the snakes and lizards, reading, and enjoying the beautiful sunsets. By 1891, however, Judge Wenner's health had rapidly declined, and on 19 September he died. Kate, the hired man, and the children buried Wenner on the island in a homemade coffin lined with a shawl. Following the burial, Kate and the children left the island, ending their five-year stay. For the next half-century, the island would be used to raise sheep. It continues to be a significant landmark in Weber County with its distinctive rock crown on the northern end of the island.

### *Industry*

Pioneer industries related to building were further developed after the arrival of the railroad. Adobe was often used for building homes and buildings, and several adobe yards produced adobe bricks for sale. Also, individual builders might make the needed adobes on the building site they were developing if the native clay was suitable. The clay for the adobes was dug and molded into bricks which were dried in the sun.

During the 1870s and 1880s, fire-cured bricks and stone began to rapidly replace adobe as building materials. Stone masons used both native stone as well as imported stone for construction. In 1889 a carload of Vermont marble was shipped by rail to Ogden for use in buildings in the county. Brickmaking flourished in the county, as more than two dozen brickmaking yards were in operation during the last half of the nineteenth century. The Joseph Jackson brickyard was one of the largest and employed twenty laborers at its Ogden location between 32nd and 33rd streets. Another product which was produced locally in the county was lime from limestone, which was used both to plaster and whitewash homes; the lime also served as the base for mortar.

Flour milling was begun in Ogden by Lorin Farr in 1850, and over the next several decades eleven flour mills were begun in the county. Farr's gristmill was built on Canyon Road to take advantage of water from the Ogden River. Daniel Burch's Riverdale gristmill was constructed in 1853 and sold to Mormon apostle John Taylor in 1858; it became known as Taylor's Mill. Chauncey West built a gristmill on Mill Creek in 1866 which was eventually sold to David Peery.

After a fire destroyed this mill in 1882, Peery and James Mack rebuilt the mill in 1883 and named it the Phoenix. Newman G. Blodgett and James Barker operated a flour mill on Cold Water Creek in North Ogden beginning in 1854. Chauncey West build the Weber Mill at 1440 Washington Boulevard in 1866, and it was housed in a two-story building with a lower floor of rock and a second floor of adobe. It was powered by a huge waterwheel driven by the water of Mill Creek. David Peery purchased the West Mill in 1872. Flour mills were also built during the decade of the 1860s in Huntsville, Slaterville, and Hooper.

David Eccles consolidated much of the flour milling in the county in 1886 with the creation of the Ogden Milling and Elevator Company, with James Mack as president. This combined operation included the Advance Roller Mill established earlier by Lorin Farr, the Eagle Mills which were earlier the Stevens and Stone mills, and the newly rebuilt Phoenix Mill. During the 1890s, Eccles added the Taylor Mill to his milling group. By 1900 Eccles's Ogden Milling Company purchased and milled 30,000 bushels of wheat. Much of this came from farmers in Weber County and northern Utah. The brands of flour produced by the Eccles company were Phoenix, Ogden's Best, and Straight Grade.

The cloth flour sacks which were used in the flour mills of this era were often used and reused in a variety of ways. Ben Rich, a grandson of Lorin Farr, commented on such uses:

> I remember the old water wheel on the grist mill and the mill race and the dam across the Ogden River. The River dam backed the river up for more than a mile which in the winter time furnished the finest skating I have ever seen. The flour mill became unprofitable when newer methods came into use and larger mills ground finer flour. Grandfather had a great many bolts of cloth for flour sacks, and from time to time these bolts were distributed among the family. We had in our family several times several of these bolts. They were all branded "Pride of the West" in red letters, and in blue letters "Farr Flour Mills," or some such thing. For several years all our underwear was made out of this material and what sport it furnished in the summer time when we would all go swimming to strip off our shirts and breeches and have on our under-

> wear "Pride of the West," and I am told that the girls in the family had panties made of the same material with the same brands upon them. Some of the families had sheets made of them.[12]

Sawmills and lumberyards contributed to the growth of Ogden and Weber County. Initially, trees in the vicinity of town and homes were used for firewood and building materials. Lorin Farr established a sawmill in 1851 on the Ogden River on Canyon Road. Joseph Harris was the first sawyer in the county and worked at the Farr mill. Logs were cut in Ogden Canyon and floated down the river to a mill pond which was constructed on the river near the Farr sawmill. In 1858 Levi J. Wheeler and Chauncy W. West built a sawmill in Ogden Canyon just west of Wheeler's Canyon. In that same year, construction was begun on a road through Ogden Canyon which made the upper valley and timber more accessible. The cost of constructing the road from Ogden to Huntsville was $19,000 and it was operated from 1860 to 1862 as a toll road. Ogden Canyon tolls were one dollar for a loaded wagon, fifty cents for an unloaded wagon, and twenty-five cents for a person on horseback. Lorin Farr, Isaac Goodale, and John Taylor owned most of the stock in the toll road company. A toll road into Wolf Creek Canyon was completed in 1868. The new roads contributed to expansion in the lumber business: David Garner put a sawmill in Broadmouth Canyon in 1867, Thomas Durfee constructed a mill in Durfee Canyon in 1870, and several mills were developed along the North Fork of the Ogden River during this era, including a hand-driven shingle mill owned by Thomas Bingham.

The largest sawmill on the Ogden River was built in 1873 by Billie Wilson, a Scots immigrant. Wilson built his mill on the river at what would later become the site of the Hermitage and he built a dam and a millrace which delivered water to power his mill. The Hermitage Hotel was established by Wilson in 1905 and the dam for the Wilson sawmill was used as a boating area for the resort. It was on this pond that two of Wilson's children drowned in a boating accident.

Logging expanded into the canyons east of Ogden and in the valleys surrounding Monte Cristo. The first lumberyards in Ogden were established in 1869 by Joshua Williams and Barnard White. The

Williams lumberyard was located on the corner of 25th and Wall and the White lumberyard was located on the corner of Wall and 24th.

David Eccles built his multifaceted financial empire on the foundation of his success in the lumber business. Eccles emigrated from Scotland with his family as Mormon converts in 1863, and the family settled in Eden. In 1872 he signed a contract to provide pine logs to a sawmill located forty-five miles east of Ogden on the east side of Monte Cristo. Henry E. Gibson and W. T. VanNoy managed the sawmill where Eccles hauled his logs. By the summer of 1873, Eccles, VanNoy, and Gibson were partners in a portable sawmill on Monte Cristo. They were successful enough in cutting trees and sawing lumber that they purchased a retail lumberyard in Ogden in the fall of 1873 to sell their own lumber. At one point, Gibson and Eccles advertised that "our prices defy competition." In 1875 Eccles married Bertha Jensen and the newlyweds moved into their first home, a small adobe dwelling on Lincoln Avenue adjacent to the lumberyard that Eccles jointly owned with his two partners. By 1881 Eccles moved into the timber and lumber business on his own. During that year, he purchased his own sawmill as well as his own lumberyard in Ogden—David Eccles & Company.

David Eccles was a diligent worker and became a very successful businessman. In 1888 profits in his Ogden lumber company reached $100,000. His company had begun to harvest timber in the area around Scofield in 1883, and eventually the Eccles ventures in that area included three sawmills, a shingle mill, a lumberyard, and a general store. Eccles expanded his investments into banking, railroads, and agriculture. A number of shingle mills, including a mill operated by Stephen and Ephraim Nye and a mill operated by Thomas Bingham, were established in Weber County to produce singles for homes and businesses.

Sorghum cane was grown in Weber County as early as 1852, and much of the mature cane was made into molasses in the county. A molasses mill included a crusher run by horse power and a tin boiler about three feet in width by six or eight feet in length and about eight or ten inches deep. The cane was fed a few stalks at a time by hand into the crusher, which was powered by a horse which traveled around a neverending circle to squeeze the juice out of the cane.

George Hill, John Cardon, Peter Boyle, James McIntrye, and Amos Pease Stone were operators of early Ogden molasses mills. Charles Parker operated a molasses mill in Hooper, and Francis M. and Noah Shurtliff operated a molasses mill in Harrisville. David Moore owned and operated the largest molasses mill in Weber County, initially located on the corner of 25th and Washington; Moore moved the mill several times as building increased in downtown Ogden.

Breweries flourished in Weber County in the nineteenth century, with many of them beginning in the decades of the 1860s and 1870s. The U.P. Brewery was located on 25th and Washington and produced both bottled and keg beer. It continued to increase its production into the decade of the 1880s with R.A. Wells and Henry Woolner as owners. The Grove Brewery was begun in 1873 by Herold, Hunt & Company and by 1883 was under the ownership of John J. Fry. It was located in Jones Grove on the Ogden River, just west of the Washington Boulevard river bridge. The Grove Brewery included a storage cellar with a capacity of 2,000 barrels as well as a beer cellar and icehouses. The Grove Brewery suggested it was the largest brewery in Ogden, with an annual production of 10,000 barrels and a specialty of bottled beer. The Ogden City Brewery was located on the south side of the Ogden River directly south of the Grove Brewery. Moritz Richter was the owner and the annual production of this facility was about 4,000 barrels of beer a year. Another Ogden brewery was the Becker brewery. The breweries of Weber County were conveniently located near good water and excellent railroad connections.

Ice for cold drinks and for keeping food cold was cut into blocks from ponds during the winter and kept insulated in sawdust during the spring and summer in icehouses. Pond ice, usually called natural ice, was harvested by Lorin Farr for public sale as early as 1863 from the Mill Pond located west of the Ogden City Cemetery and east of Washington Boulevard. Ice plants for producing ice throughout the year were introduced after the coming of the railroad by the W.F. James Company, the Becker Products Company, the Asael Farr Ice Company, and the Utah Ice and Storage Company.

## *The Mormon Cooperative Movement*

Brigham Young was continually concerned with the impact of the outside world on his Great Basin kingdom. With the coming of the railroad, he began to put some of his specific ideas into action. In the fall of 1868 he proposed the establishment of a churchwide cooperative system which would bear the name Zion's Cooperative Mercantile Institution—ZCMI. The establishment of ZCMI was aimed at having Latter-day Saints trade only with that institution and discouraged trading with outsiders. The parent ZCMI was established in Salt Lake City and branch stores were established throughout the territory. All of the stores were identified with a sign which illustrated an "all-seeing eye" which was placed under the inscription "Holiness to the Lord." The bottom of the sign usually included the words "Zions Cooperative Mercantile Institution." Some called it the Cooperative Sign while others referred to it as the Bull's Eye.

The first Weber County branch of ZCMI was established in Ogden in May 1869 and was located at 24th and Washington. Mercantile stores owned by Peery and Herrick and by Lorin Farr were absorbed into the Weber County ZCMI. Some non-Mormon merchants found staying in business was difficult and sold their inventories to the new store and left the territory. David H. Peery was the president of the Weber County ZCMI from 1869 to 1875; the store was then managed by John Watson. Peery had arrived in Utah from his native Virginia during 1864 after serving in the Confederate Army and had moved to Ogden in 1866. He enjoyed a successful career in business and banking in Ogden. He owned flour mills, began the Ogden Herald Publishing Company, served on a number of governing boards of companies, and built a beautiful mansion on the corner of Adams and 24th that he named the Virginian.

A variety of other Mormon cooperatives spread across the territory during the 1870s. Small cooperative textile mills were established at several sites, including Ogden. Woolen goods produced locally were sold or traded in competition with goods imported on the railroad. The first woolen mill in Weber County was established by the firm of Farr, Randall, Pugsley, and Neal in 1867 and was built near the Farr gristmill and sawmill sites on Canyon Road. The mill was housed in a large three-story stone building. The mill was powered by Ogden River water and supplemental power was added by a forty-horsepower engine and boiler. By 1883 there were twelve looms operating in the facility as well as one spinning mule, two carding and two picking machines, one shearing machine, one washing machine, and one scouring machine.[13]

Brigham Young also organized united order groups throughout the territory. These communitarian united order experiments varied in nature, and in Ogden and other large towns and cities were based on having each Mormon ward establish a cooperative effort among its members. Young was particularly interested in having his Mormon flock use goods produced by local congregations and avoid the drain of money from the territory. He was instrumental in forming "retrenchment" groups to avoid many of the current fashions of dress which he felt were costly, frivolous, and wicked. The Weber County Retrenchment Association was organized on 14 February 1877 under the direction of Eliza R. Snow, Zina D. Young, and Jane S. Richards. Snow and Young were from Salt Lake City, but Richards was a Weber County resident and the wife of Franklin D. Richards. This young women's organization paved the way for the organization of the Mormon Young Women's Mutual Improvement associations throughout Weber County under the direction of Weber Stake Relief Society president Jane S. Richards. There were four Mormon wards in Ogden and eight wards throughout the rest of the county. Although the united order experiments did not last much longer than Young's death in 1877, they had a decided impact on efforts to promote economic unity among the Mormons.

In March 1875 a cooperative company was organized in the east end of the Harrisville district to operate a molasses mill on Four Mile Creek; two months later a similar organization was put in place in the west end of the Harrisville settlement. A cooperative mercantile company was organized in Lynne in 1869; five years later, in 1874, a branch of the united order was established in that community.

In the spring of 1869, a cooperative store was organized in Huntsville and William Halls was appointed the business manager. In 1873 the Mormon community in Huntsville purchased a farm of 450 acres for which they paid $2,000. It was to be used as a cooperative farm, and Andrew Lofgren was appointed farm manager. In 1878 the cooperative store was sold to Christian Petersen and the cooperative farm was purchased by William Halls and his brothers. Two years later the Halls brothers produced about 8,000 pounds of cheese from dairy cattle on their farm.

As early as 1856, families in Weber County had begun to use Ogden Valley as a range for their cattle. It was an excellent place to keep cattle in the summer, as the weather was cool and the forage was of good quality. Cattle were herded from western Weber County over North Ogden Pass into the Ogden Valley. Cattle did not stray from the mountain-ringed valley, but Indian raids were sometimes a problem. As the valley began to be permanently settled in the 1860s by Thomas Abbott, Isaac and David McKay, and Jefferson Hunt, cattle remained throughout the year in the valley. Grasshoppers and crickets provided difficulties for farmers throughout the county, particularly in the spring of 1870 when grasshoppers devoured much of the early crops.

The Mormon Relief Society women of Weber County formed a co-op mercantile and millinery institution which was located on 25th Street in Ogden in May 1869. The women raised money for the building and store furnishings from donations, by making and selling rag carpets and quilts, and by sponsoring social gatherings. One of their cooperative endeavors was the making of straw hats, and children in the county gathered straw from wheat and oat stalks to be used in the braiding of the hats.

The production of silk was advocated by Mormon leaders in the territory in the 1870s. In 1875 Eliza R. Snow, general president of the women's Relief Society, visited Weber County and encouraged the cultivation of mulberry trees and the production of homegrown silk. Women of the county planted mulberry trees—usually from seed—and raised silkworms from eggs. In order to have the experiment work successfully, some women warmed the silkworm eggs with their own body heat until the eggs were ready to hatch and then established the silkworms in their homes in order to keep them warm and able to eat dry, chopped mulberry leaves. The special care of the silkworms often meant that the women and their families spent much time in barns and granaries or shared their homes with the worms.

The silkworms would go through four moultings and eat increasing quantities of mulberry leaves. After the worm spun a cocoon, the silk threads of the cocoon—which were often a thousand feet long—would be wound onto a reeling machine. The silk threads were then woven into cloth. In July 1875 Brigham Young visited Weber County and in a speech said, "There is a sister before me with a silk dress on. She raised the silk and made it herself." Young continued to encourage sericulture in his speeches, but sericulture began to decline in Weber and the other counties in Utah. However, for the next two decades there would continue to be some silk production by the women of the county.

### *Politics*

Elections in Weber County during the decades from 1850 to 1870 generally consisted of meetings held at "early candle light" where a single slate of proposed officers was presented and confirmed by a voice vote of those in attendance. There was little difference in the methods of voting in Mormon church affairs and voting in early Weber County and Ogden City elections. Church officials and government officers were often the same, and the voters were generally the same. Lorin Farr served as mayor of Ogden for ten consecutive two-year terms from 1851 to 1871 while also serving in the most significant Mormon office in the county, president of the Weber LDS Stake. Farr was called to serve a Mormon mission in 1871 to Great Britain, and upon his return he served another term as Ogden mayor, from 1877 to 1879. In 1855 an Ogden city ordinance was adopted which allowed written ballots; but the ballots were numbered and the number of each person's vote recorded, so it was possible for each individual ballot to be tied to the person who cast it.[14] Voting in elections in Weber County from its beginnings to the coming of the railroad was done either by voice vote or by the raising of hands. In virtually every case, the voting was unanimous. The Mormon church leaders of Weber County, particularly Lorin Farr, often sought the advice of Brigham Young on matters of both church and state including potential city, county, and territorial election candidates.

The Ogden city government moved around in the early years from private residences, school buildings, and the tithing office until in 1857 the Ogden City Council bought a building from James Brown for $1,200. In 1870 the city used the LDS Seventies Hall on Grant Avenue as city offices, and in 1882 a two-story brick building was erected on the southeast corner of municipal square that was known as the city hall and jail. It housed the city recorder and council chambers, a courtroom, twelve jail cells, and two large rooms that provided sleeping quarters for paupers and transients. This facility soon proved to be not large enough to meet the needs of the city. In 1888 a new building was started on the north side of the municipal square; it was finished in 1889. It was an ornate three-story structure composed of red Kyune stone, capped with a clock and bell tower with a compartment where a night watchman could keep watch over the city for fires. This building served until the winter of 1942–43 when it was torn down to make room for the new city and county building.

With the coming of the railroad, Mormons throughout the territory were concerned about the political ramifications of the new immigrants who would come with the railroad. In January 1869 the Ogden City Council passed an election ordinance which required voters to have been residents of the city for six months prior to voting; those standing for election or appointment to city office had to have been residents of the city for one year. As the leaders of Ogden tightened the voting restrictions, other developments were taking place in Salt Lake City which would affect Weber County. Mormon apostle Franklin D. Richards noted in his diary on 10 January 1869 that it was decided "at Council that I be appointed to go and live at Ogden take charge and preside over that stake of Zion and be elected Judge of Weber County & that B.Y. Jr. [Brigham Young, Jr.] be Mayor of Ogden City."[15] During the next six months, Farr and others in Ogden corresponded with Brigham Young and suggested they would accede to his wishes. One of Farr's letters to Young suggested that he would resign from the mayor's office if Young desired to appoint his son, but Brigham Young, Jr., did not move to Ogden. Franklin D. Richards did move to Ogden, however, and became the probate judge in Weber County from 1869 until 1883. He directed the affairs of the Weber Stake for a half-dozen years during the 1870s and he began the *Ogden Junction* newspaper. Richards played a significant role in

Weber County and in the Mormon church from 1869 until his death in 1899. Franklin Street, the first major Ogden street east of Wall Avenue, was named for him.

The two decades following the arrival of the railroad in Weber County saw significant changes take place in Utah Territory and Weber County, and the railroads were in the forefront of the changes. Mining activity, which had begun with the blessings of Patrick Edward Connor, blossomed and grew rapidly following the arrival of the iron horse, with much of the mining equipment transhipped from Ogden. The coming of the railroad seemed to bring to a head the protests and programs of the New Movement, or Godbeite Movement, headed by E.L.T. Harrison and William S. Godbe. This movement in 1869 and 1870 protested some of the economic programs advocated by Brigham Young, particularly his response to the railroad and outside trade. Many Godbeites left the Mormon church and advocated spiritualism. Members founded the *Mormon Tribune*, which subsequently became the *Salt Lake Tribune*. They also helped to found and promote the Liberal party, a territorial political party which ran candidates in opposition to the Mormon People's party. These two political parties emerged as antagonists in major Utah cities following the coming of the railroad. The basic support for the Liberal party came from the non-Mormons of Corinne, Ogden, and Salt Lake City; the Godbeites; and those who migrated to Utah for mining purposes.

To meet the challenges to the economy, society, and politics brought about by the railroad, Brigham Young and his colleagues advocated a number of changes in both the society and the politics of the territory. The Mormon School of the Prophets was reinstituted in Salt Lake City in 1867 and began in Ogden on 1 January 1869. The School of the Prophets provided a forum for leading priesthood members of the church to discuss matters of church government, doctrine, and temporal problems facing the community. More than 900 adult males formed the Salt Lake school, while branch schools throughout the territory had about 5,000 members. Admission to the school was by identification card and the matters discussed in the sessions were to be confidential.[16] The formation of economic cooperatives throughout the territory, particularly ZCMI, was a major effort to control the economic and social impacts of the railroad. The organization and support for the People's party was a significant effort to keep all government officials in the territory either Mormon or sympathetic to the Mormon faith. Particularly during the 1870s and 1880s, the People's party and the Liberal party skirmished with each other for political control of cities, counties, and the territory.

The Liberal party was first organized in the territory at Corinne during the summer of 1870. Ogden's representatives to the convention were Fred J. Kiesel, Oliver Durant, William Gilbert, M. Meyer, and Simon Bamberger. Kiesel and Gilbert were elected to serve on committees of the new party. The first Liberal party victory over the People's party in Utah came in 1874 in Tooele County, and during that same year many of Corinne's Liberal party members moved to Ogden as Corinne declined. Elections in Ogden over the next two decades were vigorously contested.

The practice of plural marriage, or polygamy as it was commonly known, by the Mormons became a major political and legal issue. Following the Civil War and with the completion of the railroad, the U.S. Congress became more committed to end the practice among the Mormons. Two congressional acts passed during the decade of the 1880s put teeth in the effort to end polygamy. The Edmunds Act of 1882 defined cohabitation with a polygamous wife as a misdemeanor which could be punishable by a fine not to exceed $300 and/or imprisonment not to exceed six months. The act further stated that those (both male and female) guilty of practicing polygamy were ineligible for jury service and were disfranchised and declared ineligible for public office. To enforce the terms of the Edmunds Act, a five-member Utah Commission was appointed by President Chester Arthur and approved by the Senate. The Utah Commission began to supervise voters, office holders, and candidates as well as elections in Utah. The Edmunds-Tucker Act, which passed Congress in 1887, dissolved the Corporation of the Church of Jesus Christ of Latter-day Saints, declared much of the property of the church to be forfeit, dissolved the Perpetual Emigration Company and the Nauvoo Legion, abolished women's suffrage in the territory, disinherited children of plural marriages, and prescribed a comprehensive "test oath" to eliminate polygamists from voting, holding office, and serving on juries. The enforcement of these acts brought about significant changes in the political life of Weber County and other counties in the territory.

From 1869 to 1883 Franklin D. Richards headed the People's party efforts in Weber County; but in 1883 Lewis W. Shurtliff became the new president of the Weber LDS Stake and the leader of the Weber County People's party.[17] During the 1870s, the first decade of the People's party in Weber County, the candidates for office for the party were chosen by a small group of church officials and later ratified by a meeting of male church members in a School of the Prophets meeting (from 1869 to 1873) and later in a general priesthood meeting.[18] After 1881 the general Mormon male leaders were given more involvement in the selection of candidates. Whether the nomination process took place in small caucuses or in larger priesthood meetings, both general and local Mormon church authorities were very involved in the selection of candidates. By 1887, nominations from the People's party began to be more democratic among Ogden Mormons and less controlled by the church hierarchy.

Lester Herrick was elected mayor of Ogden for five separate two-year terms. He was elected in 1871, 1873, 1875, 1879, and 1881, while Lorin Farr was elected to the 1877 term. Herrick served as the first counselor to Weber Stake president David H. Peery during part of this period and he was also elected sheriff of Weber County prior to his death in 1892. During January and February 1879, with the mayoral election to be held in February, the political solidarity of Mormons in Ogden began to splinter. It appears that some were not happy with the fact of their candidates being "chosen" by church leaders. Apostles Joseph F. Smith and Daniel H. Wells visited Weber County and spoke on three occasions trying to bring unity to the Mormon political camp and, even more importantly, trying to continue the process of selection of candidates by church leaders. In order to underline the legitimacy of the 1870s candidate selection process by the church leadership in 1881, Mormon church president John Taylor, his counselor Joseph F. Smith, Apostle Franklin D. Richards, Weber Stake president David H. Peery and his two counselors (both of whom were sitting Ogden officials—Mayor Lester J. Herrick and Alderman Charles F. Middleton) made the People's party nominations for the Ogden City elections. The proposed People's party ticket was sustained by a voice vote of the Ogden citizenry, meeting in the Ogden LDS tabernacle on 7 February 1881. In the election held one week later, 575 People's party votes were cast for the winners and seven write-in votes were registered for the other candidates. From this time onward, however, the Liberal party would begin to flex its political strength in Weber County.

In 1882, with the passage of the Edmunds Act and the creation of the Utah Commission, politics in Ogden, Weber County, and Utah began to change dramatically. Charles Middleton reported the 15 March 1882 actions taken in Weber County with the passage of the Edmunds Act:

> I met with the High Council in Forenoon. . . . At night we Rec'd Council from Salt Lake that it was thought wisdom for the Poligamous members in the County Court & City council to resign their offices and have them filled by appointment while we had the appointing power in our own hands. Consequently both these bodies met and carried out the suggestions—six members of the City Council resigned & two of the County Court.[19]

Those practicing polygamy who resigned from the city council included David M. Stewart, Charles F. Middleton, Nels Flygare, Job Pingree, Winslow Farr, and William W. Burton. Appointed to fill the six vacancies were Robert McQuarrie, Edwin Stratford, William H. Wright, Thomas Doxey, Joseph Farr, and Joseph T. Johnson. Ogden mayor Lester J. Herrick was also a Weber County selectman, and he resigned from that position along with Pleasant Green Taylor; they were replaced by Lewis W. Shurtliff and Thomas Wallace. Shurtliff was appointed Weber LDS Stake president in 1883 and served in that position until his death in 1922. Franklin D. Richards resigned as Weber County probate judge, and for the next four or five years he would be looked upon by many as the public head of the Mormon church while other prominent general authorities including John Taylor and George Q. Cannon were hiding "on the underground" to avoid prosecution for plural marriage. Lewis Shurtliff was elected probate judge of Weber County in August 1883.

The leadership of the Weber County People's party included

Lewis Shurtliff and his counselors in the Weber Stake presidency, Charles F. Middleton and Nels C. Flygare, as well as Lester J. Herrick and Joseph Stanford. Beginning with the People's party convention of 1883, the conventions began to be more open politically and less dictated by Mormon general and local authorities. The People's party continued to splinter on the edges as the Mormons who made up the party began to express differing views on candidates and issues. The Liberal party began to gain in strength as its major and less divisive goal was to defeat the Mormons and the People's party.[20]

The 1883 Ogden city election saw 1,886 votes cast—1,304 votes more than were cast in the 1881 election. In 1881 Lester Herrick was elected mayor of Ogden as the People's party choice with 574 votes. In 1883 David H. Peery, the People's candidate for mayor, received 1,059 votes to defeat Ogden jeweler and Liberal party candidate John S. Lewis, who received 818 votes. Peery was a Mormon convert from Virginia who had become an influential Ogden businessman, church leader, and politician. In 1885 Peery was reelected, with 1,129 votes cast in his favor out of a total of 2,075 votes. Ogden newspapers began to campaign vigorously in this political race, with the *Daily Herald* campaigning for Peery and the *Ogden Pilot* pushing for the Liberal party candidates. Rural Weber County remained solidly in the camp of the People's party while the struggle for the control of Ogden continued between the People's and Liberal parties.

Although the 1880s were an era of intense political conflict in Weber County, they were also the beginning of an era of cooperation. Far-sighted political, social, and economic leaders decided that cooperation and compromise would bear important dividends which conflict, contention, and confrontation could not bring about. A cooperative movement developed slowly but surely. A chamber of commerce for Ogden and Weber County was organized in April 1887 with David H. Peery, who represented the Mormons, elected president for the first year and Judge Philip H. Emerson, who represented the Liberals in the community, elected president of the chamber for the second year. The chamber acted in support of economic development throughout the community and was the first broadly based commercial organization of its kind in Utah. It became a significant conciliatory influence, although partisanship continued to dominate politics for a time.

Frank Jenne Cannon made important contributions to the political and social life of Weber County. He was born in 1859 as the eldest son of George Q. Cannon, who became an LDS apostle the same year as Frank's birth. Frank Cannon was trained in the printing and newspaper business, and he spent part of his teenage years working in Weber County at the county recorder's office and at the office of the *Junction* while he later worked to complete his education in Salt Lake City at the University of Deseret (Utah). Cannon became a journalist and a newspaperman. During the 1880s with Ogden as his chief residence, his writing skills increased but he also became a heavy drinker. Frank Cannon enjoyed the pleasures of the flesh with many of Ogden's prostitutes, including those under the supervision of Kate Flint, Ogden's most prominent madame. By 1887 Frank Cannon was the editor of the *Ogden Herald,* and the newspaper supported Mormons and the People's party in politics. Cannon was an activist in his writing and in politics. In 1886 he spent three months in jail and was fined $150 for being party to an attack on U.S. Attorney William A. Dickson, who it was alleged had questioned in court in an indelicate way Cara Cannon, one of George Q. Cannon's plural wives.

David Eccles, one of Ogden's most prominent businessmen and a founding member of the chamber of commerce, was the People's party candidate for the office of mayor of Ogden in 1887. Eccles had two wives and was therefore not qualified to hold political office under terms of the Edmunds Act; but, like some Mormon men who practiced plural marriage, he did so in secret and had already served a term as an Ogden city councilman. Eccles's Liberal party opponent in the 1887 race was Fred J. Kiesel. Kiesel, who had been a businessman both in Corinne and in Ogden, had been defeated for the office of mayor in 1885 by David Peery. The 1887 race of mayor was close, with Eccles winning by only 110 votes—1,364 to 1,254.

Fred Kiesel was vehemently opposed to the union of church and state, something he believed was happening with the People's party in Ogden, and after his loss in 1887 Kiesel and his Liberal party colleagues worked toward a possible victory in 1889. Several political and social changes pointed to a very close race in 1889, including the passage of the Edmunds-Tucker Act, the influx of more non-Mormons to Weber County, the increasing independence of many Mormon voters, and discussions about the need for national political parties rather than territorial political parties.

John Boyle was selected as the People's party candidate for Ogden mayor in 1889 and Kiesel was nominated by the Liberal party. Election day was 11 February and enthusiastic crowds mobbed the city hall voting windows during much of the day. Both of the political parties made extraordinary efforts to get out their voters while hindering when possible the voters for the opposition. The Liberal party knew that its success depended on the voting of the railroad men, and Southern Pacific, Utah Northern, and Rio Grande trains all worked hard to reach Ogden before the polls closed in the evening. The Union Pacific train was delayed in western Wyoming on election day, but the crew made special efforts to move the train from Green River to Evanston and then on to Ogden, reaching the city just in time for the men to vote. From Echo to Ogden, a brakeman kept an overheated box operating by pouring a steady stream of cool water on it. Both sides suggested that ineligible voters were allowed to vote for the other side and that the ballot box was being stuffed.[21]

Crowds milled around the city hall and the Broom Hotel after the polls were closed, and it was late in the evening when the election results were announced. Kiesel defeated Boyle by 391 votes, and the Liberal party candidates also captured every other municipal office. Ogden was the first major Utah city to be captured politically by the Liberal party, and the headline in the *Utah Daily Union* summed up the election: "OGDEN AMERICANIZED."[22]

By the time that Fred J. Kiesel was elected mayor of Ogden, he had been in and around Utah Territory for more than a quarter of a century. He arrived in Utah in 1863 and worked as a clerk in several grocery stores before opening his own wholesale and retail grocery business in the 1870s in Corinne. As Corinne declined, Kiesel moved his growing business to Ogden, where he developed it into a million dollar a year business, with transactions conducted throughout northern Utah, Idaho, and Oregon. He served only one term as Ogden mayor and was involved in many business ventures in the Ogden area. He also played a major part in founding the Great Salt

Lake resort at Syracuse. He represented Weber County at the 1895 state constitutional convention and, after Utah gained statehood, he served two terms in the state senate representing Weber County. Kiesel was the first president of the Ogden City School Board.

On 5 April 1889, Ogden's mayor and city council moved to further "Americanize" the city. Three of the original north-south city street names had been named in honor of prominent Mormons: Franklin (for Franklin D. Richards), Young (Brigham Young), and Smith (Joseph Smith). With the exception of Wall Avenue, the north-south running streets were renamed at the 5 April meeting for presidents of the United States, beginning with Lincoln (former Franklin Street), Grant (Young), Washington (Main), and moving eastward to eventually include Pierce and Buchanan as the years passed. Washington, Monroe, and Harrison avenues became major city thoroughfares. To allow for city growth, the east-west running streets were renumbered and the Ogden city boundary extended. Old 5th Street, for example, became 25th Street, and the new 1st, 2nd, and 3rd streets were on the far northern end of the newly expanded city.

The social, political, and economic rivalry of the 1870s and 1880s between Mormons and non-Mormons did not die easily with one election; but both groups became increasingly more cooperative in society, politics, and business. Most residents of the county and of the territory were interested in statehood, and the next decade would see that goal accomplished. In 1890 Mormon church president Wilford Woodruff issued the "Manifesto," which suggested that plural marriage would cease being a practice of the church. The 1890 manifesto was reinforced by a 1904 pronouncement by church president Joseph F. Smith called the Second Manifesto which drove the last nail in the coffin of official polygamy practice by Mormon church members. Along with abandoning plural marriage, there was a decided effort to reorganize the territory along national political lines and replace the old territorial People's and Liberal parties. Ogden and Weber County set the example for the rest of the territory in moving toward political harmony between Mormons and gentiles as well as moving into the national political mainstream in the 1890s.

### *Transportation and Other Growth*

As the railroads changed Weber County from the outside, they also began to have an impact on transportation within the county. In 1883 the Ogden City Railway Company had its beginnings when mules were used to draw passenger rail cars over Ogden streets. Mule teams were changed every four hours and passenger fares were ten cents. Each street train had both a mule driver and a conductor. The passenger rails were soon expanded to other parts of the county. By 1889 small steam engines known as dummies began to be used on the street railway system in Ogden, and many of the mule drivers became engineers. During the 1890s, the rail lines were extended to the Utah Hot Springs Resort. Some of the dummies were used as late as the 1930s, although the urban streetcar system was electrified during 1890 and 1891.

The Ogden Street Railway Company was initially organized as a private company in 1883 and it maintained its original name although it changed ownership several times over the next several decades. When the line was extended to the Utah Hot Springs in 1890, that branch of the line was known as the Ogden Hot Springs Railway and Health Resort Company. In 1890 David Eccles and his associates purchased the line and Eccles was particularly responsible for constructing a line up the north side of Ogden Canyon to Huntsville. This picturesque line went into operation in 1913. Riders from the upper valley used the line to attend school, to shop, or to move back and forth from their work in the lower valley. The Ogden Valley people called the streetcar the "Toonerville." Many from the lower valley took the streetcar for pleasure; boarding on Washington, they traveled up Canyon Road past Lorin Farr (then Glenwood) Park, on to the Hermitage in Ogden Canyon, and then to the artesian wells just below Huntsville. By 1935, in part due to the popularity of the automobile, ridership on the electric streetcar railway system had declined to such a point that the system was replaced by buses.

By the mid-1880s transportation in Weber County was significantly aided by three major river bridges extensively used by foot, horse, and wagon traffic. The first, which bridged the Ogden River just to the north of Ogden City on Washington Boulevard, was completed in 1876. The second bridged the Weber River west of the railroad depots and was completed in 1880. This Weber River bridge provided a double wagon track for ease of transportation. The third bridge, which was begun in 1881, spanned the Weber River in Riverdale; it was paid for in part by the territorial legislature and in part by Weber County.

In 1888 the territorial legislature appropriated $50,000 for the construction of the territorial reform school in Ogden. An imposing four-story building with a large tower steeple was designed and erected on a fifty-acre tract at 20th and Monroe. The height of the building to the top of the tower was 140 feet and the building was 142 feet by 60 feet. The reform school was planned to provide rooms for juvenile offenders, who were referred to as inmates. Living space at the facility was also planned for officers and their families and for teachers. The building included a hospital as well as offices and rooms for school and for church services. The building included a dust chute, down which all the dust and debris from any floor was thrown; it was then gathered in the basement and taken from the building. Another feature of the building was the dumbwaiter which operated with an opening on every floor. Joseph Jackson was the contractor for the building and the brick was made at Jackson's brickyard in the south part of Ogden.

In March 1875 Isaac Blake prepared a petition for the Ogden City Council suggesting that Ogden should become a depot for the storage and distribution of oil. Blake suggested to the council that Ogden would be the reception depot for oil from the surrounding states and territories and that it would then be put into cans and distributed. He proposed that his company be incorporated and called the Continental Oil Company (Conoco), but the city council tabled his proposal. Several months later, in November 1875, Blake's company was incorporated in Council Bluffs, Iowa; but Ogden did serve as a storage and distribution center for the new company's products including coal oil, kerosene, candles, bulk wax, axle grease, and ready-mixed paints.

Ogden and Weber County businesses continued to expand, taking on a more cosmopolitan nature though remaining part of the American frontier. Ogden had no paved streets, and in early spring and late autumn streets became a quagmire where wagons and buggies had difficulty in moving. During the winter, sleighing was popular as the snow was piled high on the sides of the streets. Snow removal was unheard of.

On 11 May 1881 the Ogden Electric Light Company was incorporated with David F. Walker as president, James Horrocks as vice-president, G.S. Erb as secretary, and H. Schwabe as assistant secretary. As the company made its first attempt to light the city with electricity in mid-May 1881, it constructed a high steel tower on the corner of Adams and 24th. Four large light bulbs were hooked on the tower in such a way that when lit they would illuminate a good portion of the area below the bluff of the hill. The electricity was turned on with a great deal of fanfare. Although the lights burned brightly for a few seconds, they quickly fizzled and the crowd went home disappointed. A month later, on 20 June, Ogden stores were lighted by electricity supplied by a steam generating plant. In 1883 a hydroelectric plant was built below the mouth of Ogden Canyon to produce electricity for Ogden. Ogden store owners were charged seventeen dollars a month for one light, and each owner had only one light, which was turned on at dusk and off at midnight from a central switch at the powerhouse. During 1884 Ogden homes began to receive electrical service.

The George A. Lowe Company installed the first telephones in the state in their Ogden business in 1879. The company ran a private wire between its warehouse and store to provide the initial telephone service. Within a year, public telephone service was provided by the Ogden Telephone Exchange Company and several other smaller telephone companies in the area. In 1883 these companies were consolidated into the Rocky Mountain Telephone Company. By the end of 1883 there were about "120 sets of instruments" (telephones) in Ogden and the surrounding areas including North Ogden, Plain City, Hot Springs, Uintah, Riverdale, and Kaysville. Two switchboards were in constant use in the Ogden central office, where operators were on duty both day and night.

The George A. Lowe Company began in Salt Lake City in 1870. The company sold Schuttler wagons and built and repaired both wagons and buggies at both its Ogden and Salt Lake City locations.

A stock of 200,000 pounds of bar iron and steel for the repair of wagons was stockpiled as well as hardwood of all kinds to repair buggies and wagons. The Lowe Company also sold agricultural implements to the farmers of Weber County.

The Ogden Broom Factory was begun by H. B. Scoville in 1873 using broomcorn purchased from Utah and Nebraska. By 1883 the factory was producing from 300 to 500 brooms a month. The Utah Vinegar Works began in Ogden in 1876 and by the mid-1880s was producing about 5,000 gallons of vinegar a month under the guidance of E. H. Orth and C. W. Orth, the owners of the company. Black blasting powder was produced at the Utah Powder Company located in Ogden Canyon, and the production schedule noted that about one hundred kegs of black powder were produced daily.

William H. Wright founded the W. H. Wright and Sons Company in 1875. Wright and his six sons built an elegant two-story brick building on the west side of Washington Boulevard in 1885 to house their dry-goods business. Prices in the 1880s included children shoes, $1.00 to $1.60; women's shoes, $3.00 to $4.00; corsets, 50 cents; mittens, 75 cents; and children's bonnets, 25 cents to $1.50. In 1907 the Boyle Furniture Company purchased the Wright Building and moved their furniture business into the graceful building. Peter A. Boyle and his son, John, had begun their pioneer furniture company in Ogden in 1862. The Wright Building was the second building in Ogden which the Boyles' company occupied, and they remained in the building from 1907 until 1978 when they moved to make room for the Ogden City Mall. Peter and John Boyle began in 1862 to make spinning wheels and sole pegs. In 1874, after rebuilding his original Washington Boulevard building following a devastating fire, Peter Boyle added a wholesale undertaker's department including caskets and other funeral materials to the furniture store. Fred Kiesel's large wholesale grocery built during the 1880s was located on 24th Street.

Josiah G. Read and his brothers William S. and Oscar began the J. G. Read Company in Ogden in 1876. The Read brothers made saddles, harnesses, and other leather products and set up their business initially on the east side of Washington between 24th and 25th. About 1905 the business was moved to a building on the corner of 24th and Kiesel Avenue where the firm began to sell automobile tires as well as leather goods. In 1912 a statue of a black champion race horse was placed on the top front corner of the three-story Read building, and this cast-iron white-stockinged black horse became an Ogden landmark for the next six decades. Local folklore suggests that the black horse after which the statue was patterned was captured near Promontory Point and sold to J. G. Read. He trained the horse and it became a champion racehorse which ran races on Ogden and northern Utah racetracks for seventeen years at the turn of the century.

Blacksmith shops, which had existed in the county since Ogden's earliest pioneer days, continued to dot the towns of the county. Blacksmiths kept busy shoeing horses, oxen, and mules as well as sharpening plows, setting wagon tires, and making nails, fire tongs, fire shovels, and pokers. The smiths also made and repaired farm implements. Some blacksmiths made brass cowbells, washboards, branding irons, iron door latches, and animal traps.

In 1888, under the leadership of Mayor David Eccles, Ogden City decided to proceed with plans to build a new city hall as well as extend the waterworks of the city and improve the city sewer. On 7 February 1889, just before leaving office, Eccles reported to the city council that the cost of the newly completed city hall including all of the fixtures for the building was $52,275.15. The council agreed to pay for the improvements by issuing bonds.

One evidence of the advancing cosmopolitan nature of Ogden was the wide variety of food served at various restaurants. Not far from the Ogden city hall was Goodey's Place, located near the railroad depot and owned by J. B. Goodfellow. Goodfellow advertised that his bar and lunch stand had "all the toothsome delicacies usually kept in such place such as oysters, sardelles, anchovies, herrings, cheese of all kinds, sardines, crackers, and a skillful mixologist is in charge of the bar."[23]

The Broom Hotel included on its breakfast menu fresh raspberries or blackberries, sirloin steak, ham, mutton chops, veal cutlets, liver, bacon, and Spanish steak, as well as oatmeal, rolls, and corn bread. Dinner entrees included rollet of beef à l'Espanole, stewed kidneys on butter toast, oyster patties à la creme with apple fritters and wine sauce, boiled salmon with egg sauce, shoulder of mutton in caper sauce, ox heart with jelly, and a selection of cold meats which included beef, mutton, and ham. At 150 25th Street, the Chapman House dinner selections included mountain trout, Columbia River salmon, oysters San Francisco, antelope steak, shoulder of venison, beef Chicago, breasts of sage hen, prairie chicken in cream, mourning doves, and Canada goose. The Chapman House menu included a list of cocktails which were named after railroad presidents, Indian chiefs, and mining camps. Irish whiskey sold at the Chapman House for fifteen cents a glass.

Working conditions and beginning jobs improved as the county grew. E. A. Stratford began his career as a printer for the Ogden *Junction* in 1872. His beginning wage was three dollars a week, to be paid in produce and orders for merchandise from stores in Ogden. By his second year on the job, his wages rose to five dollars a week in produce. A variety of produce was available for the newspaper workers including a quarter of beef which was delivered to the *Junction* office each Saturday from the farm of James Hutchins of Slaterville. G. J. Wright, who operated the Taylor hand-press at the paper, was the butcher who cut the quarter of beef into as many pieces as there were *Junction* employees. A number was placed on each cut of beef and a duplicate number placed in a hat. After all of the meat cutting was completed, a drawing was held. Each worker drew a number and then received the piece of beef which had the same number. When the drawing was completed, each worker knew what his family would have for Sunday dinner.

Sidney Stevens arrived in Ogden in 1865 with his wife, Mae J. Thick Stevens. Together they would become the parents of twelve children. Stevens had a major effect on business in Weber County. In order to finance his new business opportunities as well as the couple's trip from their home in England to Utah, Stevens purchased a stock of sugar, tea, coffee, and other staples in St. Joseph, Missouri, for resale in Utah. He had the talents of a natural-born businessman. His initial businesses in Ogden and North Ogden included a tannery and a shoe and harness factory. After the arrival of the railroad, Stevens moved into the machinery and implement business, with his major operations run from his Ogden store and a branch store in North Ogden. By the mid-1870s Stevens had added vehicles including wagons and carriages to his trade. His agents sold wagons and carriages throughout Utah, Idaho, Wyoming, and Nevada. In 1889 he built a commodious three-story building in Ogden with large warehouses at the rear to accommodate his growing business. The Stevens Company was involved in both the sale and the repair of implements, carriages, and wagons. He suffered severe losses by fire both in 1893 and 1894, but he rebuilt his buildings and continued his business efforts.

William Driver and his wife, Charlotte Emblem Boulter, arrived in Ogden in 1870. They emigrated from England and Driver operated a drug store for William S. Godbe in Ogden. The store proved to be profitable, and in 1874 Driver started his own drug store, which he named the City Drug Store. He built a new three-story building on Washington Boulevard to house his drug store and rented the third floor to the Masonic Order, which used it for their activities for the next decade. By 1878 Driver's son George became a partner in the business and Driver and Son became a well-known retail drug store business throughout the region. Branch drug stores were established in Logan, Brigham City, and Montpelier, Idaho. As well as being a successful businessman, Driver was involved in a number of civic activities, including serving a term as mayor of Ogden.

John S. Lewis and his family arrived in Ogden from Corinne in January 1870. Lewis, originally from Tennessee, was involved in the Montana gold rush of the 1860s where he worked both as a miner and a watchmaker. In the late 1860s, Lewis and N. B. Hale operated jewelry businesses near Denver, Colorado, and in Virginia City and Helena, Montana. They made jewelry from gold nuggets which were melted and formed into various shapes such as watch chains, belt buckles, rings, and buttons. When Lewis moved to Ogden in 1870, he believed that the area would become prosperous because of the newly completed railroad. The Lewis Jewelry firm began at 2463 Washington Boulevard in 1870; in 1882 the name of the firm was changed to J. S. Lewis and Company. The firm then included John Lewis's two sons, Hiram and John. John S. Lewis, Jr., and his wife built a beautiful and substantial home which they named the Cobbles in Ogden Canyon at Rock Ridge.

John Farr was born in Ogden in 1863, the son of Lorin and Nicholine Erickson Farr. In his autobiography, *My Yesterdays,* Farr wrote of his efforts to make a living for his family beginning in 1884. He first tried his hand at homesteading 160 acres of land in Idaho near Eagle Rock which was available under the Desert Land Act. Homesteading proved to be difficult and Farr returned to Ogden where he worked part time for his father before he began working for the Ogden City Mule Street Car Company. He noted that he worked ten to eighteen hours a day, seven days a week on the mule teams and was paid $1.50 a day. The mules included some that were broken and trained and others that were brought in from Promontory and were still "vicious, wild mules."

After two years with the mule car company, John Farr left and began to farm and raise stock on West Second Street. Water for his adobe house had to be carried from Mill Creek, more than 500 feet from the home. John and his wife, Rachel Ann Witten Farr, worked hard on the farm, sometimes arising at one or two in the morning for farm chores as well as taking care of their four young children. Farr described the black clouds of mosquitoes which would rise out of Mill Creek, the pasture swamps, and the bulrushes in the summertime just before dusk and move in a horde toward the house and barn to attack the people and the animals. The family tried to cover the windows and doors with mosquito cloth or they would be fighting the insects most of the night. In 1888 John Farr began a feed and grain business, and by the spring of 1890 he entered into the ice business, forming a partnership with Mark Hopkins and his brothers Lorenzo and Elijah. The four partners purchased the Thomas Farr Ice Company and the G. Griffith Ice Company. The demand for more ice by the railroad companies that were shipping fresh produce encouraged competition in the ice business. New ice companies in Weber County included the Ogden City Ice Company, the Farr Brothers Ice Company (under the management of Valasco, David, and Asael Farr), the Mountain Ice Company of Salt Lake City, the Zion Ice Company, the James Ice Company, the Gordon Ice Company, and the Trecedar Ice Company. The wholesale ice houses also supplied ice to shops, saloons, and stores. At one time John Farr delivered ice on a daily basis to fifty-six saloons. The retail ice wagons delivered ice to family homes; each of Farr's wagons delivered to about 200 homes each day.

John Farr also entered the retail coal business in 1888, with much of his coal coming on the Rio Grande Western Railroad to Weber County from Carbon County. Coal was delivered to individual homes and businesses by team and wagon and by horse-drawn sleigh in the winter. Farr paid from thirty-five to fifty cents a ton for the coal he received and charged from seventy-five cents to $1.25 a ton for delivery to homes and businesses.

John Scowcroft was an example of a self-made man in Weber County during the last two decades of the nineteenth century. Scowcroft was born in England and, following his conversion to Mormonism, he traveled to Utah and Weber County with his family in 1880. Scowcroft began by establishing a confectionery and bakery and then expanded into an Ogden general merchandise store. In 1885 he established the firm of John Scowcroft and Sons, and the subsequent expansion of this wholesale house was spectacular. By 1893 the Scowcroft Company was the largest wholesale establishment between Omaha and San Francisco. After John Scowcroft's death in 1902, the company continued to grow and expand, including producing Never Rip Overalls, which became famous throughout the West. The emergence of the Scowcroft Company was much like the emergence of Weber County in the nineteenth century. Both started off small and somewhat unknown; but, with the assistance of the railroad, both grew and were known nationwide by the end of the century.

## ENDNOTES

1. Franklin L. West, *Life of Franklin D. Richards* (Salt Lake City: Deseret News Press, 1924), 169–70.

2. As cited in Robert G. Athearn, *Union Pacific Country* (Lincoln: University of Nebraska Press, 1982). Athearn reported that the diary was held by Ellsworth W. Cardwell of Salt Lake City.

3. Athearn, *Union Pacific Country,* 85–88.

4. Brigham D. Madsen, *Corrine, The Gentile Capital of Utah* (Salt Lake City: Utah State Historical Society, 1980), 10.

5. Ibid., 14.

6. Book A. Abstract of Title Lots, 249, 253, 254, Weber County Recorder's Office, Ogden, Utah.

7. *Ogden Standard-Examiner,* 26 June 1924.

8. David L. Wood, "Emperor Dom Pedro's Visit to Salt Lake City," *Utah Historical Quarterly* 37 (Summer 1969): 344.

9. Don Maguire, "The Story of Ogden's Catholic History," quoted in Dale L. Morgan, ed., *A History of Ogden* (Ogden: Ogden City Commission, 1940), 51.

10. For a more extensive discussion of water in the county, see Richard W. Sadler and Richard C. Roberts, *The Weber River Basin* (Logan: Utah State University Press, 1994).

11. David E. Miller, ed., "A Great Adventure on Great Salt Lake—A True Story by Kate Y. Noble," *Utah Historical Quarterly* 33 (Summer 1965): 221.

12. T. Earl Pardoe, *Lorin Farr, Pioneer* (Provo: Brigham Young University Press, 1953), 182.

13. Kate Carter, ed., *Our Pioneer Heritage* (Salt Lake City: Utah Printing Company, 1968), 15:477.

14. Richard E. Kotter, "An Examination of Mormon and Non-Mormon Influences in Ogden City Politics, 1847–1896," M.A. thesis, Utah State University, 1967; Jean Bickmore White, "The Right to Be Different: Ogden and Weber County Politics, 1850–1924," *Utah Historical Quarterly* 47 (Summer 1979): 254–272.

15. White, "The Right to Be Different," 257.

16. Leonard Arrington, *Great Basin Kingdom* (Cambridge: Harvard University Press, 1958), 245.

17. Kotter, "An Examination of Mormon and Non-Mormon Influences," 56.

18. Henry J. Middleton, "The Life of Charles Franklin Middleton, a Man and his Times," M.A. Thesis, Utah State University, 1965; Kotter, "An Examination of Mormon and Non-Mormon Influences," 58.

19. Middleton, diary, 15 March 1882, as quoted in Kotter, "An Examination of Mormon and Non-Mormon Influences," 77.

20. Kotter, "An Examination of Mormon and Non-Mormon Influences," 100.

21. Ibid., 105.

22. *Utah Daily Union,* 12 February 1889.

23. *Directory of Ogden City and North Utah Record* (Ogden: S.A. Kenner and Thomas Wallace, 1878).

4

# Nineteenth Century Social and Cultural History

The society of Weber County changed during the nineteenth century. Initially, the society was one of Native Americans, and then the fur trade developed a society where Native Americans and trappers mingled together, as described by Osborne Russell. In the two decades following 1847, Weber County society became dominated by the Mormons; and, following 1869, the railroad and the changes it brought affected society drastically. With the arrival of the Mormons in 1847, the Native American culture and the Mormon culture of settlement clashed, much as the Mormon culture and the changes brought by the railroad later came into conflict.

The journals and diaries of the early Mormons relate their joys and tragedies, including establishing homesites, planting crops, working the fields, daily house chores, harvesting crops, relating to Indians, surviving the heat of the summers and the cold of the winters, bearing and raising children, tending the sick, burying the dead, and hoping for a better future. Women worked the fields and herded cattle along with the men and boys. Most families were involved with farming in order to subsist, and farm crops included hay, grain, potatoes, corn, beans, and garden vegetables.

Families generally had horses, cattle, and sheep. After the sheep were shorn, the wool was washed by the women, who also carded it, spun it into yarn, and then wove it into cloth. The cloth was made into dresses, shirts, and overalls. The family washing was done by hand, and stockings and mittens were knitted for the whole family. The early settlers had no coal and so they gathered sagebrush and other timber to burn for both summer and winter. Grain was cut with a cradle and threshed by pounding it out by hand. Bathing often took place in the rivers, during most seasons of the year.

Settlers spread out over the county during the first decade of Mormon settlement, and most sought the increased protection of neighbors and forts. The Frederick and James Barker families settled in the area of Mound Fort and began to farm the land adjacent to later 12th Street and Washington Boulevard. Their farm included milk cows from which they produced butter. They dried fruit from their orchards. Elfrida Gay Barker Farley remembered how grain was harvested:

> After the grain had ripened and hauled in stacks, the thrashing machine would drive into our lot. The children would gather from far and near to watch the process. This made lots of work for mother and the girls, preparing a big feed for the hungry men, usually twelve or fourteen. But oh, how lovely the table would look, the knives and forks and spoons all scoured and placed around the plates, shining glasses and cups and saucers, for nearly all thrashers drank tea or coffee, large roasts of beef and rich brown gravy. Kettles of mashed potatoes, hot biscuits with plenty of butter, extra dishes of vegetables, rice puddings, pies and cakes, dishes of fruit, etc.[1]

Straw along with corn shucks was used to fill bed ticks. Fruit was dried on roofs, sheds, and platforms, and the dried fruit filled tubs, baskets, and boxes. Both work and play brought about picnics which included food, dances, recitations, singing, and making molasses candy.

### *Recreation*

The Ogden River provided many places for recreation which were widely noted not only in the county and territory but also in transcontinental guide books. Jones Grove, located on Canyon Road and Jefferson Avenue, was one of the first resort areas in the county. This grove developed into Farr's Park and then Glenwood Park and eventually present-day Lorin Farr Park. Kay's Grove was located east of Gibson Avenue and north of the Ogden River. The Ogden Canyon Hot Springs Resort at the mouth of the canyon was in use as early as 1890.

The Utah Hot Springs located at the north end of the county between Pleasant View and Willard became a recreation area which was visited particularly by Weber County families during the latter part of the nineteenth century. Those who visited the hot springs enjoyed both swimming and soaking in the warm natural water. The first swimming and bathing pools at the Utah Hot Springs were built in 1880 by Rason D. Slater of Salt Lake City. He was fascinated by the hot springs and felt he could establish a profitable health resort. Patrons of the springs drank the water and bathed in it to seek cures from arthritis and other ailments. In an 1883 advertisement, Slater noted:

> The simple bathing and drinking of these waters has proved to be a CERTAIN SPECIFIC for Rheumatism, Catarrh, Asthma, Erysipelas, Syphilis, Salt rheum, Paralysis, all affections of the Kidneys, Nervous diseases, General Debility, and all the peculiar complaints and disabilities to which females are subject.[2]

In 1896 the Hot Springs resort owners made major improvements. They added a saloon where a mug of beer could be purchased for a nickel, and they also added a commissary, a dining hall, a dance hall, and a forty-room hotel. A horse racing track was added west of the resort. By the 1890s it was possible to travel the eight miles to the Hot Springs from downtown Ogden by the "dummy" line. The "dummy" was an enclosed steam engine which pulled two or three passenger cars along a track. Visitors to the Utah Hot Springs as well as to other resorts also traveled by a variety of means including walking, riding horseback, riding in buggies and wagons, and riding bicycles.

The Winslow family established a hotel and eating establishment on a grassy flat on the Ogden River bank near where the Thiokol Center now stands below Pineview Dam. The dam, built by Utah Power and Light Company in 1889 above the Winslow property and below Wheeler Canyon, made a small reservoir that provided a scenic view and boating. Idlewood Resort was built on the south side of Ogden Canyon near where Wheeler Creek flows into the river. Patrons of the Idlewood Resort could eat at the resort, rent boats to use on the small reservoir, have picnics, and enjoy the atmosphere of the canyon.

The Hermitage Hotel, which was established in 1905, was the most famous spot on the river. The hotel was visited by many national as well as international visitors, and it was well known for its trout and chicken dinners as well as its rugged mountain and canyon setting. The hotel, located above the river valley about halfway between Ogden and Huntsville, was built by and under the direction of Billie Wilson. It was constructed of pine, maple, and oak, with many of the logs hewed by Wilson, a Scots immigrant. Wilson took over the old Hermitage Camp on the Ogden River in 1889 and gradually improved the area. He believed that a hotel would attract visitors, and he began construction in 1904. The hotel included about twenty-five rooms; another sixteen were later added to the second floor. The floors were carpeted with Navajo rugs, and a large fireplace covered much of one wall. Visitors from around the world stayed at the Hermitage, and they arrived by both motorcar and horse and carriage. As many as thirty waitresses were employed at peak times, with four desk clerks working on staggered shifts.

The menu for the hotel was famous; it included a T-bone steak dinner for one dollar, ox-tail soup for fifteen cents, lobster salad for forty cents, a sardine sandwich for ten cents, and a pot of coffee for ten cents. The lifespan of the famous Hermitage Hotel was only about thirty-five years, for on 4 January 1939 it burned to the ground. The view from the famed hotel is still available for those who climb the steps to the hotel site. Both up and down the canyon are vistas that those on the river and highway cannot possibly see.

Billie Wilson had died two decades earlier, in 1918. In his prime he was 6 feet 4 inches tall and weighed 310 pounds. Below the hotel on the river valley floor was the Hermitage Resort. It included a picnic place, a dance hall, a merry-go-round, and a place to buy food for those who couldn't or didn't want to eat at the hotel. After Wilson's death, the Hermitage passed to a number of owners, and in the 1920s it was rumored to be the largest whiskey-producing site in Weber County. A 400-gallon still and a 300-gallon still were found during a Prohibition raid along with barrels of mash and gallons of whiskey.

In 1870, Lester Park at 24th Street and Jefferson Avenue was initiated as a public meeting place for parties and other activities in Ogden. The Ogden Driving Park was opened on 21 November 1879, and horse racing was a major activity at its location on Monroe Avenue and 20th Street. Summer activities throughout the county included picnics, orations, band concerts, swimming, and baseball games. July Fourth, Independence Day, and 24 July (Pioneer Day) were particularly celebrated. Charles Middleton recounted the 24 July 1871 celebration:

> July 24, 1871 We had a grand celebration. procession formed on Tab. Square & marched to Union Square, around our block & hence to the bowery where an oration by D. H. Wells was read by G. Q. Cannon, also speeches, songs, toasts and music, President Young was present. There were present for the occasion some 20 carloads from S. L. C. & intermediate settlements. Lees Circus performed afternoon & evening. There were more people in Ogden than every before. Everything passed off very quietly—no arrests made.[3]

Families and other groups often spent holidays on canyon excursions or took a day trip by train to the Great Salt Lake resorts including the resort at Syracuse or Lake Park near Farmington. They also liked to visit Saltair or other Great Salt Lake resorts such as Garfield Beach and Black Rock. Large groups would occasionally use county parks. On 21 June 1881, for example, an old folks excursion from Salt Lake City arrived in Ogden. The group of about five thousand in number including Mormon church president John Taylor, George Q. Cannon, and Wilford Woodruff met at Farr's Grove on the Ogden

River. Singing, feasting, dancing, and speeches were all part of the entertainment.

Baseball had begun to catch the nation's fancy and northern Utah found teams in Corinne, Ogden, Willard, and Salt Lake City all claiming to be the champions of the territory. In one game played in 1870 the Corinne team bested the Ogdenites by a score of 46 to 44. The territorial championship game that year was played in Ogden but was between the Corinne and Salt Lake City teams—Ogden appeared to be a neutral field—and the Corinne team won 12 to 8. The two teams that played for the territorial championship in 1871 were from Corinne and Ogden. In the first game, Corinne defeated the Ogden Echoes 81 to 9 in Ogden. The second game of the championship series was played in Corinne, where the Ogden team was victorious by a score of 54 to 38, only to have the Corinne team win the third and deciding game in Ogden by a score of 65 to 31.

Shooting was also a means of recreation in the county. For example, the Amateur Shooting Club advertised that it would put up live chickens as targets, and individuals could shoot at them for ten cents a shot. Asa Farley killed six chickens with eight shots.

## *Life in Weber County*

Charles Middleton's recollections give good evidence of what life in Ogden and Weber County was like for many just before and following the coming of the railroad. Much of life was spent working, including planting onions, cabbages, carrots, beets, corn, beans, and wheat, as well as attending prayer meetings, militia meetings, and church meetings. Other work included chasing cattle, cutting browse, grubbing willows, spending days in Ogden Valley picking "sarvis" (service) berries, hauling hay, lumber, and poles, and shucking and shelling corn. There were parties, some sleighing in the winter, and swimming and fishing in the rivers in the summer. Middleton also used whiskey on numerous occasions to help him with his headaches.

The *Ogden Junction,* which was published for about a decade following the joining of the rails at Promontory, revealed in its advertisements and columns what life was like in the county. Prices on 1 January 1870 included: coffee, 31 cents a pound; tea, from 50 cents to $1.50 a pound; bacon, 27 cents a pound; tobacco, 85 cents a pound; corn, $1.00 a bushel; beef, 10 cents a pound at the butcher shop and 8 cents a pound on the hoof; chickens, 50 cents each; and cheese, 30 cents a pound. The newspaper included humor in its columns. The Railroad Saloon on Washington Boulevard wished everyone a Happy New Year and noted that it received fresh oysters by the case on a daily basis from Baltimore. The Ogden Circulating Library advertised that it contained several hundred volumes available from librarian C. B. McGregor, who was located at the Ogden Post Office. A lifetime library membership could be purchased for five dollars, while others could check out volumes at a cost of ten cents per volume per week.

Advertisements suggested that the services of attorneys, dentists, doctors, shoemakers, tailors, medicine dealers, undertakers, midwives, and artists were all available in Ogden, which also featured saloons, shooting galleries, hotels, and eating establishments. Dealers in coal, ice, furniture, and general merchandise advertised their products. The Saddle Rock Restaurant advertised "Oysters in Every Style." The U.P. Brewery and Malting House offered beer at fifty cents a gallon for both saloons and families. James Allen's Staple and Fancy Dry Goods advertised free delivery within the city or to the railroad depot as well as a magnificent assortment of gent's underwear for all seasons. Sharp Brothers Dentists promised painless extraction of teeth, modest terms, and a neatly furnished private room for ladies.

A number of lodges and fraternal organizations were established in Weber County in the two decades following the arrival of the railroad. The IOOF Lodge for Odd Fellows was established in 1874 in Ogden and a decade later had forty members. Other groups organized during this era included the Union Lodge (1878), the Wasatch Tribe (1882), the Grand Army of the Republic (1881), the Wasatch Lodge (1881)—an active temperance organization, and the Knights of Pythias (1881).

### *Religion*

The railroad brought a much greater diversity of religious groups to Weber County and to Ogden. Utah's Mormon religion was very controversial in nineteenth-century America, and many of the religious groups that moved to Utah with the railroad came with the intent of converting Mormon children and adults away from the error of their ways and their current religious practices, particularly plural marriage. An observer writing in the *Atlantic Monthly* in May 1869 expressed the feelings of many Americans who were curious about Mormonism and polygamy but also convinced that the Utah practices were un-American:

> The visitor will busy himself, of course with a dozen questions and a dozen theories about Mormonism, about polygamy and Brigham Young, and when and how it is all coming to an end. Perhaps if he hears earnest Mormons talk, he will wonder in his heart whether it is possible they are right,—whether this little leaven in Utah is, as they say, bound to leaven the whole American lump, and polygamy is to become the law of the sexes, and Mormonism the religion of the future;—which is all well enough, if he keeps his wondering doubt to himself. But no social, political, and religious organization so foreign to all our principles of life and growth as this of Brigham Young in Utah, exists elsewhere in America, or even in Europe; it proceeds from and depends on a single will; and a very little knowledge of history and its philosophy, and less of our national instincts and faith in progress, will enable the observer to see that the Mormon system must give way, and be swept almost into forgetfulness by the advancing tide of American emigration and American civilization.[4]

Many American churches sent missionaries and clergy to Utah both to serve members of their own flocks as well as to convert Mormons. Church schools were sponsored to educate Mormon children and to expose them to other religious ideas and thoughts. Weber County became an area in which religious activities were multiplied.

The first Roman Catholic mass in Ogden was celebrated during Christmas week in 1871 at the home of Michael Maguire, which was located on 25th Street between Lincoln and Grant. Associated with the Maguires during the 1870s were other Catholic families including the Delaneys, the Hassetts, the Grills, the Langsdorfs, the McDonalds, the McCabes, the Biels, and the McCormicks; they formed the nucleus of the Catholic congregation in Weber County. Father Patrick Walsh traveled from Salt Lake City to perform the first service in the county in 1871, and other Catholic priests from Salt

Lake City continued to travel to Ogden until 1878 to perform services for the mostly Irish congregation in Ogden. In 1878 Father Lawrence Scanlon became the resident pastor of St. Joseph's, a wooden-frame structure built on 25th Street between Lincoln and Grant. Funds for this first church were raised in part by holding a church fair which was attended by "Catholics, Mormons, Protestants, Jews, Gentiles, and aristocratic Chinamen of those times,"[5] and services for this occasion were held on Easter Sunday, 1877, at the first St. Joseph's Church. This was the second Catholic church built in Utah, and it barely escaped destruction by fire in 1879.

By 1881 there were 150 Catholics in Ogden and the county, and by 1884 this number had grown to 400. Father Patrick M. Cushanhan, who arrived in Ogden from Maghera, Ireland, in 1881, spearheaded the building of a larger church. The site for the new St. Joseph's was purchased on the northeast corner of 24th Street and Adams Avenue in 1889. A beautiful new church was completed in 1902 and dedicated in that year as St. Joseph's by Bishop Lawrence Scanlon. The exterior structure of the new church was completed in gray and red sandstone, and the beautiful stained-glass windows added dignity and solemnity to the building. St. Joseph's Church was 150 feet in length and 90 feet in width and still stands.

Almost as soon as Catholic services were begun, the educational needs of Catholic and other children were addressed. In September 1878 seven sisters who were members of the order of the Sisters of the Holy Cross arrived in Ogden and began Ogden's Sacred Heart Academy in a three-story building located at 26th Street and Washington Boulevard. By 1883 there were 200 students in attendance at the academy. In the spring of 1882, St. Joseph's School was built as an adjoining building to the academy. In 1889, under the direction of Sister Pauline, a decision was made to purchase a five-acre lot on upper 25th Street and plans for a new academy were drawn. Ground was broken for the new school in September 1890 at the property at 25th and Quincy, and in September 1892 the new school was opened to students. The beautiful new building could accommodate 600 boarding students and a faculty of twenty-one sisters. The Sacred Heart Academy operated at this location from 1892 until it was closed in 1938. This building was later razed to make way for a medical complex. In 1923 a new St. Joseph's School for boys was completed at 28th and Lincoln.

Episcopal services were first held in Ogden on 17 July 1870 in the waiting room of the Union Depot. The Reverend James L. Gillogly and his wife lived in a boxcar situated in the Ogden railroad yards for several months as they awaited the purchase of a site for their church. The Episcopal Church of the Good Shepherd located on 24th Street which is admired today for its attractive gothic design was completed in 1874 at a cost of $11,000. James Hammersley of New York City paid for the construction of the church in memory of his daughter, Mrs. Catherine L. Livingston, who had died in Ogden en route to California. The stone for the building was quarried near Mendon, Utah. During the 1870s and 1880s a church school was conducted on the church grounds, with a yearly enrollment during the 1880s averaging 175 students. Tuition ranged from one to two dollars a month for each student. Episcopal church membership in Ogden and Weber County grew from ninety-five in 1883 to 600 by 1915.

The Reverend Daniel Tuttle, Episcopal Bishop of Salt Lake City, recorded in his diary that he had often visited Ogden in the 1860s and had eaten dinner at Mormon bishop Chauncey West's hotel, where the chicken dinners were cooked by one of West's plural wives. Tuttle described Rev. James Gillogly as being straightforward and fearless, as he "from the first assumed an attitude of strong and square opposition to Mormonism." Tuttle went on to describe one of the first Episcopal services held in the old tannery:

> Soon after opening the "old tannery," some hoodlum Mormons gathered at the services one Sunday evening, bent on making a disturbance. At first Mr. Gillogly contented himself with looking sternly at them when they were noisy. On the continuance of the disorder, however, he stopped in the services and said: "We are glad to welcome one and all here, but we expect respectful and reverent behavior from those who come. Young men in yonder corner, unless you are respectful and quiet, I shall take off my surplice and come down and put you out of here." He was a square-set, sturdily built man, and the youths deemed it wise to be quiet.[6]

Methodist church services in Ogden were begun on 28 June 1870 when a sermon was preached in the Ogden passenger depot by the Reverend G. M. Pierce. Early Methodist meeting sites included the Ogden Theater building (Grant Avenue and 24th Street, rented for five dollars a Sunday), Leavitt's Hall (24th Street and Washington Boulevard, rented at eighteen dollars a month), and a hall located at 2364 Washington Boulevard which was purchased in 1871 for $1,200. Two church buildings were constructed on this site, with a small adobe building used first as a church. It was later replaced by a larger building. A Methodist grade school was located at this site and was opened in 1871 with one teacher and six students. In 1872 there were three teachers and between sixty and eighty pupils. This school was the first Protestant church school in the area. In 1889, the Washington Boulevard church and school site was sold and new property secured at 454 24th Street. The first services were held in the new building in May 1890. The new church had been built at a cost of $65,000. This new facility served as Methodist church headquarters in the city and county until 1925 when a new church was erected at 26th and Jefferson on property purchased from the James Pingree estate.

Congregationalists held services in Ogden as early as 1876 under the direction of Reverend A. W. Safford. Ten Congregational communicants formed the core of the group which met for six months in Driver's Hall, a room over William Driver's drug store; the group included Mrs. Jane Taylor, Mrs. Aura Thompson, and Alex Bruckman. For several years this small group did not have a formal organization; but, in 1884, the First Congregational Church of Ogden was formed with twelve members, and the Reverend H. E. Thayer was elected pastor. By 1895 membership in this congregation had grown to 137 people. The educational arm of the Congregational church, the New West Educational Commission, constructed a two-room building in 1884 on the corner of 25th Street and Adams Avenue and named it the Ogden Academy. In 1887 the academy building was enlarged into a two-story brick building, and in 1896 the building was leased to the Ogden city school system. The New West Educational Commission also maintained schools in Hooper, Lynne, and South Weber. A second Congregational church group was organized in 1884 at Lynne (Five Points) and remained in operation until 1918.

Presbyterian worship in Ogden began in 1878 under the direction of the Reverend G. W. Gallagher. At the first meeting, twenty persons were received into membership and three elders were elected. During the 1880s services were held in a building at Lincoln and 24th Street, and by 1906 a new building was completed on the corner of 24th and Adams at a cost of $30,000. The Rev. John Edward Carver served as pastor of Ogden's Presbyterian Church for more than three decades, beginning as pastor in 1900, and he also served as chair of the Ogden Carnegie Free Library Board for twenty-nine years. The Central Park Presbyterian Mission was organized with a membership of sixty-two on 11 January 1890 by F. W. Hastings and Charles May in the public school building on 29th Street.

The Reverend Dwight Spencer was Ogden's first Baptist minister and he attended the organizational meeting which was held on 22 May 1881 with thirteen members in attendance in the Odd Fellow's Hall. A church was built at Grant Avenue and 25th Street for $10,000 to accommodate the growing congregation. Early Baptist baptisms were performed in the Weber River. In 1915 the membership of the Baptist church in Ogden was 350 people, and a new church building was constructed for the congregation at 2519 Jefferson in 1925. A Baptist mission church was organized in 1883, with the first services being held on Wilson Lane in Weber County. This church remained in operation until 1905.

The African Methodist Episcopal Church was organized on 20 May 1908 with J.C. Owens as presiding elder. The first meetings were convened in a store building on Washington Boulevard. The Embry Chapel at 2817 Pingree Avenue was constructed and dedicated in 1913. B. F. McCully served as the first pastor of the church from 1910 to 1912; J. H. Brown was the second pastor, serving from 1913 to 1914. In 1916 the Wall Avenue Baptist Church was organized, with its membership consisting primarily of African-Americans. A chapel which seated about 100 people was dedicated for this congregation in 1919; it was located at 1701 Wall Avenue. A. J. Billingsly served from 1917 to 1919 as the first pastor of the Wall Avenue church, and he was followed by J.L. Marque from 1919 to 1920.

Other denominations founded congregations in the area during the latter part of the nineteenth and early part of the twentieth century including the Spiritualists (1874), the Salvation Army (1887), the Church of the Nazarene (1924), and the Pentecostal Lighthouse group (1931). The Jehovah's Witnesses organization was formed in Ogden in 1909, with the first services being held in the homes of members of the International Bible Society until a small store building was obtained at 2701 Lincoln Avenue. In 1929 the name of the national organization was changed to Jehovah's Witness, and J.T.M. Kingsford was the director of this group in the Weber County area during the first two decades of its existence.

During 1888 Lutheran services were held at the home of Mrs. Hannah Lund at Five Points, and in October of that year Frans August Linder organized the Elim Lutheran Church in Weber County. In 1889 a building lot was purchased at 575 23rd Street and a frame structure with gothic-type windows was constructed on the property and dedicated in January 1890. The Elim Lutheran Church was authorized under the sanction of the Evangelical Lutheran Augustana Synod of North America, and the Reverend Frans August Linder served as clergyman from 1888 to 1891.

Christian Science missionaries organized the First Church of Christ, Scientist, of Ogden in 1892; regular services were begun during 1895, at which time the church had eighteen members. A Christian Science church building was constructed during 1914–15 on the northwest corner of Monroe Avenue and 24th Street at a cost of $15,000.

The Jewish congregation Brith Sholem began in 1890 as Ohab Sholem in Ben Oppman's clothing store at 352 25th Street, with Sam Rosenbluth as president. Charter members of Brith Sholem included D. Kraines, J. Kraines, J. Benovitz, W. Benovitz, and Ben Oppman. In 1921 a red brick synagogue with an oval roof was erected at 2756 Grant Avenue. By April 1939 the congregation had increased to twenty members.

A branch of the Greek Orthodox Holy Trinity Church was organized in Ogden in 1905 by Parthenios Lemberopulos, a priest of the Salt Lake City church. Meetings were held in the Church of the Good Shepherd from 1905 until 1936.

Japanese residents organized the Ogden Buddhist Temple in 1913; and early church meetings were held at 236 24th Street, at 2430 Lincoln, and at 225 Capitol until 1937. In May 1937 a Buddhist temple building at 2456 Lincoln began to be used. C. Kiwahara served from 1913 to 1916 as the first Buddhist priest, and he was followed by Manzoe Ishimuri, who served from 1916 to 1920.

The Weber Stake of the Church of Jesus Christ of Latter-day Saints was organized on 26 January 1851, and at that time the Latter-day Saints located on the old Goodyear claim were organized into two wards—the Ogden North Ward (centered on Farr's Fort), with Erastus Bingham as bishop, and the Ogden South Ward (centered on Brown's Fort, the old Fort Buenaventura), with Isaac Clark as bishop. As Weber County was organized and as its boundaries changed, these boundaries in general became the boundaries for the ecclesiastical organization called the Weber Stake. The stake had expanded to twenty-six wards by 1908 when it was divided into three stakes. Weber Stake presidents and the time periods that they served included Lorin Farr (1851–1870), Franklin D. Richards (1870–1877), David H. Peery (1877–1883), Lewis Warren Shurtleff (1883–1922), and George Browning (1922–1930). Presiding bishops who served only in Weber County were Chauncey W. West (1855–1870) and Lester J. Herrick (1870–1875).

A major event in the history of religion in Weber County was the Mormon Reformation of 1856 and 1857. This religious movement was begun by the forceful preaching of Jedediah M. Grant, a counselor in the Mormon First Presidency, and was followed up in local areas with speeches and calls to repentance. In order to make efforts to ensure widespread repentance, church members were visited by male members who had been designated to query each member with a score of probing questions which underlined church activity and faithfulness. Luman Shurtleff was one of the special missionaries called to present this catechism to Mormon church members in the Weber area. Shurtleff noted that the work for him and his colleagues included asking each member the questions from the catechism, after which each was to confess sins related to the questions asked; then members were to be rebaptized in renewal of their covenants and in reaffirmation of their religious commitments. Shurtleff recorded in his diary in February 1857 his commitments to the Reformation:

> This is Sunday the twenty second the last week I catechised nine persons and attended several meetings which finished the catechiseing of all the district alloted to me to catechise in all two hundred persons or a little over. . . . This is March 22 since the 22nd of last month we have attended 18 publick meetings rebaptized confirmed 87 persons married one couple and past my fiftieth birthday thankfull to God that I enjoy good health.
>
> 1. Have you committed murder by shedding inosent blood or consenting thereunto?
> 2. Have you betraid your brethren or sisters in anything?
> 3. Have you committed adultery by haveing any connection with any woman that was not your wife or a man that was not your husband?
> 4. Have you taken or made use of property not your own without the consent of the owner?
> 5. Have you cut hay whare you had no right to or turned your animals into another persons grain or field without his knowledge or consent?
> 6. Have you lied about or malissiously misrepresented any person or thing?
> 7. Have you borrowed anything that you have not returned or paid for?
> 8. Have you borne false witness against your neighbor?
> 9. Have you taken the name of the Deity in vain?
> 10. Have you coveted anything not your own?
> 11. Have you been intoxicated with strong drink?
> 12. Have you found lost property and not returned it to the owner or used all diligence to do so?
> 13. Have you branded an animal that you did not know to be your own?
> 14. Have you taken anothers horse or mule from the range and rode it without the owners consent?
> 15. Have you fulfilled your promises in paying your debts or run into debts without the propects of paying?
> 16. Have you taken water to irrigate with when it belong to another persons at the time you used it?
> 17. Do you pay your tithing promptly?

18. Do you teach your family the gospel of salvation?

19. Do you speak against your brethren or against any principle taught us in the Book of Mormon bible book of Doctrine and Covenants Revelations given through Joseph Smith the Prophet and the Presidency of the Church as now organized?

20. Do you pray in your family night and morning and attend to secret prair?

21. Do you wash your boddies and have your family do so as ofton as helth and clenliness requires and circumstances will permit?

22. Do you labor six days and rest or go to the House of Worship on the seventh?

23. Do you and your family attend ward meetings?

24. Do you preside over your household as a servant of God and is your family subject to you?

25. Have you labored diligently and earned faithfully the wages paid you by your employers?

26. Do you oppress the hireling in his wages?

27. Have you taken up and converted any stray animal to your own use or in any manner appropriated one to your benefit without accounting theirfor to the proper authorities?[7]

In 1855 construction for a tabernacle was begun in Ogden to house large religious meetings for the Church of Jesus Christ of Latter-day Saints. The building was completed and dedicated on 10 October 1869; it was located on the southeast corner of Tabernacle Square at Washington Boulevard and 22nd Street. This original tabernacle was constructed in part of pine lumber which was initially cut in Ogden and Strong's canyons and then sawed at Farr's Mill. The two-foot-thick walls were constructed of adobes which were manufactured in Weber County. The roof arches of the building were fastened together with wooden pegs.[8] The completed building had a seating capacity of 1,200. By 1896, after two and a half decades of use, it was decided to remodel the original tabernacle. Funds for the remodeling were acquired in part from large county fairs. The newly remodeled tabernacle was much more ornate in appearance with its somewhat Moorish design resembling the design of Saltair Resort. It included a choir loft and electric lights, and it would be the central meeting place for large Mormon services for the next half-century.

In 1856 the city of Ogden was divided into four LDS church units—the Ogden 1st, 2nd, 3rd, and 4th wards—and only one other Ogden ward was organized over the next half-century. Robert McQuarrie was bishop of the Ogden Second Ward for forty years (1877–1917). Huntsville, which was settled in 1860, became the main Mormon meeting place in Ogden Valley from 1860 until 1877. Huntsville had a population of 1,051 in 1870, and by 1900 had a population of only 1,022. Francis Hammond was the first bishop of the Huntsville Ward, serving from 1877 to 1885, and he was succeeded by David McKay from 1885 to 1905. From 1905 to 1932 a small new ward was established east of Huntsville; it was named the Middleton Ward in honor of Charles Middleton, and for a time church meetings were held in the old Middleton schoolhouse.

Although Eden was first settled in 1859 and the first schoolhouse was built in 1866, Eden Mormons were part of the Huntsville Ward until 1877 when the Eden Ward was organized with Josiah M. Ferrin as bishop. As late as 1930 there were about 300 people in Eden. The Liberty Ward was organized in Ogden Valley in 1892 with Joshua B. Judkins as bishop. The original Liberty Ward chapel was built of brick in 1910 at a cost of $4,000.

The Uintah and South Weber wards were organized in the lower Weber River Valley near the river's exit from the Wasatch Mountains. The Uintah area was also known as East Weber, Easton, and Deseret, while the South Weber area centered on Kington Fort, where the Morrisite "War" occurred in 1862. The South Weber Ward was located south of the Weber River in Davis County, and the ward was for a while tied to the Mormon Davis Stake; but, in 1904, because most of the residents of the area were oriented economically to Weber County, the ward became part of the Weber Stake. Abiah Wadsworth was the first Uintah bishop (1852–1858) and he was followed by Jefferson Osborne (1858–1861). Church meetings in Uintah were held in the homes of the members until 1855, when an adobe building was built which served as a schoolhouse, meeting place, and dance hall. In 1874 the adobe building was replaced by a frame building constructed on the same site. Thomas Kington, who served from 1853 to 1857, was the first South Weber bishop; Richard Cook, who served from 1857 to 1860, was the second; and Philo Allen served as presiding elder from 1860 to 1865. In 1861 Richard Cook and fifteen other members of the South Weber Ward were excommunicated from the Mormon church for following Mormon dissenter Joseph Morris and his teachings. A log schoolhouse had been built in South Weber in 1854 and Cyrus Canfield and Sarah Woodruff, a plural wife of Wilford Woodruff, were the first teachers. In 1859, with the opening of a new adobe school in South Weber, the Farmington brass band celebrated its opening by playing at the settlement.

The Morrisite episode along the Weber River in South Weber was a chapter in the history of the area which was not soon forgotten, both because of the doctrines Morris preached and because of the violence which accompanied the demise of the new sect. Morris was born near Chester, England, in 1824 and converted to Mormonism in 1848. He traveled to the United States in 1848 and worked in the East until 1853 when he and his wife journeyed to Utah. Over the next several years, Morris became increasingly disenchanted with the teachings and leadership of Brigham Young and wrote Young several letters to express this dissatisfaction and to announce that he (Morris) should become the leader of the church. In the spring of 1860, Morris moved to Slaterville and began to openly proselyte potential converts to his doctrines. Initially he had some success, but by the fall of 1860 he began to have great success in advocating his teachings in the community of South Weber. By February 1861 Morris had produced more than forty written revelations. The central theme of his religious teachings was the immediacy of the Second coming of Jesus Christ and the Millennium and the necessity for believers to live communalism and dedicate their property and their goods to the movement. By 1862 Morris had produced several hundred revelations.

On 10 February 1861 Mormon apostles Wilford Woodruff and John Taylor traveled to Ogden, where they ordained the first Weber Stake High Council. Brigham Young had chosen six of the men and Lorin Farr, the stake president, had chosen the other six. The next day, 11 February, Woodruff and Taylor traveled by sleigh driven by Bishop Chauncey West to South Weber to investigate the situation surrounding Joseph Morris and his followers. The meeting at Kington Fort in South Weber was confrontational in nature between the followers of Brigham Young and the followers of Joseph Morris, as Woodruff detailed in his diary. Morris was not at the initial meeting; but, after some discussion, Woodruff noted, "We then sent for there fals [*sic*] Prophet & Called upon him to speak." Morris spoke for about thirty minutes. His remarks were summarized by Woodruff: "He said Brigham Young was not a prophet & Joseph smith did not hold the Keys of the Priesthood & was ordained of man while He Joseph Morris was ordained of the Father, & Held six times more keys of the Priesthood than Joseph did. He said he was the seventh Angel . . . "[9]

The meeting continued, with Woodruff, Taylor, and Chauncey West speaking. At the conclusion of the meeting, sixteen of Morris's followers at South Weber were excommunicated from the Mormon church.[10] Philo Allen was placed in charge of the South Weber Branch and, as the meeting concluded, it was stressed that the branch was placed under the supervision of the Ogden area and the Weber Stake, whose president was Lorin Farr.

The confrontational meeting between Woodruff, Taylor, and Morris did little to stop the growth of Morris's congregation. Converts to Morris's message continued to flock to South Weber and Kington Fort, which also became known as Morris Town and Weber Camp. By early 1862 it is estimated that there were about 500 members of the new church, with Morris as its prophet, and another 500 sympathizers. During 1861 conflicts concerning both theology and society grew between Morrisites and Mormons, and Morris continued to receive revelations confirming the immediacy of the return of Jesus Christ. By early 1862 incidents of dissension and violence had begun to mar the Morrisite camp and its relations with outsiders. Some who had joined the Morrisite movement began to question it and their own actions and also began to demand the return of their property. The dissenters were sometimes jailed at the settlement for protesting, but some escaped to report their lack of freedom.

On 24 May 1862 Morris was delivered a writ which ordered him to surrender himself to answer complaints by former commune members at the Morrisite fort that they had been held against their will and that their property was also being kept from them. Territorial judge John Kinney issued the writ on the testimony of William Jones,

John Jensen, and Lars Geertson. Morris ignored that writ as well as a second, which cited him for contempt of court.

On 13 June 1862, 500 men who were considered members of the Utah Territorial Militia, under the direction of colonel of the militia and territorial deputy marshal Robert T. Burton, surrounded the Morrisite fort and demanded the surrender of the camp. A contingent of the Weber County Militia took positions on the north bluffs of the river, while the main militia force occupied the south bluffs. Shots were first fired from the militia and then from the Morrisite camp, and several Morrisites were killed in the ensuing battle. Two of those killed were women, and Mary Christofferson, a sixteen-year-old girl, was horribly wounded when a cannon ball struck her head, knocking away part of her face and jaw. After a two-day battle, the marshal entered the fort on 15 June to arrest Joseph Morris. A struggle ensued in which Joseph Morris and John Banks, one of his chief associates, were killed. A score of the Morrisite men who were captured were charged with murder in the deaths of some of the territorial militia members and were found guilty in district court. Utah territorial governor Stephen Harding pardoned these men, and the Morrisite movement began to gradually fade away. When General Patrick E. Connor established a military post at Soda Springs, Idaho, in May 1863, he offered Morrisite families free transportation to that area; about eighty families responded to his invitation. A few Morrisites remained in South Weber and were later buried in the town cemetery. The casualties of the Morrisite War included not only the dead (six Morrisites—two men and four women—and two militia men) but those displaced from their homes and property. Bitterness continued after the confrontation.

North Ogden was organized as a separate branch of the Weber Stake in 1852, with Thomas Dunn as the presiding elder. Dunn was a veteran of the Mormon Battalion and was ordained a bishop in 1853 by Brigham Young when North Ogden became an independent ward. During the Reformation of 1856–57, eighty-three of the members of the North Ogden Ward were rebaptized in a renewal of their earlier baptismal covenants.[11] The Pleasant View Ward was organized in 1882 as the area north of Ogden grew and developed; Edward W. Wade became the first Pleasant View bishop.

Plain City, which was settled in 1859 largely by Mormon settlers from Lehi, began its ecclesiastical history at the time of settlement. William W. Raymond was initially in charge of the Plain City Branch of the Mormon church and served from 1859 to 1863. John Carver was the presiding elder from 1863 to 1870; he was followed by Lewis W. Shurtliff, who served from 1870 to 1877.

After a little more than a decade of settlement, Edwin Dix, Jonathan Moyes, and George Musgrove organized a branch of the Godbeites in Plain City in 1871. A number of people in Plain City joined this group, and later that same year many of them became affiliated with the Reorganized Church of Jesus Christ of Latter Day Saints.[12] Thomas Robinson was the leader of the Reorganized church in Plain City for a short time before the church was disbanded. Many of the members of the earlier Godbeite movement in Plain City became involved in spiritualism. The religious dissension in the Mormon congregation in Plain City must have appeared to close observers that a religious opportunity was now available to those who wished to draw dissenters and other Mormons away from the Mormon church. The Reorganized LDS church and the clergy from the Episcopal church began to take immediate advantage of the situation. St. Paul's Episcopal Church in Plain City was organized in 1873 by the Rev. J. L. Gillogly from Ogden and Bishop Daniel S. Tuttle from Salt Lake City. The initial Episcopal services were held in homes in Plain City, and by 1877 St. Paul's Episcopal Church, built of red brick in English style, was completed.

Religious services were held in Warren during its early years of settlement early in the 1870s. Most of the settlers were Mormons, and LDS church services were held in homes until 1884 when a brick schoolhouse was built which provided a place for both school and church meetings. Christopher Folkman was appointed the first branch president. On 7 June 1896 a Mormon ward was organized and named Warren in honor of local stake president Lewis Warren Shurtliff.

The early Hooper settlement was also known as Muskrat Springs, and in 1869 Gilbert Belnap became the presiding Mormon elder in the area. An adobe schoolhouse was completed in 1871 and was used for both school and religious meetings. Edwin Parker, the first choir leader, made a tuning fork out of hard wood.

During the 1870s Mormon residents of Kanesville settled that area and attended church services in Hooper. The Kanesville LDS Ward was organized in 1886; Peter B. Peterson was appointed bishop and remained such for the next twenty-two years. The west area of Weber County was organized into a Mormon branch in 1859 with William McFarland as the presiding elder. Wilson became a separate Mormon ecclesiastical unit in 1877 as a branch of the West Weber Ward and by 1882 was organized as the Wilson Ward with Brigham H. Bingham as bishop.

A Mormon branch was organized in Harrisville in 1863 with Luman A. Shurtleff as the branch president; fourteen years later, in 1877, Harrisville was organized into a ward, with Pleasant Green Taylor appointed as bishop. The community of Farr West was created in 1890; it originally was a part of Harrisville. In that same year, William A. Taylor became the bishop of the Farr West Mormon Ward. Mormon settlers in Marriott were organized into a branch in 1856, with John Marriott appointed as presiding elder. Slaterville, which was named after Richard Slater, an early settler, was organized into a Mormon branch in 1856 when Thomas Richardson was made the presiding authority.

Riverdale was settled during the 1850s and Mormon church services began to be held in private homes during that decade, initially under the direction of Adam Fife. The Roy Ward of the Mormon church was organized in 1899 when it was separated from the Kanesville Ward. Thomas Hollands was appointed the first bishop of the Mormon ward in Roy.

## *Polygamy*

Nineteenth-century Mormons, much like seventeenth-century Puritans, looked upon themselves as "God's chosen people." Perhaps the most peculiar aspect of Mormon religious practice in nineteenth-century America was the practice of plural marriage, also called polygamy or celestial marriage. For many of the faithful, it was designated "The Principle." Polygamy was practiced in Weber County by Mormon settlers for more than half a century—from the beginnings of settlement into the first decade of the twentieth century. It appears that about 20 percent of adult Mormons were involved in the practice of plural marriage. About two-thirds of the men involved in polygamy had only two wives, and many of those who had more than two wives were Mormon church authorities.

Franklin D. Richards, Mormon apostle and Weber County probate judge, married his first two wives in Nauvoo, Illinois—Jane Snyder in 1842 and Elizabeth McFate in 1846. In 1849 Richards married Sarah Snyder, sister of wife Jane, and Charlotte Fox. Four years later, in 1853, following a mission to Great Britain, Richards married Susan S. Pierson; a year later, in 1854, he married Laura A. Snyder and then married Josephine de la Harpe in 1857. Franklin Richards's uncle Willard Richards died in 1854; and, in 1857, Franklin was married to four of Willard's widows by Brigham Young. These wives were Nancy Longstroth, Mary Thompson, Susannah Bayliss, and Rodah H. Foss. Richards eventually married eleven wives and had twenty-eight children.

In an 1880 interview, Jane Snyder Richards, Franklin's first wife, spoke with Hubert Howe Bancroft in San Francisco concerning her experiences in plural marriage. She reflected that a plural wife necessarily saw her husband less than would a woman living in a monogamous marriage, and that this allowed her to develop more independence. Though all his wives did not live in Ogden, Jane Richards's account suggests that her husband's plural wives (including two sisters and their niece) generally made an effort to get along with one another. She suggested that, on the whole, polygamy was not too dissimilar in many respects to the conventional monogamous form of marriage. The interview underlined the difficulties of plural marriage, and Jane noted that as time went on it was not such a trial to live plural marriage as she had initially feared.[13]

Ogden Mayor Lorin Farr (1820–1909) had six wives and thirty-four children. Farr was a resident of Weber County during the last six decades of his life, and he married most of his wives during the 1850s while he was living in Weber County and serving as Ogden's mayor. In 1845 he married Nancy Bailey Chase (born in 1823). In 1851 he married Sarah Giles (born in 1831), and in 1852 he married Olive Ann Jones (born in 1829). In 1854 Farr married Mary Bingham

Freeman Snow (born in 1820), and in 1857 he married Nicoline Erickson (born in 1837).

Luman Andros Shurtleff was an early resident of Ogden and Weber County who regularly recorded his daily activities in his diary. He was born in Massachusetts in 1807 and resided in Weber County from 1851 until his death in 1884. Shurtleff was first married in 1830 to Eunice Gaylord, and the couple had a family of eight children before Eunice died in 1845. The Shurtleffs had become Mormons in 1836; and, in 1845 following Eunice's death, Luman married her sister Altamira at Nauvoo. Together, Luman and Altamira had six children. In January 1848 at Winter Quarters, Nebraska, Luman became involved in plural marriage as he married Cynthia Noble Bent, the widow of Samuel Bent; and, at the same time, he married Melissa Adaline Noble, the daughter of Cynthia Noble Bent and Samuel Bent. At the time of their marriage, Luman was forty-one and Melissa was fifteen (Altamira was thirty-two). Luman and Melissa had eight children in the years from 1855 to 1874; the last of their children was born in 1874 when Luman was sixty-seven and Melissa was forty-one. Luman's last marriage came in 1854 to Mary Eliza Adams, who was seventeen. Luman and Mary had eleven children during the years from 1856 until 1873, and Mary was thirty-six years old at the birth of her last child.

In 1854 Luman and his four wives made their home at Bingham's Fort, and he began to note in his diary that Altamira was involved in dissension both against plural marriage and against her marriage to him. As Luman, Altamira, and other family members traveled from Weber County and attended the October 1856 LDS church general conference in Salt Lake City, they heard Brigham Young give all wives their liberty to leave their husbands if they wished. Luman noted in his diary that, although Altamira had been threatening to leave him, after hearing the sermon of Brigham Young, she changed her mind. Three years later he recorded that "she is feeble, cross and ugly" and gave him "much trouble." During the summer of 1860 their marriage ended in a divorce which was arranged and authorized by Bishop Chauncey West and Bishop Edward Bunker and agreed to by Lorin Farr.[14]

Plural marriage often was not easy for the participants, and federal laws enacted against the practice made it even more difficult. Although the 24th of July celebration was usually the most celebrated of the year in Utah, the Fourth of July was also celebrated as a holiday. Luman Shurtleff described the 4 July 1856 Ogden celebration:

> July 4 at sunrise a salute was fired the marshall and string bands marched through the main streets of the city playing their enlivening tunes to enliven and cheer up the Saints at 8 oclock the militia paraded and at ten marched to the bowery I in command of the company of Silvergrays consisting of forty rank and file here we spent about three hours under the flag of the United States wafted by a gentle breeze on the top of a pole seventy-fie feet in height after the constitution of the united States was read speeches recitations and many toasts presented we dismissed until three oclock then to meet for danceing singing &c and a sundown desmissed.[15]

Two decades later, on the same holiday celebrating the independence of the United States, Shurtleff was somewhat disaffected. He wrote, "July 4, 1876 I find my ardor somewhat cooled in celebrating the birthday of a nation which will not allow me the rites of a common citizen that is to worship God & keep his commandments."[16] This comment was, no doubt, in reaction to the anti-polygamy laws passed by the Congress of the United States beginning in 1862. Shurtleff and his families lived both in Ogden and at his farm in Harrisville.

Plural marriage was practiced by others in Weber County, including a number of residents of North Ogden. Alfred Randall married Margaret Harley as a second wife; Edward Davis Wade married Mary Ellen Page as a second wife; and Frederick Barker married Jane Barber and Elizabeth Thomas as additional wives. Cyrus H. Wheelock married three additional wives (Marion Dallen, Mary Ann Broomhead, and Desdemona Jemima Rose) in 1853. A number of North Ogden men who practiced plural marriage were jailed during the 1880s and early 1890s for what was termed in the newspapers and courts "UC" (unlawful cohabitation). Jail terms were usually six months and were often accompanied by a fine of from $100 to $300. Among those jailed were Amos Maycock, Abraham Chadwick, Fred W. Ellis, William F. Garner, Thomas Bennett Helm, Lorenzo Waldron, and Levi H. Wheeler. Jail terms were usually served in the territorial penitentiary, located in Sugar House near Salt Lake City. To avoid arrest, Mormon men who practiced polygamy often went "on the underground," which included hiding in the area of Weber County, moving to another area of Utah until law officers stopped looking for them, or going on an extended church mission.

Wilmer Wharton Bronson was a resident a Huntsville, where he was captain of the militia, justice of the peace, a member of the school board, and owned a 120-acre farm. Bronson's first wife died, leaving him with two daughters; and in 1867 he married a second wife, Lizzie, with whom he fathered nine children. In 1878 a Danish Mormon convert whose first name was Marian arrived in Huntsville, and Bronson courted her as a polygamous wife through an interpreter. He received Marian's consent to marry him and Lizzie's permission to have Marian become a polygamous member of their family. As Wilmer and Marian started down Ogden Canyon for the Endowment House in Salt Lake City where the marriage was to be performed, Lizzie decided she could not share her husband with another and sent a hastily scribbled note to the pair by a horseback rider. The note read, "If you go through with this, I'll burn the house down." Wilmer read the note and deliberated, then handed the note back to the rider and said, "Tell her to fire away." Wilmer and Marian drove on. Lizzie did not fire the house; but emotions often ran deep and strong during plural marriages. Some couples involved in plural marriage had very good relationships; others had many difficulties. One second wife reported that she could not even peel potatoes to suit the first wife.[17]

A number of men in the Ogden Valley were arrested by federal marshals on a charge of unlawful cohabitation during the 1880s including Soren L. Petersen, Peter Andersen, Niels Mortensen, Albert G. Slater, Knute Emmertsen, Andrew E. Berlin, Christian Peterson, Lars Nielsen, Jens Frandsen, Jens Peterson, Jens P. C. Winter, Gustave A. Stromberg, and Andrew H. Anderson. Jail terms for those convicted were usually six months in the Utah penitentiary.

Charles F. Middleton was born in 1834 and lived in Weber County from 1850 until his death in 1915. During much of his life in Weber County, Middleton kept a diary which recounted his life and experiences including being a captain in the Nauvoo Legion, a policeman and constable in Ogden, a justice of the peace, an alderman in Ogden, a school board member, and a tax collector. Middleton also served as a counselor in the LDS Weber Stake presidency for thirty-eight years. He married Martha Caressa Browning in 1854 and they set up housekeeping in a granary shed until they could build a home. In 1865 Charles married Martha's younger sister Melinda Vastia Browning in plural marriage. In 1877 Charles served as a Mormon missionary in Illinois and wrote to his wives on one occasion chiding them for not writing to him. From 1865 until 1883 Charles and his two wives lived together in their common home located on 6th and Main streets in Ogden. In 1883 Charles completed a separate dwelling for his second wife and family. In large measure, the separation of his families came as a measure to avoid federal law officers.

In 1879 George Reynolds had become the first Mormon jailed for the practice of plural marriage. To strengthen the federal assault on Mormon plural marriage, the Edmunds Act of 1882 and the Edmunds-Tucker Act of 1887 were passed. These acts put teeth into the anti-polygamy movement, with provisions for fines and confiscation of property as well as imprisonment. Between 1884 and 1893 there were more than a thousand convictions in Utah Territory for unlawful cohabitation under these laws. The Edmunds Act specified that men practicing plural marriage could not vote or hold political office. These laws and their enforcement began to have a decided impact on politics in Ogden and Weber County as well as on county social life. With the passage of the Edmunds Act, those members of the Ogden City Council and Weber County Court (similar to the county commission) who were living plural marriage resigned; they included Ogden mayor Lester J. Herrick and alderman Charles Middleton.

Charles Middleton noted in his diary that on 14 May 1885 Joseph Taylor was the first person arrested in the county by Marshal Vandercook for being married to more than one wife. Middleton was charged by a grand jury in July 1885 with unlawful cohabitation, and his trial took place during February 1886. Middleton was found not guilty on the charges because it appeared to both the judge and jury that soon after the passage of the Edmunds Act in 1882 he had separated his two families into two homes and had ceased living with his second wife. The acquittal of Middleton was the exception, not the rule. Many Mormon male polygamists were arrested, tried, and sent to jail or they went into hiding. For example, William W. Burton went into hiding to avoid prosecution, and Winslow Farr took his families to Mexico to avoid the law. City officials Francis A. Brown, Job Pingree, David M. Stuart, Nels C. Flygare, and Lester J. Herrick were all found guilty under terms of the Edmunds Act. Through the 1880s, much of what was considered normal life was disrupted for Mormon families practicing plural marriage.

### *Crime and Law Enforcement*

The first law enforcement officer in the county was B. W. Nolan, who was elected Ogden City marshal on 7 April 1851. The Weber County Sheriff's office had its beginnings in 1852 when probate judge Isaac Clark of the Weber County Court appointed R.W. Cummings to the office of county sheriff. The city marshal and the sheriff worked closely with the city and county courts to enforce the laws. In 1876 a county courthouse building was completed on 24th Street. This two-story building was constructed of brick and rested on a rock basement. A jail was eventually constructed in part of the basement. In 1895 the inmates of the jail set a fire which destroyed the interior and caused considerable damage to the tower and roof of the courthouse.

The early Ogden police force was organized somewhat like a quorum of the Mormon priesthood. When the police and guests gathered to celebrate the "Policeman's Ball" on 23 January 1860, they spent the evening in "praying, singing, recitations, preaching, and dancing." Charles Middleton became affiliated with the Ogden police, and he recounted the case of T.J. and H. H. Wilson, who were arrested for "steeling" horses in 1859 from an emigrant and then reselling the horses to the same man. They confessed their guilt and were fined twenty-five dollars each and were charged to pay the emigrant horse owner fifty dollars. H.H. Daulssamin and N. Coffin were arrested for stealing cattle. As their punishment, these culprits were sentenced by the court to be "sold to the highest biders [*sic*] for nine months hard labor."

The Ogden police were instructed among other things to try to curb the sale of whiskey, to clean the sidewalks, and to see that cattle did not roam at large through the streets during the night. Middleton arrested six men for "fast driving and loud hollowing in the streets," and, along with other policemen, he was on the look-out for drunkenness, profanity, fist-fighting, keeping cattle and horses out of the streets, and watching for liquor which was being imported from Salt Lake City. On 2 August 1868 Officer Thomas S. Doxey reported that there were "some lose [*sic*] women in our town that would bear watching."[18]

The coming of the railroad increased crime and violence in the county. In 1869 it was decided to have two policemen on the streets of Ogden every day, and the officers were expected to stay on duty until everyone was off the streets. It was noted that some parties lasted almost all night. Officers were to be paid three dollars a day. Police officers including Charles Middleton began to purchase revolvers, clubs, and handcuffs to assist them in their duties. On 29 April 1870 the county was thrown into considerable excitement with the news that a "Negro woman," Susan Jones, had been murdered by being struck on the head with a railroad coupling pin. Two men who were camped in a clump of thick brush near the Weber River were arrested for the murder. Nineteen-year-old Thomas Knapp from Wisconsin confessed to the murder; in his confession, Knapp recounted the events surrounding the killing, including stealing a trunk from Jones which the killers later found contained thirty-five cents. Other murders occurred; in August 1871 charges were brought against a Mrs. Harrison and two male friends for the poisoning of her husband, R. J. Harrison.

The areas of Ogden closest to the railroad station became known for violence, crime, gambling, prostitution, hotels, and saloons. Lower 25th Street became notorious as "Two Bit Street," and lower 24th Street was almost its equal for a time. For three-quarters of a century, Ogden's 25th Street was notorious for its saloons, opium dens, prostitution, gambling, and violence.

Late on Saturday evening, 19 April 1884, George Segal, a twenty-seven-year-old Japanese emigrant, shot Elizabeth Gudgell with a .38-caliber pistol. Gudgell was part owner of the Gem Restaurant on lower 24th Street, and it was at the restaurant that the shooting took place. Gudgell died about thirty-six hours after being shot with four bullets. Although the motive for the shooting was a bit unclear, it seems that it was in part a lover's quarrel as well as a dispute over back wages not paid. Following the shooting, Segal ran two or three blocks through Ogden streets before he was arrested by police officers Thomas H. Ballantyne and James M. Brown. They placed him in the city jail at 25th and Washington under the care of Moroni F. Brown, assistant jailer. About five hours after the shooting, at about 4 A.M. Sunday morning, policemen and jailers manning the jail saw an armed mob of thirty to forty masked and disguised men approaching the jail. Most of the mob had turned their coats inside out and many were masked to avoid giving away their identity. Several of the mob were armed with shotguns, and by armed force they gained entrance to the jail and sledgehammered and chiseled open Segal's cell door which was made of boiler iron. Segal was then dragged from his cell and hanged from the south end of the fire-bell tower. The entire mob action and hanging took no more than ten minutes. No indictments for this tragic incident were issued by a special fifteen-member grand jury which was asked by Judge P.H. Emerson to investigate the lynching. The lynching of George Segal and the murder of Lizzie Gudgell were clear evidence that Ogden and Weber County were participants in the major aspects of violence prevalent in the frontier era of the American West with its associated vigilante action. Civilized law and order hid its face during this "darkest hour" of Ogden's history.[19]

Gilbert R. Belnap was elected sheriff of Weber County in 1884 and served fourteen years in that position. As sheriff, he was involved in arresting a variety of criminals, including train robbers, gamblers, and other law-breakers. Belnap was paid eighty dollars a month and had to furnish and feed his own horse and supply his own equipment. One of his most famous arrests was that of Joseph Nay and E.K. Fisher, who had robbed a Denver and Rio Grande train in September 1889 and were captured in an Ogden pool hall. When they were captured, Belnap noted that they had enough "dynamite cartridges" on them to blow up the building.

Sheriff Belnap described one of his arrests in an Ogden newspaper:

> One time a dangerous gunman held up a saloon here and was suspected of having taken part in several Nevada train robberies. With his partner the outlaw rode off through Ogden Canyon up South Fork, through Beaver and over to Monte Cristo with myself and a deputy trailing them. On noticing one of the bandits just as he topped a ridge ahead, we separated and I got off my horse and walked on leading it. Pretty soon I came on a horse standing in a clump of brush and knew then that the rider who was one of the men I wanted was near. I had two guns with me, a .38 caliber and a .44 caliber, as I had to be prepared. The bandit had sworn to kill me on sight. Knowing that he must have me covered I walked on slowly, trying to figure out where the man was hidden. I took my .38 revolver and removed three shells, so that the hammer would strike three empty chambers in the cylinder before hitting a bullet. Then I shouted the man's name several times and asked him to surrender. He yelled back a curse and said that my time had come because he had the drop on me. So I agreed to give up and he walked out in the open never suspecting my ruse, keeping me covered with his rifle. I handed him my pistol and he laid down his rifle, and then commenced to pull the trigger, not knowing I had another gun on me. The hammer had fallen twice, and was raising for the fatal shot when I drew and ordered him to throw up his hands. Thinking the gun was empty he did so. I tied his hands with bailing wire and brought him back.[20]

It was rumored that Butch Cassidy spent some time in Ogden and rented rooms in the Broom Hotel and that in 1896 he and some of his men spent time along the Weber River bottoms calculating how they might break Matt Warner out of jail. Warner was being tried before Judge Rolapp and was eventually sentenced to five years in the state prison.

Robberies and violence of all kinds were problems for the Weber County sheriff and his men as well as for the Ogden City police department. In January 1911 a Southern Pacific train, the Overland Limited, was robbed at the Reese siding near the Great Salt Lake; the two bandits escaped by walking back into Ogden. Passengers were shot and pistol-whipped by the bandits, who took as much money and jewelry as they could find. The robbers also accosted several young people in Warren on their way back to Ogden before they disappeared from view and capture by the law.

On 30 April 1899 Ogden police captain William A. Brown was shot while assisting in the apprehension of two bandits who had committed a robbery near Willard. One of the bandits was shot in a gun battle that occurred near the Hot Springs, and Brown was then shot and killed by Abe Majors, who was also known as James Morgan. In the trial which took place in Brigham City during the middle of May, Majors was found guilty and sentenced to be executed on 7 July 1899 in Brigham City under the direction of the Box Elder County sheriff. Hundreds of people in Ogden and Weber County mourned the death of Captain Brown, and for the first days of May 1899 there were discussions and threats of a lynching. Brown and his wife, Hattie Lewis Brown, were the parents of five children. He had joined the police force on 22 February 1891 and had just been appointed captain on 9 April 1899. The position had just been created by the Ogden City Council, and it appears that Brown was the first captain to be appointed on the Ogden police force.

Ogden's reputation as a wide-open western town with a variety of unsavory activities on 25th Street spread throughout the West. Prostitution was prevalent in the area of 25th Street for eight decades—from the coming of the railroad through the era of World War II. One of the first to organize prostitution on the street was a woman who received the appellation "Gentile Kate." Bernard Devoto in his somewhat tongue-in-check description of early Ogden titled "Sin Comes to Ogden" suggested that, following the death of Brigham Young, Kate purchased his ornate carriage and traveled around Ogden in the conveyance, much to the chagrin of the Mormons of the town and county. Kate and her co-workers operated on 25th Street and in "Electric Alley," located between 25th and 24th streets. Kate was followed by "Belle London," who was known as the "Queen of Ogden's underworld." Belle's real name was Mrs. Dora B. Topham, and she was a most effective businesswoman on lower 25th street at the turn of the century. During 1908 Belle went into partnership with some Salt Lake City businessmen to open the "Stockade" in Salt Lake City, where prostitution would be legally regulated. During this period, Belle moved to Salt Lake to operate the stockade where "cribs" were rented to prostitutes for from one to four dollars a day. Each crib was about ten feet square, with a door and window in the front.[21] The cribs along "Electric Alley" in Ogden were of a similar design.

## *Immigrants*

Most of Weber County's residents prior to the arrival of the railroad had their family roots in the British Isles or in northern Europe. The railroad brought a diverse group of people with many different ethnic backgrounds—some came as immigrants and some as laborers. Many of the Chinese workers who had built the Central Pacific railroad stayed on to maintain that route. They established small communities in Corinne and in Ogden. Some moved to mining towns like Park City and Silver Reef. In 1880 Ogden had thirty-three Chinese residents, and by 1890 this figure had grown to 106. This was an era of intense anti-Chinese and anti-Asian prejudice, and the local Chinese usually established themselves in the near vicinity of the railroad station. Many of the early laundries in Ogden were established by former Chinese railroad workers including Ching Wah (at 2438 Grant), Hang Yei (at 2222 Grant), Saw Wah (at 271 25th Street), Sue Wah (at 123 25th Street), and Wong Lee (at 229 25th Street). Chinese laundry workers picked up and delivered laundry from private homes. The Sing Lung Store was an early Ogden Chinese grocery owned and operated by Wong Leung Ka.

The largely European community which formed Weber County looked on with wonder as the Chinese ate with chopsticks, used Chinese lanterns, and appeared to celebrate funerals in what appeared to be a party style, with a brass band and a parade leading to a grand funeral pyre which was burned, consuming the dead body and the associated gifts which accompanied the body. A number of Chinese restaurants were opened in the county, particularly along 25th Street. Early Chinese restaurants included the Senate, the Vienna, and the Bon Ton, where a full-course dinner could be obtained for twenty-five cents.

Many of the original Chinese immigrants came as single men to work on the railroad; but later, as Chinese women arrived and families were formed, the Chinese community developed more stability and branched out, particularly to the north of 25th Street. Lee Ben became the best known of the Chinese businessmen and was called the "King of the Chinamen." Among other businesses, Ben owned a gambling casino located on 25th Street. A number of Chinese people moved into the county and began to farm the land, usually raising crops like onions, peas, beets, carrots, squash, radishes, potatoes, and celery—all of which could be sold to other residents of the county as well as being used for subsistence. Leo and Joe were English names given to two Chinese workers who farmed in the Mound Fort area and along with other Chinese farmers like Leo Sun, Leo Lung, and Lee Wong sold their produce throughout the county.[22]

Before the arrival of the railroad, some Italians migrated to Ogden as Mormon converts. This population grew as other Italians came to seek work with the railroad. Greek workers began to arrive in the Ogden area near the turn of the century; many were single men seeking work and hoping to return home with a small fortune. In many cases, both single Italians and Greeks sent home for brides and began to establish themselves in new communities in America. A number of Mormon Scandinavian emigrants settled in Ogden Valley at Huntsville during the 1860s. They included Soren L. Petersen, Andreas P. Mortensen, Christian F. Schade, Peter C. Geertsen, Niels C. Mortensen, and Thomas Lund.

African-Americans also began to settle in Ogden with the arrival of the railroad. Some worked as laborers, but many came as porters, waiters, and cooks. As Ogden's black community developed, most of the black families were segregated into an area near the railroad depot. From the beginning, blacks as well as other minorities experienced discrimination and segregation in all aspects of life.

The first Japanese visitors to come to Utah arrived in 1872 on the railroad and visited Ogden and other areas in northern Utah as well as in the western United States. By the 1880s, a decade later, Japanese laborers arrived to work on western railroads and in mines. By the turn of the century, many Japanese laborers began to turn to farming to make a living, and the Japanese had farms in Box Elder, Weber, and Salt Lake counties. The major employer for Japanese labor by the turn of the century continued to be the railroads. A superintendent was quoted in the Railroad Notes column of the Ogden *Standard* in

July 1900 as noting, "A number of Japanese are being employed because contractors can't depend on white men although they prefer to employ white labor."[23]

Jewish immigrants to Utah and the West often arrived in Ogden before venturing to other areas of the state and the region. Many Jewish immigrants stayed in Ogden for a time to look at business opportunities before moving on. Some of the first Jewish men to settle in Weber County include Ben Oppman, Sam Rosenbluth, D. and J. Kraines, J. and W. Benowitz, Samuel Kline, Hyman Lewis, L. Siegel, and H. L. White. Frederick J. Kiesel was perhaps the most prominent Jewish early settler of the area. Kiesel was born in Germany in 1841 and arrived in Utah in 1863 after serving a short time as a teamster in the Confederate Army. Kiesel was a particularly successful merchant in both Corinne and Ogden before settling permanently in Ogden. The Fred J. Kiesel Company was a wholesale and retail grocery business which operated from its headquarters in Ogden throughout northern Utah and southern Idaho. Kiesel was in partnership with Gumpert Goldberg in the grocery business in both Corinne and Ogden for nearly a decade before Goldberg died in 1881. Goldberg, who was born in Germany in 1832, and his wife, Helena Morris, had met in Colorado and were married. They traveled to Montana during the 1860s, where he established himself in business and where the town of "Last Chance Gulch" took Helena's name as its own in 1868. After living in Corinne for a short time, the Goldbergs moved to Ogden. M. Isadore Marks, who was born in Germany in 1845, established a clothing business in Ogden in 1876. In 1881 Marks took Louis Goldsmith as a partner, and the new name of their clothing business was Marks, Goldsmith & Company. Goldsmith was born in Bavaria. The Kuhn brothers, Adam and Abraham, were born in Germany; they opened a clothing and dry goods store in Corinne in 1869. By 1880 they had moved the headquarters of their business to Ogden.

### *Lifestyles and Culture*

Early entertainment in Weber County began with celebrations like Pioneer Day (24 July) and Christmas Day. The 1856 Pioneer Day Celebration included a parade and the presentation of *Luke the*

*Laborer* by the Ogden City Dramatic Association under the direction of W. Poulter. By 1861 plays were presented in Chauncey West's barn located at 2375 Washington Boulevard. Lorenzo Hadley remembered that during the 1860s the Ogden City Dramatic Association put on plays such as *Ten Nights in a Barroom* and *The Prosecuted Dutchman* and that the association had a "collapsible stage" which was transported in a wagon to various parts of the county where the plays were performed.[24] The Ogden Brass Band was involved in theater productions. In 1864 Shakespeare was performed in Ogden by the traveling professional actor George Pauncefort, who was described as being "plump, round-faced, and eccentric."

The railroad began to bring a wide variety of performers to Weber County. Dan Costello's circus and menagerie arrived in Ogden on 4 July 1869, and the midget General Tom Thumb performed that year in the Ogden Tabernacle on 15 July. Phil Margetts, a well-known Salt Lake City comedian, visited Ogden in March 1870 with his company of performers; they appeared at Woodmansee's Hall, where the admission was seventy-five cents for reserved seats and fifty cents for back seats. Halls like Woodmansee's and Jennings in Ogden and another in North Ogden which were used for performances, dances, bazaars, and parties had a major workday function housing mercantile goods and other kinds of economic pursuits.

Dancing was an activity which accompanied many social events, and most dances were either square dances or line dances. Square dances included the quadrille or cotillion, while, in the line dances and reels, the men and women lined up in parallel lines and danced. Round dances (especially the waltz) which arrived in the United States during the second quarter of the nineteenth century initially were not well received. Waltzing all around the hall was looked upon by many in the nation as being vulgar, and Brigham Young was quoted, "With regard to round dances, he was opposed to them, from beginning to end, from top to bottom. Round dances were first commenced in and still continue brothel-house dances."[25]

During the last two decades of the nineteenth century, the waltz and the two-step gradually became more acceptable—first among the young people and then gradually among most of the other members of Utah society. The price of admission to dances was often paid in produce, including wood, vegetables, molasses, wheat, and beans. Dances provided opportunities for socializing among married couples and for dating and courting among those who were not married. Dances were sponsored by churches and social organizations as well as being held at commercial dancing sites including Glenwood Park, where dancing "on new hardwood floors" was advertised, and Utahna Park on 25th Street and Washington Boulevard, which was advertised as "strictly a Temperance Resort."[26]

Music for dances might be provided by several persons or by only one with a violin. Marinda Allen Ingles, a resident of Huntsville for part of her life, remembered an experience related to dancing:

> One time all the boys and girls were going to a dance and I vowed I would have a pair of hoops for my skirt if I had to go without shoes the next winter. My father, after much coaxing, bought me a pair and everything went well until that evening when we were on our way to the dance. Something went wrong with the bridle on the horse and father called back to my young man to get out of the wagon and fix it. Then as he went to step out of the wagon he caught his foot in my hoops and fell out of the wagon on his head. The girls tried to get me to go back home and fix my skirt, but I refused. I was dead set on going to that dance. Well, when we arrived at the dance, all the girls formed a circle around me and I tugged and pulled at my hoops until I got them straightened. But my escort was suffering with such a bad headache from his tumble that he didn't feel much like dancing.[27]

Residents of small communities in Weber County as well as those who lived in Ogden enjoyed a variety of community activities including hay rides, parades, picnics, swimming parties in either of the rivers or the Great Salt Lake, candy pulls, sleigh rides, competitive hunting parties, ice skating, family reunions, baseball games, county fairs, and community singing. Riding in carriages, wagons, automobiles, streetcars, and trains was not only a way of getting from one place to another but also was looked upon as a form of enjoyment. Traveling circuses also provided entertainment for Weber County residents, and all of the communities of the county usually had their own July 24th celebration. The fall harvest was celebrated throughout the county with a variety of activities including a county fair where prize animals and home creations could be displayed and awarded a prize.

The railroad continued to bring new and exciting forms of entertainment to Weber County, particularly to theaters in Ogden. Some of these entertainments included Japanese acrobats and jugglers, the Overland Minstrels, Hermann the Illusionist, the United Mastodon Minstrels, Professor Willie and His All Star Specialty Group, Buffalo Bill and his traveling company, the Conley-Barton Company, Man Fish and Water Queen, who "ate, drank, smoked, sewed, knit, and slept under water," and Anthony and Ellis's Uncle Tom's Cabin Company. As many as thirty traveling companies a year made one or more performances in Ogden during the 1880s. Weber County actors, sometimes with assistance from outside actors, put on such plays as *Uncle Tom's Cabin, The Married Rake, Seven Clerks and Three Thieves, My Wife's Friend, Ben Bolt, Nobbs Will Turn Him Out, Lost in London, Rip Van Winkle, Fanchon the Cricket, Husband to Order,* and *We All Have Our Little Faults.*

Salt Lake dramatic companies often traveled to Ogden to put on their plays or to collaborate with Weber County actors. Although many of the plays and events took place in Ogden, the audiences were made up of residents from throughout Weber County. Sometimes there could be minor trouble. In 1873, during the intermission of a performance by a traveling company, the *Ogden Junction* noted than an "altercation ensued between some boys from Riverdale and the doorkeeper.[28] A year later a performance of *Pizarro* by the Ogden Dramatic Company with music by the Ogden Tabernacle Choir was disturbed by the "hoodlum element." Ogden and Weber County players and the Weber County Old Folks often sang and/or acted at benefits for needy causes such as aiding the victims of the Chicago fire or supporting the Free Library and Reading Room or the Ladies' Centennial Fund.

In July 1879 the Union Opera House was opened in Ogden in what was originally the Union Hall, located on the south side of 24th Street between Kiesel and Grant avenues. The new house seated 600, with additional seating for fifteen in the orchestra area, and it was located on the second floor of the Union Building. It was lit with gas after its first years, and after the building was torn down it was replaced by the Berthana Dance Hall. Visiting companies and local players both enjoyed performing in the new theater.

Amateur theater enjoyed very good success in Weber County during the 1880s. On 8 May 1880 the students of the Sacred Heart Academy put on the one-act operetta, *The Twin Sisters*, which played to a packed house at the Union Opera House. Mormon children in the Primary organization as well as teenagers in the Mutual Improvement Associations also began to act in and present plays throughout the county. Mormon adults also participated in theatrical productions which played to local audiences. The Ogden Fourth Ward schoolhouse was the site for the presentation of *Ireland As It Is* in December 1880, and the Ogden Third Ward actors put on *Once Upon A Time* in December 1881. The Fourth Ward Brass Band assisted with the productions of *All That Glitters Is Not Gold* and *The Plague of My Life* in 1882. In March 1882 students and teachers of the Central School presented scenes from *Hamlet*. The Ogden Second Ward players presented their theatricals in the Firemen's Hall. The Episcopal Ladies' Aid Society gave performances, including *The Box and Cox* in 1884. The Ogden Dramatic and Musical Society was formed by non-Mormon actors and musicians. In 1885 the production of *Blow for Blow* by the Third Ward Dramatic Association was assisted by Ole Berkoel's orchestra and toured many of the "settlements." The Weber Comedy Company, made up of Weber County residents, also toured the various towns of the county giving performances.

After two or three years of the successful operation of the Union Opera House, Woodmansee's Theater, which had served Ogden's cultural life well, was remodeled into a grocery store. Ogden was also served by two smaller theaters—the Lyceum Theater, which was a vaudeville theater, was located on 25th Street between Grant and Wall avenues, and the Novelty Theater, which was also located on lower 25th Street. By 1889 a number of prominent Ogden businessmen began to consider the need for a new theater in Ogden. Property was acquired on the east side of Washington Boulevard from Joseph Clark. Clark, Matthew Browning, John Browning, and David Eccles proposed to build an opera house for the city without other financial aid. Construction of the Grand Opera House, as it was called, began in June 1890 and was completed in late December. The building was modeled on the California Theatre in San Francisco, and the interior furnishings were estimated to cost about $25,000.[29] A striking feature of the Grand Opera House was the turret located in the center of the building which seemed to be "Moorish" in style. The opening of the building on 29 December 1890 received the attention not only of Utahns but also of visitors from Wyoming and Colorado. The stage was forty-two feet wide and seventy feet deep, and the auditorium seated 1,700 on the main floor and balcony. Emma Abbott, a noted grand opera performer, with her troupe of eighty-five performed on the opening evening for the Grand Opera House. Peter McCourt, who managed the Denver Tabor Grand Opera House, commented, "Ogden has the grandest Temple of the Muses in the West, with the exception of the Tabor Grand."[30]

The productions and the scenery at the new opera house allowed Weber County patrons to see some of the best theater of the day. The Grand Opera House became the site for performances of opera, plays, minstrel shows, vaudeville, and burlesque. In 1894 it was Lincoln J. Carter's *The Fast Mail Train* which included "Niagara Falls by moonlight, with furling mist, 14 freight cars, illuminated cabooses with practical working engine."[31] Neil Burgess and the *County Fair* included new scenery and "horses running three-fourths of a mile in full continuous view of the audience." *Uncle Tom's Cabin* was an ongoing favorite for Weber County audiences and included Shetland ponies, Egyptian donkeys, and real bloodhounds. A 1902 production of *Foggs' Ferry* included electrical effects, a torpedo explosion, and a steamboat scene; while another 1902 play, titled *The White Slave,* involved a rainstorm of real water and a shipwreck.

The greatest and most elaborate productions that appeared at the Grand Opera House included *The Palace of the King, Ben Hur,* and *The Heart of Chicago.* In May 1891 John L. Sullivan appeared in the opera house in a twenty-round exhibition prizefight. *The Heart of Chicago,* which opened in 1908, included a simulation of the great Chicago fire with a villain and a heroine so real that the "first two rows of the 'Grand' stood up and screamed in terror." Forty-six men were needed to prepare the stage for the 1908 performance of *Ben Hur* which featured a chariot race on the stage. A treadmill for the horses allowed them to run at full speed while the wheels of the chariot spun.

For nearly two decades following its grand opening, the Grand Opera House of Ogden provided the citizens of northern Utah culture and entertainment. Opera, drama, comedy teams, and one-person shows entertained hundreds. Edwin Booth, W.C. Fields, Maude May Babcock, William S. Hart, John Phillip Sousa, and Lillian Russell all appeared at the opera house, generally in the first decade of the twentieth century. In 1909 the Grand Opera House was remodeled and its name was changed to the Orpheum. The Orpheum Theater became part of the Orpheum Circuit and was devoted in large measure to vaudeville during the second decade of the twentieth century. Elephants and leopards appeared on the stage of the theater as well as musicians, magicians, singers, and speakers.

Local amateur theater declined in the 1890s, and although some local amateur performances appeared at the Grand Opera House, most acts there were by professional and traveling companies. In 1897 the movies were introduced when a motion picture was shown between the scenes of a play; two years later, in 1899, a motion picture shared the bill with an acting company. Even though theater changed in Ogden rather drastically after the completion of the Grand Opera House, theater in Weber County communities continued. In April 1896, for example, the elocution class of D.C. Johnson of Pleasant View presented the four-act play *The Creole* in Pleasant View.

During the first decade of the twentieth century, theaters in Ogden began to show moving pictures on a regular basis. Initially movies were shown as one of several acts, usually filling in between two or more live acts or following a baseball game and a dance at Glenwood Park. By the end of the decade, the movies had become sufficiently established and the quality had improved to the point that they became the major attraction rather than just one of many attractions. Live music for these silent movies was furnished by one or more musicians, usually a piano or organ player. The same small orchestras could provide music for both movies and vaudeville shows. Songs which were illustrated on the screen and sung by the audience accompanied many of the early movies. The Lyceum

Theater showed both movies and live theatrical productions. African-American patrons were forced to sit in the balcony in this and other Ogden theaters during the first several decades of the twentieth century.

Theaters began to be built specifically to show the new moving pictures; they included the Ogden Theater (1910), located on the northeast corner of 25th Street and Washington Boulevard; the Alhambra Theater (1915) at 2429 Kiesel Avenue; and the Egyptian Theater (1924) on Washington Boulevard. The Penny Arcade at 2406 Washington Boulevard became the Pastime Theatre when it started to present movies, including *The Great Train Robbery* in 1905. In 1912 the population of Ogden was 26,000 and there were twelve theaters which showed movies in the city. Prices ranged from five cents for children and ten cents for adults at the movie theaters to one dollar for operas and vaudeville presentations at the Orpheum.[32] The Alhambra showed movies and had live wrestling matches.

Ogden hosted Utah's first chautauqua, which was a traveling program of education and entertainment. People from all over the county would gather, often outdoors or in a large tent, to listen to lectures by celebrities, scholars, and world travelers. The first Weber County and Utah chautauqua was held in July 1911 on the Ogden River. This community effort included both observers and participants camping along the river in the vicinity of Lorin Farr Park. The multi-day event included lectures from "the men of the hour, the leading statesmen and orators," and also featured singers, pageants, and outdoor demonstrations. Speeches concerned religion, history, geography, and evolution; special attention was given to presentations on farming and agriculture. Junior chautauqua programs were organized for children. The first chautauqua was a great success, and Ogden became a regular stop on the annual chautauqua circuit. Lester Park at 25th Street and Jefferson Avenue was the site for many chautauquas.

### *Malan's Basin*

One of the unique places for residents and visitors to Weber County to visit was the Malan Heights Hotel. Beginning in 1892, Bartholomew "Tim" Malan and his family began to build a wagon road up Taylor's Canyon and then up a series of switchbacks on the south face of the canyon to Malan's Peak. Malan had purchased one and three-fourths sections of land from the Union Pacific Railroad, and the area became known as Malan Heights and included Malan's Peak and Malan's Basin. After reaching the dividing ridge between Taylor's Canyon and Waterfall Canyon, the road swung to the east and descended gradually into Malan's Basin.

The hotel was completed in 1894 in the heart of Malan's Basin and was surrounded by some small log cabins and a campground for tent camping. The hotel was in operation for twelve years, from 1894 to 1906, when it closed. A visitor could depart from the end of the 25th Street streetcar line at Iowa Avenue every summer morning at 8:15 A.M. and travel by wagon or carriage up the steep and scenic route to the basin. Cost of the round-trip ride was one dollar, and for an additional thirty-five to fifty cents the visitor could enjoy a meal at the hotel in the cool mountain air. The carriages and wagons which plied the mountain road were usually filled with hotel supplies, groceries, local residents, and visiting vacationers. Railroad guide books featured Malan's Hotel as an important sight to be seen. Views of the countryside from the peak or in ascending the road were extraordinary. The panoramic views of the valley and the Great Salt Lake were matched by the immediate views of the canyons and mountains. A sawmill was operated in the basin by the Malan family. Lumber from the mill was used to build buildings in the basin, and some of it was transported down the mountain road to be used for construction in Ogden.

The social and cultural life of Weber County had changed in a major fashion during the nineteenth century. Religion, recreation, politics, and the economy all had been transformed by both the times and the railroad.

## ENDNOTES

1. Mary Elfrida Farley Shaw, comp., "Elfrida Gay Barker Farley," in J. Malan Heslop, Nona Bunderson Knighton, and Lisa Knighton Delap, comps., *Malan Book of Remembrance; Descendants of John Daniel Malan* (Ogden: n.p., 1993), 97–98.

2. *Directory of Ogden City and Weber County, 1883* (Ogden: Ogden Herald Publishing Company, 1883), 176.

3. Charles Middleton, Diary, LDS Church Historian's Office, Salt Lake City.

4. *Atlantic Monthly* 23 (May 1869): 619.

5. *Ogden Standard-Examiner,* 3 October 1981.

6. Daniel Sylvester Tuttle, *Missionary to the Mountain West, Reminiscences of Episcopal Bishop Daniel S. Tuttle* (Salt Lake City: University of Utah Press, 1987), 255–56.

7. Luman Andros Shurtleff, *His Personal History, 1807–1884* (Salt Lake City: Litho grafics, n.d.), 103–4.

8. Milton R. Hunter, ed., *Beneath Ben Lomond's Peak,* 448–49; *Ogden Standard-Examiner,* 15 December 1938.

9. Scott Kenney, ed., *Wilford Woodruff's Journal: 1833–1898,* 5:549.

10. These people included Richard Cook, William Kendall, Nels Morrison, Mrs. Hannah Cook, John Cook, Robert Farley, Nathan Brooks, Mrs. Margaret Cook, John Firth, John Parsons, John Trolsom, Mrs. Hellen Cook, Mrs. Sarah Cook, Mrs. Mary Cook, and Mrs. Joanna Kendall.

11. Floyd J. Woodfield and Clara Woodfield, comps., *A History of North Ogden: Beginnings to 1985* (Ogden: Empire Printing, 1986), 68–69.

12. *Ogden Standard-Examiner,* 26 June 1924.

13. Hubert Howe Bancroft, "Inner Facts of Social Life in Utah," 1–20, Bancroft Library, University of California, Berkeley. See also Connie Duncan Cannon, "Jane Snyder Richards: The Blue-White Diamond," in Vicky Burgess-Olsen, *Sister Saints* (Provo: Brigham Young University Press, 1978), 173–200.

14. Richard W. Sadler, "Fair Ogden and Its Early Settlement," *Encyclia* 59 (1982): 1–20.

15. Shurtleff, *Personal History,* 101.

16. Ibid., 122.

17. LaVerna Burnett Newey, *Remember My Valley, A History of Ogden Canyon, Eden, Liberty, and Huntsville* (Salt Lake City: Hawkes Publishing Company, 1977), 112–13.

18. Dale L. Morgan, ed., *History of Ogden* (Ogden: Ogden City Commission, 1940), 47.

19. Larry R. Gerlach, "Ogden's 'Horrible Tragedy': The Lynching of George Segal," *Utah Historical Quarterly* 49 (Spring 1981): 157–72.

20. Belnap interview in scrapbook pages in possession of authors.

21. John S. McCormick, "Red Lights in Zion: Salt Lake City's Stockade, 1908–1911," *Utah Historical Quarterly* 50 (Spring 1982): 168–81.

22. Kate Carter, ed., *Our Pioneer Heritage,* 10:475–78.

23. Helen Z. Papanikolas, ed., *The Peoples of Utah* (Salt Lake City: Utah State Historical Society, 1976), 339.

24. Harold R. Oaks, "An Evaluation of the Beginnings, Purposes, and Influence of Drama in Ogden from 1840 to 1900," M.A. thesis, Brigham Young University, 1962, 27.

25. Davis Bitton, *The Ritualization of Mormon History and Other Essays* (Urbana: University of Illinois Press, 1994), 103.

26. William W. Terry, "Weber County is Worth Knowing," 234.

27. Morgan, *History of Ogden,* 54.

28. *Ogden Junction,* 16 April 1873, as quoted in Oaks, "An Evaluation of Drama in Ogden," 75.

29. Oaks, "An Evaluation of Drama in Ogden," 183.

30. *Ogden Semi-Weekly Standard,* 31 December 1890, as quoted in Oaks, "An Evaluation of Drama in Ogden," 185.

31. Ronald W. Jenkins, "A History of the Grand Opera House and Ogden's Golden Age of Theatre, 1890–1909," M.A. thesis, Utah State University, 1965, 12.

32. Terry, "Weber County is Worth Knowing," 245.

# 5

# Riding the Rails into the Twentieth Century, 1889–1920

Politics, education, agriculture, and industry formed several of the essential building blocks of Weber County during the three decades from 1889 to 1920. These blocks were tied together by the railroad, whose influence continued to pervade much of the county during this era. The foundation for society in Weber County had been laid in the previous half-century: extensive Mormon colonization and agricultural activity followed by the coming of the railroad and its economic, social, and cultural influence on Ogden, Utah, and the nation. In 1889 Weber County had a population of 22,875; by 1910 it had grown to 35,179.

Although politics would occupy much attention in Weber County both before and after 1889, the county and particularly Ogden had its share of promoters. The 25 June 1889 issue of the Ogden *Standard* suggested that Ogden and the county had much of what was needed to make it successful. The paper noted Ogden had:

> Three newspapers. The best water supply in Utah. Fruit canneries and vinegar works. The finest water power in the land. A leather tannery and shoe factories. The finest business blocks in the

> Territory. A number of machine shops and a gun factory. A large woolen mill and a knitting factory. The best nurseries and greenhouses in the Territory. Good gas works furnishing light to the business houses. The most beautiful streets and avenues to be found in the Union. More shipping business than the whole of the remaining Territory. Facilities for the establishment of almost any industry conceivable. A fine steam creamery, with a capacity of two thousand pounds of butter per day. A large number of various industries which are in constant and healthy operation. A good system of street railway, belting, and grid-ironing City with steam motors. A large number of magnificent church, academy, university, college and school buildings. Twice as much railroad business as the whole of the remainder of Utah Territory combined. An electric light plant, illuminating the streets of the city and lighting business institutions. A large area of fruit and grain producing country. Several iron foundries. A magnificent avenue, running in a straight line through the center of the city, of six miles in length and eight rods in width. Numerous brick manufactories. The most magnificent flouring mills in the Territory. Men of business, brain, energy, push, and capital, always ready to assist in the establishment of all industries of beneficial character.

Many supporters felt that Ogden would soon become the leading city in the territory, and the *Standard* was a booster of Ogden and Weber County.

There were many activities at the turn of the century to increase Weber County's status as a major force in Utah. By 1910 the Business Men's Association of Ogden, which referred to itself as the Weber Club, issued *A Glimpse of Ogden,* a prime example of booster literature at the turn of the century. Included in the brochure which extolled Ogden and Weber County's virtues was a poem titled "Fair Ogden." Two of the poem's stanzas follow:

> Have you ever been to Ogden, in fairest Utah state,
> Where the cloudlets kiss the mountains
> And the birds sing mate to mate;
> Where Nature, smiling broadly upon the fertile land—
> Deals out her richest blessings with open, lavish hand.

> Have you ever been to Ogden, the best town in the West,
> Which by natural advantage
> Simply walks and leads the rest;
> A city, too, kind stranger, if you'd look this country o'er—
> You'd choose for your abiding place and dwell there evermore.[1]

The brochure was filled with pictures and pages full of reasons to settle in Weber County. Health, wealth, the railroad, and manufacturing were a few of the reasons suggested for settling in and around "Fair Ogden."

In the two decades (1869–1889) following the arrival of the railroad, Ogden changed from a small agricultural community to a major transportation center. The next three decades (1889–1920) would see equally dramatic changes. By the beginning of World War I, Ogden had about eight miles of paved streets (the total for Utah at this time was thirty-four miles) and almost 100 miles of paved sidewalks. Ogden's street-railway system, which extended north and east into the county, had about 100 miles of track. The city had sixty-four miles of water mains and about thirty-eight miles of pipe in the sewer system. The population of the city had grown, paralleling the vigorous economic growth of the area. By 1880 the population of the junction city was 6,069; by 1890 it had doubled again to 12,889. During World War I, Ogden had a population of about 32,000 people. The population of Weber County grew rapidly following the introduction of the railroad: in 1870, 7,358 people; 1880, 12,344; 1890, 22,273; 1900, 25,239; 1910, 25,179; and 1920, 43,465. Ogden's population was about 75 percent of the total Weber County population in the opening decades of the twentieth century.

## *Politics*

During the two-year period from 1889 to 1891, Weber County politics continued to splinter. The Liberal party split into factions, one headed by J. W. McNutt, pharmacist, incumbent city treasurer, Liberal candidate for mayor in 1891, and rumored liquor dealer. Another faction joined with a group from the People's party to form the Citizen's party. Of the twenty individuals elected to office in 1891, the Liberals won thirteen offices and the Citizen's group won seven. Among the seven elected to office were two Mormons—Frank J.

Cannon and Thomas D. Dee. The success of the Citizen's party was evidence that Mormons and non-Mormons could work together in common political efforts. William H. Turner, a non-Mormon who was the Citizen's party candidate for mayor, won that office by fifteen votes in a very close race with his Liberal opponent.

On 11 February 1891, two days after the Ogden city election, a petition was circulated in the city calling for the organization of the Republican party in the county and asking all who were interested to meet at a mass meeting on 16 February in the federal courtroom. At this organization meeting, D.H. Baldridge (a non-Mormon) was elected chairman of the Republican club and Frank J. Cannon (a Mormon) was elected vice-president. Ben E. Rich (a Mormon) moved that Republicans throughout the territory should be encouraged to organize, and the resolution was approved along with other organizational resolutions. In this initial organizing meeting, the Republicans described themselves as the party of "advanced thought, patriotism, and courage."[2]

Frank Cannon's Ogden *Standard* celebrated the success of the Republican organization and urged the Democrats to do likewise. Under Cannon's editorship, the *Standard* became a leading voice for the Republican party in Weber County and in the territory. On 21 February Ogden Democrats met at the Grand Opera House and elected Henry P. Henderson (a non-Mormon) as president and Charles C. Richards (attorney and son of Mormon apostle Franklin D. Richards) as vice-president. Henderson had recently retired as a Utah territorial supreme court judge. The Democrats endorsed several ideas in their initial organization meeting including being in favor of freedom from class legislation, favoring individual liberty, opposing the interference of churches in the affairs of the state, opposing free trade, and favoring the free coinage of silver.[3]

In both national party organization efforts in Ogden, the gentiles had led the way, with interested Mormons invited to participate. As the division into national political parties took place in Weber County, Weber LDS Stake president Lewis W. Shurtliff continued to consult with the Mormon First Presidency, who advised him and "other church authorities to use their influence to keep the parties about equal numerically."[4] Some folklore concerning the division into national political parties during this era suggests that in order to achieve political balance some Mormon congregations were divided down the middle, with one side asked to become Democrats and the other side asked to become Republicans.[5] In May 1891 national political parties were organized in Salt Lake City.

On 10 June 1891 the People's party of Weber County was formally dissolved, and in December 1893 the Liberal party was terminated. During 1895 a state constitution was drafted in Salt Lake City at a convention which included delegates from all of the counties. Delegates to the constitutional convention representing Weber County included Louis B. Adams, William Driver, David Evans, Lorin Farr, Frederick J. Kiesel, James N. Kimball, Theodore B. Lewis, Thomas Maloney, Robert McFarland, Hiram H. Spencer, and Charles N. Strevell. One of the most heated issues debated at the constitutional convention was woman suffrage, and, although the convention eventually approved equal voting rights for both men and women, a vocal minority at the convention spoke against it, including Fred J. Kiesel. Jane Snyder Richards and her daughter-in-law Emily S. Richards, although not members of the convention, had been longstanding Weber County advocates of woman suffrage. Jane's son and Emily's husband, Franklin S. Richards, gave a well-received speech at the convention which advocated the right of women to vote. In the territory-wide vote that followed to accept the constitution and move toward statehood, a majority of Weber County voters approved the constitution, but nearly a third voted against it. The territorial vote was 31,305 for the new constitution and 7,687 against it.

Utah achieved statehood on 4 January 1896. Frank J. Cannon had played an important role in the move toward statehood and had been involved in organizing grass-roots Republican party groups throughout the territory. In 1894 he was elected as the territorial delegate to Congress, a position his father had earlier held. In 1896 Frank Cannon was elected as one of Utah's first two United States senators by the state legislature. Although Cannon drew the shorter of the two terms (a two-year term), he represented Ogden and Utah well in the Senate during his term, although he limited his national effectiveness as a Republican by espousing the free coinage of silver. Many western Republicans including Cannon rebelled against the single gold standard for coinage. Frank Cannon gradually grew apart from the Mormon church, particularly after the death of his father in 1901.

That Ogden and Weber County were much more diverse in politics and society than most of the rest of the state was evident in the decade of the 1890s with the rather slight showing of the Populist party. The Populist party participated in two national elections—1892 and 1896—before dying. Never a strong party in Utah, most of the strength of this third party came from Salt Lake City and Ogden. William Hope "Coin" Harvey, who agitated for the free coinage of silver during the 1890s, arrived in Ogden in 1888 from West Virginia. Harvey planned to practice law and also had plans to build a mansion on the slopes of Little Mountain. Harvey was a booster who promoted Ogden and Weber County through the "Order of Monte Cristo," which he organized to promote Ogden as a mining and livestock center. As the free coinage of silver became a national political issue in the decade of the 1890s, Harvey pushed for silver coinage through his magazine *Coin.* He gained national prominence as the silver issue gained national attention; and early in the decade Harvey moved from Ogden to be more deeply involved in the "silver crusade."

In the 1894 election for Congress, Populist candidate H. L. Gaut ran a distant third, receiving the large majority of his votes from Salt Lake City and Ogden. James Hogan of Ogden, who was a national organizer of the American Railway Union and a friend of Eugene Debs, was also the main speaker at the Salt Lake County Populist convention in September 1895 and was nominated at that convention to run for Congress. The Populists met in the spring of 1896 in their state convention in Ogden and like their colleagues throughout the country became "fusionists," as their party and the Democratic party both supported William Jennings Bryan for president and advocated the idea of free coinage of silver. In 1898 in Ogden city politics the Populists were generally aligned with the Democrats, and fusionist candidate John A. Boyle was elected mayor in an extremely close contest. He defeated his Republican party opponent by only eighteen votes.[6] Boyle was the first Mormon mayor elected in Ogden since the election of David Eccles in 1886.

Woman suffrage was a major issue both in Utah and in the

United States during this era. Utah women had been allowed to vote in 1870 by a bill which became law in the territory, and women voted throughout the territory for seventeen years. However, a provision of the Edmunds-Tucker Act then disfranchised all women in Utah Territory. In 1895 Sarah Elizabeth Nelson Anderson of Weber County raised the banner of woman suffrage. Anderson, who was born in 1853, was the mother of five children when her husband of eighteen years, Dr. Porter L. Anderson of Ogden, died in 1888. As the new state constitution was completed in 1895, registration of "qualified" voters for the new constitution and for the new state officers occurred throughout the territory during the fall of 1895. The Utah Commission was responsible for overseeing the fall 1895 election. On 6 August 1895 Sarah Anderson, who lived in Ogden's Second Precinct, asked deputy voting registrar Charles Tyree to be allowed to vote in the fall election on both issues—the new constitution and the first state officers. Tyree refused to register Anderson on the grounds that she was a woman. A number of attorneys who were members of the Democratic party volunteered to represent her in court on the voting issue, and her case was filed in court on 7 August 1895. Anderson and her attorneys were granted a successful decision in the District Court in Ogden, which was presided over by Judge H. W. Smith; but the territorial supreme court by a vote of two to one ruled in favor of Tyree and refused Sarah Anderson's plea to vote.[7]

Sarah Elizabeth Nelson Anderson lost her plea to vote in 1895, but she was elected as a member of the House of Representatives in Utah's second legislature. A newspaper reporter described Sarah Anderson as being occupied with her children and her property interests and being "remarkably well posted on matters of current interest and public concern."[8] During her term in the state legislature from 1897 to 1899, Sarah Anderson was the chair of the House Committee on Public Health and introduced two bills—one regarding police and fire commissioners and the other related to teaching schoolchildren about the effects of alcohol and narcotics. Weber County and Utah women were allowed to vote by the new state constitution, and, by the turn of the century four years later, only four states of the forty-five states in the nation—Wyoming, Idaho, Colorado, and Utah—had granted full political rights to women.

The first session of the first state legislature of Utah among other actions in 1896 passed acts to establish a "Uniform System of County Government" throughout the state. The counties as they existed in 1896 were reconfirmed as "bodies corporate and politic." Counties were given certain powers, including the power to sue and be sued, to tax, to purchase land, and to make contracts. The powers of the county were to be exercised by a board of three county commissioners who had previously been called county selectmen. The three new county commissioners were to be elected at a general election to be held in 1896. The newly elected commissioners would take office on the first day of January after their election and would hold office for two years. W. G. Wilson, J. C. Child, and E. W. Wade were the last Weber County selectmen; in fall elections of 1896 J. C. Armstrong, L. B. Hammon, and John Seaman were elected and became the first county commissioners, taking office early in January 1897.

The fourth legislature of the state of Utah, which met during January, February, and March 1901, changed the terms for county commissioners. The members of the legislature had observed that it might be better to have some continuity as well as experience among those serving as county commissioners. The new law stated that beginning with the general election of 1902 one commissioner would be elected for a term of four years and two would be elected for a term of two years. In 1904, and thereafter, one commissioner would be elected for a term of four years and one for two years. With this new method of election, two commissioners would serve alternating four-year terms and one commissioner would be elected to a two-year term.

In the quarter-century following statehood, the voters of Weber County generally followed the trend of voters statewide. In 1896 William McKinley was elected president of the United States, but the majority of the voters of Utah and Weber County voted for Democratic candidate William Jennings Bryan, particularly because he and they favored the free coinage of silver. In 1900 McKinley won the presidency again, and this time Utah and Weber County generally voted Republican. Theodore Roosevelt became president when McKinley was shot and killed in 1901, and he received the majority of Weber County and Utah votes in 1904, as did his Republican successor William Howard Taft in 1908. In 1912 Weber County voters and Uintah County voters cast the majority of their votes for Teddy Roosevelt, who ran on the Progressive, or Bull Moose, ticket; the majority of the other voters in Utah counties cast their votes for William H. Taft, who had been "endorsed" by Mormon church president Joseph F. Smith. The 1912 presidential election saw *Ogden Standard* editor William Glasmann endorse the Bull Moose candidacy of Teddy Roosevelt, and Ogden voters voted primarily for Roosevelt; but Weber County voters outside of Ogden cast the majority of their ballots for Taft.

During the campaign for the presidential election of 1912, Theodore Roosevelt stopped in Ogden to campaign and spent part of his time in the city visiting the Hermitage resort. Roosevelt and his party traveled to the Hermitage by automobile; his presence in the canyon created a Sunday traffic jam, but he posed with Weber County residents for photographs which included Weber County Sunday drivers, a narrow road, a rocky canyon, and a presidential candidate. Woodrow Wilson won the 1912 presidential election as a Democrat, and, in 1916, Utah and Weber County voted for Wilson as he won reelection. The majority of voters in Weber County and Utah also voted for the Republican presidential winner in 1920, Warren G. Harding.

Ogden voters were known to favor minority political causes much more than their rural Weber County neighbors and much more than their neighbors from most of the rest of the state of Utah. Ogden City voters favored both Populist and Bull Moose/Progressive issues with their votes more than did rural Weber County voters. Ogden voters were also much more supportive of Socialist party issues during the first two decades of the twentieth century than were their rural county neighbors. In the 1908 presidential campaign, Socialist candidate Eugene Debs received 4.5 percent of the Utah vote but received 5 percent of the Weber County vote and 7.2 percent of the Ogden City vote.[9] Rural Weber County districts gave Debs only about 3 percent of their vote. This same pattern was mirrored in many of the elections from 1900 to 1920, with the city of Ogden emerging as one of the strongholds of the Socialist party in Utah during this era.

Studies about Socialists in Utah during this period have noted that about 42 percent were Mormons, 91 percent were men, and 66 percent were born in the United States. In terms of occupations, 40 percent of the Socialists were skilled laborers, while another 20 percent were unskilled, and 19 percent were farmers. There were strong ties between labor organizations and the Socialist party, particularly in mining areas as well as in Salt Lake City and Ogden. In 1906 a Union Socialist Labor and Propaganda League was formed by labor union members in Salt Lake City and Ogden. The league was organized to advance the cause of socialism and to elect Socialists to office.[10] One of the leaders of the Socialist party in Ogden was Kate S. Hillard, who wrote a weekly column in the *Ogden Morning Examiner* from 1905 to 1909 that was titled the "Socialist Column."

Lucy Hoving was an Ogden educator who became immersed in the general socialist movement. Hoving was born in Holland in 1856 and moved to Utah in 1888 after her conversion to Mormonism. She spent the next eleven years in Logan both as a student and a faculty member at Brigham Young Academy before moving to Ogden in 1899. In Ogden, Hoving taught in the public schools as well as establishing a kindergarten and a private training school for teachers. She studied socialism through correspondence classes from the International School of Social Economy, and, at the same time she began to espouse socialism, she also began to abandon her Mormon faith. She eventually wrote an anti-Mormon tract, *The X-Rays Turned on Mormonism*. She suggested that Mormon polygamy was instrumental in the oppression of women and children, and saw the Socialist party as an advocate of equality for women. Hoving's involvement in the Socialist party lasted only about three years, as she was killed on 7 August 1902 when she was struck by a carriage on an Ogden street near her home.[11]

## *Labor*

The growth of labor organizations in Weber County was tied to the railroad and many of the enterprises which grew along with and because of the railroad. The Deseret Telegraph, a Mormon cooperative system, was completed in 1866 and served towns from St. George to Logan and connected in Salt Lake City with the transcontinental telegraph line which had been completed across the West in 1861. In 1869, with the completion of the transcontinental railroad, Western Union extended its lines to Ogden, and Ogden thus had two telegraph offices. As the junction city, Ogden became the most important relay point between Chicago and San Francisco; by 1885 Western Union employed thirty telegraph operators in the Ogden office. In 1903 the relay office was moved to Salt Lake City.

By the 1880s Ogden was the second largest city in Utah and was the most cosmopolitan town in Utah because of the influence of the railroad. Ogden's population of 8,000 was about one-third of Salt Lake City's population of 25,000. The Brotherhood of Locomotive Firemen was the first railroad union to be organized in Utah; Lodge 98 of the Locomotive Firemen was organized in Ogden on 1 September 1882 with twenty-seven members.[12] The first trainmen's lodge was organized in Ogden on 22 February 1885, and it was through the railroad organizations that the Knights of Labor, a national umbrella labor organization that included many labor unions, began to be an influence in Utah. On 18 August 1885 the Ogden Knights of Labor published a front-page statement in the *Ogden Daily Herald* which opposed Chinese immigration and strongly suggested that Chinese laborers in the United States should be sent home. That same day a mass meeting sponsored by the Knights of Labor was held on the corner of Fourth and Main streets (Twenty-Fourth and Washington). The meeting, which included as many as 500 members of the Knights of Labor, was addressed by Judge Heed and Robert Wilson, who advocated the immediate and forceful exclusion of Chinese labor as it was a threat to the "economic status of the white working class."[13] In a further move, the Knights of Labor in Ogden organized an October 1885 boycott against Chinese peddlers and workers as well as those who did business with them.

Although the Knights of Labor were in decline nationally during 1886, they remained a relatively strong organization in Ogden that year. The second annual reunion of the Knights of Labor was celebrated in Ogden on 17 September 1886 and was held at the Ogden City Pavilion. The reunion was a grand affair which included illuminating the pavilion with electric lights; several speakers spoke to the theme "Labor is Noble and Holy." During 1885 and 1886 the

Mormon church–owned *Deseret News* suggested that labor organizations like the Knights of Labor might be considered "secret combinations" and as such should be avoided by church members. By 1887 the membership of the Knights of Labor began to decline drastically both across the nation and in Utah.

Trade unions, particularly as advocated by Samuel Gompers and his American Federation of Labor (AFL), began to replace the Knights of Labor. The Printers' Union in Ogden was organized in 1887 as a part of the International and Typographical Union. In Utah a painters' union was formed in 1884 and a brewery workers' union in 1885. In 1889 the Utah Federated Trades and Labor Council was organized by Robert Sleater, a member of the Deseret Typographical Union. The Federated Trades organization had as one of its purposes binding Utah's small trade unions together to work for common goals. Two day-long celebrations for labor and labor organizations were held in Salt Lake City during 1889—a 4 July and a Labor Day celebration, and both of these were "strengthened by a large delegation from Ogden." Represented in the celebrations were printers, cigar makers, plumbers, gasfitters, barbers, painters, decorators, stonecutters, masons, iron moulders, hod carriers, blacksmiths, and horseshoers. By the end of 1889, there were about 1,000 members of trade unions in Utah, with the vast majority of them located in Salt Lake City and Ogden.[14]

Early in 1890 the *Salt Lake Tribune* commented that the beginning of labor unions in Utah had been very helpful in breaking down the former territorial barriers of religion and politics. It was suggested that unions had allowed workers to join together for their common labor goals and put aside religion, race, and politics.

The Panic of 1893 was a very serious economic downturn in the nation's economy. The economic depression and unemployment related to this panic was the most serious of any depression in the nineteenth century. Nearly one-fifth of the non-agricultural laborers in the country were thrown out of work. By the spring of 1894, according to one report, Salt Lake City experienced a 48.3 percent rate of unemployment among its urban laborers.[15] Many Weber County workers also were thrown out of work. Mass meetings of workers were held throughout the United States, and in the spring of

1894 the idea of an industrial army was born when Jacob S. Coxey of Ohio suggested that the federal government build roads throughout the country with unemployed workers. Coxey suggested that industrial armies made up of unemployed workers should march on Washington, D.C., in order to demonstrate their wants and needs to Congress.

Charles H. Kelley of San Francisco became the leader of "Kelley's Army," one of several groups which made up "Coxey's Army." All of the disparate arms of Coxey's Army marched and rode the rails with a final goal of reaching Washington, D.C. On 9 April 1894 Kelley's Army reached Ogden. This "army" had traveled across California and Nevada in crowded boxcars furnished by the Southern Pacific Railroad. The Union Pacific and Denver and Rio Grande railroads refused to carry the protesters east of the junction city, and Ogden became the temporary home for the 1,200 men of Kelley's Army. Ogden and Salt Lake City units of the Utah National Guard which had been formed only two weeks earlier on 27 March 1894 were called into service to control the protestors. The members of Kelley's Army remained in Ogden for three days, from 9 to 11 April, and during this period they were closely guarded by five companies of militia as well as policemen from both Ogden and Salt Lake City. The protestors were confined to the Southern Pacific Railroad yards and they lived in the boxcars in which they had been transported from California.

Union laborers in Utah criticized territorial governor Caleb West for calling out the militia; but many residents of Ogden and Weber County who faced an unemployed army of more than one thousand men applauded the governor's actions. Even before the "Industrials" arrived in Ogden, there was fear of their arrival; but it was soon apparent that many of those in Kelley's Army were sick and weakened by their journey. Some Ogden residents formed a parade of protest with both banners and slogans which denounced the use of the militia, and the Ogden *Standard* was particularly outspoken in its criticism of Governor West. After two days of negotiations, on 11 April 1894 the industrial army marched from the Southern Pacific Railroad yards and turned south on Washington Boulevard. The men were flanked by police and militia, and as they all marched southward an

Ogden band played "Marching Through Georgia," which had been made famous three decades earlier in 1864 when the Union Army under General William T. Sherman marched through Georgia. Kelley's Army marched peacefully out of Ogden to Uintah where the men boarded a Union Pacific train which headed eastward up Weber Canyon and out of the territory.

The nationwide Pullman strike which occurred two months later also had a major impact on Ogden and Weber County. The American Railway Union under the leadership of Eugene V. Debs organized the strike beginning on 21 June 1894. As the strike began, Ogden and Weber County railway workers voted to join with the national union, and strikers throughout the nation refused to allow any trains to move that included Pullman cars. Trains that were stopped by the strike in Ogden stranded 300 passengers. Some fighting broke out in the junction city, but the most serious consequence of the strike was a series of twelve separate fires which were started by oily rags set ablaze in buildings in downtown Ogden beginning on 8 July 1894. The Sidney Stevens Implement House and the George A. Lowe Hardware Building were destroyed by fire. The fires caused $135,000 in damage in the heart of the Ogden business district. Fifteen strikers were arrested, including local union leaders Robert Stirrat and Robert Brenan. Although the charge was never proven, many Weber county residents believed that the fires were related to the Pullman strike and had been started by union members. By 13 July, the trains began to move as the federal government intervened to end the strike.

In the decade following the Pullman strike, trade unions in Ogden and Weber County gradually grew in both numbers of members and in the establishment of individual trade unions. On 1 January 1903 the Ogden Trades and Labor Assembly, a citywide union council, was organized to coordinate among and between Ogden's trade unions. National labor leaders like Samuel Gompers and Eugene Debs visited Utah, became acquainted with Utah laborers, and made speeches throughout the state. With the formation of the Utah State Federation of Labor on 5 May 1904 in Salt Lake City, Grant Syphers of the Ogden Trades and Labor Assembly and member of the Lathers Union was chosen as first vice-president. This statewide federation worked to promote eleven principles for laboring people including equal pay for equal work for both sexes, the eight-hour work day, and labor free of competition from convict labor.[16]

On 12 September 1904 the second convention of the Utah Federation of Labor was held in Ogden with sixty delegates in attendance who represented unions from across the state. Unions represented from the Ogden area included the Ogden Trades and Labor Assembly (which included several trade unions) as well as the cigarmakers, teamsters, painters and decorators, cooks and waiters, and boilermakers. Ogden, Salt Lake City, and the various mining towns were the strongholds of union labor organizations in early twentieth-century Utah. At the September 1904 meeting, J. J. Jones of the Ogden Boilermakers Union was elected fourth vice-president. Ogden was usually represented by one person out of the seven or eight officers elected each year to the Utah Federation of Labor board; and in 1908 W.M. Piggot of Ogden was elected first vice-president of the organization. Ogden regularly hosted the Utah Federation of Labor convention.

Social events were an important part of union organizations. These often included an annual outing to Lagoon Resort in Farmington on Labor Day. Union socials were often referred to as "smokers," and the Cigarmakers Union would supply union-made Havana cigars for such events. The Barber's Union of Ogden gave a ball for several hundred guests in February 1914 at the Colonial Academy. Union-brewed beer was another staple of the "smokers." Union members and their families often gathered funds both individually and through benefit balls to assist themselves and others during lengthy strikes. In September 1911, 40,000 employees of the Harriman Railway system, which included the Southern Pacific shops in Ogden, began a strike. Shortly after the strike began, 125 workers at the Southern Pacific Ogden railway shops were laid off and a wire fence was erected around the shops in order to keep strikers away from the shops. This strike included violence between strikers and strikebreakers and lasted for three years, having a devastating effect on many families.

In general, the more radical union efforts in Utah were centered in mining camps prior to 1910; but during the first decade of the century the Industrial Workers of the World (IWW), or Wobblies, began to organize laborers in Ogden and Salt Lake City as well as in the mining camps. M. Dezetel was a national organizer for the IWW who had his headquarters in Ogden and worked to enlist Weber County workers. The philosophy of the IWW movement suggested that the capitalistic system throughout the world should be overthrown by the workers, and many of Ogden's trade-union workers as well as businessmen suggested that the IWW was alien to the American culture. Although some socialists and the IWW opposed World War I, some 2,000 Ogden laborers marched in the 1918 Ogden Labor Day parade with the motto "Win the War."

The growth of labor organizations in Ogden and Weber County paralleled the growth of the railroads, business, and industry in the state and throughout the nation. Agriculture remained the primary occupation in the county through this period of time, but the manufacturing and mechanical industries and trade and transportation were growing. A segment of Weber County supported labor organizations and union growth, but others were not happy with such organizations and their growth. In 1919, as the Utah State Legislature considered repealing the "picketing law" which allowed peaceful picketing to occur in the state, both the Weber Club of Ogden and the Rotary Club of Ogden joined with other business and civic organizations across the state in petitioning the legislature to repeal the law. In spite of large demonstrations by workers in the state, the law was repealed by the legislature, and in 1919 labor organizations in Utah began to decline.

## *Mining*

Mining for precious metals (silver and gold) in Utah began in the 1860s and was pursued in earnest with the arrival of the railroad. The discovery of gold in California in 1848, followed by gold and silver discoveries in other areas of the West, made thousands of men "experts" in identifying what they hoped to be productive mining claims. Like the rest of Utah, the mountains and valleys of Weber County were scoured by miners in search not only of gold and silver but also copper and other valuable metals. In 1871 a firm named the

Nebraska and Utah Mining Company suggested they found gold-bearing quartz ledges on Fremont Island, and several mining claims were filed including the Miller, Omaha, Queen Ann, Island, Davis, and Shoebridge claims. Although the island claims were filed and worked, there was little metal produced.[17]

During the last three decades of the nineteenth century the Weber County Wasatch Mountains were probed and explored in hopes of finding precious minerals. Evidence of gold mining in Taylor's Canyon is still apparent at the Red Rock Mine, located near the entrance to the canyon. More than two dozen mining claims with names like White Queen, Regina, Red Bird, Lucky Boy, and Young America were filed in the mountains surrounding North Ogden by area residents. John Jones of North Ogden was nicknamed the "Bonanza King" by his friends, and he filed claims for eleven mines. His "Ben Loman" and Eureka mines were both successful silver mines.

Mount Ben Lomond was mined by men looking for both silver and copper. Don McQuire found lead and silver outcroppings two miles north of Pleasant View. He employed Italian workers to tunnel into the mountain and they cut a shaft 100 feet long into the mountain at the Santa Marie site. Ore cars carried the blasted rock out of the tunnel on rails. The Eldorado was another mine that McQuire located and worked. It was situated southeast of Willard and northwest of Pleasant View. The Eldorado was located high on the mountainside, and a cable-and-bucket system was constructed to transport the ore down the canyon. Ore from these mines was delivered by wagon to the Utah Hot Springs and then shipped by railroad. Israel Elliott Brown found a small iron mine on the West slope of Willard Peak in 1873 and mined a small quantity of iron ore, which was processed at the Ogden Iron Manufacturing Company located at 21st Street and Wall Avenue.

The most famous silver and lead mine associated with Weber County was named La Plata and was located in the rugged mountains at the southern end of Cache County, less than a mile from the Weber County-Cache County line. From 1891 to 1893 La Plata appeared to be the bonanza that many northern Utahns were looking for. Although substantial mining claims had been found throughout much of Utah prior to 1890, no major claim had been found north of Salt Lake City. In the summer of 1891, P.O. Johnson was herding sheep and picked up a rock which he found to be rich in silver ore. Johnson shared his discovery with his boss, W. H. Ney, and, after some surface exploration of the area, they filed a mining claim in Logan on their find, which they identified as being located near the head of Bear Gulch in the Paradise Mining District.

Rumors of the rich discovery spread like wildfire, and by the end of the summer mining fever had infected many in both Weber and Cache counties. Some rushed to the La Plata area in hopes of finding immediate wealth; others decided to capitalize on the silver find by means of investment and speculation. Members of the Ogden community who rushed to the La Plata site included Tom Harrison, who had mining experience in both Eureka and Park City, H.C. Wardleigh, Joseph Farr, Gid R. Propper, and C. K. Westover. The *Standard* estimated that during August 1891, one hundred people a day traveled through Ogden to La Plata to get a look at the town and the mining area.[18] The route to La Plata was not easily traversed from either Logan or Ogden. Travelers taking the Weber County route began at Ogden, traveled up Ogden Canyon to Huntsville, and then up Middle Fork Canyon to La Plata. Although both county governments were petitioned to build roads to the mining camp, Cache County was successful in having the first road built by 17 September 1891. The Weber County road through Middle Fork Canyon was completed on 30 October 1891 and even then was considered a very difficult route. The roads were needed to carry supplies and people to La Plata and then to carry the ore by wagon to a railhead in either Logan or Ogden.

The mining camp was named La Plata on 13 August. Tom Harrison proposed the name of La Plata, which was derived from the Spanish word for silver. Town meetings were held, the camp was laid out in streets—including Harrison, La Plata, Logan, and Washington—and the roads were graded. Businesses including sawmills, stores, and saloons sprang up. The Ogden *Standard* and the Logan *Journal* both promoted the mining boom and worked to tie the boom to their respective communities. During the initial boom period, newspaper reporters suggested that as many as 1,200 to 1,500 curious people visited the La Plata area on a daily basis.[19] The excitement and fever related to the mining boom spread through Ogden and Logan as well as smaller communities in each area. Supplies, visitors, equipment, and mail were carried to La Plata from both Ogden and Logan. David O. McKay was one of the mail carriers who hauled mail from Huntsville to La Plata, and he reported that he carried the mail from Huntsville to the mining camp on horseback three times a week.

The La Plata mining rush was typical of western mining surges. Many of the curious rushed in to see what was happening and then stayed, hoping to get rich. Local farmers rushed in for quick riches and soon found they were working alongside of seasoned miners from across the West. The town grew quickly during the summer and fall, but as the winter of 1891–92 approached only the most hearty remained at the mining camp, which included as many as seventy buildings. The buildings were generally constructed of logs with sod roofs. Most mining activity was halted as snow piled high and temperatures often fell below zero, leaving miners who remained through the winter to drink, sleep, read, gamble, and tell stories.

With the spring and summer of 1892, the population of the mining camp grew. Cache County and Utah territorial laws set the requirements for government at La Plata; but in many ways the mining camp was a shared enterprise between Cache and Weber counties. Cache County license rates set for La Plata included $800 for a liquor saloon, $40 for a boarding house, $20 for a lunch counter, and $40 for a meat market. By the summer of 1892 there were seven or eight places of business which served liquor and allowed gambling; there were also assorted boarding houses, hotels, barber shops, drygoods and grocery stores, and restaurants. By the summer of 1892, most of the mining areas were controlled by companies rather than by individuals. These included the Sundown-La Plata, the Ogden-La Plata, and the Red Jacket-La Plata. Miners were hired to work below ground at three dollars a day or above ground at $2.50 a day. Reporters suggested that a miner could live in La Plata for about twelve dollars a month, that bread was about ten cents a loaf, and that beef was cheaper in La Plata than it was in Salt Lake City.[20]

By 1893 La Plata had already begun a rapid decline. It is estimated that the La Plata mines produced about $3 million worth of ore; but conflicting land claims, a decline in silver prices, harsh winters, transportation difficulties, and a deterioration in the quality of ore brought about a rapid decline of the mining area. Most of the early ore shipments went to Logan, but enough went to Ogden to keep both communities very competitive in terms of who was profiting the most from the mines. After 1894 the mines were worked sporadically for the next decade, with virtually all of the ore transported to Ogden in wagons. La Plata never became the "next Leadville," as was hoped, but it did provide two years of rather intense mining excitement and competition to northern Utah.

### *Hospitals and Medicine*

When Weber County and the Territory of Utah were founded in the middle of the nineteenth century, medical practices in the United States were wide and varied. Almost any man could become a doctor after one year's training. Scientific medicine had made some advances, and physicians had founded the American Medical Association in 1847 to reform medical schools. Homeopaths and Thompsonian doctors continued to challenge "regular" doctors regarding both patients and cures. Herbalists and botanic physicians continued to look for cures using nature and the medicinal properties of herbs. Amos Pease Stone made stomach pills, cathartic pills, and a third preparation of lobelia and other medicines which were sold throughout early Weber County. William H. Pidcock was known for his "Pidcock Pills," and Edwin Bingham and his wife, Phoebe, concocted a potion called "Bingham Cough Syrup." Most settlers used natural herbs or cures of their own understanding in treating their ills. Four decades later, as Utah prepared to become a state in 1896, medical science had made great advances and medical school attendance of from two to three years was required for those seeking to become licensed physicians.

Ogden's first doctor was William Ludlow McIntyre, who graduated from the College of Physicians and Surgeons of the western district of New York in 1838 and arrived in Weber County in 1852 after serving in the Mexican War. McIntyre, who was raised as a Methodist, was the city physician as well as having a private practice, and he was engaged in every sort of medical difficulty. He delivered babies, pulled teeth, and amputated limbs, and he made house calls throughout the county on horseback. Rooms in the Ogden Hotel on the southeast corner of 25th Street and Grant Avenue were used to house sick and injured travelers.

Henry H. Wadman arrived in Weber County in 1861 and settled in Warren, where he farmed and practiced medicine. Wadman suggested that his medical proficiency was based on thirty years of studying botany, which gave him the "remedies for all the ills that human nature is heir to." He practiced medicine for seventeen years before he was given formal recognition as a physician by the Salt Lake City Council.

Regula Anna Furrer Cardon was another pioneer doctor in Weber County. She was born in 1826 and received her medical training in Switzerland; she then journeyed to Utah after her conversion to Mormonism. She practiced medicine in Weber County after her arrival in 1857 and continued her practice during much of the last half of the nineteenth century. She lived first in Marriott and later in Ogden and traveled on horseback to visit the sick.

Midwives were an essential part of pioneer medical practice. These women who had been trained by working on the job were particularly helpful in childbirth. With no professional training, midwives practiced their trade throughout Weber County, beginning with Polly Barker Child, who arrived in the county in 1852 and worked as a midwife for the next two decades. Elizabeth Ivins Phillips Williams served as a midwife in Weber County for nearly five decades beginning in the late 1850s. Weber County had as many as thirty women who worked as midwives in the period before 1900. Midwives often were an important source of herbs, which they gathered in the summer and fall for year-round use in poultices, ointments, teas, and cures for diseases. Mary Ann Lewis Bingham was a midwife in Riverdale, and a Mrs. Colvin and a Mrs. Eggleston were midwives in Eden. Mary Heathman Smith served as both a midwife and a doctor in Huntsville. Other midwives in the county included Helen Blackwood Russell, Hannah P. Child Elmer, Jane Pavard, Mary Ann Blanch Gibson, and Polly Chapman Bybee Hammond.

Frontier settlements in the West, including those in Weber

County, were particularly susceptible to quacks and medicine show doctors who claimed to be able to cure diseases as well as aches and pains in an almost miraculous way. One such "doctor," who took out a full-page advertisement in the 1883 *Ogden City Directory*, was Andrew Lepper. Lepper established a bath house on the corner of Washington Boulevard and 23rd Street and suggested that his "HOT, COLD, MEDICATED, AND ELECTRIC BATHS" could treat all diseases without medicine. He further suggested that he could "DIAGNOSE ANY DISEASE without asking any questions, locate the symptoms and tell the cause." Lepper, like other charlatans, did not stay long in Weber County, but he is a prime example of many who followed the railroad and traveled country roads to put on a show and bilk the sick and unaware of their hard-earned money. H. J. Powers advertised himself as a medical doctor with specialties of practice in venereal diseases and diseases of the throat and lungs.

The need for medical services and hospital care became acute during the first years of the railroad. Diseases like smallpox, diphtheria, scarlet fever, and typhoid fever seemed to run rampant across the countryside. A.J. Metcalf became superintendent of the hospital rooms in the Ogden Hotel and Dr. J.J. Powers worked with him as the Ogden city physician. In 1879 sixty Huntsville children died of smallpox; Ogden had suffered a similar epidemic three years earlier. In 1882 Ogden City built a hospital, which was called by some a "pest house," on Burch Creek at what would now be about Washington Boulevard and 40th Street in South Ogden. The hospital included six rooms, each of which was twelve feet square. This isolation facility was devoted to the care of patients with smallpox and other contagious diseases.

In 1883 the Union Pacific Railroad Company purchased a two-story adobe building at 28th and Adams and converted it into a hospital. The original building had been completed in 1860 by Chauncey Hadlock. The Union Pacific Hospital at this location was in use for fourteen years, until 1897. The railroad hired doctors T.E. Mitchell and George W. Perkins and also brought Catholic sisters from St. Mary's Hospital in Notre Dame, Indiana, to serve as nurses. They included Sister Ledevina, who was the Mother Superior, and sisters Edwina, Visitation, and Benito.

The City of Ogden built another hospital in 1892 on 28th Street between Madison and Monroe avenues at a cost of $25,000. A year later, in the midst of the Panic of 1893, the hospital was closed and remained so until 1897. In 1897 a group of Weber County doctors leased the facility from the city and remodeled the building to include a surgical ward, operating rooms, and an office on the first floor as well as six or eight private rooms for convalescent patients on the second floor. Sleeping quarters for nurses were located in the attic. Patients were charged ten dollars a week for care in the general wards and fifteen dollars a week for care in private rooms. Hospital departments included surgery, obstetrics, eye and ear, general practice, children's diseases, diseases of women, and nervous diseases. Maude Edwards was the first head nurse, and this was the first hospital in Weber County where nurses were trained. Some of the first nurses trained at this facility included Nell Carruth Becker, Coral Tyler, Jessie Adams, Elizabeth Knowles, Janet Thwaites, Marie Rasmussen, and Nell M. Dilley Johns. The hospital operated from 1897 until the end of 1910 when the Dee Memorial Hospital was opened.

On 10 July 1910 Annie Taylor Dee broke ground on three acres of ground at Harrison and 24th Street for the Thomas D. Dee Memorial Hospital, which was completed less than six months later on 29 December 1910. The hospital was built by the Dee family in remembrance of their husband and father. Thomas D. Dee was born in Wales in 1844 and immigrated to Utah in 1860 with his family who had been converted to Mormonism. In April 1871 Dee married Annie Taylor and they made their home in Ogden, where Thomas made his living as a carpenter and was also involved in the city as assessor and tax collector, councilman, and police judge. With his friend David Eccles, Dee became involved in a number of business ventures including Anderson Lumber Company, the Ogden Sugar Company, the First National Bank, the Ogden Savings Bank, and the Utah Construction Company. Dee's lifelong interest in education led him to become a member of the Ogden City School Board, where he served as president for eight years. The oldest son of the Dee family, Thomas Reese, died in 1894 as the result of appendicitis and Thomas D. Dee died of pneumonia at age sixty-one in 1905 after falling into the south fork of the Ogden River and becoming chilled. Annie

Taylor Dee and her family decided to memorialize their husband and father and provide a much-needed hospital facility to Ogden and Weber County. The cost of the building was $75,000 and the hospital equipment was another $25,000.

On 29 December 1910 Annie Taylor Dee presented the hospital to the public and Ogden mayor William Glasmann and Weber County commissioner Oscar B. Madson accepted the hospital on behalf of their constituents. Mormon bishop James Taylor pronounced the dedicatory prayer and the Reverend John Edward Carver of the Presbyterian church gave the benediction. Rates at the new hospital were three dollars a day for private room, two dollars a day for a ward bed, twenty-five dollars for fourteen days as a maternity patient, and the operating room charge was ten dollars. Nurses were to work twelve-hour shifts with one-half day off per week when the patient load permitted. There were thirty-four physicians on the original hospital staff. During its first year the hospital housed 895 patients, 481 operations were performed, and five babies were delivered. In order to encourage mothers to have their babies delivered at the hospital, Annie Taylor Dee agreed to pay for the cost of the births.

The hospital was a significant contribution to the general health of Weber County residents and also served as a facility to train medical interns and nurses. In 1913 the hospital acquired its first x-ray machine and doctors performed its first blood transfusion, a gravity flow between two brothers. In 1915 the hospital was given to the Church of Jesus Christ of Latter-day Saints in order to maintain needed funding. The Dee Hospital served the citizens of Weber County and northern Utah for nearly six decades before the building of the McKay-Dee Hospital, and today the site continues to serve the community as a city park.

The hot springs near the mouth of Ogden Canyon had attracted visitors for centuries, and in 1904 the Ogden Canyon Sanitarium was opened there by G. W. Perkins and John D. Carnahan. In 1906 the Ogden Rapid Transit Company extended its lines to the sanitarium, and visitors suggested that their bodies were relieved by soaking in the mineral waters of the thermal springs. They also purged their bodies by drinking the mineral water, not unlike the actions of visitors to Bath in England. In 1919 a dance hall and lunch room were built adjacent to the sanitarium; however, in 1927 the all-wooden structure burned to the ground. The next year A. V. Smith bought the resort and rebuilt it, naming it El Monte Springs. Smith promoted his resort, which featured wrestling, gaming, swimming, private mineral baths, and marathon dances. Smith was unable to pay his bills, however, and from 1932 to 1942 the site remained vacant. It was purchased in 1942 by Harman W. Peery and renamed Riverside Gardens. This historic and scenic site is now known as Rainbow Gardens.

## *Newspapers*

More than fifty newspapers have been established in Weber County since the arrival of the railroad. Because of the large number of papers started in Ogden that were short-lived, the junction city has been called the "graveyard of Western journalism." The county had no newspapers before 1869, but the railroad and the growth and excitement it brought to Weber County seemed to provide fertile ground for newspapers. Many of those that began died almost immediately after being born. Thomas B.H. Stenhouse made plans to move his *Telegraph and Commercial Advertiser* to Ogden in April 1869 and publish the newspaper in the old Seventies Hall. The presses and type were shipped from Salt Lake City to Ogden by wagon, but Stenhouse's newspaper lasted only three months, from May through July. The first number of the *Telegraph* was issued on 11 May 1869, with John Jaques as editor and T. G. Webber as business manager.

The *Ogden Junction* was the leading Weber County newspaper from its first issue on 1 January 1870 until it ceased publication in 1881. Initially, Mormon apostle Franklin D. Richards was the editor of the *Junction* and Charles W. Penrose was the associate editor. By April 1871, Penrose had become editor. The paper continued to be published on a twice a week schedule, Wednesday and Saturday. On 28 July 1872 Penrose was walking down a Salt Lake City street when he was attacked by W.R. Keithly, a lawyer who was angry because of a recent article published in the *Junction*. Keithly struck Penrose two hard blows on the head with his cane—hard enough to break the cane and to stagger Penrose. Keithly was fined $100 for the attack; Penrose was able to continue editing.

By 1875 the *Junction* was published every morning but Sunday;

two years later, in 1877, Richard Ballantyne became the manager and proprietor and Scipio Africanus Kenner became the assistant editor. Penrose gained good newspaper experience in the decade he was with the *Junction,* and in 1879 he moved to the editorial staff of the *Deseret News.* He was replaced by Kenner as editor. At this same time, Frank J. Cannon began his involvement with the Ogden paper. Both the *Junction* and its successor, the *Ogden Daily Herald,* were pro-Mormon in their editorial bias and news reporting. The *Herald* was issued from 1881 to 1887 and was edited successively by John Nicholson, Leo Haefeli, Charles W. Hemenway, and Frank J. Cannon. Hemenway, who edited the paper during 1885 and 1886, was fined and thrown in jail after having been found guilty of libel in three separate cases.[21]

The *Standard* began publication on 1 January 1888 under the editorial leadership of Frank J. Cannon. Cannon, a son of Mormon apostle George Q. Cannon, was a skilled writer. Edward Tullidge in his *History of Northern Utah* wrote of Frank Cannon:

> No sooner had Frank J. Cannon taken editorial charge of the Ogden Herald than both sides were made to comprehend that a Journalist had "risen in Israel." . . . Like your true Journalist, Frank J. Cannon took the editorial sceptre which belonged to him, and shaped a policy and created a typical character for his paper. The very character of such a paper required a new and typical name; so "the boy" evidently remembering his great father, as the founder of the Western Standard (San Francisco) prevailed upon his company to change the name of the Ogden Herald to the Ogden Standard.[22]

By 1892 the *Standard* was published in two editions—a daily with a circulation of 1,500 and a twice-weekly (Wednesday and Saturday) with a circulation of 2,000. Cannon was an effective newspaperman, boosting Ogden, Weber County, the Republican party, and the free coinage of silver. From 1889 and for the next several years, Mormon apostle John Henry Smith noted that the Mormon church assisted the *Standard* with both advice and money, beginning with some "help of $8,000" in 1889.[23]

Late in 1893 Frank Cannon resigned as editor of the *Standard.*

He had been involved in politics for some time, but had recently been elected Utah's territorial delegate to Congress as a Republican. Cannon would serve one term as territorial delegate and then a short term as one of Utah's first two senators. The editorship of the *Standard* passed to William Glasmann, who managed the paper until his death in 1916. Glasmann became both manager and editor of the paper, and on 13 April 1896 he stated that the *Standard* would begin publication twice a day—mornings and evenings. In 1904 the *Morning Examiner* began to be published under the editorship of Frank Francis. In 1920 the *Examiner* merged with the *Standard* and became the *Standard-Examiner*, with J.U. Eldredge, Jr. and A.L. Glasmann as publishers.

There were a number of other papers published in Ogden; they included the *Ogden Freeman*, the *Amateur*, the *Weber County Chronicle*, the *Morning Rustler*, the *Daily Pilot*, the *Ogden News*, the *Utah Daily Union*, the *Ogden Argus*, the *Ogden Commercial*, the *Utah Democrat*, the *Ogden Post*, the *Leader*, the *Evening Sun*, the *Utah State Journal*, the *Sun*, and the *Ogden Times*. The *Ogden Freeman* advertised itself as "aggressive and progressive and Anti-Mormon, Anti-Chinese, and Anti-Indian." Charles King, editor of the *Morning Rustler*, was tarred and feather by a mob in Ogden in 1880. King moved on to the *Utah Daily Union*, but he apparently did not learn to temper his writing style; in 1889 King was shot in the throat and leg by Edward W. Exum of Ogden, an ex-deputy who was enraged about an article that tarnished the reputation of his wife. The newspapers and city directories furnished information about life in Weber County as well as advertisements for businesses and entertainment.

## *Education*

For more than fourteen decades, education has been a major priority for the residents of Weber County. The first school in Weber County was held at Brown's Fort on 30th Street and Wall Avenue in 1849, with Charilla Abbott as the teacher. Her rudimentary school included pens made from chicken feathers, letters pasted on paddles for the children to learn the alphabet, and children drawing letters on their hands with charcoal to practice writing and remembering them. The cabin in which the school was held was a one-room log cabin with a dirt floor and doors hung on wooden latches. It was used as both church and school. Later that same year, a twenty-by-thirty-foot building was constructed at Farr's Fort and was used as a school. Sanford Bingham and a Mr. Walton were the first teachers at Farr's Fort.

Schools were established in most of the communities of the county as population increased, and the tuition for the children was usually paid with produce. On 10 May 1851 the Ogden City Council divided the city into four school districts and passed an ordinance to provide for a free school system for students between the ages of four and twenty-one. The school system was to receive three dollars a year for each student. Ogden's free school experiment was abandoned after one year, however, because of the difficulty in collecting taxes to maintain the system. In 1867 a system of "tuition schools" was established, and the Central School, built in 1879–80, operated on that basis.

For the first four decades schools in the county were tied closely to religion. Schools sponsored and supervised by Mormons were begun in Ogden and in all of the smaller communities in the county. Church buildings were sometimes used during the week for school, and in some communities separate school buildings were constructed. An adobe schoolhouse was constructed in Ogden in 1853, and school buildings were also constructed in North Ogden (1852), Uintah (1852), Bingham's Fort (1852), Slaterville (1855), Riverdale (1859), Plain City (1860), Harrisville (1863), Wilson (1864), Huntsville (1862), Marriott (1863), West Weber (1861), Eden (1866), Mound Fort (1867), Hooper (1869), Kanesville (1883), Roy (1885), Warren (1884–86), and West Warren (1898).

As increasing numbers of Catholics and Protestants moved to Ogden, particularly after the coming of the railroad, new schools sponsored by these religious groups were opened to educate children and to expose Mormon children to ideas from the outside world, particularly about the "evils" of plural marriage. In 1878 the Catholic Sacred Heart Academy was opened by the Sisters of the Holy Cross, and in 1882 St. Joseph's School was opened. In 1892 a beautiful new Sacred Heart Academy was opened on the corner of 25th and Quincy; it remained in operation as a boarding school from 1892 to

1938. The new Sacred Heart Academy occupied a building which was 80 feet by 250 feet in size and was built at a cost of $129,000, with financing coming primarily from Saint Mary's College in South Bend, Indiana. The faculty included twenty-one sisters who taught subjects ranging from English to Latin and bookkeeping to shorthand. Classrooms were located on the first and second floors, while dormitories were included on the third and fourth floors. The school was built to accommodate between 500 and 600 young women, many of whom would board as well as attend school in the beautiful building.

An Episcopal school was conducted for two decades during the 1870s and 1880s at the Church of the Good Shepherd; and a Methodist school was begun in 1872 in Ogden. The New West Educational Commission sponsored by the Congregational church maintained schools in Ogden, Hooper, Lynne, and South Weber.

On 26 September 1880 the Central School building of Ogden was dedicated by territorial school superintendent and Mormon church president John Taylor. The schoolhouse was located on Grant Avenue between 25th and 26th streets; it was a substantial two-story brick building which cost $15,000 to construct and housed 800 students in 1883. Students were charged a quarterly tuition fee to attend Central School, and the school provided education for many of Ogden's students—from those who were beginning their education to others who were preparing for higher education. Louis Moench was then principal of the school. With tuition payments coming from the parents of the schoolchildren, school teachers began to take home wages on a monthly basis. During the 1885–86 school year, the following salaries were paid to Ogden school teachers per month: W.H. Jones, $100; Mosiah Hall, $80; Marian Treseder, $50; Ruthinda Moench, $50; Ellen Pingree, $35; Georgiana Fellows, $30; Nellie Dana, $30; M. N. Staples, $30.[24] The three Ogden school trustees, who until 1889 were generally Mormons, were paid an annual salary of $200 during the 1880s.

The Utah Territorial Reform School was established in Ogden in 1888, in part, because "Ogden was so accessible" to all parts of the territory by railroad. The site for the school was selected at 20th Street and Monroe; it opened in 1889 and initially housed twenty-three inmates. The building included three floors and a basement. In 1896 what had become the Utah State Industrial School was moved to the old military academy site on north Washington Boulevard. Boys were taught vocational trades and girls attended regular school for part of the day and devoted the remainder to learning domestic and social skills. The 20th and Monroe site became the home for the Utah State School for the Deaf and Blind. The same board of trustees had responsibilities for both deaf children and blind children, and they essentially operated two institutions at the same site. Initially the Deaf School offered kindergarten, primary, and grammar grades; in 1907 it began to offer a four-year high school course. High school courses for girls included domestic arts, domestic science, music, and dancing; the curriculum for boys included carpentry, shoemaking, printing, animal husbandry, horticulture, dairying, and poultry raising. Frank M. Driggs was superintendent of the school from 1896 to 1940.

In 1886 T. B. Lewis moved from Salt Lake City to Ogden and was placed in charge of the schools in Ogden. Lewis reported to E.H. Anderson, who was superintendent of all schools in Weber County, and Lewis immediately began to champion free schools in Ogden. In a series of reports to Anderson, Lewis continually maintained the idea that the schools should be supported by public taxes and that they should not be tuition schools. In 1889 Ogden school officials adopted the idea of free schools. The 24 August 1889 *Standard* wrote, "Ogden has free schools, something that no other place in the Territory can boast of." An Ogden school census for 1889 suggested that there were 6,250 children in the city, with about half being Mormon and half being non-Mormon. A year later, in 1890, the territorial legislature of Utah adopted a free school law for the entire territory. In 1890 the Methodist church proposed a "University of Utah" for Ogden to be built in the vicinity of 30th Street and Tyler Avenue. A foundation of red sandstone was laid that same year, but the building was never completed.

The 1890 territorial free school law noted that city boards of education should include the mayor and a trustee from each municipal ward. The first Ogden City school board included Raisford Smith, W. W. Funge, L. B. Adams, Thomas D. Dee, W. E. Cary, and Mayor Fred Kiesel. The board began to make plans to bond to build new schools, to acquire sites, and to provide education for children in Ogden from six years to eighteen years of age. W. N. Schilling was selected as the first superintendent of Ogden city schools in 1890; he was followed by R. S. Page, William Allison, and John M. Mills.

Elementary schools in the city grew out of the LDS ward schools. In 1892 the Madison School was built on Madison between 24th and 25th streets and across the street from Lester Park. Ogden City also enlarged or rebuilt the Grant School, the Washington School, and the Mound Fort School. The city school district built the following elementary schools: Dee, Lewis, Pingree, Lorin Farr, Polk, Quincy, Lincoln, and Hopkins. Dee School, built in 1904, was named after Thomas D. Dee, school board president at the time. Pingree School, built in 1893, was named for Job Pingree and was built for $17,157. In 1890 the Five Point School district became part of Ogden City and a new building built at a cost of $16,770 was named the Five Point School; it was renamed Lincoln School in 1919. The Quincy School was built in 1892 at a cost of $15,490. The Lewis School, named in honor of Theodore B. Lewis, was placed in a remodeled four-room building which had previously been a railroad hospital at 28th and Adams. The Lorin Farr School was built in 1910–11 at a cost of $25,000. The West Ogden School, built in 1893, was remodeled in 1919–20 at a cost of $200,000 and renamed the Hopkins School in honor of Karl Hopkins, school superintendent at that time. The Polk School was built from 1926 to 1929 at a cost of $103,000.

The budget expended to operate the Ogden city schools grew over the years, beginning with a $50,000 budget in 1891–92. There was a $110,168 operating budget in 1904–05 and a budget of $232,162 in 1912–13. The 1927–28 school year saw expenses of $584,976, and 1942–43 expenses were $814,608.

The Ogden School District added junior high schools to the district in 1912. The junior highs were separated by both curriculum and distance from elementary schools and included grades seven, eight, and nine. As the Ogden District was being born in 1890, it added to its curriculum some high school courses, particularly in English. By 1898, 185 high school students were enrolled in the Ogden District. In 1896 the Ogden District leased the New West Educational Society school building at 25th and Adams for use as a high school; and in 1898 the district purchased the building for $15,000. High school courses were held in the building from 1896 to 1909. In 1909 a new Ogden high school building was constructed at 25th and Monroe on land donated by Fred J. Kiesel. The Eccles Lumber Company built the building at a cost of $100,000.

The schools in Weber County outside of Ogden City were consolidated in a county school district in 1905. The first elected members of the Weber County School Board included F. W. Stratford, J. B. Carver, A. C. Christensen, B. F. Blaylock, and Lester H. Froerer. Superintendents of the Weber County School District after its consolidation in 1905 included W. N. Petterson, Thomas E. McKay, Lars E. Eggertsen, B. A. Fowler, and Keith Wahlquist. The new county school district was faced with the task of bringing the twenty-one schoolhouses of the county, some of which had been used for several decades, up to current standards. Under consolidation, a uniform school tax was adopted for the entire county, and the school board noted that consolidation not only provided greater efficiency but also provided fair opportunities for all children in the county to receive an adequate education. In 1905 school property in the district was valued at $102,713; in 1920 this value had increased to $315,870. The county district was making efforts to provide "comfortable school wagons" to transport children to school, and as the roads were improved the wagons were replaced with trucks. By 1920 the Weber County schools included 2,969 students in twenty-one schools taught by ninety-four teachers in grade levels one through nine.

Weber County students who wished to complete high school during the first two decades of the twentieth century could choose to attend the Weber Academy or Ogden High School. There was no high school elsewhere in the county. A $300,000 bond issue to build a county high school was approved in 1926 by the voters of Weber County by a vote of 733 to 480. A site on the east side of Washington between 11th and 12th streets was chosen for the new high school, and construction began in 1926. The school was completed in 1927. Even though the building was still under construction, school was held in the facility beginning in the fall of 1926. A new south wing was added to Weber High School during 1953–54.

In 1888 the Church of Jesus Christ of Latter-day Saints established a general LDS Church Board of Education with a major goal to make efforts to combine secular and religious education, initially with the establishment of church academies and later by providing LDS religion classes in locations adjacent to public schools. In September 1888 the Weber LDS Stake Presidency organized the Weber Stake Board of Education with stake president Lewis W. Shurtliff elected as president of the board. Other members of the board included officials of the stake—Charles Middleton, N. C. Flygare, Joseph Stanford, Louis F. Moench, Robert McQuarrie, Thomas J. Stevens, and David McKay. The Weber Stake Board advertised that in January 1889 the Weber Stake Academy would begin classes, with Louis Moench, then serving a mission in Germany and Switzerland, as principal.

Opening day for the academy was 7 January 1889 at the Second Ward building, with one hundred students gathering to hear speeches during both the morning and afternoon. By the end of the first term, 171 students had registered for academy classes. Tuition ranged from three to six dollars per ten-week term, depending on in which department (preparatory, intermediate, or academic) students were registered. A complete school year consisted of four terms. As principal, Moench was paid a salary of $125 a month; his two assistants, Lorenzo Waldram and Edwin C. Cutler, were each paid seventy dollars a month. The large majority of the students of the academy came from Ogden City; about 20 percent came from the communities in the county. Mormon theology was taught along with elocution, rhetoric, physiology, philosophy, botany, zoology, geology, algebra, surveying, astronomy, bookkeeping, vocal music, ladies fancy work, phonography, German, Latin, architectural drawing, instrumental music, U.S. history, and calisthenics.

The Weber Stake Academy struggled during the Moench years (1889–1902). After meeting in ward buildings and the Ogden LDS Tabernacle, the academy by early 1892 was housed in its own building, built on the west side of Jefferson Avenue between 24th and 25th streets. The Weber Stake Board of Education with great effort and personal sacrifice paid off the mortgage on the building after more than a decade of gathering funds. The Weber Academy received annual appropriations from the LDS Church Board of Education, including $900 in 1899 and $5,000 during the 1901–02 school year. The academy celebrated Utah's statehood, began to compete in athletic events, including girls basketball, held debates, and moved from being primarily a preparatory or elementary school to becoming more of a high school by the time Louis Moench retired in 1902.

In April 1902 David O. McKay was "unanimously elected" to become principal of the Weber Stake Academy at an annual salary of $1,500, and he presided over the school from 1902 until 1908. McKay, who had grown to manhood in Huntsville, had attended the Weber Stake Academy and was a graduate of the University of Utah with a Normal degree. He taught at the Weber Academy from 1897 to 1902 and in April 1906 was appointed a member of the Quorum of Twelve Apostles of the Church of Jesus Christ of Latter-day Saints. McKay's interest in the Weber school remained strong over the next six decades.

During the first two decades of the twentieth century, Weber moved from being an academy to becoming a college. Ernest W. Nichols was hired to head the music program, and he remained for eighteen years at Weber. At the end of the 1911–12 school year, all preparatory courses were ended at the Weber Academy; from that time until the beginning of the 1916–17 school year only high school classes were offered at the academy. Normal school curriculum was added to the academy classes, and the academy now served two purposes—to educate high school students and to educate and prepare teachers. Henry Aldous Dixon became the first head of the Normal Department in 1916. Dixon presided over Weber on two different occasions and later represented Utah in Congress from 1954 to 1960. Weber Academy now offered both high school and junior college courses, and this arrangement continued until the end of the 1922–23 school year, when the high school program was completely eliminated. During the 1924–25 school year, a new gymnasium was completed on the 25th street side of the campus.

In 1912 the Ogden Rapid Transit Company offered the following round-trip fares to Ogden students of the academy and to students of Ogden public schools: Farr West, 20 cents; Plain City, 25 cents; Pleasant View, 20 cents; Harrisville, 15 cents, and North Ogden, 15 cents. Enrollments grew gradually. In 1912 there were 456 high school students enrolled at the academy; by 1920 that number had reached 812. During the 1922–23 school year, there were 258 college students enrolled and twenty-four graduated; by the 1930–31 year there were 412 students and ninety graduates. During the fall of 1922, the students and faculty of Weber began the traditional Mount Ogden hike by hiking the trail through Taylor's Canyon and Malan's Basin and planting a flagpole at the summit of Mount Ogden.

Aaron W. Tracy was president of Weber College from 1922 to 1935 and presided over the transition of the college from church ownership to state ownership. Tracy was born in Marriott and served as student body president of the Weber Academy and of Brigham Young University. By 1928 the Mormon church had begun to divest itself of many of its academies and other educational institutions in favor of supporting adjunct seminaries. Weber College was faced with several choices, including becoming a college dependent on support from Ogden City and Weber County, becoming a state-supported junior college, becoming a branch campus of the University of Utah, or being phased out as a college.

The 1931 Utah legislature passed a bill which provided for the transfer of two LDS church-owned colleges to the state of Utah; Snow College was transferred in 1932 and Weber College in 1933. Ira Huggins, J. Francis Fowles, and George Fuller were three of the Weber County legislators who were particularly instrumental in pushing the Weber College bill through the legislature. Enrollments at the college reached 1,030 in the 1932–33 school year. For the next three decades Weber College grew and developed under state sponsorship before becoming a four-year college in 1964.

### *Railroads*

In many ways, life in Weber County had been dominated by the railroad since 1869. After two decades of growth and development, it was decided to build a new railroad depot. In 1888 the Ogden Union Railway and Depot Company was organized to oversee the 131 acres given originally by Brigham Young to be used as the "permanent junction of the two roads." Charles Francis Adams, Jr., president of the Union Pacific Railroad, commissioned his friend Henry Van Brunt, one of the leading architects in America, to design the new railroad station at Wall Avenue and 25th Street. Van Brunt was the architect for several Union Pacific depots in the West. Van Brunt began his designs in 1886 and, after numerous changes, the building was completed in 1889. Between 5,000 and 6,000 people attended the cornerstone-laying ceremonies on 5 November 1888 as the stone was placed by the Grand Master Mason from Salt Lake City, Samuel Paul. The building was completed on 31 July 1889 and was described as a station/hotel, with the south end of the building providing thirty-three guest rooms on the second floor; the kitchen and dining rooms were on the first floor. Ticket offices, a telegraph office, and Pullman offices were located on the lower floor in the center of the building. This handsome two-story brick and stone building served as the Ogden depot from 1889 to 1924.

Railroad traffic through Ogden continued to increase; in 1910 millions of passengers passed through the city. That year saw 33,040 engines, 74,750 passenger cars, 33,987 baggage cars, and 31,034 mail cars pass through the Ogden yards. The Southern Pacific Railroad did the greatest amount of railroad business in Ogden. It had three large shop buildings made of white brick and stone. The Southern Pacific employed more than 500 men in its shops in the Weber County area, while the Union Pacific and Denver and Rio Grande each kept more than 125 men employed in their shops.

By 1915 it was reported that fifty-one passenger trains passed through the Ogden yards every twenty-four hours. There were 2,503 workers employed by the steam railroads at an annual payroll of $3,872,568, and there were 797 employed by the Ogden Union Railroad and Depot Company, with a payroll of $817,000. The Southern Pacific Railroad was the county's largest company and employed about 1,000 people. There were 606 employed by the sub-urban electric lines, with a payroll of $678,300; and sugar companies in the area employed 1,500 with an annual payroll of $980,000. By 1924 the Southern Pacific employed 1,683 people in Weber County, with an annual payroll of $2,400,000.

The railroads and Ogden's stockyards made it possible for Ogden to handle more cattle, hogs, and sheep than any other city in the Twelfth Federal Reserve District, which was essentially composed of the western United States. Ogden had also become a grain center second only to Portland, Oregon, in the West in grain commerce. New mills and storage facilities established in Ogden included the Sperry Flour Company, the Globe Grain and Milling Company, the Albers Brothers Milling Company, and the Hilton Flour Mills. The Columbia Club Cigar Company, which was organized in Ogden in 1892, employed about thirty people and produced about 1.25 million cigars a year.

Ogden's role as junction city grew as the railroads brought immigrants and visitors to Weber County. In 1891 President Benjamin Harrison came to Ogden by train, and in September 1909 President William Howard Taft visited the city. On 13 September 1912 ex-president and Bull Moose candidate Theodore Roosevelt made a major speech in Ogden during his presidential campaign, and in September 1919 President Woodrow Wilson passed through Ogden on his way to Salt Lake City and Pueblo, Colorado. In Pueblo, Wilson suffered the physical breakdown which essentially ended his political career. The railroad depot saw Weber County soldiers leave for the Spanish–American War and World War I; and, as the soldiers came home, they greeted their loved ones at the depot.

The Bamberger Electric Railway was built under the leadership of Simon Bamberger, pioneer Utah coal-mine operator and railroad entrepreneur. Bamberger projected the Ogden-Salt Lake City line as a steam line as early as 1891; and in 1908 Ogden was connected to Salt Lake City on what was known as the Bamberger. The line was electrified on 28 May 1910 and renamed the Bamberger Electric Railway. The business of the line included commuter and shopper travel between Ogden and Salt Lake City as well as heavy summer traffic to Lagoon resort. Bamberger had developed Lagoon at Farmington to compete with the Denver and Rio Grande's resort, Lake Park, on the shore of the Great Salt Lake. In 1908 the Bamberger had five daily trains running both directions. The Ogden depot of the Bamberger was located on Lincoln Avenue just north of 24th Street. On 7 May 1918 the Ogden station, car barn, and some of the passenger equipment were destroyed by fire. Replacement equipment was difficult to obtain until the end of World War I. The advantage the Bamberger had over the Union Pacific line from Ogden to Salt Lake City was that it made stops at most of the small towns on the way, while the UP trains did not normally stop between Ogden and Salt Lake City. In 1914 the electrified Utah-Idaho Central was established, connecting Ogden with Preston, Idaho. A branch line of this road was extended to Plain City.

The Ogden City Railway Company (OCR) made connections for passengers who arrived in Ogden by train. The OCR was begun in 1883 with mule-drawn cars. The lines were extended in 1889 and steam engines replaced the mules. In 1891 tracks were re-laid to prepare to electrify the system. In 1900 David Eccles and some of his associates purchased the company and reorganized it as the Ogden Rapid Transit Company. In 1913 a line was extended to Huntsville up Ogden Canyon; another line extended to the hot springs on the North.

In 1901 a revamping of Southern Pacific (SP) lines was begun. William Hood, chief engineer for the SP, proposed routing SP trains directly west from Ogden across the Great Salt Lake to avoid the route around the north end of the lake over Promontory Summit. The Lucin Cutoff, as the lake route would come to be called, would save forty-three miles and would eliminate sharp curves and steep grades associated with the northern route. Hood's proposed route began to be built in March 1902 and included a combination of fill in shallow areas and trestles in deeper parts of the lake. The cutoff was engineered to cross the tip of the Promontory peninsula. Workmen on the route often worked ten-hour shifts, with shifts running around the clock. They were usually quartered on the bridge they were building across the lake. Charges were four dollars a week for board and room on site, and liquor was forbidden. Work on the cutoff was completed in 1904, and the route was opened to freight traffic on 8 March 1904; passenger traffic began on 18 September 1904. The cutoff needed continued maintenance because of storms on the Great Salt Lake. High winds and heavy waves continually caused severe damage to the manmade dike. Rocks weighing as much as twenty tons were dumped on the sides of the cutoff to mitigate wave action from storms. In 1929 a new station called Bridge was built on the cutoff to assist in maintaining the dike and its double track. A stern-wheel, double-stack steamboat, *Promontory,* was involved in the construction of the Lucin Cutoff.

### *Banking*

In the years between 1890 and 1910, employment in the steam railroad industry in Utah jumped from 2,094 in 1890 to 3,414 in 1900 and then to 8,199 in 1910. The railroad industry became the primary export-based employer in the state in 1910, and Weber County's role as the railroad center of the state benefited by this growth. Stock raising was the number two export-based industry in the state during this two-decade period, and Weber County also became a central player in this industry. Export-based industries brought capital to the state and provided for other economic development. The first cattleman's congress in the United States was held in Ogden in 1892, and the Ogden Packing and Provision Company began to operate in 1901. Meat-packing became an important business. The annual Ogden Livestock Show became a noted high point in the county and state beginning in 1919.

The railroad promoted commerce and industry, which in turn promoted Ogden as an important banking center. In 1875 John William Guthrie began to do banking business in Corinne and soon established a branch in Ogden on 24th Street. In 1878 H. O. Harkness acquired the Guthrie bank, and in 1884 Harkness's bank received a national charter and a new name—the Commercial National Bank. A second Ogden bank was established in 1875 by J. E. Dooly, a non-Mormon agent for the Wells-Fargo Company; in 1880 Guthrie became a partner in the Dooly bank. Three years later, in 1883, Dooly and Guthrie pooled their resources and organized the Utah National Bank in Ogden. Dooly became president of the Utah National Bank and remained in that position until his death in 1911. Ralph E. Hoag then became president of the bank, and he was succeeded in 1917 by David C. Eccles.

By 1881 the directors of the Deseret National Bank, which was organized in 1872 in Salt Lake City under the direction of Mormon church leaders, decided to expand to Ogden and gain some influence on financial affairs in the junction city. Ogden First National Bank began operations on 3 January 1882 and received deposits from ZCMI and many Mormon businesses and families. David Peery, David Eccles, and Matthew Browning became investors in Ogden

First National, and by the end of the 1880s they were heavily involved in the decisions related to the bank. Peery became the first Ogden president of the bank in 1888 and remained president until 1894. He was succeeded by David Eccles, who remained president until his death in 1912. Eccles's widespread financial interests included his involvement in nine banks, serving as president of six of them, including the Ogden Savings Bank.

Although a bank president several times over, David Eccles kept his office at the Eccles Lumber Company on 24th Street in Ogden. He often kept his banks afloat during difficult periods with his own resources. He refused to liquidate the assets of his banks during periods of panic, and with his banking colleagues Peery, Browning, and others Eccles established a strong financial community in Weber County. When Eccles died in 1912, his close banking associate Matthew S. Browning became the president of the six banks. Marriner S. Eccles, one of David's sons, was particularly involved in continuing the banking tradition in the Eccles family, and in 1924 Marriner and his brother George formed a partnership with the Browning family in Ogden to form the Eccles-Browning Affiliated Banks, which developed into the First Security Corporation by 1928.

The Utah Loan and Trust Company was established in 1888 by Charles Comstock and Franklin S. Richards, who were sons of Mormon apostle and Ogden resident Franklin D. Richards. This new banking institution experienced extreme financial difficulty during the 1890s and was saved from failure through the efforts of another Mormon apostle, Heber J. Grant. Grant had become involved in Ogden business circles a decade earlier when Heber J. Grant and Company, an insurance firm which had its headquarters in Salt Lake City, opened a branch office in Ogden. Brigham H. Goddard, a partner of Grant in the insurance business, ran the Ogden operation for the company during the 1880s. In 1892 he purchased the Ogden branch for $1,500 and formed the B. H. Goddard Agency. Goddard's son Kelly and his grandson Jack continued to develop the business, and from it, in 1958, the United Savings and Loan Association was formed.

## *Agriculture, Industry, and the Economy*

Subsistence agriculture had been a major part of the economy and lifestyle of Weber County since its settlement. By 1890 the economy, which had begun to depend so much on the railroad, began to change in other ways throughout the county. Sugar beet cultivation, sugar factories, and canneries began to appear in the county and would become a significant segment of the county economy during the next three decades. By 1890 county farmers sought new sources of water for irrigation to increase crops under cultivation. Included in the water discussion were possible new sources of water as well as the construction of dams, canals, and ditches.

During the period from 1889 to 1910, Ogden City water rights were controlled by the Bear Lake and River Water Works and Irrigation Company; however, in 1910 Ogden City repurchased these water rights for $100,000 and resolved not to let control of city water pass into private hands again. The decades surrounding the turn of the century saw numerous suits filed within Weber County to clarify water rights between towns and villages.

In 1884 the Davis and Weber Counties Canal Company was formed with its prime stockholders including Feramorz Little, William R. Smith, William Jennings, Anson Call, and William H. Hooper. Initially, the company began to dig a canal which started in the canyon of the Weber River about a mile from the canyon mouth and a half mile below Devil's Gate. The canal was to carry water to Ogden, Kaysville, and "Hooperville." By 1894 the directors of the company decided to build a storage dam on East Canyon Creek twelve miles south of Morgan in the Narrows, also called Red Rock Gorge. This site would become the location for five different dams during the next several decades until the last (and current) East Canyon Dam was built in 1966. In 1913 the canal from the mouth of Weber Canyon was lined with concrete and an electric power plant was built about seven miles west from the canyon mouth. This small hydroelectric plant was called the Bostaph Electric Plant and was located adjacent to the Weber County–Davis County boundary.

The Pioneer Electric Power Company was organized in Ogden in 1893, and the company organizers made plans to dam the Ogden

River about ten miles east of Ogden and use the water behind the dam for culinary water and for the irrigation of an additional 20,000 acres in Weber County. Electricity would also be produced by using the stored water to turn generators, and the electricity would provide power for Ogden, for developing factories, and for electric railways in Ogden and Salt Lake City. First counselor George Q. Cannon of the Mormon church's First Presidency became the president of the company, and this appointment in part recognized the $520,000 investment of the church in the project. The total investment was $2,500,000.

Pioneer Electric projects included a temporary dam on the Ogden River just below Wheeler Canyon which was completed in 1896. This temporary dam was followed by a permanent dam across Ogden Canyon at the Pineview site. It was completed at a cost of $250,000 in 1898 and was 340 feet long from canyon wall to canyon wall, 93 feet thick, and 60 feet high. The Pioneer Power Plant, which was located downstream from the mouth of Ogden Canyon at 12th Street and Harrison, was completed in 1897 and had a capacity of 10,000 horsepower. This plant was supplied with water from the dam by a six-mile-long wooden-stave pipe which was reinforced with bands of steel. The construction of the dam and the pipe was a major engineering achievement. In August 1897 the Pioneer company merged with Union Light and Power Company of Salt Lake City; it would later become part of Utah Power and Light Corporation.

The sugar beet industry became an important part of the Utah economy during the last part of the nineteenth century. In 1891 a beet sugar factory was constructed at Lehi by the Utah Sugar Company, which was largely owned by the LDS church. David Eccles and Charles W. Nibley began to see the success of the sugar beet industry, and with other investors they built factories in Ogden in 1898 and Lewiston in 1905. The Ogden Sugar Company was organized in 1897 in a meeting held at the Weber Club. Directors of the Ogden Sugar Company included David Eccles, Thomas D. Dee, Hiram H. Spencer, Joseph Clark, George Q. Cannon, John R. Winder, John Scowcroft, Fred J. Kiesel, and Ephraim P. Ellison. In 1898 the Ogden Utah Sugar Factory began production and in its initial year produced 25,716 100-pound bags of sugar from 15,205 tons of sugar beets. Weber County farmers and others in northern Utah were sought by the company to contract to grow sugar beets for the Ogden facility. In 1915 the Amalgamated Sugar Company was organized and included the Ogden Sugar Company. In 1899, 58,348 100-pound bags of sugar were produced at the Ogden factory; in 1900, 59,126 bags were produced. The sugar beet industry continued to grow during the first two decades of the twentieth century. In 1916, on the eve of U.S. entry into World War I, Utah ranked third in the nation in sugar production. Sugar beets became a major source of income for many Weber County farmers during the era from 1890 to 1920.

The increase in home-grown sugar stimulated the candy industry in Utah. The Ogden-based Shupe-Williams Candy Company was incorporated in 1900 and located its large four-story candy factory on Wall Avenue and 26th Street. Shupe-Williams began in a one-room candy kitchen just below Grant Avenue on the south side of 25th Street. This candy company became well known throughout the region, as salesmen were sent out to adjoining states. The Shupe-Williams factory had a whistle which was blown whenever important local, state, or national events occurred.

The food-canning industry in Weber County and in Utah began in 1886 in Ogden. Alexander McKinney and Robert Lundy began their Colorado-Utah Canning Company in an old pickle factory on west 29th Street. Although this first company operated for less than one year, it provided an impetus to the canning industry, particularly in Weber County. In a 1929 *Ogden Standard-Examiner* interview, Mrs. McKinney remembered that they paid farmers six dollars a ton for their tomatoes, paid their tomato peelers four cents a bucket to remove the tomato skins, and sold a twenty-four-can case of tomatoes for $1.85. She also noted that tomatoes were the first vegetables to be canned in Ogden; but over the next decade plums, peas, apples, corn, pears, catsup, berries, pumpkins, string beans, and peaches were canned and shipped across the country. In 1888 Lundy and McKinney dissolved their partnership; each went his own way although both continued to work in the canning business in Ogden.

By 1890 Robert Lundy had established a partnership with I. N. Pierce in the Utah Canning Company and they began to process Pierce's Pork and Beans. In 1897 Thomas D. Dee became the president of the Utah Canning Company. With the assistance of his partner David Eccles, the Utah Canning Company became one of the most stable and enduring canning companies in the state. In 1904 the Utah Canning Company produced 45,000 cases of canned tomatoes. In 1960 the Utah Canning Company merged with the Pleasant Grove Canning Company to form the multimillion dollar Utah Packing Company.

Two dozen canneries were organized in the Weber County area in the period from 1890 to 1920. Some of the most significant companies were McKinney's Ogden Canning Company; Utah Canning Company (Lundy and Pierce); Wasatch Gardens and Orchard Canning Company; Utah Packing Corporation, a subsidiary of California Packing (products from Weber County sold under the Del Monte and Sunkist labels); Hooper Cannery; Star Canning Company; and Ogden Canning Company. The three decades from 1890 to 1920 were a period of great growth in the cannery industry in Weber County; county farmers found many markets for their produce but were not always happy with the prices paid. By 1915 farmers were receiving forty-two dollars a ton for peas and fifteen dollars a ton for tomatoes. In the decade from 1900 to 1910, eleven canneries operated in Weber County; from 1910 to 1920 twenty canneries were in operation, and this number was impacted in part because of World War I.

The highest number of canneries to operate in any decade in Weber County came in the 1920s when there were twenty-two canneries in operation. William J. "Jake" Parker was particularly active in the cannery business in Weber County, and in March 1917 he organized his five canneries into the Utah Packing Company, which in 1924 became the Utah Packing Corporation, the largest operator of canning factories in the state. Nephi Preston Hardy and his son Nephi Edwin Hardy were important early canning operators in Hooper and Roy and had a major impact on Utah canning in Spanish Fork.[25]

Fresh fruit and vegetables also were shipped out of Weber County on the railroad. Peaches, pears, and apples grown in the Farr Orchards along the Ogden River and in the McGriff Orchards in North Ogden were wrapped in paper, packed in boxes, and shipped by railroad, particularly to the east of Utah. North Ogden cherries became well known throughout the West, just as Hooper tomatoes had become famous.

The livestock industry in Weber County began when Miles Goodyear began to collect a variety of animals. It evolved to 1892, when the first cattlemen's congress in the United States was held in Ogden, with representatives from fifteen states. In 1906 the Ogden Packing and Provision Company began to operate as a meat-packing house, and by 1914 two meat-packing houses were in operation in the county. During that same year, these packing houses employed 130 people and produced $1.9 million worth of dressed animals. During the world war, Ogden became a major center for shipping, feeding, and marketing livestock. By 1916 the Ogden Packing and Provision Company employed 240 people, and a year later it was the largest packing house west of Omaha. During 1919, the year following the end of the war, the Ogden Union Stockyards dealt with shipments of from three thousand to seven thousand animals a day.[26]

World War I and the increased supply of electrical power which came after the turn of the century both stimulated the flour milling industry. By 1919 Utah's milling industry, centered in Ogden, had become one of the ten leading flour milling centers of the United States, and Utah became an exporter of flour.

The Utah Construction Company was organized in 1900 with capital of $200,000. The beginnings of this wide-ranging construction company were found in the Corey brothers' railroad construction company, founded by W.W., C.J., and A.B. Corey in 1881. In 1887 E.O. and W.H. Wattis became partners in the Corey brothers' firm. This railroad construction company experienced financial difficulties during the 1890s along with many American businesses and was reorganized in 1900 under the leadership of David Eccles as the Utah Construction Company. During the next half-century, Utah Construction became involved in a wide variety of projects including the completion of numerous railroad lines and participation in the six-company consortium which built Boulder Dam in the 1930s.

The Browning Arms Company was one of Ogden's and Weber County's most well known businesses. The company was founded by John Moses Browning, one of the most famous gun inventors in the world. Jonathan Browning, John's father, was born in Tennessee in 1805 and died in Ogden in 1879. Jonathan became a skilled gunmaker, converted to Mormonism, lived in Nauvoo, traveled to Utah in the Mormon exodus, and became a polygamist and the father of several families. John M. Browning, who was born in 1855 in Ogden, and his brother Matthew S. Browning grew from childhood to adulthood in Ogden and Weber County. John's first invention was a single-shot .22-caliber rifle that he pieced together in 1878. From then until his death in 1926 he was continually involved in inventing guns and improving his inventions. In general, John handled the inventing and Matthew handled the banking and business affairs. They advertised their business as the "Largest Arms Factory between Omaha and the Pacific," and with their staff, including Ed Browning, Frank Rushton, Sam Browning, and George Browning, they made and repaired rifles and sold a variety of sporting goods. Between 1883 and 1900 John Browning sold Winchester Arms Company some forty-four gun patents; and by 1900 Winchester had a virtual monopoly on sporting arms in the United States. At that same time, at the turn of the century 75 percent of sporting arms sold in the American market were weapons that had been invented by John Moses Browning.

Browning invented rifles, shotguns, pistols, and machine guns. His weapons were produced particularly by Winchester and Colt in the United States and by Fabrique National d'Armes de Guerre in Belgium. His 1894 30/30 rifle, which made use of the new smokeless powder rather than the older black powder, was produced by Winchester; by 1914 Winchester had sold more than 1,500,000 rifles of the 1894 model. Browning's pump-action and automatic shotguns set the standards by which other shotguns were measured. His .45-caliber pistol and machine gun were particularly helpful in aiding the U.S. in World War I and World War II. John and Matthew Browning joined with G. L. Becker and A.P. Bigelow in the 1890s to become Utah's premier bird-shooting team—the Four B's; they also were known nationally as a champion trap-shooting team.

## *War and Weber County*

Soldiers from Weber County went to war in the Spanish-American War, the Mexican border incident of 1916, and World War

I. Batteries A and B of the Utah National Guard Artillery saw action in the Philippines in 1898 and returned by train to Ogden in 1899 to a jubilant welcome from a crowd of 10,000 assembled at the Ogden depot. The railroads were major supply routes between the east and west coasts for war materials, and Ogden's junction status was important as war efforts geared up.

In 1916, as World War I raged in Europe, revolutionary activities in Mexico spilled over into the United States. Pancho Villa, leader of one of the revolutionary factions, raided towns along the Mexican-U.S. border to protest among other things the involvement of the United States in the Mexican Revolution. In 1916 Troop B, First Squadron, of the Utah National Guard Cavalry was dispatched to the Mexican border to protect the border from further raids by Villa and his troops. The Mexican border "police action" lasted about a year; by March 1917 most of the U.S. units had returned from patrol duty near Nogales, Arizona.

The United States entered World War I in April 1917, and by November 1918 when the armistice was declared nearly 5,000,000 Americans had served in the armed forces of the United States. During the war, a number of Weber County volunteers and conscripts were assigned to the 362nd and other regiments of the 91st Division, which fought in the Argonne-Meuse campaign in France and in the Ypres-Lys sector in Belgium. About sixty citizens from the Ogden area served in Battery B of the 145th Field Artillery Regiment of Utah, which was a part of the 40th Division, known as the Sunshine Division. The 40th Division was made up of troops from California, Nevada, and Utah and trained at Camp Kearney near San Diego; it then was shipped overseas to Camp De Souge near Bordeaux. Just as the regiment prepared to move to the front lines, the armistice was declared in November 1918.

As the United States entered World War I, war hysteria began to grip much of the country, including Weber County. Anti-German sentiment and feelings were widespread. The teaching of the German language was banned in both public and private schools in Utah. Reverend B. Henry Leesman, pastor of the German Evangelical St. Paul's Church in Ogden, was arrested in May 1918 as he became involved in conducting church services in the prison camp for

German prisoners which was located at Fort Douglas in Salt Lake City. Although Leesman was later acquitted, the backlash related to his arrest and the anti-German feeling in the community led to the collapse of the German Lutheran Church in Ogden. In March 1918 Otto Heinrich Thomas, who had been a photographer and soldier in the Austrian Army, was arrested in Ogden. Thomas had escaped earlier from a Russian prison camp and had fled to the United States, where he opened a photography shop in Ogden. He was arrested and charged as an enemy alien who owned a motion picture camera.[27] The anger against Germans which was shared by most Americans did not subside until well after the end of the war.

Ethnic prejudice raised its head against other groups as well as Germans during the war. Many emigrants from central and eastern Europe found it wise to carry Liberty Bonds on their person in order to prove their loyalty to the United States. One Greek emigrant traveling from Utah to Montana was stopped in Idaho and nearly lynched. The Liberty Bonds he carried in his pocket saved his life, but he was told to get out of town immediately.[28] Of the 21,000 men who served in the U.S. armed forces during the Great War, about 10 percent were immigrants and American ethnic minorities. The largest ethnic groups represented in the armed forces from Utah included Italian, Greek, and English immigrants. Ogden and Weber County had become the home for many immigrants who sought work related to the railroad, agriculture, or the canneries.

The combat veterans of the 362nd Regiment were released from the army at Fort Russell, Wyoming, and returned to Weber County as private citizens; but the members of the 145th Field Artillery Regiment arrived at the Ogden depot on 17 January 1919 to an enormous welcome. Utah officials were very much concerned about mixing the soldiers with the crowds at the depot because of the threat of an influenza epidemic in the communities of Weber County. The orders were given that the troops would march on parade from the depot up 25th Street and along Washington Boulevard to 28th Street and then north to 21st Street and back to 25th Street, where the parade would end. Crowds were not allowed to gather at the depot, the troops would not be allowed to speak to anyone in the crowds, and the soldiers would not be allowed to break rank until the end of the parade. The enthusiasm of the Ogden crowd altered the orders, however. At the depot, families and friends clamored to greet their returning soldiers, and the homecoming embraces were left uninterrupted by officials. Governor Simon Bamberger and state officials then led the 1,117-man regiment in the biggest military parade in the history of the city of Ogden. After the parade, the soldiers returned to the train and proceeded to Logan where they were mustered out of federal service.

Louise Owen, who graduated from the Dee Hospital School of Nursing in Ogden in 1916, was one of the many nurses from Utah who served during World War I. Having contracted pneumonia, she was released from military service, and throughout the remainder of her life she suffered respiratory problems. She became a member of the Disabled American Veterans and for the next four decades worked as a registered nurse at both the Dee and St. Benedict's hospitals.[29]

## *Twentieth Century Growth*

As the citizens of Weber County moved into the twentieth century, a number of technological developments including the automobile, the airplane, the increasing use of electricity, and the increasing use of the telephone changed life in the county and in the country. N.T. Moore, who had joined the Ogden Fire Department in 1874 when the department had nine members and horse-drawn equipment, was injured in 1906 as he and his colleagues were traveling to a fire in their motorized fire engine when it skidded on an ice-covered street. Moore suffered a fractured hip and had to remain in bed for several weeks. Moore also had been injured rushing to a fire a year earlier when the driver of the truck in which he was riding suddenly swerved to prevent striking a streetcar and Moore was thrown from the truck.

World heavyweight boxing champion, African-American Jack Johnson, fought former title holder James J. Jeffries, who had come out of retirement and was known as the "great white hope," in a 4 July 1910 world title bout in Reno, Nevada. Johnson handily defeated Jeffries and on 5 July 1910 arrived by train in Ogden traveling through to Chicago. A crowd of 500 people greeted Johnson, who shook hands with some of his admirers. As Johnson returned to his seat next to his wife, several "young toughs" called through the open train window with some "vile epithets" to Johnson. Threats of "shooting" also were made by the tough element of whites that had gathered. Police officers rushed to the scene and forced the crowd back from the train, and the conductor waved the engineer to start the train. Race riots occurred across the country including Boston, Cincinnati, Houston, New York City, and Norfolk. Three black men were killed in Georgia, as white bigots expressed their rage as Johnson continued to maintain his supremacy as the first black heavyweight boxing champion.

As Weber County moved into the twentieth century, the number of women working outside the home began to increase. Occupations of the women included launderers, servants, lodging housekeepers, dressmakers, nurses, bookbinders, and school teachers. About 13 percent of the women studied in Salt Lake City were employed outside of the home.[30]

Child labor was a concern addressed by many groups at the turn of the century. Many children were involved in agricultural endeavors on family farms, but children working for wages was primarily an urban problem in Utah at the turn of the century.[31] Fawn McKay Brodie recalled growing up in Huntsville with inflation in the economy and animals in the farmyard in an essay published in 1972 in which she suggested that Mormon farmers were generally more fruitful with children than with the soil they worked.[32]

The end of World War I brought two significant problems home to the United States and to Utah—the Red Scare and the influenza epidemic. Shortly after the end of the war in November 1918, the nation fell into a severe economic depression. Utah wheat declined from a price of $3.50 a bushel at the end of the war to 98 cents a bushel in 1921. In 1919 the mineral industry of the state produced 54 percent less copper, lead, zinc, and silver than it had in 1918. As thousands of workers lost their jobs, strikes and labor demonstrations became common across the nation and the state. Utah war veterans returned to difficult economic times with high unemployment. Many Americans were fearful of events which had occurred in Russia with the communist Bolshevik Revolution. Utah as well as the rest of the nation became involved in what became called the Red Scare of 1919 and 1920.

In the spring of 1919, thirty bombs were sent to leaders and prominent citizens across the country. General labor strikes and May Day riots along with the formation of domestic Communist party groups led to a general distrust of many foreigners, particularly those who might be classified as labor radicals. The 2 May 1919 *Salt Lake Tribune* headlines announced that the 362nd was welcomed home that day from Europe and that "TWO BOMBS FOUND IN MAILS HERE." One of the bombs, which was in a package addressed to Utah Senator William H. King, was intercepted by Ogden postal authorities. The other was discovered in Salt Lake City in a package sent to Frank Nebeker, who had been the prosecutor in the Illinois trial of William "Big Bill" Haywood, a noted IWW organizer.

In June 1919 the Elks clubs of Utah held their state convention in Ogden with the theme "The Elks vs. Anarchy." The Kiwanis and Rotary clubs joined the crusade as did also the American Legion. An *Examiner* editorial suggested that foreign-born radicals should be "shown the way to their homeland" to test their ideas. Still, the Ogden Socialist party continued to meet and listen to local party secretary O. A. Kennedy as he talked of the awakening of the working classes of the world. Although the Red Scare was evident in Utah in 1919, the repercussions of that year were mild in Utah in comparison to reactions in much of the rest of the country. By 1920 much of the hysteria related to the scare had died down.[33]

Influenza arrived in Utah as the war in Europe was grinding to a halt. The first cases in the state were discovered in early October 1918. Ogden became a principal target of the virus. During the period from 3 to 26 October, 2,638 cases of flu were reported along with seventy-three deaths. This was an epidemic of major proportions for Weber County along with the rest of the state. The Dee Hospital quickly was filled to capacity and a temporary hospital was created by using the amusement hall of the Ogden LDS Third Ward. Myrtle Swainston, a nurse who had recently graduated from nursing school in Salt Lake City, was placed in charge of the Third Ward facility. On 17 October the emergency hospital in Ogden was moved from the Third Ward to the Congregational church building. An addition was added to the north end of the Dee Hospital to provide bed space for new flu patients. On 30 October Salt Lake City reported 2,300 cases of flu, with 117 deaths since the beginning of the epidemic. Ogden averaged fifty people a day who came down with the virus. Ogden deaths included the minister of the First Baptist Church, the city editor of the *Standard,* and Albert Scowcroft of Scowcroft and Sons manufacturing company.

The worst of the epidemic occurred during the fall and winter of 1918–19. Cities and counties required different precautions to try to stop the spread of the disease. Many cities required homes to display a sign with the large letters INFLUENZA if flu patients were on the premises; quarantines also were established. Public gatherings became unlawful, and many cities required that gauze masks be worn in public. Some schools were closed for three or four months. Patients were required to be kept in bed and warm, and some suggested that fresh air would help. Efforts were made to keep the lungs of the patients warm, including using alcoholic beverages which were administered by doctors and nurses—usually brandy and whiskey. Although Prohibition had begun in Utah on 1 August 1917, alcohol was looked upon during the epidemic as a medicine. By 25 November there were 225 influenza-related deaths in Ogden and more than twice that many in Salt Lake City.

As more people began to contract the dreaded disease, more precautions were taken. Ogden began a citywide quarantine effort to ban from the city citizens from other communities which did not enforce strict influenza regulations. This created a confrontation between Ogden and Salt Lake City. Ogden officials had chosen to be more strict in their regulations than were Salt Lake City officials, and for a period in late November and December 1918 no agreement between the two cities was reached. Ogden police and highway patrolmen turned back cars whose passengers did not have certificates of compliance with Ogden's ordinances. Train passengers were also checked and told not to leave the platform in Ogden if they could not provide a certificate which declared they had a clean bill of health. On 2 December 1918 the Elks Club Building, which had formerly been the Central School of Ogden, began to be used as a hospital, replacing the First Congregational Church. At this time there were about fifty new cases of flu reported every day in Ogden along with two or three deaths.[34]

Although public gatherings were banned, two events seemed to demand some large-scale public gatherings which superseded the need to prevent the spread of influenza. The first was the celebration of the armistice which ended the war on 11 November 1918; the second was the spontaneous celebration which erupted when the soldiers of the 145th Field Artillery were welcomed to Ogden in January 1919. The 1,174 returning enlisted men and forty-three officers were dressed in battle gear and met by hundreds of friends, family, and well-wishers. About 20,000 cheered them along the welcoming route. Many of the cheering crowd were Weber County residents; they celebrated loudly in the streets and cheered Governor Bamberger, who led the returning troops.

The influenza epidemic gradually began to slow during December and January, and by February and March 1919 it began to disappear. The influenza epidemic and the Red Scare along with casualties associated with World War I seemed to indicate to many in the United States and Weber County that it was best to withdraw from world events and attend to affairs at home. These events set the stage for the Roaring Twenties and the Great Depression.

## ENDNOTES

1. *A Glimpse of Ogden* (Ogden: A.L. Scoville Press, c. 1910), 1.

2. Edward Leo Lyman, *Political Deliverance, The Mormon Quest for Utah Statehood* (Urbana: University of Illinois Press, 1986), 150–54.

3. Richard E. Kotter, "An Examination of Mormon and Non-Mormon Influences in Ogden City Politics, 1847–1896," M.S. thesis, Utah State University, 1967, 117.

4. Lyman, *Political Deliverance,* 153; Kotter, "An Examination of Mormon and Non-Mormon Influences," 119.

5. Lyman, *Political Deliverance,* 165–66.

6. David B. Griffiths, "Far Western Populism: The Case of Utah, 1893–1900," *Utah Historical Quarterly* 37 (Fall 1969): 396–407.

7. Jean Bickmore White, "Gentle Persuaders: Utah's First Women Legislators," *Utah Historical Quarterly* 38 (Winter 1970): 40–42.

8. Ibid., 40.

9. Jean Bickmore White, "The Right to Be Different: Ogden and Weber County Politics, 1850–1924," *Utah Historical Quarterly* 47 (Summer 1979): 271.

10. John S. McCormick, "Hornets in the Hive: Socialists in Early Twentieth-Century Utah," *Utah Historical Quarterly* 50 (Summer 1982): 226.

11. John R. Sillito, "Women and the Socialist Party in Utah, 1900–1920," *Utah Historical Quarterly* 49 (Summer 1981): 220–38.

12. Sheelwant Bapurao Pawar, "An Environmental Study of the Development of the Utah Labor Movement: 1860–1935," Ph.D. diss., University of Utah, 1968, 94.

13. Ibid., 94–95.

14. Ibid., 115.

15. Leonard J. Arrington, "Utah and the Depression of the 1890's," *Utah Historical Quarterly* 29 (1961): 6.

16. Pawar, "An Environmental Study of the Development of the Utah Labor Movement," 229.

17. Kate Carter, ed., *Our Pioneer Heritage* (Salt Lake City: Utah Printing Company, 1968), 11:435–36.

18. David Rich Lewis, "La Plata, 1891–1893, Boom, Bust, and Controversy," *Utah Historical Quarterly* 50 (Winter 1982): 8.

19. Ibid., 9.

20. Ibid., 13.

21. Sherilyn Cox Bennion, "In and Out of Mormondom: Charles W. Hemenway, Journalist," *Utah Historical Quarterly* 61 (Spring 1993): 150–63.; J. Cecil Alter, *Early Utah Journalism* (Salt Lake City: Utah State Historical Society, 1938), 152–53.

22. Alter, *Early Utah Journalism,* 154.

23. Jean B. White, ed., *Church, State and Politics: The Diaries of John Henry Smith* (Salt Lake City: Signature Books in association with Smith Research Associates, 1990), 217.

24. Clifford B. Doxey, "The History of the Ogden City Public Schools," MA. thesis, University of Utah, 1944, 24.

25. William W. Terry, *Weber County is Worth Knowing* (Weber School District, 1987), 180–225.

26. Leonard J. Arrington and Thomas G. Alexander, *A Dependent Commonwealth: Utah's Economy from Statehood to the Great Depression* (Provo: Brigham Young University Press, 1974), 39–40.

27. Allan Kent Powell, "The German Speaking Immigrant Experience in Utah," *Utah Historical Quarterly* 52 (Fall 1984): 304–46; Allan Kent

Powell, "Our Cradles Were in Germany: Utah's German American Community and World War I," *Utah Historical Quarterly* 58 (Fall 1990): 371–87.

28. Helen Z. Papanikolas, "Immigrants, Minorities, and the Great War," *Utah Historical Quarterly* 58 (Fall 1990): 361.

29. Miriam B. Murphy, "If Only I Shall Have the Right Stuff: Utah Women in World War I," *Utah Historical Quarterly* 58 (Fall 1990): 349.

30. Michael Vinson, "From Housework to Office Clerk: Utah's Working Women, 1870–1900," *Utah Historical Quarterly* 53 (Fall 1985): 326–35.

31. Martha S. Bradley, "Protect the Children: Child Labor in Utah, 1880–1920," *Utah Historical Quarterly* 59 (Winter 1991): 52–71.

32. Fawn M. Brodie, "Inflation Idyl: A Family Farm in Huntsville," *Utah Historical Quarterly* 40 (Spring 1972): 112–21.

33. Andrew Hunt, "Beyond the Spotlight: The Red Scare in Utah," *Utah Historical Quarterly* 61 (Fall 1993): 357–80.

34. Leonard J. Arrington, "The Influenza Epidemic of 1918–1919 in Utah," *Utah Historical Quarterly* 58 (Spring 1990): 165–82.

6

# Boom, Bust, and War, 1920–1955

The history of Weber County has been deeply affected by national events. As the nation felt some economic surge from the effects of World War I, so too did Weber County, and that growth continued for a few years after the war. By the mid-1920s, however, there were signs of an economic downturn and the depression which followed. By the end of the 1920s, the economic situation was dismal. During the 1930s Weber County received assistance from New Deal programs and became in many ways a "Federal Colony," as historian and Ogden native Thomas Alexander has described the era.

## *Agriculture*

By 1920 Weber County was enmeshed in three main trends of economic development—agriculture, railroading, and business. In the period from 1920 to the mid-1950s agriculture continued to play a major role in county economics. Farmers in the area grew a variety of crops, which was in some ways a protective measure against bad markets or diseases that might destroy specialized crops. The major commercial farm activities in Weber County were dairying, which produced milk and butterfat products; the cattle and sheep industry, which produced meat and wool; the field crops of wheat, oats, barley, corn, alfalfa, timothy, clover, and other grasses, in which most production was used as feed for animals; commercial garden crops that consisted of sugar beets, potatoes, tomatoes, onions, and some lesser crops of carrots, celery, asparagus, cabbage, pumpkins, squash, and melons; fruit orchards that produced peaches, apples, cherries, pears, apricots, and plums; and some berries, mainly strawberries.

In the 1920s most of the population of the county lived in a rural setting; not until the census of 1930 was it reported that 52.4 percent of the population of the state of Utah lived in urban communities. A large portion of the people was engaged in farming activities. In Weber County in 1930, however, the population had reached 52,172, with 77.2 percent living in Ogden City and the rest (22.8 percent) living in the outlying county. By 1950, 85.5 percent of Weber County's population was urban.[1] The agricultural censuses showed the following numbers of farms in Weber County during various years: in 1924 Weber County had 1,253 farms; in 1930, 2,040 farms; in 1940, 1,693 farms; and in 1954 the number of farms had decreased to 1,477.[2]

Along with the changes in the number of farms through these years, there were also changes in the acreage used in farming. There was a certain amount of shifting of crops and land use as some crops became more profitable or were more or less productive because of weather conditions, diseases, or marketing problems. In the early 1920s Weber County was one of the most agriculturally productive counties in the state; however, over time the county became more urbanized and the overall production declined compared to other larger counties which had room to expand their farming operations. This made Weber County one of the less productive counties agriculturally. Weber County's total land area of 581 square miles ranks Weber as the second smallest county in the state, with only Davis County being smaller with 297 square miles. As farms became larger and expanded onto new undeveloped lands, Weber County was limited by the total space available for farming. Also, as the population grew and as industries expanded, more farmland would be used for housing and industrial development.

In 1930 Weber County had a total land area of 346,000 acres (the total was 371,840 acres, including the area of the Great Salt Lake), and, of that total, 319,000 acres were farm lands and 52,000 acres of the farm land was in cultivated land, as distinguished from range land or pasture lands. The average size of the farms in the county was 180 acres and the crop farms averaged 29 acres.[3] In 1945 Weber County had 300,107 acres in farm land; in 1954 agricultural land had fallen to 264,752 acres. In 1940 the average size of a farm in Weber County was 244.7 acres; by 1954 it had declined to 179.2 acres.[4]

In 1929 Weber County had 7,427 dairy cows that were being milked, which was 7.24 percent of the total for Utah. Weber County was surpassed only by Cache County, Utah County, and Salt Lake County in this category. In 1939 there were 7,036 dairy cows on Weber farms; in 1944 there were 8,563, the highest level reached; in 1949 there were 6,816; and, in 1954, 6,855 cows.[5]

Beef cattle numbers in Weber County in 1920 totalled 7,034 animals, which was small compared to other larger counties; but the number of cattle increased over the next several decades as beef consumption largely replaced mutton and other fabrics replaced wool. By 1940 Weber County had 19,056 beef cattle, and in 1954 there were 31,104 such animals. The number of sheep in the county in 1920 was 51,082; in 1940 that number had declined to 39,097, and it continued to decline to 24,509 by 1954. The number of hogs in 1920 was 7,729; this declined to 2,918 in 1940 and to 2,216 in 1954. The poultry industry apparently did not begin keeping statistical accounts until recent times. In 1939 the farm census showed that there were 103,023 chickens, used both for meat and egg production, in Weber County. In 1945 there were 163,628 chickens; and, in 1954, there were 95,086 chickens. Egg production was 1,221,363 dozen in 1944 and 903,292 dozen in 1954. Turkey production is a rather recent industry in Weber County. In 1939 the agricultural census showed that there were 27,339 turkeys in the county; in 1944 there were 23,675; and in 1954 there were 25,130.

Field crops of hay and grains and garden crops of vegetables also indicated some interesting trends in the years between the 1920s and the 1950s. Hay production statistics show that Weber County in 1939 had 19,708 acres devoted to hay; and that land yielded an average of 2.8 tons per acre, with a total production of 54,891 tons. Production stayed close to that same level, except for the year 1944 when it went up slightly; by 1954 production was still steady at 19,317 acres in hay and a yield of 2.7 tons per acre, for a total production of 51,961 tons. There was also some acreage devoted to alfalfa seed production during these years; it varied from 854 acres in 1939 to 239 acres in 1954. Seed production dropped off considerably over the years.[6]

A significant number of acres was devoted to wheat, but Weber County was not a large producer in comparison with other counties. Records of 1930 show that Weber County had 6,129 acres in wheat, with a total production of 166,233 bushels.County consumption that year was 121,807 bushels used in feeding poultry, 9,193 bushels used for seed, and 218,078 bushels consumed by humans. This total consumption of 347,078 bushels for the county was more than the county produced and meant that 182,845 bushels of wheat had to be imported into the county to meet its needs. Acreages in wheat fluctuated over the years, with 4,279 acres in 1939; 10,702 in 1949; and 3,112 in 1954. Barley production was based on 1,205 acres in 1930; 3,084 acres in 1939; 4,061 acres in 1949; and 4,181 acres in 1954. Oats were produced on 2,981 acres in 1930; 1,430 acres in 1939; 1,854 acres in 1949; and 1,515 acres in 1954. Corn for all purposes in 1930 used 140 acres; in 1949 corn for silage used 2,085 acres, and in 1954 it used 2,569 acres. Corn for canning in 1939 used 34 acres; in 1949, 158 acres; and, in 1954, 50 acres.[7]

Other crops that had considerable acreage devoted to them included sugar beets, potatoes, tomatoes, peas, and onions. Sugar beets in 1930 occupied 2,630 acres in Weber County, which gave the county a seventh rank in beet production in the state. At that time, there were 34,516 tons produced in the county, which was 7.2 percent of the total state production. In 1939 Weber County farmers devoted 5,280 acres to sugar beets; in 1949, 2,594 acres; and, in 1954, 2,659 acres. Potato acreage also showed varying amounts. In 1930 Weber County had the most acreage in potatoes of all of the counties in the state—1,659 acres of potatoes, which produced 300,963 bushels. This was 15.2 percent of the total state production. In 1939 Weber potatoes occupied 1,813 acres; in 1949, 1,376 acres; and in 1954, 515 acres. Tomato production in acreage was 977 acres in 1939; in 1949, 1,541 acres; and in 1954 it was 1,410 acres. Canning peas in

1939 occupied 1,178 acres; in 1949, 950 acres; and, in 1954, 633 acres. Dry onion acreage was 156 acres in 1939; it was 213 acres in 1949; and in 1954 it was 96 acres.[8]

Fruit growing was a major activity; railroad carloads of fruit were sent to markets in the East and a large amount of fruit was processed in the local canneries. In 1939 Weber County produced 74,657 bushels of peaches; in 1944, 103,270 bushels; in 1949, 65,340 bushels; and, in 1954, 79,060 bushels. There were 46,015 bushels of apples picked in 1939; in 1944, 22,626 bushels; in 1949 the total was 35,119; and, in 1954, 15,641 bushels. The cherry industry, mainly centered in the North Ogden area, was significant in the county. In 1939, 1,441,079 pounds of cherries were picked; in 1944, 1,392,183 pounds; in 1949, 1,775,116 pounds; and, in 1954, 1,068,721 pounds. Apricots were also bountiful. In 1939, 72,598 bushels were harvested; in 1944, 40,835; in 1949, 34,156 bushels; and, in 1954, 132,050 bushels. The pear harvests were smaller: in 1939 the harvest was 5,430 bushels; in 1944, 7,067 bushels; in 1949, 6,653; and, in 1954, 8,318 bushels. Strawberries were a small but popular product, mainly grown in the Plain City area. In 1939 there were 32 county acres in strawberries; in 1944, 17 acres; in 1949, 32 acres; and, in 1954, 11 acres.

In pioneer times there was much cooperation on the farms in Weber County through the local religious organizations of the Mormon wards. Later there were some cooperative efforts through water districts and among fruit and produce jobbers who helped market the crops. There also was some talk and organizational efforts during the Populist era at the end of the nineteenth century; but, for the most part, the farmers of Weber County were on their own in making their farms successful.

Before 1920 there were several farmers who had become commercial farmers, and some had become quite successful. Abiathar Richard C. Smith of North Ogden was featured in 1901 in the *Industrial Utah* newspaper, which rated his "country home" as "the finest by far of any of the farm homes of Utah." The paper said that his barns and other outbuildings are

> in proportion and in harmony with the house and in keeping with the requirements of an extensive farmer and stockman. There are

> two large barns and monstrous sheds and feed yards. In one barn alone there is now stored 500 tons of the best timothy and clover hay, and when it is said that this is only a starter, some idea of the immensity of the scale upon which Mr. Smith conducts business may be gained.[9]

Smith owned fifty-eight acres of land adjacent to his home and a winter ranch on the bench of North Ogden which included 500 acres. Among other out buildings there were large sheep sheds. Near North Ogden he owned a higher mountain grazing area—a 14,000-acre tract of land. He had approximately 11,000 head of sheep and raised Chester White hogs, Jersey cows, horses, and chickens. Smith had also acquired approximately 212,000 acres of grazing land on and around Ben Lomond Peak, extending from North Ogden to North Fork and Avon on the east and to Mantua on the north. Some of this land he held by title, and some he rented from the government and the railroad. The size of his herds usually ranged from 6,000 to 8,000 animals, divided into bands of from 1,000 to 2,000 sheep. The *Industrial Utah* article concluded that "the holdings of Mr. Smith are wholly the result of his own efforts here in Utah. What he has he has come by through industry and careful attention to his business and good management."[10]

Another impressive cattle and sheep operation in Weber County was that of Walter J. Lindsay of Eden. At age eighteen, Lindsay homesteaded forty acres of land near the Middle Fork in Eden which was the beginning of what later became a 300-acre ranch in Ogden Valley. He began by raising cattle, and he later ran sheep on his land, which caused difficulties with those who opposed sheep grazing. Lindsay established a large sheep operation by using the Ogden Valley for his summer range and the Promontory desert a hundred miles away as his winter range. He acquired land in between the summer and winter ranges where his sheep could rest during the trailing process. He trailed both wet bands (500–1,000 ewes with lambs) and dry bands (1,000–2,000 sheep), with stops at ranches at Corinne, Connor Springs, Promontory, Rozelle, and Locomotive Springs.

Impressed with Lindsay's success, four of Ogden's prominent sheepmen—Lewis Bitton, William Hunter, Charlie Ziemer, and Jack

Spiers—joined him in the sheep business. They organized the Lindsay Land and Livestock Company, with W. J. Lindsay as president and general manager. Lindsay also had gone into partnership with his half-brother James A. Farrell, and they operated sheep ranches in Liberty and Eden. The Lindsay Land and Livestock Company, with its headquarters in Ogden, had a number of other properties including Blacksmith Fork Sawmill, Washington Meat Market, Wilson Lane Feed Yard, Connor Springs Ranch, Idaho Falls Feed Yard, Birch Creek Ranch, Eden Ranch, Promontory Ranch, Garland Feed Yard, Four-Mile Ranch, Elite Market, and the Ogden Wool Yard. At the height of its operations, the Lindsay Land and Livestock Company ran twenty-two bands of range sheep, 3,000 range cattle, 6,000 hogs, and 300 horses. At the four feed yards, 25,000 sheep and 4,000 cattle were fattened for market each year. Lindsay's vast empire later was lost in the Great Depression.[11]

Other major farm operations in the county before 1930 were the family farms of the Folkmans, Skeens, Hunts, Robsons, Maws, McFarlands, Spaldings, Stallings, Lowes, Andersons, Jones, Petersons, Ures, Widdisons, and Thompsons. Most farmers had struggled hard on their own, and they eventually realized that by working together and learning new techniques, improving seed and cultivating practices, and marketing their products they would fare much better.

A major thrust for improving agriculture came from the Utah State Extension Program and the creation of Farm Bureau chapters. On 31 July 1915 Weber County organized the first county farm bureau in Utah. D. D. McKay of Huntsville was elected president, James R. Beus of Hooper was made vice-president, and W. N. Petterson became secretary-treasurer. W. Preston Thomas was the first extension agent for Weber County. Twenty farm communities in the county outside of Ogden participated in the programs. In 1917 there was a membership of 904 farmers in the county organization, and the numbers remained relatively constant for the next decade.[12] Early Weber County farm bureau projects included eradicating noxious weeds such as Canada thistle, Bermuda grass, morning glory, whitetop, knapweed, leafy spurge, puncture vine, and burdock; combating various crop diseases and pests including potato wilt, Colorado potato beatles, rats, gophers, and ground squirrels; making experiments and improvements in crop seeds and varieties that produced best in the area, such as tomatoes, potatoes, and sugar beets; improving the breeding and production of farm animals, especially the dairy herds of Guernsey, Holstein, and Jersey cows; and marketing crops in a cooperative way. The bureau negotiated contracts with the local sugar refining and canning companies, and the price of sugar beets improved from five dollars to eight dollars a ton in 1923. The bureau developed financial programs, including rural credit, fire insurance, taxation, records keeping, and cooperative buying. The bureau educated farmers in irrigation techniques, which led to the organization of a water district for the county and the eventual development of water-storage dams such as Echo Dam and Pineview Dam.

The dairy industry was important in Weber County, and in 1923 several dairymen decided that cooperative marketing would bring them better profits and control. In that year seven cooperative dairy marketing units or receiving stations (sometimes called skimming stations) were organized; and in 1924 these units organized into one central association called the Weber Central Dairy Association. In 1926 the scattered units moved from Hooper, Warren, West Warren, Slaterville, Harrisville, Farr West, Huntsville, and other communities to a central location at 2551 Ogden Avenue in Ogden. Here milk and cream were pasteurized and bottled. In the late 1930s the Weber Central Dairy adopted the "Cream O' Weber" brand name for their products which has been used since that time. Some of the early organizers of this association were Howard Dabb, Joseph E. Garlick, Merwin Thompson, and James R. Beus. Over the years the association expanded and diversified its products and operations. In 1964 the Weber Central Dairy became part of the Federated Dairy Farms, which in 1973 became part of Western General Dairies. The Weber Central Dairy moved its plant to 1225 Wall Avenue in 1946, where it remained until 1991 when the plant operations and offices moved to Salt Lake City as part of a another merger. There also were other smaller dairy operations in Weber County during this time, including the Ekins Dairy, the Arden Dairy, and the Model Dairy.

The Farm Bureau sponsored a women's organization which in turn sponsored activities to make farm homes more comfortable, productive, and attractive. Activities included the canning and bottling of farm produce in the most efficient and safe way; improving homes with designing and decorating classes, including the installation of new bathroom facilities; making clothing and hats and sewing other household items; and planting flowers and home gardens. The women also developed projects to improve the education system, including the development of a school-lunch program that fostered the serving of nutritious food including a hot dish to be served daily in the school kitchens. Members studied student nutrition, health, and contagious diseases to identify problems they might solve. They sponsored a campaign to improve sanitation practices on the farms, especially the eradication of flies. This project came about in 1917 after sixteen Weber County dairies were identified as having a poor quality of milk because of its contamination by foreign materials and flies that made it unsafe for consumption.[13]

Another important activity of the Weber Farm Bureau program was the development of 4-H clubs. Programs to interest area farm youth in farm activities were seriously considered in the 1920s, and in 1929 a few communities adopted the 4-H Calf Club, which encouraged young people to study and prepare calves for judging at the county farm conventions that began in 1919 and were held in addition to the Weber County Fair. The intent was to teach young farm children basic farm skills that would lead them into the farming profession with a good background. The 4-H clubs participated in a variety of competitive programs. For the young men there were activities of animal raising and marketing, crop growing, and record keeping. For the young 4-H women there were activities in the culinary arts—cooking, produce bottling, sewing, clothing design, home improvement, and home management.

Many 4-H program participants went on to successful farm careers. Others such as Olene Smith, who won prizes in clothing sewing and design, and Ronald Smout, who won local honors for his raising of prize canning peas and a national prize from the National Dairy Association for a project he did on rural electrification, went on to other careers. Olene Smith became Mrs. Olene Walker, Utah Lieutenant Governor, and Ronald Smout became involved in education.

The Weber Farm Bureau also sponsored recreational activities such as excursions for farm families. The first excursion was in 1916 with 150 members traveling in thirty automobiles to Salt Lake and Utah counties to view different farms and see some of the scenery. In May 1920 the Weber County Farm Bureau organized a baseball league which sponsored eighteen teams in the first year. For more than two decades, more than twenty teams regularly participated in Farm Bureau A and B leagues; later a C League also was organized for younger participants, with the winners of each league playing for the championship. In 1920, 300 farm boys played 319 games which provided "wholesome entertainment" to some 85,000 people in Weber County. The Saturday afternoon baseball games were well-attended activities for the county farm families. These games were very competitive, and several skilled local ball players, including Elmer Singleton of Plain City, went on to play professional or semi-professional baseball.

In 1919 the Weber County Farm Bureau held its first Farm Bureau Day. Farm Bureau Day was usually held in September during the 1920s and 1930s and was not held regularly during World War II. After 1945 it was replaced by Dairy Days in Plain City, Tomato Days in Hooper, Cherry Days in North Ogden, and Utah State Fair competitions. Activities during Farm Bureau Days included parades featuring farm equipment and produce and displays of farm accomplishments and production. Dairy Days were part of this tradition, and in 1928 they were called Black and White Days in reference to the raising of black and white Holstein cows, mainly in Plain City. Other communities followed with Guernsey Days and an annual Jersey cow show. Other Farm Bureau Day events included the judging of prize farm animals in different categories, horse pulling contests, displays of sewing and handicraft, and culinary entries. Final activities included a championship baseball game of the Farm Bureau League, a banquet, and a dance.

For some Weber County farm operations hard times began in the mid-1920s; for others the Great Depression beginning in 1929 brought about failure. Many farming and ranching operations did not make enough profits to pay the debts, and some individual farms that had been prosperous went into bankruptcy. Some Weber County farmers became accustomed to a relatively low standard of living through the 1920s and 1930s.

Walter J. Lindsay lost his land and livestock operation as aggressive local bankers pushed to take control of his company; however, he went on to build another fortune in the construction business in California. Other cattle and sheep raisers received a severe setback during the 1920s and 1930s. Some cattlemen purchased young cattle, pastured and fed them for a year, grained them heavily, and sold them for prices below what they had paid for them. Many cattlemen reduced their herds drastically or sold out completely.

In the sheep business, the partnership of Hyrum, Nathaniel, Jonah, and Alma Bailey was forced to dissolve and sell its sheep during the Depression. Some were not fortunate enough to sell their herds and were forced to turn them back to the banks on loan commitments they could not honor. Frank Francis, Jr., an employee at the Ogden State Bank (which failed during the Depression), recalled that the bank had trouble maintaining its assets because some of the items the bank invested in lost their value. The price of sheep was so low that some farmers abandoned their herds in the mountains. The Ogden State Bank hired employees to go into the mountains and herd the sheep on which they had foreclosed. Frank Francis recalled that most of the farmers tried to cooperate:

> We didn't want their assets. We didn't want their cattle or sheep. We didn't want to foreclose on their homes. Most of them worked out, but we had some, of course, that were obstinate, too. We'd have to get a court order and go and repossess. So there was some of the terrifying things, to see a family destitute, and have to have them lose their livestock, or their cow, or whatever their livelihood was. I don't want to go through those days again, I tell you; they were terrible.[14]

Hooper farmer J. Levi Beus sold his potatoes for eighteen cents for a 100-pound sack. Vern Parker from Hooper suggested that his egg business failed because it cost too much to run his Model T Ford to market.[15]

The hard times of farming during the 1920s and 1930s changed the lives of many Weber County citizens, including J. Willard

Marriott. In October 1924, after attending Weber College and serving an LDS mission, Marriott took charge of driving a herd of 3,000 sheep from Cherry Creek, Nevada, around the west side of the Great Salt Lake to Blue Creek, Utah, near Tremonton, arriving there in April 1925. This proved to be a cold and difficult ordeal which included losing 500 head of sheep. Prices for sheep were down and the profits from the venture were used for the most part to pay back the bank. At this point, Marriott concluded that farming in Weber County was a very shaky business. After that experience, Marriott went east and became involved in the A and W Rootbeer business in Washington, D. C., and he later developed a chain of restaurants known as Hot Shoppes. Marriott also organized the Marriott Corporation as a worldwide corporation dealing in premium hotels, restaurants, and the food-catering business.

The Depression affected the cattle and sheep industry in Weber County severely. Few of the original main ranchers weathered the hard times, and even they were forced to cut back their operations considerably. New owners and users moved on to the upper ranges on the Ogden River after others failed during the Depression. They included Wilmer J. Maw of Plain City, Ralph W. Davis of Lehi, Harry Pappas of Ogden, Glen L. Hall of North Ogden, Raymond Jones of Pleasant View, J. S. Cook of South Weber, and Fred Taylor of Ogden. These ranchers were able to move into range areas from which others had been forced to withdraw.

The administration of President Franklin D. Roosevelt attempted to combat the Depression with a series of federal programs called the New Deal. New Deal agencies including the Federal Emergency Relief Administration (FERA), the Agricultural Adjustment Administration (AAA), the Works Progress Administration (WPA), and the Farm Security Administration (FSA) assisted Weber County farmers. In 1932, a year before the New Deal began, the federal government made 256 government livestock feed loans in Weber County for a total of $31,114 and 185 government crop production loans totaling $22,338 in Weber County. Emergency railroad rates were allowed on 404 cars of livestock feed for the county. Thirty-one railroad cars of hay were purchased for farmers, and more than two million pounds of Red Cross wheat was distributed in the county.[16]

In 1933 a county farm relief Committee was formed, and it assisted the farmers in making allotment contracts on various crops because the surplus production of agricultural commodities had driven the market prices down. It was suggested that by limiting production with acreage allotments the prices would be driven up. In 1933, 187 wheat allotment contracts were made, which included approximately 24 percent of the local wheat growers. There was also action taken under the Emergency Farm Mortgage Act to help farmers from going into foreclosure on their properties; in 1933 fourteen Weber County farms were protected from foreclosure under federal legislation.

In 1934 the FERA provided Kentucky blue grass seed to farmers to improve their pasture lands, and this agency also provided plants, seed, information, and supervision for fifty-eight subsistence gardens planted by needy families in the county. In that same year, the AAA arranged payment to farmers on 185 wheat allotment contracts and set up 192 corn-hog reduction contracts. P. J. Clark, Joseph Skeen, and James Rawson helped develop the wheat program. The federal government bought 2,067 head of cattle and 4,397 head of sheep from Weber County farmers, animals which otherwise would have gone unsold.

The year 1934 was a difficult water year, and during that year a county water committee was organized to consider water development and conservation. A. L. Christiansen, county agent, served as chair of the committee, with members of the committee E. J. Fjeldsted of the chamber of commerce; John Woodfield, president of the North Ogden Canal Company; George B. Taylor, Ogden River Water Users Association; Victor Reno, from a local canal company; Fred Williams, representing Ogden City; and G. F. Stallings, president of the Weber County Farm Bureau. A $48,732 federal government allotment was made to study the water problems of the area at this time.[17]

In 1935 the AAA added sugar beets to the allotment program, with 1,063 acreage allotment contracts made in Weber County during the year. Assisting in this program were James R. Beus, J. J. Gibson, J. D. Brown, Ralph Robson, Joseph Belnap, R. P. Greenwood, D. A. Johnston, Adrian Fife, and M. J. Davies. The WPA began to play a larger role in the county, taking over some of the responsibilities that had earlier been managed by the FERA and the Civil Works Administration (CWA).

In 1937 the WPA sponsored weed and pest control projects. In that same year, 1,427 farms enrolled in the conservation program. In 1937 the AAA sponsored an irrigation project to demonstrate how proper irrigation practices would improve soil conservation, and this project continued for several years. Weber County fruit growers in 1937 under the leadership of A. J. Howell, Clyde Jackson, O. K. Farr, John Hall, Paul Cragun, M. E. Purdy, John C. Sorenson, and Alma Ellis took action to interest the Federal Surplus Commodity Corporation to purchase fruit from county growers. From this effort three train cars of apples were purchased. In 1939 the WPA assisted in the removal of 5,424 fruit trees that had become diseased and nonproductive.

## *Agriculture and World War II*

During World War I, 2,000 young men from Weber County were involved in military service, and this caused a shortage of labor on the farms in the county. This shortage was made up by women and by young men and young women who did much of the necessary labor to keep the farms functioning. During World War II, Weber County farms were again drained when even larger numbers of men were taken into military duty. Again, women, young people, and workers from Ogden did many of the required farm tasks; but other laborers including Mexican nationals, prisoners of war, Japanese-Americans displaced by the government relocation program, and Native American laborers—mainly Navajos from the reservations of Arizona and New Mexico—also were involved in farm labor.

Even before war was declared in December 1941, the effects of war were already being felt in the county. Defense building activity, improving industrial conditions, and the military draft were drawing manpower away from the farms. By 1942 many activities such as the county fair, seed shows, Farm Bureau day, and the baseball league were discontinued because of a lack of participants. Weber County farms were generally small and did not provide large incomes. County people had gotten along without much income during the

Depression and more than half of the farms were mortgaged. The new sources of work in the war industries drew workers away from the farms. It was estimated in 1942 that there were only 500 out of 1,693 Weber County farmers who worked their farms with no outside jobs. Other family members also often were employed outside of the farm. Farmers often were too busy to attend farm meetings or activities of farm improvement, and they were increasingly involved in war efforts including war boards, labor and transportation problems, defense councils, scrap collection campaigns, machine rationing assessments, food councils, canning projects, and other similar activities.

The Weber County War Board was organized to deal with agriculture problems brought about by the war; and the board contained a labor council which tried to find ways to solve farm labor problems. In 1942 there was a greater participation in the pea harvest by women and young girls. Sugar beet thinning needed extra labor, and the War Board and Labor Committee assisted by organizing a child labor contact office headed by Parley Bates, Weber High School principal. School buses were used for the transportation of boys and girls to work projects, and drivers of buses and experienced school teachers acted as supervisors. The sugar company paid for the supervisory personnel and for the use of the buses. The Ogden Chamber of Commerce furnished attractive placards advertising for assistance on the farms. Some businessmen let their workers off to help thin the beet crop; others employed in business went to the fields after their regular day's work to help. In this fashion the beets were thinned in 1942. Bates also acted as the contact man for the fruit growers of the county to harvest the fruit crop. He recruited young fruit pickers, established bus routes, kept records, and paid the bills for the operation.

The tomato harvest was another problem; but with additional effort by farm families and some additional Japanese-American laborers who were brought to Utah relocation camps from the west coast by the War Relocation Program, the crop was harvested. The lack of labor to process the tomatoes in the canning factories was another major problem for the tomato industry; however, through close cooperation of labor committees, war boards, U.S. employment agents, canners, chambers of commerce, farm bureaus, and growers associations, the tomato crop was canned. Local schools postponed their opening dates two weeks and then adjourned school at noon so teachers and older children could work canning tomatoes, and rural women as well as the wives of Ogden's businessmen peeled tomatoes for canning. School buses carried Salt Lake City women to work in Weber County's tomato canneries.

During the war there was a shift away from crops that required a great deal of "hand labor," such as the row crops for canning and sugar beets for sugar refining. There was a trend to build up the acreage of grain, hay, and pastures. The change marked the beginning of the end for the canning industry in Weber County, which up to this time had been a major industry in the county. Canneries moved to other areas where larger harvests could be produced and mechanized harvesting could be used.

Another effect of the war was that farm land was taken up to support the national defense programs. A 1942 report showed that Ogden City had given 721 acres of land for a new airport and that the army supply depot on 2nd Street had taken 1,678 acres—a total of 2,399 acres of farm property taken over for national defense. Some farm families were displaced by this new use of land, and farm workers often began to work on defense projects. Some owners were unhappy with the offers the government made for their lands and held out for reappraisals and possible court action to get more favorable settlements. Others were outraged by the government takeovers, probably no one more so than Jerome Wheeler of Slaterville, who wrote some years later that good producing farm lands were turned into an area covered with

> heaps of steel and cement in the form of office buildings, warehouses, barracks, shops, repair buildings, storage plants, snackbars, and almost a countless list of other things, nearly all of which represent a staggering waste of material and a ruthless expenditure of billions of dollars. Unfortunately, through deceitful, underhand maneuvering of a Chamber of Commerce, working in secret and behind closed doors with the Federal Government, several of these war plants were forced on an unsuspecting public surrounding Ogden. The Chamber supposedly working to advance the welfare

> of Ogden and vicinity, bargained off property belonging to old-time residents to our government, which under the strong arm of the law, had power to condemn and take regardless of who or how many were hurt in the transaction.[18]

Wheeler claimed that the government was offering $50 to $200 an acre for land valued by other estimates at $800 per acre, and he represented a small but vocal group of people who opposed the war industry development on Weber County farm land.

By 1943 the United States Department of Agriculture War Board for Weber County oversaw the war effort of the farms in Weber County. The board was headed by J.F. Stewart, chairman of the AAA county committee; A.L. Christiansen, county agent, Utah State Extension Service; Clark Anderson, U.S. Forest Service; Julian Heppler, Farm Credit Administration; W.J. Thayne, Farm Security Administration; Don Nielson, Soil Conservation Service; and Stewart Campbell, Emergency Feed and Seed Loan Agency. They created other county committees that dealt with war issues; these included a machinery committee, a transportation committee, a meat committee, and a committee to promote the use of the pressure cooker. In 1944 Louise East of Warren was the president of the home and community farm women's organization in the county; Lillian Belnap was vice-president; Helen Lowe was secretary; and Viva Kingston and Ellen Bowns were directors. They promoted wartime programs including a float for a victory parade and clothing design and sewing projects. Canning demonstrations were sponsored by the Kerr bottling products company, and DuPont representatives sponsored demonstrations of new plastic products.

Farm labor was a problem throughout the war, and in 1943 the Weber Labor Committee and other agencies established a labor camp at Roy on land rented from private owners. The camp was used to house Japanese-Americans who worked in the local canning factories. When not working in the factories, they were engaged on the local farms, mainly in thinning beets. During that same year, Italian prisoners of war who were incarcerated at the U.S. Army General Depot on 2nd Street were used as farm laborers. Contracts for pay were made between the prisoners and the North Ogden Fruit

Growers Exchange, Utah Fruit Growers, Inc., Weber County Labor Committee, and the Ben Lomond Orchard Company. The usual contract provided for sixteen cents to be paid per bushel of apricots picked, two cents per mile for travel was allowed, meals for the prisoners were furnished by the army, and meals for the guards were furnished by the growers. Prisoners who worked on other projects were paid eighty cents a day. Some 500 Italian prisoners participated in the program, and there were only three attempts of escape. Records showed that they picked 25,775 bushels of apricots and 21,271 pounds of sour cherries while working for thirty-one different growers. Some prisoners also helped to top sugar beets.[19]

The young people of the county helped throughout the war with the fruit harvest. In 1943 they picked most of the cherries, while the prisoners picked apricots. An average of 162 young people worked in the orchards and fields for seventy-two days from 29 June to 22 September 1943. The greatest contribution toward harvesting the crops came from men and women and older boys and girls who worked in the fields and orchards after their regular shifts in industry and defense jobs. These were mainly experienced farm people who needed little supervision.

In 1944 Mexican nationals became involved in the Weber County farm effort when a farm labor camp was established in Kanesville, using the abandoned school of the community as the center of the camp. Kitchen and dining facilities were available at the camp and administrative offices were set up; tents were used for housing the workers. One hundred and fifty Mexican nationals occupied this camp after 18 May 1944. The Mexicans thinned beets, cleaned irrigation canals, picked cherries, weeded onions, and did general farm work until the tomato crop was ready for harvest. They were given some preliminary training and began picking tomatoes about 5 September. Some Mexican labor was also used to harvest peaches, sugar beets, and potatoes. The use of imported labor was not without problems, however, and it also encouraged farmers to plant more crops on the assumption that they would have more labor available in the future.[20]

In 1944 German prisoners of war began to be used on Weber County farms. The prisoners remained incarcerated at the Utah

General Depot at night and were transported under guard to the farms in school buses. They usually worked in groups of ten with a guard. Although the U.S. Army was somewhat reluctant to allow this program, 300 German prisoners participated in the crop harvests in Weber County in 1944.

In 1945 Mexican labor and German prisoner-of-war labor were again used. Up to 185 Mexican laborers had been kept at the Kanesville labor camp and some seventy had been housed on farms. Three hundred fifty farmers used Mexican labor. Some local farmers complained that the laborers of 1945 "were not as good as farm hands as those we had last year. Too many were small in stature and unwilling to work in certain jobs, especially in harvest of beets." Another complaint was that laborers tried to force wages up by "bickering or walk offs." Wage rates were finally established after public hearings were held.[21] Twenty fruit growers used German prisoners to prune about 110 acres of orchards. Prisoners thinned and hoed 1,046 acres of beets; picked 413 tons of tomatoes; weeded 107 acres of onions; picked up 7,734 sacks of potatoes; picked 2,274 tons of fruit; and harvested 2,006 acres of beets, 1,964,400 pounds of onions, and 222 tons of string beans. They also sorted 241 boxcars of potatoes and 77 boxcars of onions. Area canneries used 44,445 man hours of prisoner-of-war labor. The prisoners were a major source of farm labor in Weber County in 1945.[22]

During 1945 Weber County youngsters were heavily involved in picking the cherry crop, with 1,000 youth harvesting 712,000 pounds, or 356 tons. The average age of these pickers was eleven years of age. Ross Rutherford, age twelve, picked 1,984 pounds of cherries in thirteen days to win a prize as champion cherry picker. Harold Ray and Russell Wood were also recognized as top pickers. Victory gardens were grown throughout the county to provide vegetables for local consumption. Various organizations including garden clubs, radio clubs, railroad companies, and oil companies sponsored these wartime gardens. One of the more successful gardens was in Roy; it was worked by fifty-two individuals who were from families of war plant workers. The Weber County Commission provided a light tractor to plow these community gardens; and this tractor was used to plow about 225 gardens in the county.

Prisoners of war were used for farm labor until 24 June 1946; Mexican nationals continued to be used after that time. New sources of labor that began to be used near the end of the war were migrant laborers and local adults who worked during the harvest season. It was recorded that 835 of these workers helped in 1946, especially to harvest the cherry and apricot crops. There were also efforts made to establish a permanent farm labor camp in the county to entice transient laborers to come to the area in future years. In 1947 Allen Taylor, Weber County Labor Supervisor, went to New Mexico and recruited 100 Navajo Indians to work on county farms. It was reported that "they have done good work, and the farmers are well pleased."[23] Farm labor continued to be scarce, and those responsible for acquiring labor even scouted Ogden's notorious 25th Street and its taverns.

### *The Development of Water Resources*

Farmers and other residents of Weber County had struggled with shortages of water from the natural streams each summer and in the 1890s, in conjunction with Davis County residents, had developed and subsequently improved the East Canyon Dam and the Davis and Weber Canal. From the early 1900s on there were constant efforts to develop a larger and longer-lasting water supply by building dams on the Weber and Ogden rivers. Through the years several dam sites were surveyed and proposed, but it was not until the 1930s that dams were actually constructed. All of the planning and background effort came to fruition with the completion of the Echo and Pineview dams.

The U.S. Congress approved the Echo Dam Project in 1924. The planned dam would provide supplemental irrigation water to 60,000 acres of land in the lower Weber and Ogden river valleys and, through an exchange of water from the Weber River to the Provo River, provide water to 20,000 acres of land along the lower Provo River. Among the promoters of the Echo project from Weber County were A. P. Bigelow, Ogden banker and longtime advocate of Weber River development; T. R. Jones, a farmer from Kanesville; P. F. Kirkendall, mayor of Ogden; John Maw, a farmer from Plain City; and John T. Bybee, a farmer from Riverdale. In order to meet the requirements for construction of the project set by the United States Bureau of Reclamation, it was necessary to organize a group of water users to contract with the bureau. This necessary organization was formed on 15 January 1926 when the Weber River Water Users' Association was incorporated. Following this organization, contracts were completed and construction on the earth-and-rock Echo Dam began on 26 November 1927. The dam was completed on 7 October 1930, and the debt on this $2,875,871 dam was paid in full in 1966.[24]

For several decades there also had been interest in a dam on the Ogden River. In 1915, with the organization of the Weber County Farm Bureau, there began to be increased discussion of water development on the Ogden River. J.L. Robson of Plain City, Thomas Fowles and J.R. Beus of Hooper, Norton Bowns of Slaterville, M.P. Brown of Roy, R.T. Rhees of Pleasant View, D.D. McKay of Huntsville, and H. B. Stallings of Eden were major supporters of early discussions. Progress on the project remained in the discussion phase for almost two decades, and it was a combination of the Depression and local droughts during 1933 and 1934 which helped bring development on the Ogden River to fruition. The Ogden River Water Users' Association was organized in 1933, and the Weber-Box Elder Water Conservation District and the South Ogden Conservation District were organized in 1934. These organizations were primed to push for development of the river.

On 31 May 1934 the Ogden River Water Users' Association entered into a contract with the United States government for construction and repayment of the cost of Pineview Dam, which was to be constructed upriver from Wheeler Canyon. Arrangements were made for funding through the Public Works Administration, and much of the construction labor was provided by the Civilian Conservation Corps. Included in the Pineview project was the capping of fifty-one artesian wells which provided the main water supply for Ogden City and would lie under the reservoir of the finished dam. The Pineview Dam was completed in June 1937, and the first water was delivered to farmers during the 1937 irrigation season. The cost of the project was $4 million, and the completion of the dam did not come without some complaint from upper valley people who felt that the costs to them were out of proportion to the benefits they received since most of the water went to the lower valley and to Box Elder County. Overall, however, the dam was a major benefit to Weber County.

World War II brought a delay to further water development, but it did create an increased need for water, as the construction of several federal war installations in the area pressed the water supply to its limits. The increased population in Weber County brought water matters to the fore in the years following World War II, but Davis County was the most active of the northern Utah counties pressing for water development in those years. Joe Johnson and Delore Nichols were the most active promoters of water development in Davis County, and they coaxed and cajoled Weber County leaders on ideas that led to the Weber Basin Project. Ezra J. Fjeldsted, secretary to the Ogden Chamber of Commerce, was solicited by Joe Johnson to join in the proposed water development movement. By December 1947 Fjeldsted was working with Davis County and began to push for further water development in the Weber Basin.

Fjeldsted gained support from Judge J. A. Howell, chairman of the Ogden Chamber of Commerce Water and Conservation Committee, and Win Templeton, Ogden City engineer. These men worked with mayors, town board presidents, and county commissioners to create a unified effort in water development. On 20 February 1948 the Weber County Water Development Executive Committee was formed with Thomas East, Ogden city commissioner as chair; Ezra Fjelsted as secretary; and board members including Doren B. Boyce of South Ogden, Dean Parker of Roy, M. W. Maycock of Pleasant View, and Alma Ellis of Riverdale. From the work of this group, a joint organization with Davis County was formed in 1948 known as the Davis-Weber Counties Municipal Water Development Association. This group unified water development proposals. After gaining some unity on the local level, attention was turned to convincing the federal government to recognize local needs. Targets of this lobbying were individuals in the Bureau of Reclamation and Utah's representatives in Congress, including representatives William Dawson, Walter K. Granger, and Reva Beck Bosone, and senators Arthur V. Watkins and Elbert D. Thomas. These politicians worked diligently to comply with the wishes of their water-minded constituents in Davis and Weber counties; through their efforts, enabling legislation for the Weber Basin Project was approved in the Senate on 9 August and in the House of Representatives on 15 August 1949. President Harry Truman signed the bill on 29 August 1949. Francis M. Warnick and Paul Sant were bureau employees who were helpful in gaining project approval from the Bureau of Reclamation.

The enabling legislation required the organization of a water conservancy district to move the project to the construction stage, and a large-scale campaign was organized to persuade the citizens in Weber, Davis, Morgan, and Summit counties to approve a conservancy district. Petitions with 24,671 signatures asking to form the Weber Basin Water Conservancy District were filed in the Second Judicial District Court of Utah in April 1950. Two months later the court approved the incorporation of the district. The next step was for the voters of the counties to approve funding for the building of the Weber Basin Project, which included storage facilities, diversion dams, pumping plants, drains, wells, and power plants. The Weber Basin Water Conservancy District contracted for $57,694,000, which required bonds to be issued for that amount. The actual estimated cost was about $70 million, of which the federal government agreed to provide $12,691,000 as an appropriation to the area in return for national benefits from flood control, recreation, and improvements for fish and wildlife. The bond election was held on 6 December 1952 in each of the four counties and, although the bond resolutions were approved by an overall four-to-one margin, many in Morgan and Summit counties and in the Ogden valley voted against the resolutions. Most voters in Weber and Davis counties voted in favor of them.

With the funding approved, the construction of the project began in 1952 with the construction of the Gateway Tunnel in Weber Canyon. By 1957 Wanship Dam, the Davis Aqueduct, the Weber Aqueduct, the Gateway Canal, and the Stoddard Diversion Dam had been completed. In 1957 Pineview Dam was enlarged from 44,200 acre-feet to 100,000 acre-feet capacity and the Slaterville Diversion and the Willard Canal were completed. By 1961 new cost estimates suggested that the cost of the total project had increased to $97.5 million, of which the Weber Basin Conservancy District was to pay $81.6

million. From 1964 to 1966 the Willard Reservoir (now the Arthur V. Watkins Reservoir), the Lost Creek Dam, and the Causey Dam were completed. The original projects in the Weber Basin were finished in 1969. An enlarged Smith and Morehouse Dam was completed on the upper Weber River in 1988 at a cost of $12,000,000.

Another important water development was the creation of the Weber County Watershed Protection Corporation. Following a series of floods across the Wasatch Front in the 1920s and 1930s, land conservation steps were taken in Davis and Box Elder counties to terrace upper watersheds to prevent flooding. After a flood in Jumpoff Canyon and Cold Water Canyon on the west side of Lewis Peak occurred on 19 August 1949, a committee was formed from members of the Ogden Kiwanis Club's Agricultural Committee to study flood problems in Weber County. This committee recruited others from the Soil Conservation Service, and the members reported that the Weber County mountainsides were in serious shape and that there was so much silt being deposited in the Pineview Reservoir that the reservoir rapidly might be completely filled with sediment. They recommended that much of the of the area of the upper watersheds be retired from grazing use and be held for watershed protection.[25]

As a result of this recommendation, the Weber County Watershed Protective Corporation was formed on 18 January 1947 for the purpose of acquiring from private owners lands in the upper watershed areas to be put under control of the United States Forest Service for restoration and future management in the public interest. Officers who were instrumental as this organization began were A. L. Christiansen, president; Harold L. Welch, vice-president; Charles A. Halverson, secretary-treasurer; and R. R. Rowell, John M. Mills, Charles B. Empey, and John S. Whiteley. In three decades, from 1947 to 1976, the Weber County Watershed Protective Corporation was able to raise $121,024 for the purchase of 16,417 acres of land, and it also assisted in the direct sale to the federal government of another 7,935 acres. Thus, a total of 24,352 acres of the Ogden River North Fork watershed was put under the control and management of the government. The Watershed Protective Corporation also supported the Utah state program to acquire 12,000 acres on the middle fork of the Ogden River at a price of over $4,000,000. With the urging of the

Weber County Watershed Protective Corporation, the federal government approved the Watershed Protection and Flood Prevention Act of 1956 and completed a project on the north fork of the Ogden River which restored 42,880 acres of watershed.[26] Haynes Fuller was the last president of the organization, which ceased functioning in 1984.

## *The Railroad in Weber County*

In 1929 Ogden was the second largest city in Utah, with approximately 45,000 people and eighty-nine industrial establishments, which had a volume of business of approximately $40 million. Much of the business was related to the railroads. Ogden's railyards included four steam railroad lines and three electric railroads. Ogden also was the terminus for the Southern Pacific, the Union Pacific, and the Denver and Rio Grande Western railroads. The railroads employed 3,360 employees, and most of these workers were from Weber County; their annual salaries totaled $5,610,257. These workers serviced on a daily basis 119 steam trains as well as fifty-eight trains and buses for the electric lines. Over a year's time nearly 1.5 million rail cars were handled in the yards, where there were over 609 different tracks making up eighty-five miles of track.

Extensive shops and round houses for each of the railroads were maintained in Ogden. Ogden had an icing plant which produced 400 tons of ice daily, making it possible to ice 272 cars per hour. In 1929, 82,302 cars carrying perishable products were iced at this facility. The Ogden railyards included a commissary and a laundry plant to service the trains and their passengers. In 1932 the chamber of commerce proclaimed that Ogden was the "Gateway to the West," and boasted that "You can't get anywhere without coming to Ogden," and that "You can get anywhere by coming through Ogden."[27]

Ogden was a major grain and milling center, with 15,000 cars of grain shipped to Ogden in 1932. It was also the largest livestock market west of Denver, and Weber County was a major canning center. The sugar beet industry supported a growing candy industry. In 1932 the Ogden Chamber of Commerce began to emphasize the tourist industry, which also was promoted by the railroads. It was advertised that Weber County had some of the most impressive scenery in the

West, and tourist facilities that were featured included the Hermitage Hotel and Restaurant in Ogden Canyon, the Hotel Bigelow, the New Healy Hotel, the Marion Hotel, the New Community Hotel, the Broom Hotel, the National Hotel, and the St. Paul Hotel. Tourism was becoming a significant business.

The prosperity brought by the railroads during the decade of the 1920s was ended by the Great Depression. The railroad industry declined and remained at a low ebb until World War II. Thor Blair operated the newsstand in the Ogden Depot and observed the decline of passenger traffic during the 1930s. Blair remembered that the trains were "sporadically" ridden by "gaunt men led by a faint hope of finding some employment." During those years a friend reported to him: "I've been riding this railroad for many, many years and that's the first time in my life that I have had a private car on a regular ticket."[28]

The 1940s brought a resurgence of growth to the railroads as they became a part of the nation's military system during World War II. The railroads did their greatest volume of business in history as they carried war materials and troops for the war effort. In 1944 the total railroad volume in the United States increased to 738 billion ton-miles in freight. Passenger travel increased to 95 billion passenger miles in 1944, with American railways filling 43 million seats with members of the armed forces in 114,000 special troop trains.

The Ogden Depot, being on the main east-west rail line, had a tremendous amount of freight and passenger business as both civilian and troop trains moved along the rails. LeRoy Johnson, a "Red Cap" porter at the Union Station for over forty years, recalled those busy days. He said, "At one time, during World War II, sixty-two passenger trains left the depot every day—streamliners from all over the nation carrying presidents, kings, ambassadors, movie stars, doctors, lawyers, authors, poets—and just people—thousands of them, everyday, from all walks of life." During that time, eighteen Red Caps worked around the clock at the Ogden Depot to provide service for rail passengers.[29]

## *Industry and Business in the County, 1920 to 1955*

The *Ogden Standard-Examiner* of 1 February 1920 listed 170 businesses in Ogden. These businesses ranged from automobile and motor-truck body plants to bakeries, and from candy factories to coal companies. Cement factories, chemical factories, creameries, cigar factories, and cereal food plants employed Weber County workers. Knitting factories, pickle factories, planing mills, woodworking shops, and mattress factories employed others.

In 1930 there were five banking institutions in the county. The major bank was the First Security Corporation, which had total resources of over $50,000,000 and owned and operated twenty-seven banks in Utah, Idaho, and Wyoming. The other county banks were the Ogden State Bank, owned by Archie P. Bigelow and located at 25th Street and Washington Boulevard; the Commercial Security Bank at 369 24th Street, with H. E. Hemingway as president; the First Nation Bank and the First Savings Bank, both members of the First Security Corporation; and the National Bank of Commerce at 2453 Washington Boulevard, with Charles Barton as president. In 1920 the Pingree Bank, an Ogden institution, had gone bankrupt as a result of business conditions following World War I; and, during the Depression the Ogden State Bank failed. The failure of these two important banking institutions severely affected the business climate in Weber County.

The First Security Corporation was the most successful bank in Ogden during this period, and it was organized as a holding company in Ogden on 15 June 1928 by members of the Eccles family and the Browning family. Members of the Eccles family owned the First National Bank of Ogden and the Ogden Saving Bank, while members of the Browning family owned Utah National Bank. Under terms of the new charter, Marriner Eccles became president; Marriner Browning, vice-president; Elbert G. Bennett, vice-president and general manager; and George Eccles, secretary/treasurer. There were sixteen directors including Ogdenites Spencer Eccles, W.H. Harris, John Browning, Joseph Scowcroft, R.R. Porter, and W.H. Wattis. This financial institution weathered the Depression and through its expansion became the largest financial establishment in the Intermountain West. During the 1930s the First Security Corporation moved its head office to Salt Lake City and later created the Northern Division of the First Security Bank of Utah, which was headquartered in Ogden. In 1984 there were 500 employees in the division, and they operated twenty-two different branches, ten of which were in Weber County.[30]

Another important banking firm in Weber County during this era was Commercial Security Bank. Harold E. Hemingway had opened banks in Nevada, Idaho, and Bingham, Utah, and he moved to Ogden in 1928. In 1929 he acquired the controlling interest in Commercial Security Bank of Ogden, whose roots began in Ogden in 1875. Hemingway's Ogden bank made it successfully through the Depression and expanded its operations by acquiring the National Bank of Commerce. During the Depression, Commercial Security Bank prepared bank scrip to be given to customers if the money supply ran out; but things never got to that point. One incident encouraged customers not to withdraw their money. A prominent businessman, Jim DeVine, arrived at the bank with a large amount of money in hand and proclaimed, "I'm putting mine IN! I have faith in Commercial Security." A cheer went up, and few asked for their money.[31] Hemingway made his customers feel comfortable by keeping the bank open until late at night and serving sandwiches to the waiting customers.

Harold Hemingway guided the Ogden bank and his Idaho bank with much success. He was a generous supporter of Weber County organizations, including the development of Washington Terrace as a community after World War II and the Ogden Reds baseball team. Hemingway died in 1949, and his two sons, Robert and Richard, continued to direct Commercial Security Bank until it merged with Key Bank in 1987.

Two of the largest meat-packing establishments in Ogden were the American Packing and Provisions Company on 24th Street and the Fox-Keller Dressed Meat Company on 21st Street. Together, they employed 208 people and slaughtered 18,000 head of cattle, 70,000 hogs, and 10,000 sheep in 1929. They produced fresh meats, sausage, and lard. The Union Stock Yards did a great amount of business in Weber County and employed forty workers who handled hundreds of thousands of cattle, hogs, sheep, and horses and mules annually. The Union company handled more than 13,000 railroad cars of livestock. In association with the Union Stock Yards was a stock-feeding operation that employed as many as forty-three persons. The feed yards occupied an area of 100 acres in the west Ogden area. This traffic in meat-producing animals led to the development of an annual stock show that was held in Ogden beginning in 1919 and lasting into the 1960s.

In 1930 there were thirteen canning factories in Weber County that employed 2,350 workers during the packing season, with a payroll in 1929 of $266,000. In that year the total value of the products was $3,225,000. In the entire district of which Ogden is the center, the normal pack was 3,500,000 cases, valued at $9,000,000. Tomatoes and tomato products provided the largest volume in the Weber County canning industry. Other crops canned included peas, string beans, beets, pumpkins, lima beans, carrots, sauerkraut, peaches, cherries, plums, apricots, apples, and berries. In 1914 the American Can Company built a can-manufacturing plant at 20th Street and Lincoln Avenue, and this facility became a major provider of cans to the canning industry in Utah until 1979 when it was closed. In 1929 the plant had the capability to produce 125 million cans a year.

In 1929 Weber County had five clothing manufacturing businesses including the Scowcroft Company, which produced "Never Rip Overalls," and the Zions Cooperative Mercantile Institution (ZCMI), which manufactured clothing in Ogden. In 1929 there were 383 people employed in this industry, which had a payroll of $488,000. There were 892,000 pieces produced that year, with an output valued at $1,457,030. The main items produced were work clothes, housedresses, knit goods, and hats; and the market for these goods reached from the Pacific coast to the Missouri River.

The bottling industry in 1929 employed ninety-five people in four plants in the county and produced 157,000 cases of soda water; 25,000 barrels of beer; and 12,000 gallons of cider—which brought an overall profit of $562,000. A main bottler in this period was the Becker Brewing Company. Four wholesale baking plants employed 136 people and did a volume of business of $1,156,000 in 1929. They baked and distributed 5,757,000 loaves of bread, 2,588,000 cakes, and 65,000 pies that year. They obtained all their raw ingredients from local county sources which supported the local agricultural market.

Three iron foundries employed 192 workers in 1929, with a profit of $939,745. The Ogden Iron Works specialized in machinery for sugar manufacturing, sugar beet handling, and mining. Another local factory cast a patented grinding ball for grinding ore and made a patented automatic floor-waxing machine, and it was equipped to handle all classes of iron, brass, and bronze casting. A third foundry specialized in stove and furnace parts. A sheet-metal industry made up of seven establishments employed fifty-four workers with a volume of business of $288,000 in 1929. This work was general sheet work but emphasized roofing and furnace installation.

Two brick and tile plants with 100 employees did a volume of business of $325,000 in 1929 and used local clay. These two plants were the Leek Brick and Tile Company and the Ogden Pressed Brick and Tile Company. Eight planing mills with twenty-eight employees did general mill work and cabinet work for the community that year. The Ellis Planing Mill and Wheelwright Lumber were the local mills with the longest history. Five canvas and leather shops with fifty-four employees produced 635 saddles, 700 sets of harnesses, and other accessories in 1929. Canvas items included auto tops, awnings, tents, side curtains, window awnings, blankets, and other items.

In 1929 the printing industry had eleven establishments in Ogden, and there were 153 employees with a payroll of $348,000. Printing included the daily newspaper, the *Ogden Standard-Examiner*, which advertised a daily circulation of 12,186 newspapers and a Sunday circulation of 13,009. One print shop specialized in lithography and two other establishments made outdoor signs. Twenty-eight individuals were involved in the outdoor sign business. The Thomas Young Sign Company manufactured neon signs. Five laundries served the county in 1929; the largest were the American Linen Company, the Ogden Steam Laundry, the Troy Laundry, and the Model Laundry. There were 193 employees in the laundry industry. One laundry specialized in linen service for hotels, cafes, and offices, and it also made smocks, jackets, aprons, dresses, and other similar workplace items and provided cleaning service for these products. Some laundries did both cleaning and dyeing.

Asael Farr and Sons Company, Utah Ice and Storage, and the Becker Products Company were the major ice and storage businesses in the county. These plants made and distributed ice through wholesale and retail outlets. There was a bedding factory which manufactured 4,646 mattresses in 1929; it also had a capacity to build custom furniture and to repair and reupholster furniture. Other businesses included a box factory which made large baskets and berry cups that were used by local farmers; a salad dressing factory which produced 78,750 cases of salad dressing, mayonnaise, and sandwich spreads; and a honey processing and distributing company.

The sugar refining business began in 1898 in Weber County with the Amalgamated Sugar Company. The company experienced hard times in the decade and a half from 1920 to 1936. During this period, both farmers and refiners suffered losses. In 1928 a refining plant was closed at Cornish, Utah, and moved to Missoula, Montana. Bad weather conditions and white fly infestations cut back the acres harvested to 22,421, with an average of 12.13 tons per acre. This was a considerable drop from previous years and far below the expected average predicted for the year. This reduction led to the closing of the Logan, Utah, plant and plants in Paul and Twin Falls, Idaho.

The fluctuations in sugar production from 1918 to 1928 went from a high of 1,400,000 bags in 1921 to a low of 470,000 bags in 1926, with 813,875 bags produced in 1928. In 1936 the Amalgamated Sugar Company with its headquarters in Ogden left a partnership with the American Beet Sugar Company and its successor the American Crystal Sugar Company and continued its own operations with its five sugar plants located in Ogden and Lewiston, Utah, and Burley, Rupert, and Twin Falls, Idaho. A profit of $713,816 was realized in 1936, and the years from 1936 to 1961 were typified as "years of growth and success." The company claimed profits in 1961 at $3,561,400, with 2,093,590 tons of sugar beets being purchased and 5,732,142 bags of sugar being produced. By 1940 circumstances leading to World War II in Weber County including increased population and the encroachment of military establishments on the beet-growing acreage led to a downturn in sugar production. The Ogden factory operated only forty days in 1940, and it was decided that it should be moved to a place where it could be profitable. Nampa, Idaho, was selected, and the move was completed on 8 October 1942. The headquarters of the Amalgamated Sugar Company remained in Ogden, its place of origin, and still remains there in 1996.

Beet farmers in Weber County continued to grow beets after the

Ogden plant was closed down, and the beets were shipped by rail and truck to the Lewiston, Utah, Amalgamated plant. Harold Thompson remembered that he grew his last sugar beet crop in 1980 because the Amalgamated company had found that it was too costly to ship county beets to the processing plant. It was about this date that the growing of sugar beets in Weber County came to an end.[32]

One of the major local consumers of sugar was the candy industry, which was mainly represented by the Shupe-Williams Candy Company. This company had started in 1896 with William H. Williams, David Shupe, and John Pawlas as owners. David Shupe and John Pawlas both died young as a result of accidents and William H. Williams continued in charge of the company until his death in 1928. Before the death of David Shupe, however, the two men had incorporated the Shupe-Williams Candy Company. Through the years the company had occupied three locations in Ogden; in 1907 it built a four-story structure at 26th Street and Wall Avenue. When William H. Williams died in 1928, the company came under the control of Fred Williams, a younger brother, who became president, general manager, and majority stockholder in the corporation. Fred's sons, George and Harmon, became prominently involved in the company. The Shupe-Williams Candy Company was one of the largest candy producers in Utah; it produced about 400 varieties of candy including hard-stick (all-day suckers, etc.), soft-cream candies, specialty items, chews, caramels, nougat, fruit candy, and chocolates. It also made a popular brand of pink-colored, sugared popcorn marketed as Mother Goose Popcorn.

Shupe-Williams made it through 1930 showing a profit, but in 1931 sales dropped drastically. Many consumers did not have the funds to buy candy and it often was considered a luxury item during the Depression years. The company survived, but it had to resort to taking some payments in the form of produce such as butter, cream, and honey which could be used to make candy. Overall candy production during the Depression, when compared to production during the 1920s, was down by about 50 percent. The years of World War II proved to be good years for the company even though sugar was restricted or rationed. The company found some substitutes such as canned milk and also found ways to make the sugar go farther. These years brought general prosperity because the company could sell at higher prices all it could produce. This boom lasted until 1947 when sugar was taken off the rationing list and homemakers began to do more of their own cooking of pastries and sweet items. Candy sales declined sharply after rationing ceased. In the late 1950s Fred Williams, who was then in his eighties, decided to sell the factory and retire. In 1958 the company was sold to a group of employees headed by T. Frank Williams, who had been sales manager, and James Farr, who had been the office manager. This group ran the company for another seven or eight years and then the building was sold to a plumbing-supply organization.

The Depression years of the 1930s were difficult years for businesses and people in Weber County. Businesses closed, mortgages on many farms and homes were foreclosed, and unemployment numbers grew. During this period, however, George T. Frost was able to begin a Hudson dealership in Ogden on the corner of 27th Street and Washington Boulevard for $250 which he and his partner borrowed. Brad H. Paul operated a store in Ogden, keeping it open from seven in the morning until eleven at night in order to make enough money to stay in business. Stanley Robbins managed the David H. Peery estate at the beginning of the Depression and then managed the Fred J. Kiesel estate during the latter part of the Depression. The Peery estate included the Egyptian Theatre, the Ogden Theatre, the White City Ballroom, several business houses that were rented to tenants, and farm lands in Utah and Canada. Robbins sponsored a lottery at the Ogden Theatre and the Egyptian Theatre, with the grand prize being a Chevrolet automobile. Usually, four cars were given away annually, and up to 5,000 people packed the ballroom during the drawings. The admission for a dance ticket on the night of a drawing was fifty cents; it was thirty-five cents for a dance ticket on nights when attendance gave credit toward a drawing for a car. Theatres and ballrooms in Ogden made good profits from using techniques like these, and they drew people from all over Weber County and northern Utah as well as from Idaho and Wyoming.

The Peery theatres were in competition with other Ogden theatres, including the Paramount, the Orpheum, and the Rex, which were owned by William Glasmann. It was a difficult task to obtain first-run movies since both companies wanted them for their theatres; but both survived by using special ticket sales and grocery giveaways to entice people to come to the movies. The theatres seemed to survive better than some other recreational activities because the movies provided a relatively inexpensive and satisfying diversion from the problems of the Depression.

Many wage earners and laborers in Weber County had difficulty finding jobs and providing food for their families. Lloyd E. Clark, living in Liberty at the time, recalled how difficult it was to find employment:

> Jobs were almost impossible to find. If there was a job opening somewhere, like at the beginning of canning season, there would be about 200 people waiting to get 25 or 30 jobs. It was the same everywhere—20 people for every job that came up. I got a job at the Pea Viner threshing peas for the Cannery. I was paid 15 cents per hour and then they deducted 5 cents per hour for meals. This job lasted for about three weeks.[33]

Alvornia Thompson lost his job as a boiler-maker foreman in a sugar factory and remembered:

> we moved in with my wife's folks in Ogden. We had three children at the time. My wife and I started at baking in the basement. We sold bread for 15 cents a loaf, and doughnuts for 5 cents a dozen. We also sold cakes and pies. I carried a box on my back from door to door. I paid for the births of my next three children by baked goods for the doctors services. I made enough money this way to buy a car too."[34]

Individuals, families, and communities survived in part by wearing old clothes and making over the used clothes of others. They often ate soup and beans. Wages were often only $1.50 a day for those who could get jobs, and some only worked part time or not at all. As the Depression continued, aid came from the government—both local and national—and from churches and other relief agencies, including the Salvation Army. New Deal programs helped to solve some of the unemployment problem in Weber County.

## *Weber County, the Federal Government, and World War II*

The establishment of Intermountain District Four of the United States Forest Service created the first of several agencies of the federal government to be placed in the Ogden area. As early as 1907 the Forest Service began consideration of a headquarters in northern Utah. The Weber Club, led by its secretary Ira Lester Reynolds, lobbied to have Ogden become the headquarters site. Fred J. Kiesel, Ogden businessman and former mayor, offered to construct a building that would provide a supply depot and headquarters offices for the Forest Service. Kiesel's efforts and other aggressive actions from Ogden businessmen as well as favorable railroad facilities seemed to be crucial factors in the decision. On 5 November 1908 the Forest Service announced that Ogden would be the headquarters of District Four. In 1933 a four-story art-deco style building was built on the corner of Adams Avenue and 25th, on the site of Fred J. Kiesel's former residence, to house the district offices.

Following World War I, the United States Army Ordnance Department began hunting for a suitable arsenal site to store munitions. By 1920 it had decided on a site about ten miles southwest of Ogden and east of the small city of Sunset in Davis County. This location was selected on the criteria of having adequate railway and highway routes, having suitable land in a sandy bench area, and being located away from the vulnerable coastal areas. The War Department authorized the purchase of 1,200 acres, consisting mainly of small farm plots of twenty to fifty acres. An amount of $98,000 was appropriated to buy the land; another $153,914 was used to purchase a 212-acre watershed at Military Springs in the Wasatch Mountains to the east and to provide a right-of-way to take the water to the installation. The installation was named the Ogden Arsenal.

The army assigned Ora Bundy, an Ogden businessman and mayor of Ogden from 1930 to 1934, to oversee the construction of the facility by the W.M. Sutherland Company. Construction costs were slightly more than one million dollars, and the buildings were completed and in use by 1920. From 1920 to 1935 the facility was only marginally used; but, by the mid-1930s, there began to be increased interest in the facility. New construction, including storage igloos, a bomb-loading plant, and railroad facilities, was completed at a cost of $3.5 million. The Ogden Chamber of Commerce was instrumental in the continued growth and development of the arsenal. The arsenal facilities were used extensively during World War II and the Korean War. At the zenith of its operation in 1944 the Ogden Arsenal employed 6,000 persons, more than half of whom were women.

There is probably nothing that has impacted the northern Utah economy more than the location of Hill Field to the area. Even though the air base is located in Davis County, it was the Ogden Chamber of Commerce and business community that aggressively petitioned the government to locate the base in the area. The history of the development of Hill Air Force Base began in 1934 when Salt Lake City was chosen as a hub headquarters for the western sector of the air-mail system that was operated by the Army Air Corps. Lieutenant Colonel Henry H. "Hap" Arnold was appointed commander of the Western Zone and he later became an important contact in favor of placing an air field along the Wasatch Front. This mail operation only lasted about four months, but that was long enough to make an impression on people who played a key role in the establishment of Hill Field.

The aggressive action of the Ogden Chamber of Commerce and Weber County business leaders gave the area the edge in getting the base located near Ogden. The chamber adopted the motto, "Things Don't Just Happen," and proceeded to win the decision of the War Department. The Ogden Chamber of Commerce, under the leadership of Ogden businessman W. Rice Kimball, organized an Aviation Committee to try to secure a first-class airdrome or air field for the Ogden region. On 30 June 1928, through the work of this committee and several aviation boosters, Ogden City and Utah Pacific Airways opened an airport on the plateau area to the southeast of Ogden.

In 1934 the War Department began looking for sites for air bases throughout the United States, and Colonel Arnold, who had been stationed in Utah, suggested that the Wasatch Front be considered for a major air base. After months of investigation, several possible sites were being considered to be selected. To have an air base near a community and to have the related jobs was very enticing during these years of economic depression. Sites were considered in California and Utah, and Salt Lake City was the main competitor to a site near Ogden.

In June 1934 Lawrence Clayton, an Ogden banker and chair of the chamber's Aviation Committee, petitioned George Dern, the Secretary of War and former Utah governor, to consider an Ogden location for the proposed air depot. In the fall of 1934 Clayton went to Washington, D.C., to work with Marriner Eccles, who was serving as chairman of the Federal Reserve Board in the Roosevelt administration; and Clayton hoped that Eccles's Ogden background would help in gaining the air depot. With the support of Eccles, Clayton began to conduct a forceful lobbying campaign in Washington. In 1935, Ora Bundy, Ogden businessman and city official, visited Washington, D.C., and met with Secretary Dern, now-Brigadier General Arnold, and others to push the Ogden site. Much was made of locating the new facility near the Ogden Arsenal.

Significant action in this campaign for the air base was performed by Frank M. Browning, who directed the Military Affairs Committee of the Ogden Chamber of Commerce. The committee heavily lobbied Utah's congressional delegates—senators Elbert D. Thomas and William H. King and representatives Abe Murdock and J. Will Robinson. Decisive action occurred when Browning's committee secured options on land at the proposed site. In the spring of 1936 the chamber committee secured options on 4,784 acres of land adjacent to and east of the Ogden Arsenal. To secure the options, most of the businessmen of Ogden donated to an escrow account, with the chamber and Julian Bamberger, owner of the adjacent Bamberger Electric Railway, making the largest contributions. The Ogden chamber urged the government to acquire these options; but the options needed to be extended because the government did not have the funding to purchase the land at that time.

While Ogden was pressing for the air field on several fronts, other groups tried to sidetrack Ogden's bid. David A. Smith of the Mormon church's Presiding Bishopric made objections to the Ogden site being considered over one in Salt Lake City, and the Reserve Officers Association also opposed the site. Nevertheless, the Ogden Chamber of Commerce extended the options on the land and continued to pursue the task of getting the government to rule in their favor.[35]

In the years 1938 and 1939, as the threat of a world war increased, the United States government became more serious about the effort to build several air bases throughout the country. In 1938 plans were made and $100,000 was appropriated to construct some buildings and an air strip, which was masked as improvements to the Ogden Arsenal. At that same time, the Ogden Chamber of Commerce purchased 386 acres of land. On 12 November 1938 President Roosevelt approved $55,608 through an executive order to be used in constructing an air field near the arsenal. In 1939 Congress appropriated $232,000 for an additional 2,967 acres in Davis County adjacent to the Ogden Arsenal. In October 1939 the government authorized the Works Progress Administration to begin some grading of the area, as far as its budget would allow.

In August 1939 Congress passed legislation that earmarked $8 million to develop an Ogden air base. Senator Elbert D. Thomas informed Frank Browning of that approval on 5 August 1939, and the Ogden Chamber of Commerce held a party that night celebrating the success of their efforts to bring a major air base to the area. On 1 December 1939 Frank Browning was informed that the War Department, with the urging of Hap Arnold, had designated the name of the base as Hill Field, in honor of Major Ployer P. Hill, who had been killed on 30 October 1935 at Wright Field, Ohio, while test flying a prototype of the B-17 long-range heavy bomber that became an important air weapon of World War II.

On 7 and 8 December 1939 a delegation of members of Congress, including Senator Harry S. Truman of Missouri, and several military leaders came to Ogden to tour the proposed site and inspect the Ogden Arsenal area. On the evening of 7 December the group was served an impressive buffet dinner at the Weber Club in downtown Ogden; the next day they were taken to the site of the new air depot. The delegation seemed to be impressed with the plans for the new base and its location and felt that it would play an important role in the air defense of the nation. Ezra J. Fjeldsted, secretary of the Ogden Chamber of Commerce, congratulated Frank Browning for the success of the delegation's visit and for his years of service spent in gaining the installation for the community. He wrote, "The board was unanimous in its expression that this was one of the finest conducted affairs that this Chamber of Commerce has ever attempted."[36]

Construction of Hill Field began on 12 January 1940, and Frank Browning turned the first shovel of dirt at the ceremony, which was held in a driving snowstorm. Initially, twenty-three permanent buildings for technical uses, supply, repairs, housing, and utilities were built as well as a concrete runway and ramp. By 1 September 1941 four 7,500-by-150-foot runways and taxiways were completed. Colonel Morris Berman was the first base commander, and his first major task was to oversee the construction of the base. The base had 300 civilian workers in 1941; and, as the war developed, this number increased to 7,000 by mid-1942 and to approximately 16,000 civilian workers and 6,000 military personnel by June 1943. A large number of these workers lived in Weber County. The principal workload of Hill Field during the war was the repair and maintenance of aircraft, including B-17s, B-24s, B-29s, P-40s, P-47s, P-61s, and A-20s. Another important war role for the base was to serve as a supply depot to handle parts and equipment of every type of aircraft. It is estimated that workers received a payroll of $50 million during the four years of the war.[37]

On 22 July 1946 the command of the installation was renamed the Ogden Air Materiel Area, and Hill Field was renamed Hill Air Force Base on 5 February 1948. With the demands of the Korean War, employment on the base rapidly increased; it reached 12,133 civilians and 2,531 military personnel in January 1953. In 1953 the Ogden Air Materiel Area took a major role in supporting jet aircraft, which required the building of longer runways. By 1955 a 13,500-foot runway which could handle the jet aircraft was completed for $3.5 million.

A significant contribution to the economic growth of the county and an important contributor to the war effort was the Utah General Depot. Through the years it has had eight different name changes, including the Utah General Depot from 1930s to 1962, the Utah Army Depot from 1962 to 1964, and the Defense Depot Ogden since 1964. In 1935 the U.S. Army selected Ogden, more specifically the community of Marriott, as the site for a general warehousing depot.

Reasons for selecting this site included adequate rail facilities and highway routes, geographical proximity to major west coast ports, sufficient available land, and a population of skilled and semi-skilled workers.

Much like the development of other military installations in the area, the Ogden Chamber of Commerce and community leaders played significant roles in bringing the Utah General Depot to Weber County. Ora Bundy, former mayor of Ogden, helped select the site in Marriott for the depot and Frank M. Browning of the Ogden Chamber of Commerce sparked the efforts to raise some local money to close the deal. The 1,679 acres of land chosen for the depot was priced at $409,632, and Congress had appropriated $310,000. The Ogden Chamber of Commerce acted quickly to raise the additional $99,632. In a matter of forty-eight hours, the chamber obtained $100,000 from local citizen groups, and this amount was deposited with Federal District Judge Tillman D. Johnson to complete the purchase. Local farmers were not as enamored with the agreement as the local businessmen. The farmers whose land was condemned for the purchase contested the low appraisals on their lands and denounced the use of the choicest farming land in Weber County for such a project. Because of several law suits contesting the condemnation of the properties, clear title to the land was not obtained by the government until 1943.

Construction began on 16 December 1940 with the building of eight large warehouses. By the end of World War II there were twenty-eight large warehouses and nineteen sheds. During the Korean War, four more warehouses and one shed were built. In the 1960s Defense Depot Ogden was one of the largest supply depots in the nation, with 6,189,000 square feet of covered storage space available in sixty-nine warehouses of various types; 610,000 square feet of hardstand for open storage; and 8,521,000 square feet available for other uses. It had an 800-car rail marshalling yard with forty-five miles of track and some forty-six miles of paved streets for motor access. In 1964 it was estimated that the total replacement value of the installation was $100 million. It originally had been constructed at a cost of $56 million.[38]

During World War II the Utah General Depot carried out various supply functions. The Quartermaster Section handled what mainly consisted of clothing and general supplies. The Signal Supply Section dealt with signal supplies—mainly radios and electrical equipment. The Chemical Supply Section dealt with protective clothing, toxic gas, flamethrowers, and other chemical weapons. The Ordnance Supply Section worked with motor transportation repair, including railroad locomotive repair; the assembling of tanks, artillery pieces and vehicles for long term storage; and the manufacturing of shipping and storage boxes. The depot also had a Machine Records and Training Section that trained people in many specialties. The Utah General Depot also was a prisoner-of-war camp. At its apex of use there were 4,000 Italian and approximately 1,000 German prisoners at the camp. Prisoners of war were also kept at the Clearfied Naval Supply Depot and at Hill Field. These prisoners were used extensively to do some of the non-sensitive work. In fact, in May 1945 it was reported that there were 5,000 POWs and Italian Service Unit personnel employed at the depot as compared to 4,000 United States civilian workers. Peak civilian employment during the war came in 1944 when 12,000 were employed.

During the Korean War the activities at the Utah General Depot picked up again after a decline during the interwar years. Peak shipping of supplies came in 1953 when 37,000 tons per month were shipped, an amount greater than the heaviest shipping done in World War II. Employment increased from 2,774 civilians in June 1950 to 3,919 by September of that year. There were 4,282 civilian employees in February 1951. In 1952 the government spent $9,225,853 on depot operations and equipment and an additional $1.5 million to build the firty-three-unit housing project at Harrisville Heights in Marriott. Much of the money filtered through the depot and directly affected the economy of Weber County.

In 1942 the United States Navy made the decision to build a supply depot at Clearfield, Utah. Many of the local farmers whose land would be used for the depot opposed the decision, and G. Harold Holt, mayor of Clearfield, spoke and lobbied against the depot. The Ogden Chamber of Commerce was outspoken in its support of the depot, and Ezra J. Fjeldsted, secretary of the chamber, spearheaded the efforts to have the project approved. The depot was opened in

April 1943 and for the next two and a half years made an important contribution to the war effort. After the end of the Korean War in 1953 there was a reduction of operations at the Clearfield depot, and on 30 June 1962 the depot was deactivated.

In addition to the military installations built by the federal government in northern Utah, there were some private businesses which were hired by the government to support the war effort. The American Can Company in Ogden fabricated metal containers and received $83,000 from July 1940 to August 1945 from the government. The Lion Coal Company received $219,000 from the federal Reconstruction Finance Corporation to provide coal needed by the government. The Ogden Transit Company was paid $88,000 for transportation services, and Pringle R & D Company received $98,000 for providing cold-packed fruits to the government. Utah Ice and Storage Company was paid $89,000 for warehousing space, and Weber Central Dairy received $80,000 for supplying dairy products to support the military.[39]

World War II and the Korean War changed the nature of Weber County. The population rose and economic development occurred. The ethnic mix and makeup of the population changed. As historians Leonard Arrington and Thomas Alexander wrote:

> It is difficult to overestimate the importance to the Utah economy of the federal defense installations constructed in the Beehive State during World War II. In the Ogden area alone the Army, Navy, and Air Force poured almost $100 million into permanent facilities, and the number of employees at these installations during the war was almost 52,000 persons—easily as many as in all of Utah's agriculture—50 percent more than in all of Utah's manufacturing at the time. The investment in such facilities in the Ogden area was more than twice the assessed valuation of Ogden for 1942 and more than one-half times the assessed valuation of Weber County.[40]

The mass influx of people coming to work in the Ogden area during World War II required additional housing construction. In 1942 it was estimated that housing would have to be found for 3,150 employees at Hill Field. It was determined that 17 percent of employees lived in Salt Lake City, 26 percent in small communities surrounding Ogden, and 57 percent in Ogden proper. The need for additional housing led to the building of the first federal housing project in Ogden—the Grandview Acres.

Grandview Acres was located on a thirty-acre plot of land north of 40th Street and west of Quincy Avenue. On 4 March 1941 Ogden City annexed the area to the city in order to win government approval of the project, and in April the property became the subject of Utah's first condemnation suit involving land needed for defense housing. In that same month, the government awarded a $442,000 construction contract to George A. Whitemeyer and Sons Company, and in May the city agreed to provide sewer, water, roads, and other facilities. The city could not levy taxes on this government project, so the federal government agreed to pay Ogden City 9.4 percent of the annual rent collected to repay the city for the services provided. The Ogden Chamber of Commerce lobbied the government to approve and finance the construction of this 150-unit project which consisted of fifty-one frame buildings—thirty-four duplex structures, ten two-story, four-family buildings, and seven two-story, six-family units. Construction took place during 1941, with tenants moving in between September 1941 and February 1942. Only defense workers could live in the project, and the average monthly rents ranged from twenty to twenty-four dollars a month.

More people than were first anticipated kept coming, and by January 1942 it was determined that there was a need of 2,500 housing units in the Ogden area, and the government approved the immediate construction of 2,000 prefabricated houses. With the success of the Grandview Acres project and the joint chamber of commerce-government study of the needs, these additional housing units were deemed justified. In addition, private enterprise was to construct 1,750 housing units and people were asked to take roomers into their homes to meet the demands of defense housing. At one point, housing was so desperately needed that tent frames were constructed on the dance floor of the old Roman Gardens dance plaza at the Ogden River and Washington Boulevard.

The housing areas developed under these programs included Washington Terrace, which was a 1,400-unit project of prefabricated houses built on 266 acres in the southern end of Weber County; a 600-unit project at Bonneville Park on 7th Street in Ogden; a 600-unit area in Roy called Arsenal Acres; 400 units in Layton, called Verdeland Park; 200 units south of Hill Field, called Sahara Village; and 200 units in Clearfield, known as Anchorage Acres.[41]

On 23 May 1947 the residents of Washington Terrace incorporated and became the Washington Terrace Non-Profit Corporation. The new corporation purchased Washington Terrace from the federal government on 1 September 1950 at a cost of $2,250,000, and this sum was to be repaid gradually by owners in the project as part of their monthly payment to the corporation.

Through the federal Urban Renewal Program and cooperation of the local banks, the corporation was able to work out plans to create new housing for families by separating into two houses structures that had been built as duplex buildings and by placing individual family units on new concrete basement foundations. Much of this effort effort of developing private homes was made by Robert Hemingway, Rulon Starley, Don Chambers, and Judge J. A. Howell. It was a major task since three-fourths of the 1,400-unit project were duplex structures. With good planning and cooperation and the approval of financing by the Urban Renewal Program for remodeling and refacing of the structures with brick, the community of Washington Terrace was reorganized into a permanent community of comfortable and appealing residences. A final step in this process was the creation of the City of Washington Terrace as a municipal corporation on 12 December 1958, with Stanley W. Poulsen elected to serve as the first mayor.

## *Weber County Citizens in World War II and the Korean War*

A total of 8,238 (4,622 inducted and 3,616 enlisted) men and women of Weber County served in World War II. This service brought many personal hardships and sacrifices to those who served and to their families. During World War II, 161 Weber County residents lost their lives in the war. All of these losses were tragic; most were young men and women in the prime of life, in some cases leaving behind young families. One was Bert Noorda, who left his wife,

Arlene, and two sons, Steve and Rick; another was Clyde Decker, who left his wife, Terese, and son, Robert.

The war experiences of the military people of Weber County were varied. Lloyd S. Wallace, who had worked as a locomotive engineer in Ogden before the war, performed the same job in the army. He landed at Normandy several weeks after D-Day and operated a troop train through Paris in September 1944; he later operated trains that carried German prisoners of war from Warburg, Germany. Charles Sommerville, who served in the 507th Regiment of the 82nd Airborne Division, parachuted behind Normandy Beach in the D-Day landing on 6 June 1944 to secure roads and bridges for the invading forces. He was in the Battle of the Bulge in Belgium in December 1944 and was wounded in the arm. Ogden's Kayji Oka was in the Army Military Intelligence Division, serving as an interpreter; he was on his way to Japan as part of the anticipated invasion force for Japan when the war ended. He served later as part of the American occupation force in Japan.

Clarence Charles Hetzel, Jr., entered the service in August 1941 as a medical doctor in the army reserve for a period of training; when war was declared on 8 December 1941, he became a member of the regular army. From March 1943 until the end of his service he was assigned to various islands of the Pacific—from Guadalcanal to the Philippines—and for most of that time served as a flight surgeon to various medium bombardment groups of the 13th Air Force. Wendell Saunders served in the U.S. Navy as a submariner on board the *USS Kraken.* He spent the war attacking Japanese supply ships in the Pacific Ocean. Maurice Richards flew B-29s during the war. He flew thirty-five missions, most of them from Tinian Island in the Pacific to bomb the mainland of Japan. Richards remembered that "all the missions were dangerous" because they had to fly such long distances over water. On one occasion during a bombing raid on Kobe, Japan, much of their tail was shot off, and it took both pilots to maneuver the plane back to Tinian.[42]

William J. Gibson served two tours of combat duty in the Pacific. During the second tour he was the twenty-five-year-old commander of the 484th Bomber Squadron. He piloted his B-29 bomber, *Forever Amber,* on a long flight from Japan to Washington, D.C., to carry the movie film and still pictures of the Japanese surrender ceremony. Gibson remained in the air force for thirty years before he retired and returned to Ogden. He later became the civilian manager of the Ogden Hinckley Airport. Charles Hancey spent the war years in the navy on the cargo ship *Camanga* in the Pacific. Norman Farr of Ogden and Arthur Shattuck of Pleasant View also served in the navy in the Pacific. Farr was on the *USS ATR-80,* which was used as a tow ship for disabled craft.

Paul Edson served as a dental surgeon and followed the movement of U.S. forces across the Pacific. He was on Okinawa when the war ended. In the frenzy of celebrating the end of the war, he reported, "practically every gun on the island began firing and tracer bullets streaked through the night air in every direction. They had a wild party. Everybody who had a gun shot it and we managed to kill 10 of our own soldiers."[43] Delbert Bingham of Ogden, who had been widely known in the area for his athletic accomplishments in basketball at Weber High and Utah State Agricultural College, served in the 316th Troop Carrier Group. He was in the North African and Sicily campaigns, where he flew C-47s loaded with supplies and personnel. He later transferred to England, where he continued his flying missions into mainland Europe. His most trying experience was as a glider pilot in the Market Garden Campaign in Holland; he was part of the air assault on Nijmegen in that campaign.[44]

John G. "Jack" Hayes lived his entire life in Weber County except for the war years after he enlisted in the army. He trained with the 82nd Airborne and later transferred to the 101st Airborne, where he participated in the D-Day landings as a pathfinder in the 506th Infantry Regiment. He parachuted behind enemy lines the night before the invasion took place. He also participated in the Market Garden operation in Holland and the Battle of the Bulge in Belgium, where he was wounded. He was in the American group that captured Hitler's headquarters at the Eagle's Nest in Berchtesgaden, Germany. John Lindquist, as a member of the 8th Air Force, was a bombardier-navigator in a B-24 that participated in the D-Day invasion. On one mission Lindquist had to be lowered into the bomb-bay to disarm twenty-one bombs that had become lodged there when their fins became entangled.

Those who returned home were left with indelible impressions by the experiences of the war. Many came home with battle wounds and were recipients of the Purple Heart medal. The 161 dead Weber County military personnel also received the Purple Heart. George Wahlen of Roy was recognized with the highest medal given by the government—the Congressional Medal of Honor. He received this honor for his service as a navy medical corpsman in the 5th Marine Division on Iwo Jima in February 1945. After being wounded three times, Wahlen continued to perform his duty in treating other wounded marines on the beaches. He later spent several months in army hospitals recuperating from separate wounds to his head, back, and legs. Because of his disregard for his own safety and his valiant efforts in helping his wounded comrades, he was presented the Congressional Medal of Honor on 5 October 1945 by President Harry Truman in Washington, D.C. Wahlen remained in the military and transferred from the navy to the army. His post-war service took him to many places in the United States, Korea, Hawaii, and a tour in Vietnam before he ended his military career and returned to Roy to settle down.

Many Weber County residents who served in World War II entered the service as National Guardsmen. Weber County had organized National Guard units since the beginning of the Utah National Guard in 1894. On 3 March 1941 five units from Weber County were called into federal service for a year of training, and when the war began for the United States, these units remained activated until its end. These National Guard units from Weber County were Company "G," 115th Medical Regiment from Ogden, with Howard K. Belnap, Conroy Francis, William S. Moyes, and Elmore F. Smith as leaders and medical doctors; 115th Ordinance Company (Medium Maintenance) from Ogden, with Captain Glenn Z. Nielsen as commander; Battery "B," 145th Field Artillery from Ogden, with Captain Virgil C. Toller as commander; 222nd Field Artillery Band, with Warrant Officer Herbert Snyder as commander; and Battery "B," 222nd Field Artillery from Ogden, with Captain Leonard V. Call as commander.

Except for the 145th Field Artillery, the Weber County units of the Utah National Guard, for the most part, trained in Hawaii and then went to Guadalcanal, New Britain, Luzon, Philippines (where they fought from the Lingayen Gulf to Manila), and the islands of Panay and Negros in the Philippines. Some units ended up as occupation forces in Korea.

When word was received on the afternoon of 15 August 1945 that the Japanese had agreed to surrender terms and the war was ended, the communities in Weber County responded with enthusiasm. The *Ogden Standard-Examiner* headlines announced that the "World Welcomes New Era of Peace." Businesses and federal installations closed for the rest of that day and the following day in celebration. As word of the end of the war surged through the county, crowds poured into the center of Ogden and the area became a noisy center of activity. Firecrackers and fireworks were set off. People embraced and kissed each other. Hundreds of cars formed a line that circled the block of Municipal Square. Cars sounded their horns and dragged noise-making articles such as garbage cans behind them. One car that brought a great amount of cheers had an effigy of Japan's emperor suspended from a pole tied to the front of the car. City commissioner Harold L. Welch arranged for an orchestra that provided music for the dancers. The celebration ended when a rainstorm caused the crowd to disperse.

In Plain City the citizens went to the town square and celebrated the end of the war by forming a long line of cars in an impromptu parade. Plain City held a program and dance the next day in the local chapel. The newspaper reported that "Roy residents celebrated quietly." A special thanksgiving service was held in the North Ogden LDS chapel, and in Hooper a town band "serenaded the community during the afternoon and evening and residents congregated at the town square for further merrymaking."[45]

World War II ended in 1945; five years later the Korean War began. Because it was a limited war—technically, a United Nations police action—the Korean War did not require the mobilization of the whole nation as World War II had done; but it still required much sacrifice from those who were selected to carry out the fight. Utah provided 65 percent of its National Guard ground troops and 90 percent of its Air National Guard units to the war effort. Weber County people served in the war as members of National Guard or Reserve

Forces units or as conscripted or recruited personnel. It is estimated that 2,940 Weber County people served in the Korean War.[46]

### *Politics and Government in Weber County—1920 to 1955*

The population of Weber County grew from 43,463 in 1920 to 83,319 in 1950. The biggest growth in this period occurred in the years from 1940 to 1950—from 56,714 people to 83,319. In Ogden City the population grew from 33,804 in 1920 to 57,112 in 1950. The county and city had become areas of significant growth and were faced with all the concerns and responsibilities of modern governments. County commissioner George F. Simmons later suggested that some of the accomplishments of the county from 1934 to 1940 included the building of county shops, keeping open all county roads in the winter regardless of weather conditions, the construction of new county roads, the improvement and hard surfacing of many of the county roads, the construction of cement culverts and bridges to replace inadequate wooden structures, the replacement of an old record-keeping system by a modern system, and the construction of the City and County Building.[47]

The total expenditures by the Weber County Department of Public Welfare in 1939 were $661,704.93, and the Work Projects Administration in April 1940 employed 1,132 people (981 male and 151 female) exclusive of thirty-six non-relief workers. The Work Projects Administration labor was employed for local and statewide purposes and other agencies including the Soil Conservation Service, the Building Survey, the Forest Service, the War Department, and the Bureau of Entomology. This expansion in government services made the United States government the largest employer in Ogden during the Depression and increased the size of county government.[48]

The symbol of the importance of local government at this time was the completion of the new City and County Building in November 1940. Words to that effect were stated by William R. McEntyre, chair of the Weber County Commission, in the dedicatory program of 8 November 1940:

> May it [the new building] ever symbolize harmony and good will between the branches of government, a complete unity of interest among the citizens of this community, and point the way to

> greater achievements to the end that Ogden City and Weber County may be made a still better place in which to live.[49]

This new building represented the expanded role that Weber County and Ogden City governments had acquired by 1940. Through the years previous governments often had met in inadequate quarters. In early times the government councils met in Weber schoolhouses, local church buildings, homes, and other informal places. On 26 August 1872 the city was given by the Mormon church the "Seventies Hall" located at Grant Avenue and 25th Street, and municipal meetings were held there until 1882 when a new city hall with a combined jail was constructed on the northwest corner of 26th Street and Washington Boulevard. This later became the site of the Carnegie Library. In 1888–89 a new, ornate city hall was erected on Municipal Square block facing 25th Street. That building served as city offices until the completion of the new City and County Building in 1940.[50]

The county courthouse was established on 24th Street in 187[illegible] on land that was purchased from David Moore. The courthouse building included a rock basement which had a brick vault for records storage and a jail for prisoners, a second and third floor with brick walls for courtroom and county business offices, and a roof and clock tower made of wood covered with metal. This building served as the county courthouse from 1876 to 1895. On 10 October 1895 it was severely damaged by a fire set by three jail inmates. Following the fire, the building was remodeled and served as the county center from 1895 until 1940 when the county operations were moved into the new City and County Building.[51]

The Republican party consistently dominated the elections from statehood in 1896 through the 1920s in Weber County. Weber County was a labor-oriented county because of the large numbers of railroad workers. Early in this century, organized labor favored the Republican party in Weber County because labor felt that the Republicans backed the businesses on which the county labor force depended for jobs. This loyalty lasted until Franklin D. Roosevelt became president in 1932 and his New Deal legislation favored workers. With Roosevelt's election, the majority in Weber County began to favor the Democratic party, and this political situation generally continued until 1956.[52]

One of the labor organizations that had followers in Weber County was the American Alliance for Labor and Democracy, which was organized in Ogden in February 1918. The Ogden chapter was a member of the national organization which supported the mobilization of labor behind the war efforts in World War I and worked against the radical unions. Other labor organizations active in the county included the American Federation of Labor, which held its twenty-fifth Utah convention meeting in Ogden in September 1929. Fifteen accredited delegates attended the meeting, representing seven unions—the Typographical Union, Motion Picture Operators, Garment Workers of Ogden, Streetcar Men, Ogden Trades and Labor Assembly, Ogden Brewery Workers, and Ogden Sheet Metal Workers. The main thrust of the meeting was to press for more union membership. One result of the meeting was the enrollment of about 200 employees of the American Packing and Provision Company at Ogden in 1931 as union members.[53]

As a part of the open-shop movement which opposed labor unions, businessmen organized their own groups to challenge the labor movement. This opposition culminated in 1927 in a statewide organization known as the Utah Industrial Council, which had as its driving force the Utah Associated Industries group. John G.M. Barnes was president of this organization, with M.S. Eccles as vice-president, and R.E. Bristol, G.G. Wright, and H.S. Rolapp from Ogden serving as members of the board of directors.[54]

In 1920 Weber County generally voted for the Republican ticket that included Warren G. Harding for president of the United States, Reed Smoot for U.S. senator, Don B. Colton for representative, and Charles Mabey for governor. In this election Eugene V. Debs received 351 county votes on the Socialist ticket and Parley Christensen received 1,325 votes on the Farm-Labor ticket. In 1924 Weber County voted for Calvin Coolidge for president and Republicans also won most of the state offices; however, George H. Dern, the Democratic candidate for governor, won the election, including Weber County's vote. Frank Francis from Ogden was the Democratic candidate for

Congress, and he won the majority of Weber County's votes; but the incumbent Republican representative, Don Colton, was elected.

In 1928 the Republicans won big again, with Herbert Hoover winning the presidential race and most of the state offices going to the Republicans. In Weber County, county resident William H. Wattis won the vote for governor over George H. Dern but lost on the state level as Dern was reelected to a second term. After his second term, Dern served in the Roosevelt administration as Secretary of War. In this election Republican David J. Wilson was elected to the position of district attorney over a popular Democrat, Joseph Chez.

In 1932 Weber County went strongly Democratic as Franklin D. Roosevelt defeated Hoover for president, Elbert D. Thomas defeated long-time senator Reed Smoot, Abe Murdock defeated Don Colton, and the Democrats made a clean sweep of the state offices. In 1932 William Z. Foster was a presidential candidate running on the Communist party ticket, and he received sixty-one Weber County votes. Norman Thomas ran as the Socialist party candidate in the same election and received 922 Weber County votes. O. A. Kennedy, an Ogden insurance broker and part-time writer for the *Ogden Standard*, was the secretary of the Socialist party of Utah.

The Democrats remained strong through the rest of the Depression general election years of 1936, 1940, and the war-time election of 1944. Franklin D. Roosevelt won the county vote in all of those years. In 1938 John W. Arrington won a seat on the county commission and was reelected in 1940. This began a long tradition of political service by the Arrington family that has been continued by his son, John B. Arrington, who served on the Ogden City Commission from 1969 to 1978 and has served in the Utah State Legislature from 1978 until the present (1996).

In 1940 Democrat and Weber County native Herbert B. Maw was elected governor of Utah; and he was reelected in 1944. In 1940 Dexter Farr, a Democrat following a political interest like his ancestor Lorin Farr, defeated C. Angus Wright for the state senate seat. In 1944 the Democrats almost swept the local elections, as it seemed that the public did not want to make any drastic changes during the war. The major exception in the county was that the vote for governor went to Republican J. Bracken Lee, but he did not win the statewide vote.

After the war the voting in Weber County became mixed between Democrats and Republicans. On the state level, in 1948 J. Bracken Lee was elected as governor; Weber's David J. Wilson ran for the U.S. House of Representatives as a Republican, losing to Democrat Walter K. Granger. In the 1952 elections, Republicans held a slight edge in the Weber County vote. They selected Dwight D. Eisenhower as president, Douglas Stringfellow as member of the U.S. House of Representatives, and Earl J. Glade as governor. Glade was born in Weber County, but he did not have enough votes statewide to win the election over J. Bracken Lee, who won a second term. Stringfellow's term was cut short by a major scandal—he made false claims about his military service during World War II. Stringfellow resigned after pressure was put on him by his Republican colleagues in Congress and Utah. In the election of 1954 Henry Aldous Dixon ran on the Republican ticket to replace Stringfellow. Dixon had served as president of Weber College and also as president of Utah State University. Dixon lost the Weber County vote in the election to Walter K. Granger but won the state vote and became a member of the House of Representatives.

In the 1954 election there was an important referendum on the ballot dealing with an issue created by the legislature and Governor J. Bracken Lee when they passed a law, Senate Bill 39, which would transfer Weber College, Snow College, and Dixie College out of state control back to the Mormon church. There was much opposition to this, especially in the college towns, and action was taken to override the legislation by a referendum vote of the people. After a hard campaign to get enough signatures on a petition to put the question on the ballot, the referendum was presented to the voters in the 1954 election. The referendum in favor of keeping the colleges under state control won by a vote of 137,389 in favor to 92,787 against, keeping the colleges under state jurisdiction. Weber County voters approved of keeping the college under state control by a vote of 22,879 in favor and 6,042 against. County residents felt that they had saved an important institution in the area.

In 1956 the Democrats were strong in Weber County. They won all the state-level offices and chose Alonso F. Hopkin, a Democrat, over Wallace F. Bennett for the U.S. Senate. Bennett, however, won in the statewide election. In this election Weber County supported Republican Henry Aldous Dixon for his second term in the House of Representatives. Weber County also cast most of its votes for Dwight D. Eisenhower for a second term over Adlai Stevenson. In the county Democrat L. Rulon Jenkins won the vote for the state senate, and Democrats J. Levi Beus, Elizabeth Vance, and Edward Larsen won in the state House of Representatives races. L.G. Bingham was the only Democrat to lose in this election; Fred Froerer won a local House seat in that contest by a vote of 3,802 to 2,931.[55]

Some of the Weber County commissioners who were noted for their service in the 1920 to 1955 period, particularly in dealing with agricultural needs and water development, were J. M Child, Moroni Skeen, F. W. Stratford, William R. McIntyre, Charles A. Halverson, Arthur P. Brown, and Elmer Carver.

In the period 1920 to 1955 Weber County had gone through some hard times of depression and war but had come out of the period with some renewed hope for the future. Life had never been easy in the county, but the county residents had always made it through. Good leadership and the will of the people seemed to be of importance in overcoming the difficulties. There were, however, many changes that would come in the future that would make the county much different than it had ever been, and it could not turn back to more nostalgic times again.

## ENDNOTES

1. Lyn Prestwich, comp., *Utah Agricultural Statistics, 1920–1958,* Project 519, (Salt Lake City: Utah Agricultural Experiment Station, 1959), table 40.

2. State of Utah, *Bulletin No. 5 of the Industrial Commission of Utah: Period July 1st, 1926 to June 30th, 1928,* 11; Prestwich, *Utah Agricultural Statistics, 1920–1958,* table 9; *Inventory of the County Archives of Utah: Weber County,* 25–26.

3. Charles H. Skidmore, *Utah—Resources and Activities* (Salt Lake City: Department of Public Instruction, 1933), 247.

4. Prestwich, *Utah Agricultural Statistics, 1920–1958,* tables 9, 10, and 11.

5. Ibid., table 109.

6. Ibid., tables 67 and 68.

7. Skidmore, *Utah—Resources and Activities,* 279; Prestwich, *Utah Agricultural Statistics,* tables 70, 71, 72, and 77.

8. Skidmore, *Utah—Resources and Activities,* 288, 290; Prestwich, *Utah Agricultural Statistics,* tables 73, 74, 76, 78, and 79.

9. *Industrial Utah* (Ogden), 15 July 1901, 9.

10. Ibid.; Floyd J. and Clara Woodfield, comps., *History of North Ogden: Beginnings to 1985* (Ogden: Empire Printing Company, 1986), 149; *Ogden Standard,* 17 August 1909, 4, and 20 August 1909, 7.

11. Melba and Ron Colvin, comps., *History of the Eden Ward, Ogden Stake Utah, 1877–1977* (Ogden: LDS Genealogical Society, 1977), 160–65; LaVerna Burnett Newey, *Remember My Valley: A History of Ogden Canyon, Huntsville, Liberty, and Eden, Utah, from 1825 to 1976* (Salt Lake City: Hawkes Publishing Company, 1977), 266–69.

12. W. P. Thomas, *Utah—Weber County: Annual Report of 1916,* 1; William W. Owens, comp., *Utah Extension Division: Weber County Annual Narrative Report, 1920,* 4, 31.

13. Edna W. Ladwig, "Extension Work with Women," *Annual Report from September 5, 1917 to December 1, 1918,* 1–7; E. W. Robinson, "Program of Work, Child Welfare Project, School Lunch," *Annual Narrative Report of Weber County, 1920,* 8–26; A. L. Christiansen, "History of Extension Work in Weber County," *Annual Report of Extension Service, 1939, County Agents, Weber County, State of Utah,* 9–11;

14. Mack S. Taft, "The Great Depression in Weber County, Utah," M.A. thesis, Utah State University, 1973, 11.

15. Ibid., 67–68.

16. A.L. Christiansen, *Annual Report of Extension Work, Weber County, Utah, 1932,* 2.

17. A.L. Christiansen, *Annual Report of Extension Service, Weber County, Utah, 1934,* 3, 8, 14, 15, 16, 18.

18. Jerome Wheeler, *History of Slaterville.* (n.p., n.d.), 13–14.

19. Ibid., 34–35.

20. Ray Burtenshaw, *Combined Annual Report of County Extension Workers, Weber County, Utah, 1944,* 25.

21. *Annual Report of Extension Service, Weber County, Utah, 1945,* 2.

22. Ibid.

23. *Annual Report of Extension Service, Weber County, 1947,* 12.

24. Richard W. Sadler and Richard C. Roberts, *The Weber River Basin: Grass Roots Democracy and Water Development* (Logan: Utah State University Press, 1994).

25. Richard C. Roberts and Richard W. Sadler, *The History of the Weber*

*County Watershed Protective Corporation* (Ogden: Weber County Watershed Protective Corporation, 1989), 29–35.

26. Ibid., 94–95.

27. Ogden Chamber of Commerce, "Ogden—Utah's Industrial and Railroad Center," 1932, located in Bancroft Library, Berkeley, California.

28. *Salt Lake Tribune,* 18 January 1972, 22.

29. Ibid., 14 June 1970, 21A.

30. *Ogden Standard-Examiner,* 31 August1930, 3D; Sidney Hyman, *Challenge and Response: The First Security Corporation First Fifty Years, 1928–1978* (Salt Lake City: Graduate School of Business, University of Utah, 1978), 37; "First Security Corporation," in Richard C. Roberts and Richard W. Sadler, *Ogden: Junction City* (Northridge, CA: Windsor Press, 1985), 234–37.

31. Linda Sillitoe, *Banking on the Hemingways: Three Generations of Banking in Utah and Idaho* (Ogden: Weber State University, 1992), 12.

32. Harold Thompson, interview by Richard C. Roberts, Ogden, Utah, 26 October 1995, copy in possession of author.

33. Lloyd E. Clark, interview by Troy Nye, Ogden, Utah, 16 April 1981 (Sand Ridge Junior High Oral History Project), copy in possession of the author.

34. Alvornia Thompson, interview by Wanda Thacker, Ogden, Utah, April 1981 (Sand Ridge Junior High School Oral History Project), copy in possession of the authors.

35. Roger Launius, *A Case Study in Civil-Military Relations: Hill Air Force Base and the Ogden Business Community, 1934–45* (Hill Air Force Base, Utah: Office of History, 1986), 36–42.

36. Ibid., 51–52.

37. *Hill Air Force Base Economic Resource Impact Statement* (Hill Air Force Base, Utah: Ogden Air Logistics Center, 1990), 2; Launius, *A Case Study in Civil-Military Relations,* 61.

38. Leonard Arrington and Thomas Alexander, "Supply Hub of the West: Defense Depot Ogden, 1941–1964," *Utah Historical Quarterly* 32 (Spring 1964): 100–02.

39. Leonard J. Arrington and Anthony T. Cluff, *Federally-Financed Industrial Plants Constructed in Utah During World War II* (Logan: Utah State University Press, 1969), 70–72.

40. Arrington and Alexander, "Supply Hub of the West," 99.

41. James B. Allen, "Crisis on the Home Front: The Federal Government and Utah's Defense Housing in World War II," *Pacific Historical Review* 38 (November 1969): 414–15.

42. Ralph Wakely, *Standard-Examiner,* 2 September 1995, 1A.

43. Ibid.

44. Delbert Bingham, interview by Richard C. Roberts, 21 December 1995, Ogden, Utah, copy in possession of the authors.

45. *Ogden Standard-Examiner,* 15 August 1995, 1A.

46. According to David Phillips of the Veterans' Administration and Terry Schow, Weber County Veterans' Association, this number is as accurate as can be determined.

47. George F. Simmons, "Statement," in *Ogden and Weber County Municipal Building Dedication Program* (Ogden: City and County Commissioners, 8 November 1940), 5.

48. Dale Morgan, ed., *A History of Ogden,* 66.

49. W. R. McEntire, Dedication Program: City and County Building (Ogden: City and County Commissioners, 1940), 2.

50. Morgan, *A History of Ogden,* 66.

51. *Inventory of the County Archives of Utah: Weber County,* 29–30.

52. Ira Huggins, interview with Patricia A. Buchanan, Ogden, Utah, 14 July 1980, copy in possession of the authors.

53. Sheelwant Bapurao Pawar, "An Environmental Study of the Development of the Utah Labor Movement," Ph.D. diss., University of Utah, 1968, 406–7

54. Ibid., 397–401.

55. "Secretary of State Election Papers, 1851–1976," Series 364, Utah State Archives, various reels according to election years cited.

7

# A Time of Change and Diversity, 1955–1996

Weber County residents over time have reflected on their lives and personal status; and some, with questions about the changes around them and the uncertainty of the future, have felt, as Charles Dickens wrote in *A Tale of Two Cities,* that "it was the best of times, it was the worst of times." This has been especially true in the four decades from 1955 to 1996. After the Korean War the world changed a great deal, and these changes were felt in Weber County. The age of relative innocence was lost and people in the United States faced a world of Cold War tension and economic change. The Korean War had done much to cause Americans to lose their confidence that they were a favored nation or a chosen people—they had come out of that war doubting that they had won a battle for good. The following Vietnam War continued that trend and even more divided the nation over the question of whether the United States should be involved in that war. In the end, the country withdrew from the war without any sense of victory and very much shaken and disrupted by the experience. Many Weber county men and women served in this war; many died and others came home wounded in both body and soul.

The old foundation on which Weber County had been established had shifted a great deal. Family ties to the county had changed. Many young men and women who had served in the wars or had been forced to take employment outside of the county or state were no longer attached to the old homesteads. Ogden was no longer the power it had been in relation to the county and surrounding cities. Much of the population was more mobile and moved into the county areas outside of Ogden. Smaller communities began to challenge Ogden's role as the governmental and business center. Business and commerce became increasingly global, and an increasingly multicultural population moved into the county. Politics, although still concentrating on local matters, had a more broad aspect to them. Old farms and open spaces were being taken up and population growth began to crowd into every possible space of the county. Empty spaces between communities began to be almost nonexistent. Social, political, and economic changes were rampant in the county during the last four decades of the twentieth century.

The term "diversity" describes the changes which have taken place in the county, and it not only describes what has happened in terms of population changes but also to changes in business and commerce, participation in government, ideas that are taught in the schools and the marketplaces, and cultural considerations.

Population growth was one of the most obvious changes in the modern era, as the number of people in Weber County increased significantly during the years from 1955 to 1996. The population changed in both numbers and ethnicity. The landscape of the county was changing noticeably as housing and community developments sprang up in various parts of the county. Two centuries ago Daniel Defoe described the growth around London, and he bemoaned the development that was taking place and asked:

> How much further it may spread, who knows? . . . We see several villages, formerly standing, as it were, in the country, and at a great distance, now joined to the streets by continuous buildings, and more making haste to meet in the like manner. . . . All this is very evident, and yet all these put together, are still to be called London. Whither will this monstrous city then extend? and where must a circumvallation or communication line of it be placed?"[1]

Ogden will never become London; but the citizens of Weber County should ask themselves those same questions as growth continues, and the debate between urban and rural development becomes more complicated.

## *The Economy—Agriculture and the Railroad*

In this period the economy was a major driving force in shaping developments in the county. There were significant shifts in the basic county economic structure which had included farming, the railroad, and business and government installations that had formed the basic foundation of the county's economy before 1955. In recent times farming no longer is the main economic factor in the county. Farms changed—the sugar beet farms dwindled; in 1994 the last green beans were canned from local county production; the sheep raising industry declined; the dairying business was severely cut back; and those farming activities that remained generally shifted to less labor-intensive farming such a grain and hay crops and cattle herds. In addition, all the food-processing industries that had relied on locally produced commodities left the area. The canning industry, sugar refining, slaughterhouse and meat-packing businesses all withdrew from the region.

The railroad industry also went through major changes in this time period. In the mid-1950s railroading shifted from being a major mode of passenger travel to become oriented to a freighting industry. As a result, the Ogden terminal became less important, and by the 1970s railroad companies wanted to divest themselves of the expense of maintaining the old station facilities. At this time Ogden took action to preserve the depot as a community center. The railroad industry, which had provided the county population with a large number of jobs and had placed Ogden on the national map as the junction city, ceased to be as important a player in the economy of the county.

Federal government facilities in the Weber County area were also cut back in the decades following the Korean War. The Clearfield Naval Supply Depot was sold by the government to private concerns. Defense Depot Ogden went through some up-and-down times during this period, including rumors of closure; by the middle of the

1990s it was scheduled for termination as a government installation, with plans to turn the property over to the private sector. Hill Air Force Base, like the other federal installations, depended on the fluctuations of national defense priorities. By 1996 Hill Air Force Base had survived several threats of being shut down, but the questions of how the changing mission of the base would finally be defined in the post-Cold War era continued to be addressed.

The changes and uncertainties of the economy in the last four decades led county business and community leaders to pursue other means of supporting and diversifying the local economy. It took some concentrated planning and effort by many leaders in the community to put Weber County on a more stable economic base. Changes in agricultural practices in Weber County that started to take place in the 1940s, especially during World War II, would have impacts that shaped the nature of farming in the county up to the 1996 period. It was in the 1940s that some of the agricultural-based industries began moving out of the area; these included major organizations such as the Amalgamated Sugar Plant, the California Packing Company, the Swift Meat Packing Company, the Becker Brewery, the American Can Company, the North Ogden Canning Company, and the Utah-Idaho Sugar Company. These moves came about in part because of a lack of sufficient farmland in the county to permit large-scale mechanical harvesting. The federal government had acquired much prime farmland for wartime government installations. Many farmers also turned away from farming to take full-time government employment with more reliable income. Urbanization also reduced much of the farm acreage as new housing projects were built to accommodate the large influx of governmental and other workers coming to the area.[2]

A study done in 1974 on farming in the county by the Weber County Planning Commission stated that "the economic importance of agriculture in Weber County has been steadily declining in the last few years. Yet Weber County still remains as one of Utah's most agriculturally productive counties."[3] It was noted that Weber County had 712 farms in 1974 and that the total acreage in farms amounted to 215,421 acres, with the average size of the farms being 303 acres. The county had 42,404 acres in crops, and 34,319 of that total was irrigated. Hay was the major crop of the county, with 15,763 acres being planted; wheat, barley, and oats were planted in 2,286 acres, 2,220 acres, and 205 acres, respectively. Most wheat was grown in the Ogden Valley around Huntsville. Field corn for silage took up 6,000 acres; sugar beets, which were still produced until 1980, took up over 1,000 acres; and 300 to 570 acres were used for various vegetables.

In 1974 there were 464 farms in the county, with a total of 30,9[illegible]9 cattle and calves and 8,753 bulls and steers. Sixty-seven farms reported having a total of 59,116 sheep and lambs which were shorn during that year. Most of these sheep were "farm flock," which meant that they were pastured near the farm and accounted for a higher sheep-to-acre ratio than range sheep operations would produce. Weber County had 135 dairy farms in 1969; that number declined to 117 dairy farms in 1974, with 5,850 cows being milked. This produced on average more than $2,500 a year income for those farms. Even though the dairy farms were on the decline, Weber County was still more productive in the dairy industry than any of the other Wasatch Front counties. The statistics show that Weber County had one of the highest market values of products sold from its farms among the counties of Utah. The average value of agricultural products sold was $39,659 per farm, with total net farm income for Weber County in 1974 being $6,024,000—only 1.5 percent of the total income of the county.[4]

By 1984, 88.4 percent of the county population lived in towns or cities of 2,500 or more people. Weber County had 13 percent of its area in croplands, and of that total 47,394 acres were irrigated and 959 acres were not irrigated. Of the total of 371,840 land acres in the county, 271,758 acres were privately owned; 70,105 acres were owned by the federal government; 4,070 acres were owned by the state of Utah; 24,365 acres were devoted to roads and railroads; and 1,542 acres were taken up in streams and small water areas. Of the total land area of the county, 48,353 acres were crop lands; 1,770 acres were pasture; 117,803 acres were rangeland; 86,346 acres were forest land; and 21,556 acres were devoted to other purposes.

Agricultural production for the county in 1983 included [illegible],600 acres in wheat, 4,000 acres in barley, 1,000 acres in corn for grain, 4,900 acres in corn for silage, and 12,300 acres in alfalfa hay. It was estimated that Weber County raised 36,300 cattle and 7,200 milk cows. In 1985 there was a federal "buy-out" program carried out by the U.S. Department of Agriculture to help the dairy industry by purchasing some of the herds to reduce milk production and thus help increase the price on milk for the farmers. Twelve dairies in Weber County took advantage of that program and got out of the dairy business. Those who participated in the buy-out were John Beus, Gene T. Wayment, Hal Stoddard, Don and Jeff Widdison, Norman J. Montgomery, Von Stauffer, Ralph Hansen, Jensen Middleford Ranch, Lee Howard, and Dee McFarland.[5]

Farm incomes in Weber County amounted to $31.1 million in 1992; that total was broken down into $23.8 million from livestock and livestock products and $7.3 million from various crops. In the 1992 farm census, Weber County had 945 farms with a total of 256,522 acres in farm land. There were 50,283 acres in crop land; 27,860 acres were harvested and 31,758 acres were irrigated. The average size of county farms was 271 acres. The average estimated market value per county farm of land and buildings in 1992 was $231,593, and the average value of farm land was $832 per acre. Most Weber County farms made under $10,000 in sales in 1992 (664 farms out of 945) and seventy farms had over $100,000 per year in sales. Thirteen farms were larger than 1,000 acres and 639 farms had less that fifty acres of land.[6]

By 1995 agriculture had declined even more. The population of the county in 1995 was 158,330, with 93 percent of that number (147,172) living in urban areas. The county had 3,600 acres in wheat production, including one-third in spring wheat and two-thirds in winter wheat; 2,900 acres in barley; 1,500 acres of corn for grain and 4,000 acres of corn for silage; 900 acres in oats; and 16,400 acres in hay, with 13,600 acres of that amount in alfalfa and alfalfa mixtures. In 1995 Weber County farmers had 33,000 cattle and 6,000 milk cows, a reduction of 1,000 milk cows from the previous year. In 1996 there were only forty dairy farms in Weber County.[7] The sheep industry in Weber County moved from 8,900 sheep in 1994 to 5,000 in 1995, a significant decline. There were only three ranchers running sheep on a commercial scale in Weber County in 1996.

In the past three decades there has been some extension of farm lands in the west part of the county because of additional irrigation water made available by the completion of Weber Basin projects, particularly Willard Bay, and the draining of land in the county. During this same period, however, other farm lands have been eaten up by new housing and industry. The number of farmers in the county has declined. The number of dairy farms in the county has also declined, but the milk production for individual animals has increased dramatically. In 1939 the annual average amount of milk produced per cow was 7,290 pounds; today the annual average is 20,000 pounds. Most of the dairy herds in Weber County today are Holstein cattle; all of the Guernsey herds are gone and there are only three Jersey herds left in the county.

There is a recent resurgence of vegetable farming in the county including sweet corn, potatoes, tomatoes, onions, watermelon, squash, pumpkins, garlic, gourds, and mini-Indian corn. Some of the major vegetable farmers in the county include Mike Panunzio in Plain City; August Favero and his sons David and Tom in Taylor; and Layne McFarland in West Weber.

In 1995 the fruit industry had declined in the county, with only three farmers doing any kind of major production: Henry Hall in North Ogden, Amos Brown in Roy, and Joe Dawson in Roy. In 1992 Weber County had 2,200 sweet cherry trees, which was 3 percent of the sweet cherry trees in Utah, and 5,334 apple trees, 1 percent of the state's total. The numbers of peach, pear, apricot, and tart cherry trees were not significant enough to list. The days of the fruit cooperatives were gone, and the fruit industry of Weber County had declined as development encroached on the orchards.

In 1994 it was estimated that there were 21,668 horses in Weber County, which amounted to about 12 percent of all the horses in Utah. Most owners use their horses for pleasure riding, youth activities, and hunting. Less than 5 percent of Utahns received any income from horses; but those who made income did so through breeding, racing, and show-related activities. Also, there are some horse stables that keep horses for urban horse fanciers.[8]

There are some new approaches to farming in the county, including the raising of ostriches for meat and leather. Eric Olsen is a major innovator in this field in the county, with 200 to 300 ostriches being raised on his Big O Ranch in Slaterville. The Dancing O farm in Hooper keeps approximately 100 ostriches. Huntsville has some llama raisers, with llamas being used for their wool and as pack animals. It is estimated that there are approximately 200 llamas in the area. There are three or four fish farms in the county which produce fish for commercial use and others which allow anglers to catch fish for their dinner.

Agriculture appears to be headed in a direction of further reduction by encroaching residential and industrial construction and a new threat that could take up a good portion of the best farm lands—the construction of a new super-highway through the western part of the county. This new highway running from Willard to Nephi, dubbed as Governor Michael Leavitt's "Legacy Project" (or the Western Transportation Corridor), proposes to cut a "300 to 400 foot right of way through the heart of some of the county's most fertile farmland," and the farmers of west Weber County are very disturbed by this proposal.[9] Controversy over the project is likely in the coming years. Farming in Weber County has changed a great deal, but it still remains an important part of Weber County life.

Another industry that had played a unique part in the history of the development of Weber County—the railroad—declined rapidly after the 1950s, and by 1996 it made only a small contribution to the economy of Weber County. This was a remarkable change considering that the railroad industry had made Ogden and Weber County prosperous and nationally important as the junction of the transcontinental railroad system; but, by the 1960s, all this would change. In the period from 1949 to 1967 railroad travel in the United States was cut in half and heavy financial losses were suffered in the passenger service business. The decline of the railroad business had a tremendous impact on the Ogden depot. The Ogden Union Station, which in past times had been bustling with passengers, was nearly deserted. One account said it was like a "mausoleum." Another said, "Now that there are no passenger trains, it's almost deserted, with the exception of maybe one-half hour when the Amtrak comes in. There is no restaurant now, no beauty shop, no red cap. It's kind of a sad looking place in the evening when the train comes in, because there are only one or two people there." Another wrote:

> Ogden is much different now than what it used to be too. Ogden was once advertised as the hub of a wheel as far as the railroad was concerned. Today it is only a spoke. It's just some place they go through. . . . The depot is just something I never saw locked and there was always the hurry and skurry of people in it up until the last ten years. It has dwindled down like that each year and they close the doors and lock everything up and open only so many hours a day when the Amtrak train comes through.[10]

With the decline of passenger service, there was a change in operations at the Ogden depot. The number of employees dropped off dramatically; some departments were transferred and others were closed down. With revenues falling, the railroads were forced to relieve themselves of many facilities which no longer had any usefulness but were only a maintenance or tax burden. Under those circumstances, in 1968 the Ogden Union Railway and Depot Company was ended and its properties and operations at Ogden were assumed by the Southern Pacific and Union Pacific companies. Other facilities suffered the same fate. In January 1970 the Union Pacific announced that its laundry facility would be closed. In February 1970 the Union Pacific commissary building at 25th and Wall Avenue was demolished. In September 1970 the Union Station telephone switchboard was closed, and on 1 May 1971 the station ticket office was turned over to the Railpax operation. In May 1971 the Railway Express Agency, immediately south of the Union Station, was demolished, and in October 1971 all but two of the passenger tracks and "protective sheds" for passenger service were torn up and removed. On 17 January 1972 the Barkalow brothers newsstand and snack bar located in a corner of the Union Station waiting room was closed down, and in June 1972 the Union Pacific-Southern Pacific freight office building located near 24th and Wall Avenue was torn down.[11]

Over the years other facilities also had been demolished, changed, or transferred. After the change from steam to diesel engines, the roundhouses were no longer needed and had been destroyed. Many of the repair shops were no longer needed because of improved equipment or reduced traffic. These shops were transferred to other places, including Salt Lake City, Green River, and Cheyenne. The ice plant at 33rd Street and Riverdale became obsolete because of new refrigerator cars and was closed. In September 1972 the railroads built a "run around track" that allowed traffic to pass through Ogden to Salt Lake City without stopping. In August 1996 Amtrak announced that the Pioneer—the last passenger train serving Ogden on the Chicago, Denver, Seattle line—would terminate its services on 10 November 1996, ending all passenger service in the city that at one time had been known as Junction City. It was sad to many that such a fate had come to Ogden.

Many prominent Ogden civic leaders and organizations had seen or been involved in the history of railroading and recognized that the same fate that had come to other facilities was a possibility for the Union Station. It was recognized that this would be a great loss to the community, and steps were taken to preserve the historic and symbolic structure. The efforts were successful, and on 21 October 1978, with proper ceremony the Union Station was dedicated by Ogden City and the railroad companies to serve as a "multi-purpose community center."[12] It was designated as a railroad station for the running of Amtrak services and railroad company offices; as a community center, with convention facilities and the M.S. Browning Theater and the Myra Powell Art Gallery; as a museum, with historic railroad, automobile, and firearms displays in the Wattis-Dumke Railroad Museum, the Browning-Kimball Vintage Car Collection, and the Browning Firearms Museum; and as a commercial facility, with the establishment of space for various businesses and restaurants. This diverse use of the historical edifice brought new life to the area and did much to keep alive the memory of the railroad years as a stimulus for new economic endeavors and as an important part of downtown Ogden.

The efforts of many people have helped railroading remain an active force in Weber County. Murray Moler, editor of the *Standard-Examiner,* worked hard to get the Union Station renovation established and get it designated on the "Railroad Hall of Fame" in the National Register of Historic Sites. Elizabeth "Teddy" Griffith served as the first director of the facility for a period of almost twenty years and worked to make the Union Station an important part of downtown Ogden. Under her guidance, the complex of museums and conference facilities became an important place for displays and a place for teaching and informing schoolchildren, community members, and tourist groups of the railroad history and important happenings which took place in Weber County and in the region. Dr. Michael Burdett heads a project to restore the track and a vintage rail system from Ogden to Promontory, where the National Transcontinental Railroad Monument is located. Burdett, a Weber County dentist, is also the president of the Golden Spike Chapter of the National Railway and Locomotive Historical Society, which was organized in Ogden in 1991. Robert Geier, current director of the Union Station, Burdett, and their organizations are working for greater support of the Union Station and the restoration of the original transcontinental line from Ogden to Promontory as a part of the national railroad grid. This project is estimated to cost $30 million, of which some $400,000 has been raised to make feasibility studies, which seem to indicate that the project would pay for itself and add additional tourist revenues to the region. Weber County and some of its residents are working hard to keep the memory and history of railroading in the area preserved in one way or another.

### *The Economy—New Directions*

With the decline of agriculture and related businesses in the county and the decline of the railroad industry, there was a need in Weber County for new businesses to shore up the economy. Businesses related to government agencies became somewhat unstable as the agencies tied to national defense fluctuated according to the national political and economic factors. Because of Weber County's location and labor force, some defense industry businesses came into Weber County; they included the Marquardt Corporation, a producer of the Bomart Missile, and the Boeing Company, which also was involved in missile production. Thiokol Chemical Corporation was located in northern Utah and was also closely tied to the military complex. The uncertainty of the military-industrial climate had an effect on many of these companies. The Marquardt Corporation discontinued its defense-oriented business and sold out to the White Truck manufacturing company, which later became White Volvo. Robert Marquardt, however, remained in the area as the founder of the Management Training Corporation, which organized and ran several U.S. government Job Corps sites, including the Clearfield and the Weber Canyon Job Corps. Marquardt kept his corporation headquarters in Ogden and made many contributions to the Ogden community, including the Marquardt Pavilion at Mount Ogden Park, the Ogden River Parkway Project, and the Eccles Dinosaur Park.

Thiokol Chemical became the Morton Thiokol Corporation, which was divided in 1989 into Morton International Incorporated and Thiokol Corporation, with Thiokol keeping the missile program and Morton International branching out into other business endeavors. Morton International developed two major manufacturing plants in the area: the Morton Automotive Safety Products Group in Weber County near the Ogden Municipal Airport and another in Brigham City. The company shifted much of its business away from defense-related industry. In October 1996 Morton International merged with Autoliv AB of Sweden, a leader in the European airbag and seatbelt market. The new company became Autoliv, Inc., the largest automotive safety-restraint systems supplier in the world.

These moves by private business away from reliance on the defense industry were also augmented by efforts of the Weber County Chamber of Commerce and community leaders. By the 1950s Weber County's business leaders were well aware of the ups and downs of businesses that relied on government spending and of the decline of agriculture and the railroad industry. They began to take action to realign the local economy along new trends. Dean Morrin, president of M. Morrin and Son Construction Company, and John A. Lindquist, president of Lindquist and Sons Mortuary, played key roles in changing the direction of business development in Weber County. Morrin remembered that "when the railroads began to disappear, the rippling effect on the community was traumatic. Had Hill Air Force Base closed for any reason in the 50s or 60s we would have been thrown into some terrible economic conditions."[13]

On 17 January 1954 the secretary-manager of the Ogden Chamber of Commerce, Bernie Diamond, announced that the chamber was opening a drive to raise $150,000 to establish a Weber County Industrial Development Bureau. Richard Hemingway was appointed as chairman of the funding drive, with committee members H. A. Benning, A. L. Glasmann, Ted G. Schmidt, George S.

Eccles, Frank M. Browning, James Devine, George (Ted) Hone, Harmon B. Barton, Frank M. Edwards, and Ernest H. Balch. With the successful conclusion of the funding drive, Daniel B. Dale was hired as the first director of the bureau; but he stayed only a year. D. Keith Hunt was hired to a reconfigured position in the bureau which combined fund-raising with fostering industrial development. The first businesses to relocate to Weber County as a result of the efforts of the bureau created an estimated 10,000 new jobs; they included Thiokol Chemical, Marquardt Corporation, Pacific Iron and Steel (which later became Jetway Corporation), Flameco, and McBee Corporation.

After a few years, the industrial development leveled out and seemed to have little direction, so a committee was formed to try to find some solutions to the problems. After a few years of study of programs in other states, it was decided to seek a "county-funded, Chamber-administered industrial promotion organization" that "would not be subject to partisan politics." With the help of Weber County commissioners Art Brown, Elmer Carver, and George Frost, state laws were passed to allow local tax monies to be used to support a business-controlled county industrial development agency.

With a new source of funding, the development program was rejuvenated and continued to use the name of the Weber County Industrial Development Bureau. Under the direction of successive directors Ed Peters and David Allred, the bureau made plans to create a Weber County Industrial Park, which would include the undeveloped areas of the communities of Harrisville, Farr West, and Pleasant View. In 1968 a 476-acre plot was identified which had nearby railroad and highway access to service the industries and companies that would locate there. In order to create this industrial park, the land had to be disincorporated from the communities involved and money had to be raised to acquire the properties. Key figures in procuring the money for the project were Dean Morrin, John Lindquist, Richard Hemingway, Marion (Red) Cummins, Joe Neary, Keith Hunt, Stephen Denkers, Mark Darney, and Nathan Mazer. Nathan Mazer was hired to head the Weber County Industrial Development Bureau in 1969. He had been a colonel in the U.S. Air Force and was involved in the community as chair of the centennial celebration of the driving of the golden spike before leading the

A country road in west Weber County during the 1920s. (Richard Roberts Collection)

county development effort. Mazer and the group organized the Committee of 100, which was made up of prominent community businessmen and members of the chamber of commerce who were put to the task of determining how to develop the industrial park and how to raise the money for it.

The Weber County Industrial Development Bureau borrowed $1 million from Weber County, which was to be repaid as the property was sold; but it was determined that another million dollars would be needed to complete the park. One of the disagreements about the development of the industrial park related to how much development should be done in the park to attract businesses. Abe Glasmann was of the opinion that very little should be done, while Dean Morrin was of the opinion that to be competitive basic utilities and infrastructure to the sites should be provided, so that they would have "more than a weedpatch to entice new industry." This became the source of a bitter argument between the two men. The Committee of 100 decided that the park needed more rather than less development and took on the task of raising the second million dollars for development of the site. Hockenbury System, Inc., of Harrisburg, Pennsylvania, a well-known community fund-raising organization was hired to help in the money-raising effort. As a result, a consultant from the company, Larry Lidstrom, came to Ogden to help in organizing the drive. Through his efforts and that of the Committee of 100, $1.4 million from 537 contributors was raised. In order to keep track of the funds and to determine how they would be expended, the Ogden Industrial Development Corporation was incorporated on 9 November 1971. Richard K. Hemingway was made president; Robert Heiner, executive vice president; Joseph Breeze, vice president; Roderick Browning, treasurer; Richard Mercer, assistant treasurer; and E. Lynn Foley, secretary. Lynnwood Islaub acted as accountant, with the responsibility of collecting the money and managing the books. Major contributors were Commercial Security Bank ($100,000); *Ogden Standard-Examiner* ($50,000); Bank of Utah ($35,000); Bank of Ben Lomond ($7,000); First Security Bank ($100,000); Utah Power and Light ($75,000); Mountain Bell ($40,000); Ogden First Federal ($35,000); Federal Building and Loan ($35,000); Mountain Fuel Supply Company ($25,000); Western General Dairy ($25,000); Church of Jesus Christ of Latter-day Saints ($25,000); and Smith Management Corporation ($20,000).[14]

Nathan Mazer also hired Charles Kelley, a capable consulting engineer and former city manager who had a great deal of understanding of Weber County, to design and manage the Weber Industrial Park. With support from county commissioner George Frost, the bureau trustees, and the Ogden Industrial Development Corporation directors, Mazer and Kelley were able to put together a well planned, full-scale industrial park. Kelley was able to design a park with wide roads, landscaped areas, and restrictive covenants which required buildings to follow certain design guidelines, including required setbacks from the roads, which provided green areas in the park.

With the plans in place, the groundbreaking ceremonies were held on 28 June 1972 with approximately 150 area residents, civic, business, and government leaders in attendance. Within five weeks of the opening of the park, the Bradley Corporation of Menomonee Falls, Wisconsin, which manufactured plumbing supplies, was the first business to buy property in the park,. This was a $500,000 investment for the Bradley Corporation, with another nearly matching amount awarded by a business grant. The arrangment to have them as tenants required a building swap of the old Shupe-Williams Candy Building in Ogden and an offer to build a structure at the industrial park by the Morrin and Son Construction Company at no profit to the Morrins. This was a demonstration of the county and citizen commitment to ensure the success of the Weber Industrial Park; and this type of commitment was needed to get the enterprise going. Other companies soon became involved in the park, including the West Bend Company, which purchased twenty-three acres and erected a $2.5-million facility to manufacture cookware; the John Ingles Frozen Foods Company, with a $3.5-million plant, which the Williams Research Corporation later took over; and the M & M Trailer Manufacturers Company.

Eventually eleven companies located at the park. Those that had the largest employment impact were Aviation Materials Management, Inc., with thrity-five employees; Bourns, Inc., manufacturers of electronic potentiometers, with 210 employees; Cerro Wire and Cable Company, with forty-four employees; Chromalox, manufacturer of industrial heating elements, with 475 employees; Loren Cook Company, maker of air-moving equipment, with sixty-five employees; Kimberly-Clark Corporation, maker of Huggies diapers, with 585 employees; Parker Hannifin Corporation, manufacturer of flight-control systems, with 321 employees; United Foods, Inc., producers of frozen foods, with eighty employees; Vermont American Corporation, packaging hand tools, with ten employees; and Western Coating, which recoated steel products, with twenty-five employees. The Weber Industrial Park was considered the flagship of industrial development in the county, and, in 1992, the eleven companies of the park provided work for 1,777 people and had a total value in property and personal earnings of almost $110 million, a tax assessment of over $1.6 million, and a sales tax return estimated at over $2 million to the county.[15]

With the initial development of the Weber Industrial Park for larger companies, it became clear that something needed to be done both to accommodate smaller businesses and to have a location closer to the city. With these goals in mind, the development of the area in the vicinity of 2550 South and 1500 West was begun. This property had been acquired by various businessmen but was largely owned by the Abe Glasmann family. Glasmann had not been very anxious to allow development of this area; but, after his death, the Weber County Industrial Development Bureau approached Blaine Glasmann about selling the property, and an agreement with the family was made. As a result, the Ogden Commercial and Industrial Park began operating in 1977. In 1992 the Ogden Industrial Park had more than eighty businesses as tenants and employed approximately 1,815 people. Market value of this park and personal earnings were assessed at $37 million, with a tax assessment of $582,633. It is evident that the work done for industrial development in Weber County has done much to bring employment and tax monies to the county. The industrial park concept and its advertisement also brought other economic investments to other parts of the county.

The industrial park developments gave life to the economy of Weber County, but for a period of time the downtown Ogden area had an appearance of neglect and deterioration. In the period from the 1960s into the early 1980s many of the old landmarks of Ogden were torn down as they became vacant eyesores to the community. In that space of time, many of the buildings at the Union depot had been torn down. Other structures that met the fate of the wrecking ball included the Sacred Heart Academy at 25th and Quincy; the Ogden Mormon Tabernacle at 22nd Street and Washington; the 2nd Ward Mormon Chapel; the Moench Building on the old Weber College campus at 25th Street and Jefferson Avenue; the Carnegie Library at 26th Street and Washington; several of the old schools of the city, including Grant, Lincoln, and Pingree; the Orpheum Theater near 25th and Washington; the White City Ballroom on 25th east of Washington Boulevard; the Peery Mansion at 24th Street and Adams; the Moose Hall which had served as a Methodist church on 24th Street; the Broom Hotel at 25th and Washington Boulevard; the Healy Hotel at 25th Street and Wall Avenue; and the Dee Hospital at

24th Street and Harrison Boulevard. In 1993 the Golden Spike National Livestock Coliseum in West Ogden, which had been the home of annual livestock shows from 1926 until it closed in 1988, burned to the ground. In addition, a number of business and hotel buildings on 25th Street and Washington Boulevard that had been a representation of earlier Ogden in the pioneer, railroad, and war eras, were demolished.[16]

It seemed to some that buildings with historical and community significance were being destroyed with no consideration of their historical and community value. It appeared as if the wrecking ball was going to destroy any building that did not have the appearance of being new and in the mode of new economic development. Beginning in 1981 some local leaders started to push to save some of the earlier representative buildings for reasons of historical or architectural significance. As a result of this, the Ogden Landmarks Commission was organized to try to preserve some of the remaining structures as significant parts of local history. The commission was organized on 21 February 1980 with a membership that included David Roth, chair, and members Ann Peck, Pete Poggemeyer, James Harmston, Margaret Hunter, Justin Eccles, Lani Prout, Bill Terry, Sterling Sessions, Susan Curtis, and Virginia Andrews.[17] The commission had been organized too late to save some of the truly significant and fine examples of early Ogden; nevertheless, the Ogden Landmarks Commission has been active through the years to preserve major representative structures and encourage their use as viable places of business or habitation.

The Weber County Industrial Development Bureau also had an interest in stimulating the revival of the downtown business district. As a result, under the leadership of Nate Mazer, Tom Peterson, and Cal Jeanselme as successive directors of the industrial bureau, continued efforts were made to promote business not only in Ogden but throughout the county. Among the new companies brought in were the Admiralty Beverage Corporation; the Great Salt Lake Mineral and Chemical Corporation; Western Zirconium; Williams International; Golden State Castings; Levelor Lorentzen Blinds; Kremco; and, more recently, the H. C. Brill Company, America On Line, and the Payless Drug Distribution Center, which merged in 1996 with the larger national Rite Aid Corporation. Other companies that were already in Weber County included Iomega; Smith and Edwards; Petersen Engineering Fabrication and Machining; the Kier Corporation; the R and O Construction Company; and the Big D Construction Company. All found Weber County a comfortable and profitable place to do business.[18] The new or expanded businesses represent an added value of investment and an increased tax resource for Weber County.

In addition to an emphasis on the development of industrial growth in the county, there was also concern about the retail and consumer aspects of business in the county. This led to plans for constructing the downtown Ogden City Mall in the area of Washington Boulevard between 22nd and 24th streets. The Ogden Industrial Development Corporation (OIDC) pledged $44,000 for appraisals on the property that would be taken over by the mall. This began the difficult job to convince property owners in that area to sell their property and have it demolished for the mall. The OIDC also promised an additional $150,000 as front money for title searches and to obtain options on the properties. Alan Nye and Thomas Dee were appointed to raise the needed money, which amounted to $17 million, and later, with some added improvements, the value increased to $23 million. Others who played major roles in this project were Richard Hemingway, Dean Morrin, Fred Froerer, Jr., Richard Mercer, A. J. Staples, and Stephen Dirks, who was then mayor of Ogden. Bonding for the project was arranged with the Goldman Sachs firm of San Francisco and Ernest Hahn, a California developer, was hired to construct the mall. The mall began operating in 1980, and in 1996 it has three major retailing stores as its main anchors—Nordstrom, ZCMI, and J.C. Penney stores. The mall has had some difficulties bringing and keeping permanent businesses in the complex. There were initially some public complaints about the mall structure, especially the back portion of the parking plaza and the sculptured piece in front of the building, and some reinforcement of the parking plaza was done. There is a current problem of the financial repayment of the debt on the mall that has put the owners into a receivership situation. It has been suggested that this is only a short-term problem and that it will be successfully resolved.[19]

Additional emphasis on improving the Ogden downtown area became a matter for other groups. As a result, the chamber of commerce and others became more active in dealing with some of these questions by creating several councils and committees to work on the downtown problems. The Weber Economic Development Corporation and the Ogden Industrial Development Corporation were reorganized and revitalized. A convention and visitors bureau was created to oversee the Union Station and bring more visitors and tourists to the county. As a part of a state program to promote tourism, "The Golden Spike Empire" was created which linked the efforts of Weber, Davis, Morgan, and Box Elder counties together with the railroad theme to promote regional tourism.

Tourism centered on the development of a railroad and firearms museum in Union Station, the winter sports development of Snow Basin, Powder Mountain, and Nordic Valley ski resorts, and the fishing, boating, and water recreation resources of Pine View Reservoir, nearby Willard Bay, and other reservoirs and tributaries of the Weber and Ogden rivers. This development of recreational areas has become part of the environmental and development debate. A major question revolves around how much development of Snow Basin Ski Resort area will be allowed in association with the Utah Winter Olympic Games of 2002. Some estimates indicate that with the building of hotels, condominiums, a golf course, ski lifts, lodges, and more than 1,000 private residences there will be a city of 8,000 people in the Snow Basin area. That would do much to change the nature of the mountain resort and add additional pressures to the water supply and the general environment as well as significantly increase traffic up the canyons. This continued debate will likely leave a lot of disappointed citizens in Weber County regardless of how it is resolved.[20] In September 1996 the United State Congress passed a national parks and public land bill that included approval of the exchange of 1,320 acres of United State Forest Service land to be added to the adjacent land of the already established Snowbasin Ski Resort. In return, Earl Holding, owner of the resort, turned over 4,100 acres of less useable land he owned—some located in the resort area and some of it in the Taylor Canyon area.[21]

Another organization, Mission 2000, was established to focus on some of the long-range goals of the community; and, in 1995, special committees were organized to save Hill Air Force Base and the Defense Depot Ogden from closure. They succeeded in helping save Hill Air Force Base but had to concede on the closing of the Defense Depot. This meant that Hill Air Force Base would keep its workforce of approximately 13,000 and perhaps add another 187 workers as the base picked up additional work from bases that were being closed down in other parts of the country. Defense Depot Ogden, however, would close and would lose a civilian workforce of approximately 1,100 workers. Overall, the commitment to keep government workers in the Weber County area seemed to be firm.[22] Other groups took direct action to help businesses in the downtown area; they included Downtown Ogden, Incorporated, and the 25th Street Development organizations, made up of property owners and businessmen in downtown Ogden and on 25th Street.

Ogden City and Weber County governments did much to support the downtown businesses. A study was financed in 1987 to bring a group known as the Regional/Urban Design Assistance Team of the American Institute of Architects (R/UDAT) to try to determine the overall direction that the city should take in developing the downtown area of Ogden. The group gave several important suggestions and commented that the area has a lot to be proud of and much to offer the community and its visitors. It was suggested that this good image of the region should be better portrayed. Suggestions were made on improving entrances into the city and on the need to have better planning for traffic, parking, pedestrian ways, and greenspaces to make the area more appealing. The report has given the city and county a plan to follow.[23]

The Ogden city council and mayor supported the building of a new city public safety building for the police and fire departments as well as plans to save and remodel the historic City and County Municipal Building. A bond of $23 million was approved by city voters to complete these projects. City, county, and private monies have gone into the restoration of Peery's Egyptian Theater and the building of the David Eccles Conference Center and the Downtown Center for the Performing Arts at 24th Street and Washington Boulevard at a cost of $22.7 million. Funds of $4.6 million have been approved for the building of a baseball/community stadium on the location of the old Ogden Iron Works property on 23rd and Grant Avenue.

The Weber County Commission supported many of these same projects and also decided to keep its county office complex in the downtown area by approving a renovation of a ZCMI store at the corner of 24th and Washington Boulevard into the Weber County Center at a cost of $14.5 million.[24] The political leaders put themselves out on a political limb many times by supporting some of these projects. Some community activists opposed many of these proposals and debated in the committee and council meetings; some even went to the courts to try to bring a stop to the projects. For the most part, these attempts failed, but they led to extended debate and to some increased costs to projects. There were also some political costs to some members of the county and city government who lost their reelection bids, perhaps in part because of stands they took on these projects.[25]

The Committee of 100 supported the renewal of downtown Ogden by making a $10,000 advance for a feasibility study for a proposal of the Ogden Redevelopment Agency under the direction of Scott Parkinson to see if a 300-room hotel would be successful in Ogden. The building of the Hilton Hotel, later renamed the Ogden Park Hotel, on 24th and Grant Avenue came from this endeavor. In addition, there was confidence that additional hotel rooms also could be profitable. The Ogden Industrial Development Corporation advanced $143,000 for the refurbishing of the Ben Lomond Hotel, which had been a city landmark since 1927, standing on a corner which hotels had occupied since the beginning of the city. The hotel was refinished and eventually became the Raddison Hotel, which still serves visitors in downtown Ogden. An increase in business, travel, and tourism stimulated motel development in Weber County in the 1990s, with the building of large motel complexes near the Interstate 15 exits into Ogden. In this time period Motel 6, Big Z Motel, Flying J, the High Country Inn, the Sleep Inn, and Comfort Suites provided lodging near the freeways and at other entrances into Ogden and the county industrial park areas.[26]

In 1986 the State of Utah built a new seven-story state office building in downtown Ogden on Washington Boulevard, and in 1996 the $12 million state court building is being completed on Grant Avenue west of Municipal Square. Thiokol Corporation in 1986 leased a new headquarters building on Washington Boulevard, one of the first to introduce glass-front architecture to Ogden. The thrill of having such a prestigious business headquarters in Ogden was eventually lost when the Thiokol Corporation announced that they would move their corporate headquarters to Salt Lake City in 1997. This was bitter news for the Ogden community, many of whom felt that their culture and lifestyle had been insulted by this announcement.[27]

Perhaps Ogden needed to take this decision in stride and accept the idea that it would never quite be a major city in Utah, an idea former mayor Robert Madsen suggested when he gave some parting remarks as he left Ogden. Madsen said that "Ogden needs to downsize and accept the fact that [it] is a city with little growth potential. But it can be the very best of what it is, a medium sized city."[28] There is perhaps some truth in the saying that became prominent during this time, "From Ogden to Salt Lake it's 30 miles, but from Salt Lake to Ogden it's 300." This kind of thinking is abhorrent to many Ogden and Weber County residents because in their minds there is no better place in the world to live than in Weber County. For that reason, county residents continue to build and upgrade the county and their communities.

While Ogden worked to save its downtown, county communities began to develop local strip malls or shopping centers built around major food stores or variety stores. The small family stores and shops that had served the community over a long period of the county history were almost entirely eliminated. The mall and major companies in the strip malls were usually dominated by national or regional corporate businesses that had numerous stores in the region or around the nation. Among them are food stores such as Smith's Food and Drug Stores; Albertson's; Harmon's; Macey's; Fred Meyer; and Stop and Shop—a local-oriented business. Variety stores have also created their own strip malls. Early businesses in the county such as Gibson's and Grand Central variety stores gave way to Ernst, Shopko, K-Mart, WalMart, Home Depot, Super Target, and other large corporate stores. There has been some concern about what this has done or is doing to the county and the country in general, and some of that concern has been about the amount of leverage a big store places on a community to get special favors and tax exemptions as well as what a large store does to other businesses in an area. Some of this frustration has been expressed in what has been called "The WalMart Syndrome." Several Weber County communities have been faced with pressures from large stores to give them favors.

In 1996 there was still further talk of business expansion in other areas of the county, mainly some consideration of industrial development in the old disused railyards and at the Ogden Depot, and the development of the old American Can plant on Lincoln Avenue into a retail center. There were also plans made to develop a retail complex on land on Washington Boulevard in North Ogden.

One significant development is that besides the tendency of each community to develop some of their own businesses in their own communities, a major shift of retail business has gone to South Ogden and Riverdale. South Ogden supported the building of the New Gate Mall in 1981, now owned by the General Growth Corporation of Minneapolis, Minnesota. Over the years many businesses have come and gone, but Mervyns, Sears, and Dillards are the prime large businesses in that mall. South Ogden has had a large number of businesses established along 36th Street, in the New Gate Mall area, and along Harrison Boulevard.[29] Riverdale, incorporated on 4 March 1946, until recently a small community with a small business section along Riverdale Road, has mushroomed into a thriving economic development. Robert Merrill, who in 1972 owned one of the first businesses (Merrill's Paint and Glass Company) in what was known as the Bar C Plaza in the Riverdale Road area, remembers that there were only a few businesses there at that time. Since that time, Riverdale has become a booming place of commercial growth. It is estimated that the population has grown from 3,704 in 1972 to approximately 7,000 people in 1996 and that there are an estimated 350 business and home occupations located in Riverdale.[30]

## *County Growth and County Government*

The economic status of Weber County and its various communities has been recognized as a major reason why people have come to the county to live. The railroad brought many people to the county and diversified the population; during World War II, war industries also drew large numbers of people from different parts of the country. With the recent prosperity in the state of Utah and Weber County there has been a large increase in population, and a large part of the growth has come from people moving into the area.

Population figures for the last few decades for Weber County show the amount of growth in the county and figures for the communities within the county show where the growth has spread within the county. The county has grown from 110,744 in 1960 to an estimated 175,000 in 1995.[31]

Population figures demonstrate the steady growth in Weber County, and show some remarkable growth between 1980 and 1996 in some of the county areas as well as a decline in population in Ogden until after the 1990 period. The communities that had the highest percentage of increase in the 1980s were Harrisville that had a 119.11 percent increase; Uintah, a 73.12 percent increase; and Farr West, a 50.10 percent increase.

This sharp increase in population brought a fluctuating housing boom to the county which was especially strong in the years from 1960 to 1979 and then took a downturn in the years from 1979 to 1984, with many contractors going into bankruptcy or receivership because of overbuilding or in some cases mismanagement of their operations. There were large subdivisions built in the northern and southern parts of Ogden. Among the large tracts built during the 1959–60 period were the low-cost housing developments in Ron Claire Subdivision in the north part of the city with contractor Weston Scow doing a good share of the building. In the south part of Ogden the College Heights, Forest Green Estates, and Shadow Valley subdivisions were developed. Early developers in this area were Allen Jackson, Ben Clay, and John Goddard. In the Combe Road area Ron Wright and Dan Hunter were the leading developers. In the 1980s and 1990s in the Shadow Valley and Uintah region there was a host of builders and developers including Lowell Dean, C.L. Martineau, Darrell and Greg Buxton, Kip Cashmore, Kelly Goddard and Skip Nelson, Bob Anderson and Orluff Opheikens, Kent Fisher and Lyle Stott, and Camille Cain. In South Ogden City area were Ezra Nilson,

Bruce Nilson, Ted Holtry, Orluff Opheikens, and Howard Kent. On east 29th Street Ora Hall developed some large condominium and apartment complexes, and Corey Malan developed housing on some of the old Malan family properties. In North Ogden, Bruce Jones and Jed McCormick built many homes. In the western part of the county the building trend in Roy inched its way along the main artery roads such as 5500 South, 4000 South, 3300 South, 2550 South into Hooper, West Haven and Taylor, and farther north along Pioneer Road, Harrisville Road, 1900 North, and North Plain City Road into Slaterville, Farr West, Plain City, and Warren.

Growth in the upper Ogden River Valley came slower and was somewhat different than in the rest of the county. The tendency in Huntsville, Eden, and Liberty was to build homes as single units rather than as subdivision tract homes. A major exception to that was the Patio Springs–Wolf Creek Condominium complex on the east side of the valley.[32]

Growth of population and building of houses and industrial structures on the land became a growing problem in the years from 1955 through 1996. In fact, by the 1990s growth had become the major problem for county and community governments. Weber County had formed a planning commission in January 1947 and Ogden City had organized a planning commission in 1945. The planning effort was revitalized on 8 February 1951 when zoning ordinance enforcement was added to the planning responsibilities in the city.[33]

Through the years, several plans and master plans were developed which dealt with the problems of growth; and after the 1960s these plans became more detailed and concerned about impending growth. A major study was made by the county in 1969 and updated in 1979 which dealt with development on the western agricultural land in Weber County. A conclusion made in the 1979 study was that

> the question to be addressed is not will western Weber County grow, but how should it grow? The central issue therefore before citizens and decision makers alike is how to accommodate the anticipated growth and yet maintain a desirable environment.[34]

Eventually each incorporated town and city established planning committees to deal with the problems of growth, and each had to face the problems of controlling a growing community without sacrificing some of the important elements that characterized the essence of the community or violating a sense of fairness for all of the citizens.

As growth questions became more pressing in April 1996, the Weber County Commission organized a Public Lands Advisory Board which consisted of nine members from different parts of the county, each to serve a four-year term to "advise commissioners on a variety of public lands issues including watershed, grazing and livestock, agriculture, water quality and recreation." The immediate questions that this council dealt with were a proposal of a general plan for the development of Ogden Valley, the issue of allocating mineral extraction royalties from the Great Salt Lake Minerals Corporation, and the creation of Planned Residential Unit Developments (PRUDs). A PRUD is a plan for clustering homes in order to preserve dwindling open spaces yet still allow space for planned housing, community parks, playgrounds, recreation centers, and producing farm lands. In planning for the future there is a perceived need to deal with the problems of growth while still being able to maintain some of the traditional community and agricultural ways.[35]

In the 1990s there has been much interest in annexing unincorporated areas of the county to existing cities to increase the taxable lands. There has also been a concentrated move in some of the unincorporated communities to become incorporated. In 1991 West Haven was incorporated as a city, absorbing the old communities of Kanesville and Wilson. In 1996 the state legislature passed a law which allowed unincorporated areas to form townships, allowing them to keep county services and have their own planning and zoning boards but avoid annexation. This encouraged several communities to make application for township status. Included in this group of communities were Marriott, East Huntsville, Warren, West Warren, Hooper, and Slaterville. All of these townships were approved in the 5 November 1996 election. Each township elected a township board for the first time in that election and West Warren changed its name to Reese.

The large increases in population brought related problems to the county, including planning, water supply, waste disposal, environmental concerns, and questions of overcrowding and encroachment on farm lands. Concern also was raised that the new growth was changing the nature of the society and culture in the county. Dealing with these problems brought new pressures on county and municipal governments. Politics played a major part in how these problems were approached, and during the last four decades there was a variety of approaches made by county commissioners, city councils, mayors, and other governmental leaders.

During the 1960s Arthur P. Brown, Elmer Carver, George T. Frost, Bud Favero, Maurice Richards, Albert Bott, and William Moyes served as county commissioners and formulated county policies. During that decade a main issue was the elimination of a one-half million dollar deficit; a second issue was the need to reorganize and create a more efficient county government because it had become unsatisfactory to many. Maurice Richards, who had previously served for fifteen years as Weber County Prosecuting Attorney and had been a major figure in cleaning up Ogden's 25th Street, brought that same reforming spirit to the commission from 1965 to 1968. Richards and Bud Favero carried on a reforming crusade as county commissioners. Surplus and costly equipment and property acquired by the county was sold, and further purchases were better controlled. Some county equipment was painted brown so that it could be identified and not be used for illegal or private use. Salaries of employees were improved, which also reduced the temptation of corruption. Some departments were trimmed and costs cut; the county deficit was eliminated.

Efforts were made to make Weber County a major tourist and travel hub by proposing a major highway out of Weber County along 12th Street and across the Great Salt Lake to California. This concept was also tied to the development of tourist attractions to be established at Fremont Island, Malan's Basin, and La Plata. This grand scheme never went very far, but it did stimulate some ideas that later made tourism one of the major contributors to the Weber County economy. Other county developments at this time included the approval of a garbage incineration plant that operated for approximately fifteen years before it was discontinued and a land-fill garbage project was developed. Discussions about the use of the coliseum for livestock shows, rodeos, and as a display area for large events such as car sales led to the acquisition of a larger county fairgounds facility.

During the 1970s the major leadership on the commission came from Keith G. Jensen, Boyd K. Storey, Monte Bailey, Doug Hunt, and Ron Sessions. Keith Jensen felt that the main concerns of the commissioners during that period included the county hospital in Roy; the purchase of the Hotel Ben Lomond as a county office complex; the integration of the paramedic and ambulance service into the county fire department; the need to obtain land in the Defense Depot area from the federal government for the county fairgrounds and nature center; the consolidation of the human services functions; and the question of how to dispose of the garbage of the county.[36]

The hospital in Roy cost the county over $1 million a year to operate, and leaders believed the county could not afford to be in the hospital business. In the late 1970s the hospital was sold to a private company. The same fate befell the Ben Lomond Hotel; but for a time the county benefited and saved the hotel from possible demolition by purchasing it for $80,000 and using it for county offices. It later sold to a private owner who developed it into the Raddison Hotel, with the county renting some of the space for offices. The county took over the ambulance business when a private ambulance service went broke; but when federal monies became available, the various cities of the county took over paramedic and ambulance services. The lands obtained for the fairgrounds and nature center became the beginning of the development of those facilities, and development of each area has continued to the present. During the 1970s disposal of garbage became a question of whether to continue to incinerate the garbage or dispose of it in a landfill. The commissioners made the choice of the landfill and this method has continued for a twenty-year period. The question of garbage disposal has come to a head again in the 1990s, and it has been decided by the commissioners and local governments that the disposal of county garbage will be done through county transfer stations, which will accept garbage in Weber County to be shipped to Carbon County for disposal.

In the 1980s commissioners Robert Hunter, Roger Rawson, William Bailey, and Lowell Peterson dealt with county problems which included major spring floods of the Weber River that did an estimated $750,000 damage to public lands and $1,000,000 damage to private properties. Volunteer work by many individuals and groups helped save the county from more extensive damage. The floods led to some projects developed by the state and national agencies to prevent further widespread flooding. From these flood difficulties came a federal Army Corps of Engineers project to clear the Weber River of debris and overgrowth by dredging and clearing trouble spots that build up and overflow during the heavy runoff season. A State of Utah project to build pumps to keep the level of the Great Salt Lake near an official level of 4,202 feet also came about at this time. In 1984, under the sponsorship of Roger Rawson, the plans for a new Human Services Building was approved, and this building was constructed at 26th Street and Lincoln Avenue. In the Ogden Valley Dan Cook took action to develop Nordic Valley Golf Course into a year-round resort.

Robert Hunter served on the Weber County Commission from 1981 to 1989 and spent part of that time as chair. Hunter had served in Ogden city government for several years as a public relations officer, and he was encouraged to run for the county commission by representatives of both the major political parties. Due to some scandals, some people felt that county government was deteriorating and that Hunter could give better direction to the government. During this period the county cleared the debt on the Roy Hospital and reduced the county deficit. Hunter felt that much of the trust between the city and county was restored. Voter referendums to build a new jail and save the Ben Lomond Hotel failed; still, the county commission felt that it was in the best interests of the county to move ahead with these projects. Through the provisions of the building authority law, the county was able to bond for these projects without a public vote. The Hotel Ben Lomond was saved from destruction and was sold to a private buyer. It has remained an important historical structure and continues to serve as an important hotel and meeting place. The commissioners used the same bonding structure to construct a new jail adjacent to the City and County Building.[37]

The building of the Weber County Fairgrounds on lands acquired earlier from the Defense Depot Ogden in the Harrisville area is one of the most important things accomplished during the

1980s. With Hunter as chair, the vision of William A. Bailey, and the support of Roger Rawson, the county fairgrounds was built, with the Golden Spike Arena as a major display area. The first fair there was held in 1988. This has been one of the most used and successful facilities in Weber County. On the partisan side of county politics there were questions brought up that included some opposition to the appointment of the Roy mayor Leon Poulsen to the Central Weber Sewer Improvement District and the appointment of Ken Miller as Ogden Airport Manager; an audit of Weber County investments to account for $900,000 of invested county monies; and the questionable use of tax money to send twenty-four county employees to a Las Vegas convention.[38]

In the 1990s county politics became much more lively, with the local newspaper using investigative reporters to enliven the news page. In this period Lowell Peterson served in the county commission and pressed for a number of county improvements, including the downtown conference center. Peterson resigned in 1992 to return to private business. Joan Hellstrom, the first woman to ever serve on the county commission, was elected for a term in 1990 yet lost a reelection bid in the county Republican primary in 1994 to her Republican opponent, Glenn Donnelson. Democrat Randall Williford had a similar career on the commission by being elected in 1990, serving one term, and losing in his try at reelection. Williford was defeated by conservative Republican Bruce Anderson. Joe Ritchie, former Ogden City police chief and a Democrat, defeated Glenn Donnelson in the November election for county commission by a vote of 18,963 to 17,906. These commission races centered around the financing of projects in the county, including bonding for the new county office center, county participation in the downtown conference center, the new county court building, and other financing. Financing was to be either by lease revenue bonds authorized by the municipal building authority, which did not require a public vote on the bonding, or by calling for a public vote to approve the bonds and, in reality, the projects. Election outcomes seemed to be based on how the different candidates related to this issue.[39] In June 1996 Spencer Stokes resigned as Weber County commissioner to take a position with the state Republican party, and several weeks later Glen Burton, who would have been a Republican opponent in the primary election, was appointed to fill the vacancy. Burton was elected to a four-year term in the 5 November 1996 election.

### *Ogden City Government*

Ogden did much to shape politics in Weber County. In 1948 a group known as the Ogden Metropolitan Development Conference met to organize a move to adopt the city manager-council form of government. Through the work of a charter commission, a new charter of government for Ogden City was accepted by the voters on 29 June 1951. The first election under this new council-manager form of government in 1951 brought six men and one woman to the city council; they included G. Stanley Brewer, George T. Frost, and Mary Woolley, members at large; Raymond S. Wright, representing the First Voting District; Thorstein Larsen, representing the Second District; C. Austin Seager, representing the Third District; and James R. Foulger, representing the Fourth District. W. Rulon White served for a period of thirteen months as the first city manager at the insistence of the council; later, E. J. Allison of Kansas became the first permanent city manager.[40]

In January 1992 Ogden City government was transformed into a mayor-council form of government. This form assumes that the city council is the legislative branch and has the policy-making powers while the mayor heads the executive branch and, along with the administrative departments and staff, executes and administers the policies and laws of the city. The Ogden City Council consists of seven members; one member is elected from each of the four municipal wards and three are elected from the city at large. All terms are for four years. The members of the first council elected to serve under this new form of government were Barbara Dirks, Glen V. Holley, Bonnie McDonald, Michael Miller, Ralph W. Mitchell, Darrell J. Saunders, and Adele Smith. Glenn Mecham was elected as the mayor.

Ogden City has had many problems to solve in the past four decades. Many of the problems have been related to population growth and the economy. They have included such matters as strengthening and maintaining the infrastructure of the city; fostering the well-being of adults, young people, and families; keeping the city economically strong; and managing population and business moves into surrounding areas, including losses of city revenue and businesses in the downtown area.

Merle E. Allen, a Slaterville native and a professor and administrator at Weber College, served as mayor of Ogden from November 1961 to November 1965. Some of the main accomplishments during his time in office were the extension of Harrison and Monroe boulevards into North Ogden, giving better traffic flow into the city; the building of the Golden Hours Center for the support of elderly citizens of the city; and the planning for the Marshall White Center, named for a police detective who was killed during Allen's term. During his term a tax program was put into practice to have the outlying communities and the county government share in the costs of the various public services which were mostly being paid by Ogden City. Several public services including the library and the garbage dump were taken over by the county. Other programs of note were the establishment of an Ogden City Youth Corps that did much improvement work along the Ogden River and in the parks; the covering of culinary water reservoirs to protect the purity of the water; and the annexation of unincorporated areas in the southeast section of the city.[41]

Bart Wolthuis was one member of the city government for whom the welfare of the youth in the city was especially important. Wolthuis served through the 1960s, first as a member of the city council from 1961 to 1965, and then as mayor of Ogden from 1965 to 1971. As councilman and mayor, Wolthuis did much to support youth, and he counted as a major achievement the building of the Marshall White Center to help the youth in the central city to have a place for recreation and supervised activities. This center served the needs of many of the black, hispanic, and caucasian youth who had no other resources for organized athletic play. Wolthuis also felt that the construction of swimming pools at Ogden High School and Ben Lomond High School provided an outlet for high school students during the day and the entire community after school hours. The two swimming pools and a fire-fighting training tower were approved by a bond election. Wolthuis also promoted the idea of a downtown mall, which began to be discussed during his tenure of office.

Crime increased with population, and the policing of the city was an important function of city government. One of the problems was financing the police and fire departments. During the Wolthuis administration the Ogden Riverway Park was proposed; this included the development of the Ogden River from the canyon to the confluence with the Weber River. This proposed development would provide a series of parks along the Ogden River, with hiking and bike paths along the entire route for use of the public. When this proposal was put up in a bond election, however, the issue failed and Mayor Wolthuis, who had pushed for its approval, was not reelected. At a later date this idea was carried out by a private operation with city support under the leadership of Robert Marquardt. [42]

In the election of 1972 Mayor Wolthuis did not take his somewhat unknown and young Democratic opponent very seriously, yet A. Stephen Dirks won that election. Once in office, Dirks found that there were several pressing issues to be dealt with. There was the question of the declining downtown area and whether to build a mall. Also, should 25th Street be developed and should better hotel facilities be established? A general bond election concerning the building of a downtown mall had failed to meet the approval of the public. Most officials in city government felt that something had to be done to save Ogden from further deterioration. It was decided to use a new state law, known as "tax increment financing," which used the increase of earnings on a property after improvements were made to pay the cost of the project. Ogden city officials thus were able to fund the building of the Ogden City Mall. Understandably, Mayor Dirks felt that this was one of the most important projects completed during his administration. The completed mall did not have as great an economic effect as it was hoped it would have, however, in part because of competing malls and also because a recession began at about the same time the mall was completed. Still, a question asked by Dirks seems to summarize the issue, "What would Ogden City downtown be like if we had not constructed the mall?"

There were other major improvements during this period including the development of the Union Station as a community center, the beginning of 25th Street development, further development of the Ogden Industrial Park, the building of the Hilton Hotel in the downtown section of the city, and some increases in the salaries of city employees.

During the 1970s the county and many of its cities and towns took advantage of a new state law concerning the distribution of sales taxes. Under the new law, the sales tax revenues allotted to the county were divided in such a way that outlying areas of the county received a larger amount of the sales tax than had earlier been the case. This division of tax money was much to the detriment of Ogden, which in many ways supported some of these areas with public services. The new law allowed half of the county sales taxes to be given to communities on a population basis and half on a "point of purchase" basis. Communities like Riverdale took advantage of the point-of-purchase provision by drawing businesses into their jurisdiction and then collecting the increased sales taxes. Automobile dealerships and other businesses flocked to Riverdale and brought the community much new revenue.[43]

Robert Madsen, L. Clifford Goff, and Scott Sneddon served as mayors of Ogden from 1983 to 1991. During that time the main matters dealt with were some of those continuing out of the 1970s having to do with ongoing building up of the mall, the Union Station, and the Ogden Industrial Park. Robert H. DeBoer, who served on the city council for fourteen years—from 1971 to 1977 and from 1983 to 1991—observed that the 1980s were mainly occupied by the questions of growth. The Ogden Housing Authority and the Ogden Redevelopment Agency were both kept under the control of the city council. The redevelopment agency had the responsibility to help the city deal with the problems of deteriorating and/or blighted areas. Several programs were undertaken in the downtown business area and the residential neighborhoods to rebuild deteriorated areas. The housing authority, through federal and local grants, did much to improve affordable housing for many of the people in the city. The Kier Corporation became heavily involved in such projects as the rehabilitation of the Madison School and the Marion Hotel as well as the 22nd Street and Harrison Boulevard projects to revitalize low-cost housing. The 22nd Street project constructed twenty-four low-cost houses on the site of the old Lorin Farr School. Such programs as the Rainbow Plan, which provided basic materials and paint, helped citizens of selected areas of the city fix up and paint their homes and properties. Weber State University through its Continuing Education Division introduced a program to educate residents of the city on how to improve both their lifestyles and their properties.[44]

Glenn J. Mecham, first mayor to be elected under the new mayor-council system of city government, outlined the main points of success from 1991 to 1995:

> With partnerships between the public and private sectors, the 30 year dream of developing the Ogden River Parkway, including the world famous Dinosaur Park, Big D Sports Park and Management Training Center Learning Park with its beautiful gardens, became a reality. We realized the long-awaited return of professional baseball: the Ogden Raptors. The Marshall White Center and many of our parks have been refurbished. The new Downtown Conference and Performing Arts Center is under construction. Recreational and cultural opportunities are at an all time high.[45]

As Mecham ran for reelection in 1995, he suggested that a downtown multipurpose stadium for the Ogden Raptors baseball club and a new arena for Pioneer Days Rodeo events should be constructed. He saw the challenges of the future to the city government to be the conversion and reuse of Defense Depot Ogden facilities to civilian use; the revitalization of downtown Ogden; the creation of a community-oriented policing policy; the beautification of Ogden, with special attention to the entryways into the city; and development of Ogden neighborhoods through such programs as the Enterprise Community designation.

Weber County people have played an important role in state and national politics. In the 1940s Herbert B. Maw, who was born and raised in Weber County, served as a two-term governor of Utah. Olene Smith Walker, raised on a Weber County farm, served four terms in the Utah House of Representatives in the 1980s and in 1992 became the first woman to be elected as lieutenant governor of the State of Utah. Several members of the Utah Legislature from Weber County have been elected to major positions in the legislature including Ronald Rencher and Nolan Karras, each of whom served as Speaker of the Utah House of Representatives. Marty Stephens served as chair of the Utah House Appropriations Committee. A number of Weber County politicians have been recognized for their contributions to the legislature; they include Ron Halverson, Grant Protzman, E. LaMar Buckner, John Arrington, Haynes Fuller, Winn Richards, Merrill Jenkins, Dale Stratford, Joe Hull, and Robert Montgomery. Mike Monson served as Weber County Assessor for three terms, and he was later involved in the property tax division of the Utah State Tax Commission.[46]

Henry Aldous Dixon, president of Weber College, was appointed to serve the remainder of Douglas Stringfellow's term in the U.S. House of Representatives after Stringfellow resigned. Dixon subsequently was elected to the House as a Republican for three terms during the years 1954 to 1960. N. Blaine Peterson, a Democrat from Weber County, succeeded Dixon for a term in the U.S. House, and Laurence J. Burton was elected as a Republican congressman for four terms from 1962 to 1970. K. Gunn McKay, a Democrat and a resident of Huntsville, was elected as a U.S. Representative for five terms from 1970 to 1980 before being defeated for reelection by James Hansen of Davis County. No other Weber County residents have been able to win House elections during Hansen's long tenure.

William H. Orton, a Democrat born and raised in Weber County, served as a member of the House of Representatives for the Third Congressional District of Utah (which does not include Weber County) from 1990 to 1996. Another Weber County native who served in national politics was Richard Stallings, born and educated in Weber County. A Democrat, he served several terms as an Idaho member of the U.S. House of Representatives in the 1980s. The county has had no person elected as United States Senator since Frank J. Cannon served in that position as the first senator of the new state in 1896.

Myrene Rich Brewer was prominent in local and national Republican politics. She was Republican national committeewoman for Utah from 1972 to 1976. She also served as a member of the electoral college in 1972 and was a delegate to the Republican national conventions in 1968 and 1972. Richard Richards, an Ogden attorney and a Republican, was appointed as the chair of the Republican National Committee from 1981 until 1983. Richards influenced

President Ronald Reagan to make a visit to Utah on 9 and 10 September 1982. During that visit President Reagan visited the Ogden LDS church volunteer welfare center and motorcaded through Ogden and Weber County, where crowds cheered him along the way. President Reagan and his party spent part of the afternoon in Hooper at a Republican rally, where townspeople and many other people of the county and state came to see the president of the United States at a town park.[47]

Brent Scowcroft was another Weber County native who gained national prominence. Scowcroft was born and raised in Ogden and in the 1950s began a military career when he was appointed as a cadet to the West Point Military Academy. Later in his career, he transferred to the air force and rose to the rank of lieutenant general. During the Nixon, Ford, Reagan, and Bush administrations he served as member of the National Security Council and as a military advisor to those presidents. David M. Kennedy, resident of Riverdale and graduate of Weber College, became the United States Secretary of the Treasury during the Nixon administration and also served as Ambassador at Large for the United States and as U.S. Ambassador to the North Atlantic Treaty Organization (NATO) during the Nixon years. Mark Evans Austad, raised in Ogden and student body president at Weber College in 1940–41, became a Columbia Broadcasting System commentator, United States delegate to the United Nations in 1973, U.S. Ambassador to Finland from 1973 to 1977, and U.S. Ambassador to Norway from 1981 to 1984. Another political figure of note is Alex Hurtado, who was raised in Ogden and was appointed to the Ogden City Council in 1971. He was elected to the council two additional terms before being appointed in 1981 as a member of the Republican National Committee. Hurtado has been active with the Republican National Committee from 1981 to the present (1996).

It has become apparent in recent politics in Weber County that women have become more involved in politics as time has passed. There were a few women who were elected to public office in earlier times, such as Sarah Anderson, who was in the state legislature from 1897 to 1899; Mary C. Coulter, who was elected for the term 1903 to 1905; and Jane Wilkin Manning, who was in the Utah House of Representatives from 1913 to 1915. In the 1950s Mary Woolley became the first woman elected to serve on the Ogden City Council, where she served three terms from 1951 to 1955. Elizabeth Vance of Slaterville became an important figure in the Democratic party by serving in the Utah Legislature for a total of seven two-year terms beginning in 1950. She also served two four- year terms (which ended in 1984) as Utah Democratic national committeewoman and attended eight national party conventions. She served a total of fifty-two years in Weber County politics.

Myrene Brewer was prominent in Republican state and national committees. Rosanne Peery King, daughter of Harmon Peery, was elected to the Ogden City Council and served there from 1977 until 1983. Gaye D. Littleton served on the Ogden City Council from 1983 to 1987. Barbara Dirks and Bonnie McDonald served on the Ogden City Council from 1987 to 1995, and Adele Smith has served on the council from 1991 to 1996. Joan Dixon Hellstrom set a new precedent as the first woman to be elected to the Weber County Commission when she was elected in 1990.

Unfortunately, some scandal has touched local politicians. Politics deals in power and people and, as Lord Acton said, "Power tends to corrupt." Robert Bowen was convicted of a felony while he was a county commissioner. In 1979 and 1980 there were twelve counts of class-B misdemeanors handed down as indictments accusing county commissioner Doug Hunt of alleged unauthorized acts in public office; however, the indictments were dismissed. On 1 February 1991 Weber County's District 10 Representative to the Utah House of Representatives, Dionne Halverson, was forced to resign from the legislature because of a plea of no contest to a charge of shoplifting. Patricia B. Larson was appointed to the legislature to fill the vacant position.[48] In 1992 Weber County Assessor Steven Bezell was convicted of "misuse of public funds and theft by deception." He admitted to writing 150 bad checks amounting more than $30,000 as personnel checks drawn on county accounts. He served three months in jail and forty-five days in home confinement and made restitution of the money taken.[49]

Some county towns and cities have had some difficulties. For example, South Ogden had some tumultuous times in its government in the last decade. In 1987 the city began collecting a $700 per lot impact fee on development in the Burch Creek area. During the period from 1987 to 1995 a sum of approximately $235,000 was collected from this fee. When a master plan for South Ogden was considered, questions arose about the ordinance that had established the fee. After a search for the ordinance by city workers, newspaper reporters, and others, the document could not be found. A short time later, the supposed document showed up in the files. During an investigation by the Weber County Attorney's Office, it was determined that a false ordinance had been put into the city files. Eventually the South Ogden city engineer admitted that he had prepared a fraudulent ordinance and signed the names of then Mayor Lew Wangsgard and City Recorder Kathy Vandrimmelen. Vandrimmelen had been fired by the city council.[50] The aftermath of this case led to a turnover on the city council, including the election of Kathy Vandrimmelen, the conviction of the city engineer, and a program to partially return the fee money that was collected illegally. South Ogden City then adopted a city manager form of government, which many felt would solve some of the problems that had plagued the city.[51]

In the period from 1955 to 1996 the Weber County economic situation went through many changes, but leaders on the county and community levels took action to keep the economy viable and steady and moved in new directions to meet the challenges of the future.

## ENDNOTES

1. Daniel Defoe, *A Tour Through the Whole Island of Great Britain, 1724–6,* in *London, Great Britain,* ed. by Cathrine Cullen and Michael Rapoport (New York: Alfred A. Knopf, 1993), 106.

2. *Ogden Standard-Examiner,* 11 March 1984, 1E.

3. *Western Agricultural Master Plan, Weber County, Utah: An Update of the 1969 Weber County Master Plan* (Ogden: Weber County Planning Commission, 1979), 40.

4. Ibid., 41–46, 169–70.

5. *Utah Agricultural Statistics, 1984* (Salt Lake City: U.S. Department of Agriculture and Utah Crop and Livestock Reporting Service, 1984), 6, 11–14, 76–81; James Barnhill, interview with Richard Roberts, Ogden, Utah, 21 August 1996.

6. *Utah Agriculture Statistics—1995* (Salt Lake City: U.S. Department of Agriculture, National Agricultural Statistics Service and Utah State Department of Agriculture, 1995), 26, 90–110, 116–18; *Standard-Examiner*, 13 April 1986, 1E; 8 January1995, 1F; 2 May 1984, 1D.

7. According to James Barnhill, Weber County Extension Agent, the dairy owners were Billy Gee, Blaine and Dale Wade, Larry Wade (two dairies), Richard Knight, LaMoin Larkin, Dennis Brown, Dean Barrow (two dairies), Ron and Kevin Stratford, Curtis and Kelly Wangsgard, Sherman and Eugene Bailey, LaMar Skeen, Scott Wayment, Mike Giordano, Albert Dickamore, Lyman Barker, Vern Hancock, Harold Anderson, Allan and Dale Parker, Dale Fowers, Lewis Holmes, Vern Holmes, Ray Holmes, Vaughn Allen, Larry and Blair McFarland, Tom Shupe, Tom Favero, Bob and Gene Ropelato, Harry and Jim Papageorge, Dale Chugg, Delwynn Westergard, Kim Slater, Dave Degiorgio, Dick Gibson, Wayne Gibson, LaMar Gibson, Blair Hancock, Rex Hancock, and Phillip Green.

8. James Barnhill, Horses file, in office of Weber County Extension Agent.

9. James Barnhill, interview by Richard Roberts, Ogden, Utah, 3 July 1996; Matthew McFarland, interview by Richard Roberts, Ogden, Utah, 3 July 1996; Laura Favero, interview by Richard Roberts, Ogden, Utah, 3 July 1996, transcripts in possession of the authors; *Standard-Examiner*, 31 August 1996, 1A.

10. Clarence Belnap, interview by Mary Werner, Clearfield, Utah, 26 July 1973, 4; William Price, interview by Mary Werner, Ogden, Utah, 19 July 1973, 5; Tom Zito, interview by Mary Werner, Ogden, Utah, 6 July 1973, 9, transcripts in possession of the authors.

11. *Standard-Examiner*, 31 May 1971, 1B; 25 October 1971, 12A; 18 January 1972, 22; 7 June 1972.

12. Ibid., 22 October 1978, 1B.

13. Cora Lou Glenn, *Ogden Industrial Development Corporation: Projects, Partnerships, and Progress* (Ogden: Weber State University Continuing Education and Community Services, 1992), 2–3.

14. Ibid., 6–11.

15. Ibid., 12–15, 25–26, 29–30.

16. Numerous newspaper articles trace the destruction of various historical structures in Weber County. See the *Standard-Examiner* for information about the following structures: Broom Hotel 2 November 1964, 2B; Healy Hotel, 20 November 1967; Ogden Theater, 14 July 1968; Carnegie Library, 10 February 1969; Dee Hospital, 17 August 1969 and 26 February 1973; Third Ward LDS Church, 25 July 1970; Moench Building on Weber College Campus, 28 September 1970; Lincoln and Pingree schools, 10

November 1970; Ogden LDS Tabernacle, 1 September 1971; Becker's Brewery, 26 February 1984; *Standard-Examiner,* 12 July 1996, 1A.

17. Minutes, Ogden City Landmarks Commission, 19 February 1981; Ogden City Ordinance 7–80.

18. Articles in the *Standard-Examiner* include 4 October 1995, 1C; 7 March 1996, 1D; 17 July 1994, 1F; 24 February 1996, 1A; 22 June 1994, 1B;

19. See ibid., 3 October 1980, 6 February 1996, 1A; and 10 May 1996, 15A; Glen Peterson, interview by Richard Roberts, Ogden, Utah, 12 July 1996, transcript in possession of the authors.

20. *Standard-Examiner,* 24 April 1996, 13A; 3 May 1996, 1A; 9 May 1996, 1C; 23 May 1996, 1B; 24 May 1996, 1B; 26 May 1996, 14A; 23 June 1996, 1A; 20 June 1996, 1B; 26 June 1996, 1A; 27 June 1996, 1A; 9 July 1996, 1A.

21. Ibid., 26 September 1996, 1A; 4 October 1996, 1A.

22. Ibid., 28 February 1996, 1A; 10 March 1995; 22 June 1995, 1A.

23. Regional/Urban Design Assistance Team of the American Institute of Architects, "Ogden City, Central Business District," *Standard-Examiner,* 16 November 1987, special section.

24. *Standard-Examiner,* 5 September 1995, 1A; 8 October 1995, 1A; 12 June 1996, 14A; 7 July 1996, 1A; 25 August 1996, 1A; 3 May 1995, 1A.

25. Ibid., 29 December 1994, 1A; 6 March 1996, 1B; 13 March 1996, 1B.

26. Ibid., 1 February 1994, 1D; 3 March 1994, 8A; 26 October 1994, 1A; 23 February 1996, 5B.

27. Ibid., 6 December 1995, 1A.

28. *Salt Lake Tribune,* 1 June 1991, C12.

29. *Standard-Examiner,* 19 December 1993, 5C; 21 March 1995, 1A.

30. Bob Merrill, interview by Richard Roberts, 5 July 1996, Ogden, Utah; *Standard-Examiner,* 1 July 1996, 1B; 2 June 1996, 1F.

31. These population figures come from the Wasatch Front Research Center and from the various towns and cities listed.

| WEBER COUNTY: | *1960* | *1970* | *1980* | *1990* | *1995 (est.)* |
|---|---|---|---|---|---|
| Weber Co. | 110,744 | 126,800 | 144,616 | 158,330 | 175,000 |
| Eden | | | | | 1,802 |
| Farr West | | | 1,451 | 2,178 | 2,200 |
| Harrisville | | 749 | 1,371 | 3,004 | 3,500 |
| Hooper | | | | | 4,249 |
| Huntsville | 552 | 553 | 577 | 561 | 600+ |
| Kanesville | included in West Haven | | | | |

| WEBER COUNTY: | *1960* | *1970* | *1980* | *1990* | *1995 (est.)* |
|---|---|---|---|---|---|
| Liberty | | | | | 969 |
| Marriott | | | | | 414 |
| North Ogden | 2,621 | 5,257 | 9,309 | 11,668 | 14,000 |
| Ogden | 70,197 | 69,478 | 64,407 | 63,909 | 66,000 |
| Plain City | 1,152 | 1,543 | 2,379 | 2,722 | 3,000 |
| Pleasant View | 927 | 2,021 | 3,983 | 3,603 | 3,600 |
| Riverdale | 1,848 | 3,704 | 6,031 | 6,419 | 7,000 |
| Roy | 9,239 | 14,356 | 19,694 | 24,603 | 25,000 |
| Slaterville | | | | | 920 |
| South Ogden | 7,405 | 9,991 | 11,366 | 12,105 | 12,105 |
| Taylor | | | | | 1,200 |
| Uintah | 344 | 400 | 439 | 760 | 900 |
| Warren | | | | | 500 |
| Washington Terrace | | 7,241 | 8,212 | 8,189 | 8,742+ |
| West Haven | | | | 2,172 | 2,718 |
| West Warren | | | | | 393 |
| West Weber | | | | | 1,692 |
| Wilson | included in West Haven | | | | |

32. John Shupe, interview by Richard Roberts, Ogden, Utah, 3 September 1996; Craig Barker, interview by Richard Roberts, 27 August 1996, Ogden, Utah, transcripts in possession of the authors.

33. Elizabeth Tillotson, *A History of Ogden* (Ogden: J.O. Woody Printing, 1962), 28, 32–33.

34. *Western Agricultural Master Plan Weber County, Utah,* 1.

35. Ibid.; *Standard-Examiner,* 18 August 1996, 5B, 24A.

36. Keith G. Jensen, interview by Richard Roberts, at Huntsville, Utah, 20 August 1996, transcript in possession of the authors.

37. Robert A. Hunter, interview by Richard Roberts, Ogden, Utah, 27 August 1996, transcript in possession of the authors.

38. *Standard-Examiner,* 7 August 1987, 1C; 15 March 1986, 1C; 29 July1987, 1C; 3 October 1984.

39. Ibid., 26 April 1994, 1C; 19 April 1994, 10A; 17 April 1994, 1B; 29 May 1994, 16A; 24 July 1994, 15A; 29 June 1994, 1A;

40. Tillotson, *A History of Ogden,* 25–34.

41. Merle E. Allen, interview by Richard Roberts, 28 October 1996, Ogden, Utah, tape in possession of the authors.

42. Bart Wolthuis, interview by Richard Roberts, 19 August 1996, Ogden, Utah, tape in possession of the authors.

43. A. Stephen Dirks, interview by Richard Roberts, Ogden, Utah, 22 August 1996, tape in possession of the authors.

44. Robert H. DeBoer, interview by Richard Roberts, Ogden, Utah, 4 September 1996, tape in possession of the authors.

45. *Standard-Examiner,* 6 November 1995, 3C.

46. Mike Monson, interview by Richard Roberts, 28 August 1996, Ogden, Utah, tape in possession of the authors.

47. *Standard-Examiner,* 10 September 1982, 1A, 3A.

48. Ibid., 2 February 1991, A1; 12 February 1991, A1.

49. Ibid., 18 March 1992, A1; 19 March 1992, A1; 21 March 1992, A1; 23 March 1992, A1; 25 November 1992, B1.

50. See ibid., 1 April 1995, A1; 4 April 1995, A8; 21 April 1995, B1; 2 June 1995, B1; 14 July 1995, A14.

51. Ibid., 20 July 1995, B6.

8

# The Social and Cultural History of Weber County in the Twentieth Century

Weber County's population growth in the twentieth century is illustrated by the following census figures.

| | | | |
|---|---|---|---|
| 1910 | 35,179 | 1960 | 110,744 |
| 1920 | 43,463 | 1970 | 126,800 |
| 1930 | 52,172 | 1980 | 144,616 |
| 1940 | 56,714 | 1990 | 158,330 |
| 1950 | 83,319 | 1995 (est.) | 175,000 |

The large increases from 1940 to 1960 illustrate the impact of the war industries. There not only was an increase in numbers but also a change in the makeup of the ethnic mix of population as a result of people outside of Utah moving into the area to be employed in war industry and agricultural jobs. The last half of the twentieth century has seen sustained population growth in the county, which has brought both opportunities and challenges to the people of Weber County.

## *Ogden City Politics and 25th Street*

Ogden City's growth was much more concentrated than that of the county and involved complex issues. Some have said that the railroad brought many of the problems to Ogden. Bernard DeVoto wrote:

> The overland limited stops at Ogden for fifteen minutes. The tourist, a little dizzy from altitude but grateful for trees after miles of desert, rushes out to change his watch and see a Mormon. He passes through a station that is a deliberate triumph of hideousness and emerges at the foot of Twenty-fifth Street.[1]

Twenty-fifth Street in Ogden became a center for railroad travelers seeking entertainment while stopped for transfers or layovers. It was also a place for local people to seek business and entertainment. The bustle of business and activity that centered on 25th Street created an atmosphere that allowed many undesirable activities to locate on the first few blocks of the street—the lower end of 25th Street. Many of the practices there over nearly a century were unlawful and included prostitution, gambling, and sales of prohibited liquor and illegal drugs. Regulation of these problems posed a question of how dedicated the city officials were to the enforcement of the laws. Under some mayors and city governments of Ogden, 25th Street illegal practices were allowed as long as they did not get out of hand. It was suggested by some that many government officials and police department members were "on the take" and allowed certain practices to take place as long as they got paid off. One study suggests that

> by 1916, the infection [vice in Ogden City] had sufficiently spread that the police department had begun covertly licensing vice. In fact, some of the officers had personal investments in the continued good health of vice through illegitimate licensing practices. City policy became friendly toward vice operations and by 1944, the go signal had been given to vice operators. From the mayor down through to the police department, the government of Ogden City was indulgent with vice.[2]

Generally, through the 1920s, prostitution, narcotics peddling, and gambling went on unabated; but the largest number of criminal violations related to liquor traffic because this was the era of prohibition. Moonshine stills were found on 25th Street and at various places throughout the county. Gambling and narcotics sales, notably opium, were mainly the domain of Asian people on 25th Street during the 1920s, and there reportedly were some sales of marijuana by Mexican traffickers. The 1930s saw a continuation of the crimes of the 1920s but with new names and new places being involved.

In Mayor Harman Peery's second term of office in 1942–43 there reportedly were sixty-five gambling houses in the 25th Street vicinity, with 259 people associated with the gambling operations, and there were eleven known houses of prostitution. Jack G. Meyers ran gambling activities from the basement of the Eccles Building. Rosette Duccinni Davie and her husband, Bill Davie, were perhaps the most well known operators in the late 1940s and early 1950s with their four houses of prostitution—the Rose Rooms, the Denver Hotel, the Wilcox Hotel, and the La Siesta Hotel. Rose Davie made herself more of a personality of interest because of her open flaunting of prostitution in Ogden and her walks on city streets with an ocelot on a leash and her drives around town in a rose-colored Cadillac convertible.

Mayor Peery is considered by some to be a city official who allowed a great deal of vice to take place, with the philosophy that Ogden should be a "wide open city" and that the city should tax the various vices and thus control them. Under this philosophy, criminal activities would be kept from going underground and the city would receive benefits from the extra funds that would be raised in the taxing of these "businesses." Peery held office for several terms, including 1934 through 1939, 1942 and 1943, and 1948 and 1949. As pressure grew to clean up the city, particularly during Peery's last term in office, Peery "began to plead for fairness in the treatment of the 'little people' down on Twenty-fifth Street and the same treatment for the 'big fellows' in the Weber Club, the Ogden Golf and Country Club, and others."[3]

There were many Ogden residents who did not want the city to have a "wide-open" reputation and felt that the city should be cleaned up. As a result, efforts were made to move the vice activities out of Ogden and the county. There were several mayors interested in reform, including Fred M. Abbot (1940–41), who lost his bid for reelection as he campaigned on a platform to clean up 25th Street. David S. Romney was appointed mayor in 1944 upon the resignation of Kent S. Bramwell, who had resigned because of a scandal which suggested he had taken bribe money from 25th Street criminal operators who did not want the government to prosecute crime on the street. Bramwell served only three months as mayor before joining the army. W. Rulon White (1950–51) did much to crack down on prostitution, narcotics, illegal liquor, and gambling. During White's term in office, more arrests and convictions were made than at any other time and the flagrant crimes associated with 25th Street were reduced.

Many people in Weber County did not think that the performance of the Ogden city government against crime in the county, and especially on 25th Street, was adequate. The problem required an "aggressive individual" to bring the vice to an end. For many county residents this meant having an official who would set out to clean up the county even if every other city official opposed such action. Weber County residents found such a law enforcement team in Weber County sheriff Mac Wade and his chief deputy, Jack Card. Wade interpreted his role as county sheriff broadly in the sense that he felt that the Utah code in describing the duties of county sheriff stated that the responsibilities were to "preserve the peace, and . . . make all lawful arrests" within the boundaries of Weber County. To him, this included Ogden City.[4]

As a result, the Weber County sheriff's office carried on a successful campaign against crime and vice in Weber County during the years 1947 to 1954. With the help of county attorney Maurice Richards during the years 1949 to 1952 much was done to eradicate open crime in the city and county. The position taken by Sheriff Wade led to difficulties with Ogden City police chief Maurice Schoof, however. Charges and countercharges were made by the two officers as to who was doing the best police work in cleaning up the vice in Ogden. In reality, during his years in office Sheriff Wade probably did more in cleaning up the problems. There is no complete record of total arrests and convictions made during the Wade years, but some of Wade's accomplishments included the arrest and conviction of Rose and Bill Davie, who were sent to prison for sentences of two and one-half years and five years, respectively, in 1951 and the arrest and conviction of Eddie J. Doherty, who was described as "a big-time gambler, pimp, dope peddler, and junky." The Labor Temple, Lucky's Tavern, Dick's Club, the Key Club, the Bank Smokery, the Rodeo Cafe, and the Porters' and Waiters' Club were forced to close their gambling operations. Houses of prostitution such as the Rose Rooms, the Wilson Rooms, the Wyoming Rooms, the Parkway Hotel, and the Wilcox Hotel were put out of business by action from the sheriff's office.

By 1955 commercialized vice had been driven from open view on 25th Street and throughout the county. Captain Roberts F. Carver of the Ogden City Police Department summarized feelings of the time when he stated that

> although prostitution has been driven into secrecy into the county or other cities, it is still better than having it here on Twenty-fifth Street. When vice was located on Twenty-fifth Street, it attracted the pimps, the con-men, the gamblers, and the burglars. Now, without the prostitutes, these undesirable elements have vacated the area.[5]

Carver recognized that vice still existed, but it was not in the open with the apparent sanction of government, as it appeared to be in former times. It seemed that progress was being made.

## *Crime and Tragedy in Weber County*

Beyond the problems of 25th Street, there were other crimes that caught the attention of county residents. On 10 April 1923 Marriner A. Browning and John Browning, Jr., were jailed for shooting and killing Benjamin Frank Ballantyne. Ballantyne was the husband of John Browning Jr.'s sister Elsie, and Ballantyne reportedly had abused his wife over a period of time. Marriner and John went to the Ballantyne house to persuade Ballantyne to allow Elsie to attend a Browning family party. Ballantyne agreed, but when Elsie was getting into her brother's car her husband grabbed her and dragged her back into the house. Marriner and John followed, and Ballantyne pulled a gun and ordered them out of the house. Marriner then shot Ballantyne, telling authorities that if he hadn't shot Ballantyne first, Ballantyne would have killed John. Other witnesses to this incident corroborated the story, but the two Brownings were put in jail. This story was discussed and followed by the newspaper for months. Charges of first-degree murder were filed against the Brownings and the trial was moved to the Utah District Court in Salt Lake City. Following the trial, the jury, after fifteen minutes of deliberation on 8 December 1923, acquitted the Brownings on the first ballot. It was said to be the shortest jury decision time in the state's history.[6]

In 1936 George Mortensen of Salt Lake City arrived in Ogden to persuade his wife, Grace Snyder Mortensen, to return with him to Salt Lake City. While staying at his wife's parents home on the night of 30 June, Mortensen used a pick handle to bludgeon to death his wife's parents, Adam and Mabel Snyder, and Mrs. Snyder's mother, Emma Scott Rose. He also beat his wife severely, but she recovered from the beating to testify against him in court. Mortensen was found guilty and sentenced to life in prison.[7]

Another murder trial in the county was over a water-rights dispute in 1936 in Kanesville. On 19 May 1936 David H. Johnson shot his neighbor John Kap in the chest when Kap attempted to take water, which he claimed was his water turn, from water Johnson was using. These neighbors had been arguing about their rights over a period of years. In the trial Johnson tried to prove that Kap had fired the first shot, but the jury thought otherwise and found him guilty of second-degree murder. Johnson was sentenced to serve the rest of his natural life in the state prison. His defense was complicated by two earlier accusations of assaults with a deadly weapon.[8]

In an incident on 11 February 1941, Ogden detective Hoyt L. Gates was killed while trying to apprehend an armed robber, Robert Avery of San Francisco. The incident took place at a grocery store on the corner of Grant and 24th Street. Gates was summoned to the store while the robbery was in progress. Gates drew his pistol and entered the store, and the robber fired three shots, hitting the detective in the side. The detective fired six shots in return, but none of them hit the robber. Avery ran to a back room where he was later captured by police who used tear gas to force him out. Gates bled to death, and Avery was sentenced to die on 5 February 1943 by district judge Lewis V. Trueman.

Judge Trueman himself was the next victim of a notorious murder in Weber County. On the night of 23 July 1943, while many from the community were attending the Pioneer Days Rodeo in the local stadium, Austin Cox, angry over the divorce from his wife and the decision rendered by Judge Trueman, took a shotgun and tried to hunt down his former wife and the judge. Cox went to a residence where he thought his wife resided, but she had moved away. In his anger, Cox opened fire on some innocent people at this residence who had no connection with the affair. As a result, four people were killed—Sam Nelson, Bessie Brooks, Jane Stauffer, and Mrs. T. Burton. Two others were wounded. Cox then went on to the residence of Judge Trueman and fired a shotgun blast through Trueman's kitchen window. When Judge Trueman peered through an upstairs window to see what the trouble was, Cox shot him through the window. Trueman died, and Cox proceeded to the Ogden police station where he announced that he intended to "kill every son of a bitch in here." Cox fired one shot while in the station but was overpowered by two military police officers who happened to be at the station. Cox was found guilty of the murder of Judge Trueman and was executed on 19 June 1944.[9]

On 20 July 1949 Shirley Gretzinger, a seventeen-year-old Ogden girl, was raped and killed by Ray Dempsey Gardner, a twenty-nine-year-old Ogden man. Gardner had lured the girl to 34th Street and Washington Boulevard with an offer of a baby sitting job. Her body was found the next day in an area of tall grass near the Weber River. Gardner was later arrested in a hit-and-run accident in Pleasant View in a stolen car that he was driving. In the car were found items of women's clothing and newspaper advertisements for baby-sitting jobs that linked Gardner to the murder. In a confession to Weber County sheriff Mac M. Wade, Gardner also confessed to another murder in Montana. He was found guilty of the Ogden murder and executed by a firing squad made up of Weber County volunteers on 29 September 1951.[10]

In the period from 1920 to 1955, Weber County experienced several tragic criminal incidents which took the lives of several county residents; but there were other tragedies which also affected the citizens of the county. One was a train wreck that occurred in the early morning of 31 December 1944 when a passenger train, the Pacific

Limited, traveling from Ogden, had stopped for a freight train. It was overtaken and crashed into from the rear by a fast-moving express and mail train at Bagley, seventeen miles west of Ogden on the Lucin Cut-off track. This serious accident included forty-eight deaths and seventy-nine others who were injured. Rescue trains staffed by railroad workers helped in removing the injured and dead from the wreckage, and local sheriff officers, Utah National Guard troops, and medical personal were posted at Union Station to meet the rescue trains as they returned. The depot became the initial medical center to assist the casualties which arrived at the Ogden Station in various trains. Some fifteen to thirty ambulances lined the track to receive the dead and injured as they arrived in Ogden. Howard Wade, one of the rescue workers, said that "after handling the bodies or parts of bodies of the victims it changes your life a great deal." The people of the county began the new year on a somber note.[11]

The death of Marshall White, a fifty-four-year-old black Ogden detective sergeant, was a tragedy that shook the community. White had been on the Ogden police force for fifteen years and was a highly respected officer. On 15 October 1963 White and five other officers were called to a home in the north part of the city where they found a sixteen-year-old escapee from the state industrial school who had broken into the home. The young escapee had found a .32 caliber rifle in the home which he used to shoot and kill Officer White. White's death was a tragic loss, and he was honored for his sacrifice and service in the community by the dedication of a community and recreation facility known as the Marshall White Center five years after his death, on 18 October 1968.[12]

Highest on the list of vicious crimes in county history are the "Hi-Fi Murders" of 22 April 1974 in which three people were tortured and killed in an Ogden music store. Killed were Michelle Ansley, 18; Stanley Walker, 20; and Carol Naisbitt, 52. Five victims had been shot and left for dead; the two who survived were Orren Walker, 52; and Cortney Naisbitt, 16. Convicted for the crime were three Hill Air Force Base airmen, all from outside Utah. Pierre Dale Selby and William Andrews were found guilty of first-degree murder and armed robbery and subsequently were executed more than a decade later after exhausting their appeals in the legal system. An accomplice, Keith Leon Roberts, was released from prison in 1987.

The three airmen made plans to rob the Hi-Fi Shop and proceeded to do so near closing time on 22 April 1974. They held and bound store workers Michelle Ansley, Stanley Walker, and Cortney Naisbitt. While the robbers loaded two vans with stolen electronic equipment, Carol Naisbitt, mother of Cortney, and Orren Walker, father of Stanley, arrived at the shop concerned about their children. They walked into the robbery scene and became victims. All were tied up and tortured, and Ansley was raped. All were forced to drink Drano, and Orren Walker had a ball-point pen kicked into his head through his ear. Finally all five were shot and left for dead; but two survived to testify in court concerning their grisly torture. On the day following the murders, two young men were digging through the trash bins near some barracks at Hill Air Force Base and found wallets belonging to the victims and other items from the crime scene which led to the arrest of the airmen. Robert Newey was the Weber County prosecuting attorney and John Caine was appointed by the court as public defender. John Wahlquist served as the 2nd District Court judge. This crime shocked the citizens of the county and created some difficult racial overtones because the victims were caucasian and the murderers were African-Americans.[13]

Another crime that shook Weber County was the murder of eleven-year-old Charla Nicole King, who was found raped and strangled to death in her mother's Washington Terrace apartment. The murder occurred on 23 June 1989, and in December 1989 John Albert Taylor was convicted and sentenced to death for the crime. He was executed at the Utah State Prison on 26 January 1996 by a firing squad. Another high-profile crime was the Courtney Jo Flemel murder case, in which the three-year-old girl was reported missing from the Ogden Liberty Park on 4 June 1994 by her mother. A three-day search resulted in the discovery of the body of the girl near the Ogden City Cemetery. Over a period of several months, evidence suggested that the mother, Shelly Flemel, had suffocated the child and hid her body in bushes at the west end of the cemetery. On 25 April 1996 Judge W. Brent West sentenced the mother to a five-years-to-life sentence for killing the girl.[14]

One other killing which brought a great deal of attention in the county was a shooting exchange that took place in the Union Building of Weber State University campus on 8 July 1993. At a grievance hearing in which harassment charges had been made by a married Vietnamese student couple against a twenty-eight-year-old Vietnamese refugee and student at Weber State, a shooting spree erupted in which sixteen shots were fired. The accused person, Mark Duong, pulled out a concealed handgun and began firing at people in the room. In the melee, shots struck Weber State University police officer Kent Kiernan and Weber State University attorney Richard Hill, who struggled with the gunman. Officer Kiernan shot the gunman during the exchange, and Duong died later at the hospital.[15]

Another high-profile crime in the county involved the abuse of children committed by a religious sect led by Arvin Shreeve. Shreeve's religious group was known as the "Sister Program" or the "Zion Community." In Ogden's Northwood Subdivision in the north part of the city, Shreeve had acquired several homes that were noted for their well-kept yards and the clannish activities of their residents. After an investigation and trial, in December 1991 Shreeve was sentenced to a minimum of twenty years in prison on conviction of child sodomy. Shreeve's community was made up of fifteen women of various ages who considered themselves to be "eternal companions" to the cult leader. Included in the group were several young children who were subject to sexual abuse. In all, two men and ten women were sent to prison on child-abuse charges.[16]

In the last decade Weber County has entered into an era of modern metropolitan crime problems. Drugs, gangs, graffiti and drive-by shootings have become much more common. Ogden, with its larger and concentrated population, recorded the largest number of crimes in the county. Criminal cases in the city were reported to be 4,109 in 1990; 5,536 in 1991; 6,529 in 1992; 7,656 in 1993, and 8,208 in 1994. The gang-related crime of drive-by shootings showed one in Ogden in 1993 and ten in 1994; reported graffiti crimes numbered four in 1993 and fifty in 1994. Police in 1994 identified 474 people who were considered to be gang members; of those, 393 were males. Police also listed some forty names of gangs in the Ogden area. It is estimated that gang membership in the county was 1,000 to 1,200 individuals in 1996, and Roy and Ogden both have major gang problems.[17] Studies have suggested that in Ogden a twenty-four-block area centered on the intersection of 25th Street and Jefferson Avenue is the "roughest part of the town."

For the most part, Weber County law enforcement forces have worked well together in such programs as the Narcotics Strike Force, the Gang Task Force, and the Technical Services approach pioneered by Ogden and the county. The Weber State University Crime Laboratory carried the responsibility for supporting the police departments as a state and county crime lab for two decades beginning in 1972.[18]

## *Growth and Architecture*

Weber County grew during the first half of the century, and Ogden growth included the city expanding east of Harrison Boulevard as well as filling in some of the vacant spaces of the inner city with housing. Housing developments and subdivisions sprouted after World War II both in the city and throughout the county. There were several major builders in the county following the war including W. Allen Jackson, Roscoe Hunter, Glade B. Nielsen, Delbert and Robert Moulding, Alton and Wally Wade, Elmer Brown, Lee K. Hansen, Burton Mansfield, Monty Smith, Everett Pierce, L. Weston Scow, and Clay and Duane Campion.[19]

Nineteenth-century architects including William Nicol Fife, William W. Fife, Francis C. Woods, Samuel T. Whitaker, and Obed Taylor had left their design influences on the community. Different architectural styles developed in the decades of the twentieth century. In the 1920s the styles were mainly the bungalow, the Prairie School, and period revival styles. In the 1930s the most prevalent styles were the period revivals, the Colonial Revival, the early Christian, English Tudor, French Norman, Spanish, and Pueblo styles. During World War II, fewer houses were built outside the government housing projects, but those constructed were of an International Style, Art Moderne, Art Deco, or PWA Moderne design. Houses after World War II and into the mid-1950s generally were of the Cottage and Ranch styles.[20]

In the early twentieth century, the most prominent architects in the county were Leslie Hogdson, Myrl McClenahan, Eber Piers, and S. Arthur Shreeve. Leslie Hodgson had a tremendous impact on architecture in Weber County. Hodgson was born in Salt Lake City, where he studied architecture in the offices of Samuel Dallas and Richard Kletting; he later worked in San Diego, California, as a draftsman under Irving Gill, who had been influenced by the work of Louis Sullivan and Frank Lloyd Wright. Gill in turn influenced Hodgson along those same lines, and Hodgson brought this training with him when he came to Ogden in 1906. In a career that spanned more than four decades from 1904 to 1947, Hodgson is credited with at least seventy-five architectural designs of major buildings and residences in the county. Some of his most prominent structures are his Art Deco public buildings—the Forest Service Building, Ogden High School, and the City and County Building. He also designed many of the homes in Eccles Circle. Myrl McClenahan had worked with Hodgson since 1919 and was involved with all the projects which were developed from that time. It was suggested that Hodgson did most of the conceptual work and McClenahan did the drafting.

Eber Piers began his architectural career in Denver as a draftsman, and he arrived in Ogden in 1908 where he worked in that same capacity for Smith and Hodgson for two years. During that time he drew plans for the Ogden High School at 25th and Monroe. He then went into business for himself and gained his first client in 1911. This began a career that lasted for fifty years in Ogden until his death in 1961. Over that half-century Piers produced a great volume of work including the Berthana Ballroom, the El Monte Golf Clubhouse, the Utah State Tuberculosis Sanitarium, the Central Junior High School, the North Ogden Junior High, the Ogden Airport Administration Building, the Ogden First National Bank, and residences which he designed in the Prairie Style, including those of E.O. Wattis, Marriner Browning, Royal Eccles, Gwilliam/Marriner Eccles, and Ezekiel and Edna Dumke.

S. Arthur Shreeve also was a noted architect in this period who left an important mark on Weber County architecture. He was born in Ogden in 1885 and graduated from Weber Academy. He went on to architectural studies and schooling in Pennsylvania, California, Illinois, and England; he then returned home to design and build many homes, churches, schools, and office buildings in the county. Shreeve built and developed the Utah Hot Springs health resort and the Patio Springs summer resort. Among some of the most remarkable structures he designed are a number of homes built in the 1920s and located in the 1400 and 1500 blocks of 26th Street, 27th Street, and Marilyn Drive. The seven stucco homes in two blocks of Marilyn Drive are Shreeve homes. Rock work edging the structures, Norman towers, Craftsman and Mediterranean styles, Prairie Style, California Bungalow, and Tudor Style—all can be seen in his creations.[21]

Notable buildings built in the early decades of the twentieth century included Peery's Egyptian Theater designed by Leslie S. Hodgson and Myrl A. McClenahan and built in an Egyptian Revival style in 1924; the Union Station, designed by Los Angeles architects Don and John Parkinson and built in a Spanish Colonial style in 1924; the gymnasium built on the Weber College campus on 25th Street in 1925; the Baptist church, completed in a Colonial Style on the corner of Jefferson and 25th Street in 1925; the Ogden Livestock Coliseum, erected in 1926 at a cost of $100,000; the Bigelow Hotel (later known as the Ben Lomond Hotel and now as the Raddison) designed by Hodgson and McClenahan in an eclectic style and built in 1927; the twelve-story First National Bank (now First Security Bank), Eber Piers architect, built in 1927; the Forest Service Building, with Hodgson and McClenahan as architects, designed in an Art Deco style and completed in 1933; the El Monte Golf Course Clubhouse, designed by Eber Piers in the Prairie style with cobblestone walls and built in 1936; the Ogden High School of Art Deco design, designed by Hodgson and McClenahan and completed in 1937; the City and County Building, designed in Art Deco style by Hodgson and McClenahan and built in 1940; and Saint Benedict's Hospital on Ogden's east bench, designed by Denver architect John K. Monroe and completed in 1946.[22]

Some of the major architects in the last half of the twentieth century in Weber County were Lawrence Olpin, who designed the first four buildings on the new Weber College campus and the Ben Lomond High School; Ken Jones, who designed the Jefferson Elementary School, the Golden Hours Center, and the Marshall White Center; John Piers, architect for the Weber High School, the

Weber County Library, and the Bank of Utah; and Keith Wilcox. A partial list of the buildings Wilcox designed includes the Collett Visual Arts Building, the Val Browning Fine Arts Building, and the Shepherd Student Union Building on the Weber State University campus; several buildings and renovations for the Ogden City School District, including the Mountain View Elementary School and the Mount Ogden Junior High School; several buildings for the Weber County School District—the Roy High School, the Bonneville High School, the T. H. Bell Junior High School, and the North Park Elementary School; several public and government buildings including the McKay-Dee Hospital, the Weber Memorial Hospital in Roy, the Federal Office Building on 25th Street, the Commercial Security Branch Bank on Harrison Boulevard; and several churches.[23]

Some of the most active local architects in the 1980s and 1990s have been Case Lowe and Hart Inc., who have done many commercial buildings in the Weber Industrial Park; Sanders Herman Architects, who have done the Juvenile Court Building on 26th Street, have cooperated on the Second District Court Building on Grant Avenue, and were the main architects in cooperation with a Colorado firm on the Weber Performing Arts-Egyptian Theater Center on Washington Boulevard; and Jones Richards Associates Architects, who have done several new and renovation projects including the Technical Education Building and the Health and Physical Education Building on Weber State University's campus. They are the major designers of the $12 million Second District Court Building and designed in cooperation with MHTN Architects the newly renovated Weber County Center at 24th Street and Washington Boulevard.[24]

## *Music and Dance*

Music and dancing have been a social diversion throughout the entire history of the county. Denominational churches had their local choirs, musical groups, and productions. The Mormons in the Ogden community organized a choir prior to the dedication of the Ogden LDS tabernacle in October 1859. The Ogden Tabernacle Choir remained in existence for nine decades until 1949, when it disbanded. This choir provided many organized music presentations in the county. It was first organized by John Hart as a small singing group but grew to larger numbers under conductor Squire Coop, who increased the choir to 120 voices in 1897. It grew to its largest membership of 250 under the direction of Joseph Ballantyne in 1921. Over the years it was made up mainly of amateur musicians who enjoyed the cultural experience of singing. Gerard Klomp was an Ogden grocer who became president of the Utah Grocery Association and also president of the National Association of Retail Grocers yet found time to sing in the choir and in quartets. H. Aldous Dixon sang in the choir as a young man, and longtime choir member Mary Farley worked as Ogden City Auditor and later as a clerk at the city cemetery.

The choir had twelve conductors during its ninety years, many of them without much formal training. Some brought high standards to the group, including William Pugh; John Fowler; Squire Coop, who later became the head of the music department at the University of Utah; and Joseph Ballantyne. Ballantyne took the choir on several performance tours, including appearances at the Lewis and Clark Exposition in Portland, Oregon, in 1905; the National Irrigation Conference in Sacramento, California, in 1907, and a concert in San Francisco on that same trip; the Panama Pacific Exposition in San Francisco in 1915; and the San Diego World's Fair Exposition during that same tour. Under Ballantyne's leadership, which ended in 1921, the choir received national recognition. His successor (and the last choir conductor) was Lester G. Hinchcliff. Hinchcliff's father also had been a director of the choir, and young Hinchcliff received musical training in the east and on the west coast. The highlight of his term as director was apresentation by the Ogden Tabernacle Choir over KSL Radio to a national audience on 17 September 1934. During its last three decades, the choir generally presented local programs, including many religious oratorios. Over the years, there were many tabernacle choir organists, beginning with John Fowler and ending with Samuel F. Whitaker, who served in that position from 1907 until 1949.

The annual singing of Handel's *Messiah* is a continuing tradition which has become a community event. The first local presentation was on New Year's Day 1923, with Lester Hinchcliff conducting, Samuel Whitaker at the organ, and the Ogden Tabernacle Choir singing. Since 1950 the presentation has become in part a community sing-along, with the audience participating in some of the parts.[25]

Weber College hired several noted musicians early in this century. Among them was Ernest W. Nichols, who came to Ogden as a member of the John Philip Sousa Band on one of its tours in October 1904. Shortly after the Ogden performance, his wife became ill with an asthma affliction and was advised to find a dry climate in which to live. This brought the couple to Ogden in 1905, and he became a music instructor at the Weber Academy and also conducted the academy band and the industrial school band from 1905 to 1923. Nichols trained his son, Ernest Loring "Red" Nichols, on the cornet, and Red Nichols became an accomplished musician. In 1922 he was featured as the major instrumentalist in a program performed by a band at the Berthanna Ballroom. In 1923 Red Nichols went to Atlantic City, New Jersey, where he was quickly recognized as an outstanding jazz musician. Red organized several bands in the east, and his groups were known under several different names—the Charleston Chasers, the Red Heads, the Louisiana Rhythm Kings—but were best known as Red Nichols and His Five Penneys. After a hiatus during World War II, Nichols started music groups again and continued his career until his death in 1965. Some of the great jazz artists who played with him or in his bands included Jimmy Dorsey, Eddie Lang, Miff Mole, Joe Venuti, Benny Goodman, Fud Livingston, and Lennie Hayton. Also, Glenn Miller joined him occasionally.[26]

One of the pillars in music at Weber College was Clair W. Johnson, who arrived at the college in 1937 after national recognition as a high school band leader in Provo. Johnson served as director of the band and orchestra and taught music theory, harmony, music history, and orchestration as well as serving as music department chair for a number of years. He was known outside the area, even nationally, for his band and orchestra compositions. Over a four-decade career, he published more that three hundred scores for band and orchestra; many were published by Belwin Publishers of New York City and distributed nationwide. In publishing, Johnson used two names—his own and the nom de plume Gene Ogden.[27]

Roland Parry, a descendant of a pioneer family of Weber County, joined the Weber College faculty in 1930 after completing his music studies at UCLA, Columbia University, and the University of Utah. When he arrived at Weber there was no music department, and he became the organizer and head of that department. Parry was most interested in teaching and music composition. During his career, he composed more that one hundred songs of a wide variety, three musical comedies, two cantatas, two overtures, a symphony, and other compositions. Some of his works incorporated antiphonal singing that required several choirs.

Parry also wrote an epic historical musical telling the story of the Mormon pioneer trek west, *All Faces West.* In 1951 Parry was commissioned by Ogden City to compose the work for the 24 July Pioneer Day celebration that year. Over a six-month period he composed the music and his wife, Helen, wrote the lyrics. The production was first presented on the designated day. From that time on for a period of ten years *All Faces West* was presented three or four times each year. A renowned opera star, Igor Gorin, came to Ogden to play the part of Brigham Young. Gorin enjoyed the role, and he gave the production national recognition when he presented fifteen minutes of music from the work on the National Telephone Hour radio show. Fredonna Dixon, who was known for her beautiful contralto voice, was the lead female vocalist in the production. She participated in many musical programs in the county including Handel's *Messiah.*[28]

Dancing, in either its formal style as an art form or as a social entertainment, has long been practiced in Weber County. One of the first activities in Mathew William Dalton's first home in Ogden was a dance held in his newly finished log house by the "young people of the neighborhood." Here he caught the eye of one of the young dancers, who later became his wife.[29]

During the first half of the twentieth century, formal dance was taught to many Weber County young people by Sophie Wetherell Reed. After teaching English and physical education in the Ogden city schools for a number of years, Reed opened the Reed School of Dance in 1920. Her classes were held in several locations before she established her own studio at 2360 Adams Avenue. In her first dance teaching years, she taught only ballet; however, as time went on, her teaching repertoire expanded to acrobatics, national dances, natural dances, tap dancing, and ballroom dancing. Her watchwords were "precision, culture, and etiquette." She influenced the entire community through the many young people involved in her program. All of the year's training and preparations came together each spring when a dance review was held for public audiences. In 1956 when she sold her studio there were 400 students enrolled in the Reed School of Dance.

Social dancing was a popular entertainment in the twentieth century, and dance halls and ballrooms with live bands drew large crowds. During the Depression, ballrooms added incentives of prizes being given away to draw more people. The most frequented establishments were the Berthanna Ballroom, the White City Ballroom, the Weber College Dance Hall, and the outdoor Roman Gardens. Churches also sponsored dances, as did private and public clubs such as the Porters' and Waiters' clubs and the Old Mill. On occasion, dance parties were held at the Union Station and in the Ben Lomond Hotel Ballroom. Among those who played in Ogden were Alvino Rey, a jazz banjo player of the swing era who often played at White City, and the Milt Taggert Band, which featured the King Sisters as vocalists, at the Berthanna. It was a common practice for young people to go as a group and trade dances throughout the evening.[30]

## *Drama and Motion Pictures*

Plays and movies were popular forms of entertainment. Weber College provided much of the theater repertoire and the Orpheum Theater also had vaudeville and traveling plays early in the century. The Orpheum Circuit and the Pantages Circuit provided much of the traveling entertainment along with the chautauqua programs that came to Ogden. The chautauqua program in Utah started in Ogden in 1911 when the community put on a "ten-day extravaganza" with all local talent. Frederick Vining Fisher put together a program that included the Salt Lake and Ogden Tabernacle choirs, Evan Stephens's Zion Choir, Ernest Nichol's Chautauqua Band, the Morgan Brass Band, Romania Hyde's Ladies Orchestra, and the Don Phillippini Italian Band. Several dramatic readings, three pageants, patriotic addresses including a speech by B. H. Roberts, local societies representing the Scotch, Welsh, Irish, Scandanavian, German, and Japanese people of Utah displayed their individual cultures through handicrafts, costumes, folk dances, music, and grand marches were featured, and a big Pioneer Day celebration was a highlight of the multi-day program. The chautauqua was put on by local talent until 1915 when the community contracted with the Ellison/White circuit to bring their seven-day program into town. This lasted until the late 1920s when problems of raising money for the programs became significant due to the downturn in the economy. Also, the availability of automobiles allowed people to travel out of the area easier and movies and radio cut into the chautauqua program audience.

Circuses, which drew people from throughout the county, brought different types of outside amusement to the area. Circus day was a great event for young and old, beginning with the parade of the animals and special features from the train station to the circus grounds, which could be the Tabernacle Square, City Hall Park, Jones Grove, near the Ogden Stadium, or the north side of 20th Street west of Harrison Boulevard. The circuses delighted county crowds on a regular basis for several years, but they later ran into the same problems as had the vaudeville and chautauqua programs, and they became less frequently held.[31]

The Pioneer Day program separated itself from the chautauqua program in 1913 when David O. McKay directed the event, which included a parade in which various floats featured the themes of growth and development from the Native Americans, trappers, and settlers to 1913. This continued a tradition of parades celebrating the early pioneers. Two decades later Ogden's "Cowboy Mayor" Harman Peery attracted national attention through the press with his antics to advertise what he designated as "Ogden's Pioneer Days" celebration. As mayor in 1934 he did much to try to publicize the Pioneer Days event. Late in 1934 he was presented with a pinto pony by the management of the Ogden Union Stockyards; a few days later, he accepted the challenge of the Evanston, Wyoming, fire chief to engage in a horse race. The contest seems never to have been staged but certainly attracted publicity. Early the following year, Peery challenged members of the Byrd Antarctic Expedition to a beard-growing contest, with the results to be decided at the time of Ogden's Pioneer Days celebration. That year, all men in Weber County were encouraged to grow beards, and those who complied were "forcibly" ushered into the line of the parade. Also, 1935 was the year that the first rodeo was held in Ogden Stadium during Pioneer Days.

Many in the community remember the plays and musicals put on by Weber College, with Thatcher Allred, Roland Parry, J. Clair Anderson, and Pearl Allred involved in the productions. Among the plays were *The Vagabond King, Arms and the Man, Our Town, The Taming of the Shrew,* and *The Importance of Being Ernest.* A community theater group which was established in the early 1930s took the name of the Weber Little Theater. As time passed, this group took different names, including the Ogden Little Theater, the Ogden Community-Weber College Theater, and the Ogden Civic Theater. The group presented plays in the old Lyceum and Cozy theaters on 25th Street. Early plays were presented under of the leadership of Bertha Eccles Wright, who was later joined by Leora Thatcher, from the Utah State Agricultural College in Logan, and Kathryn M. Northrup, who had gained experience in theaters in New York. Thatcher went on to become a popular radio, Hollywood, Broadway, and television actress. William Wright and Russell Thorson, who developed their talents in community performances, also moved on to professional radio, television, and motion picture roles. Eventually many of the community theater activities were incorporated into the Weber College theater productions. Thatcher Allred, John Grover Kelly, and Carl White played a major part in producing a regular schedule of plays for the college.

From 1920 to 1955 there were nine theaters that operated in the area. These included the Orpheum on Washington Boulevard; the Lyceum on 25th Street; the Ogden Theater on 25th above Washington Boulevard; the Rex at 225 25th Street; the Alhambra at 2429 Kiesel Avenue; the Utah at 2510 Washington Boulevard; Steck's Cozy Theater at 2476 Washington Boulevard; the Colonial Theater at 2465 Washington; and Peery's Egyptian Theater, built in 1924 at 2439 Washington and presently being restored as part of the Ogden Convention Center complex. Only the Lyceum, Alhambra, and Egyptian buildings still exist, and none of them currently are functioning as theaters. [32]

In the visual arts, many Weber County artists have been recognized beyond the county for their work. The list of noted artists of the county includes Corinne Damon Adams, Arthur Adelmann, Brigham Y. Andelin, Mark Biddle, Solon Borghum, Lois Breeze, Drex Brooks, Dale Bryner, Roy Butcher, Margie M. Call, Farrell R. Collett, David Cox, Florence B. Drake, Roberta Glidden, Charles A. Groberg, Calvin Grondahl, Ron Hales, Stephen Hedgepeth, Fred Hunger, James Jacobs, LeRoy Jennings, Olive Belnap Jensen, Geri Kelly, Michael Keogh, Peg Kotok, Dee Lefon, R. Eddi Malloy, James McBeth, Sandria Miller, Lee Parkinson, Al Rounds, Lillian Senior, Richard Shepherd, Clara Smith, Norman Skanchy, Steve Songer, David Mac Stevenson, Helen Stone, Doyle Strong, Dell Taylor, Richard Van Wagoner, Blanche Wilson, J. S. Wixom, and Ron Zollinger. Farrell Collett is widely known for his wildlife oil paintings that are collected widely in Utah and beyond the state. Dale Bryner is also highly respected and known for the variety of his art works. Artists' works are displayed in the county in the Collett Gallery at Weber State University, the Eccles Community Art Center, the Myra Powell Gallery, at the Municipal Park during Pioneer Days, and at other selected places.[33]

In musical entertainment, Weber County since 1970 has had some remarkable individual and organized successes. Weber State College (now University) presented musical programs of a great variety. The summer Utah Musical Theater usually presented three or four musicals. Such works as *West Side Story, Pajama Game, Fiddler on the Roof, Sound of Music, Cabaret, Damn Yankees, Will Rogers Follies,* and *Forever Plaid* are some of the major productions. Productions were staged at the Val Browning Center on the Weber State campus, but future productions also will be presented in the newly renovated Egyptian Theater in downtown Ogden. The Ogden Symphony Ballet Association and the Ogden Opera Guild also scheduled symphony and operatic performances regularly. Since 1978 the John and Telitha Lindquist family have sponsored an annual outdoor symphony concert presented at Weber State campus. It has featured over the years the Utah Symphony and the Mormon Youth Symphony orchestras.

Other well-known Weber County musicians include Donald Ripplinger, an assistant director of the Mormon Tabernacle Choir and a composer of religious music. Shi-hwa Wang was known for his violin concerts. Weber State's music department was recognized for its teachers, including Earl Erickson, who was known for his jazz interests. Yu Jane Yang instituted a children's music program, known as the Piano Preparatory Program, that was popular in the community, and Michael Palumbo did significant work in organizing and conducting the New American Symphony, made up of musicians from the university and the community.

Before 1950, after attending the theater or a movie, Weber County residents frequented the soda fountains or eating houses in downtown Ogden. Among the favorites were Greenwell's and Keeley's cafes on Washington Boulevard; John Bockus' Little John's Sweet Shop on 25th Street, and the Orpheum Shop next to the theater entrance. One of the most popular eating places during the first half of the century was Ross and Jack's, located at the corner of 25th and Washington on the ground floor of the Broom Hotel. Lou Gladwell wrote:

> In the old days Ross and Jack's was part of the joy of going downtown in Ogden. You could go to a movie—usually a cowboy show at the Ogden, Cozy or Alhambra theater—for a dime—and then go to Ross and Jack's for a piece of pie for another dime.[34]

The cafe's most popular dish was the "Burger Spuds," which consisted of hamburger advertised with "a little reindeer and beef bull meat" mixed in, with mashed potatoes, gravy, and ketchup on the side. Ross Hawkins and Jack Crane started their partnership just prior to 1920 and stayed together in business until 1957. Lou Gladwell remembered that while he was in the army during World War II in Australia, he overheard two army men talking about the delicious and plentiful servings they had been served at Ross and Jack's while passing through Ogden.

Some Weber County actors and writers went beyond local productions and became known across the state and nation. Moroni Olsen became known for his work in the theater and movies. In 1923, with Janet Young and Byron Foulger, he organized the Moroni Olsen Players, a traveling repertory company which presented productions throughout the Pacific Northwest and in California. Olsen appeared in New York productions of *Man of Wax*, with Lenore Ulric, *Mary of*

*Scotland,* starring Helen Hayes, *Romeo and Juliet,* and *Barrets of Wimpole Street,* starring Katharine Cornell. He played in about forty movies, one of which was *Kentucky,* with Loretta Young, Richard Greene, and Walter Brennen.

Robert Walker was a Weber County resident who became a star in the movies. He began acting in the late 1930s and married another star, Jennifer Jones. He received major roles during World War II in such pictures as *See Here Private Hargrove, The Clock,* and *Thirty Seconds Over Tokyo.* After the war, he starred in *Strangers on a Train, Till the Clouds Roll By,* and several other films. He died while in the process of finishing the film *My Son John* in 1951. Lila Eccles Brimhall was another actress who had her beginnings in Weber County. She spent the years 1929 to 1960 as a teacher of drama at the University of Utah and played in many local productions during those years. The seven children of Edwin F. Tout were well known in theatrical and musical circles of the county; Nannie, Margaret, "Romaine," and Hazel "Dawn" were the most prominent. Gean Greenwell was a noted Weber County baritone who became a Metropolitan Opera singer.[35]

Portia Nelson came out of Weber College to pursue a musical career. She performed in over 300 commercial, film, and television appearances, including the film *The Sound of Music.* The Osmond family lived in Ogden until 1963 when they were drawn to other places with their entertainment careers. They found fame in the *Andy Williams Show* in the 1960s and the *Donny and Marie Show* in the 1970s. Gedde Wantanbe graduated from Ogden High in 1973 and went to California to establish his acting career. He appeared in such movies as *Sixteen Candles, Volunteers,* and *Gung Ho.* Hal Ashby was born and raised in Ogden and became a noted Hollywood film director of such films as *Shampoo, Coming Home,* and *Being There.*

## *Weber County Writers*

A number of noted writers have had their beginnings in Weber County. Bernard DeVoto and Fawn Brodie each received extensive national recognition. DeVoto was a historian, critic, novelist, educator, and conservationist. He was born and raised in Weber County and used the locale of Ogden as the setting for his novel *The Crooked*

*Mile*, published in 1924. DeVoto was known nationally for many of his writings; among his most enduring were his histories of the West, including *Year of Decision, 1846* (1946); *Across the Wide Missouri* (1947), for which he received the Pulitzer Prize and the Bancroft Prize; and *The Course of Empire* (1952), which was given the National Book Award. He also edited the *Journals of Lewis and Clark* (1953). DeVoto made some uncomplimentary remarks about the culture of Ogden in which he was raised; however, he later apologized and toned-down his earlier remarks.[36]

Fawn McKay Brodie, a nationally known biographer and historian, was born in Ogden in 1915. She graduated from Weber College at age sixteen and from the University of Utah two years later. After teaching English for a short time at Weber College, at age twenty she completed a master's degree in English Literature from the University of Chicago. This precocious woman taught for several years at UCLA as a professor of history. Her writings were mainly psychological/historical biographies that stirred controversy. Her first major work was a biography of Mormon leader Joseph Smith, *No Man Knows My History* (1947). Her other books include *Thaddeus Stevens: Scourge of the South* (1959), *The Devil Drives: A Life of Sir Richard Burton* (1967), *Thomas Jefferson: An Intimate History* (1974), and *Richard Nixon: The Shaping of His Character* (1981). Brodie's biography of Joseph Smith questioned his claims and his character, and, although some critics questioned her psychohistorical approach to her subjects, she received several awards for her writing.[37]

Arthur Guy Empey was a Weber County native who wrote concerning his experiences in World War I in *Over the Top*. Empey's book received national attention. Coleman Cox, author of *May Be So*, was a reporter on the *Ogden Standard*. Another writer for the paper was Cuthbert L. Olsen, who in 1940 became governor of California.[38]

Phyliss McGinley won a Pulitzer Prize in poetry, and other local poets include LaVon B. Carroll, Brad L. Roghaar, Helen Mar Cook, Bob Urry, Maxine Jennings, Patricia Grimm, Clarence P. Socwell, Frank M. DeCaria, Sherwin W. Howard, and Sister M. Madeleva Wolff. Noted county fiction writers include Richard Scowcroft, Levi Peterson, Gordon Allred, Joan Allred Sanders, Wayne Carver, Judith Freeman, Margaret Rostkowski, and Robert Hodgson Van Wagoner.

### *Automobiles and Airplanes*

The automobile changed life in Weber County. The first car came to Weber County in 1904, and by the 1920s automobiles were a part of many families' means of transportation. The first black-top or "macadamized" roads were authorized by Ogden officials in 1904. With the introduction of the automobile, many more county residents traveled to Ogden to purchase groceries and clothing. Automobile dealers began to sell cars to county residents, and the servicing of automobiles—from gasoline and oil to major repairs—became a steadily increasing business for some Weber residents.

Weber County entered into the air travel business in the 1920s. In 1927 a few energetic businessmen and local aviation enthusiasts formed the Red Raven Flying Club. They purchased a Lincoln Standard plane and a canvas hangar, and they erected the hangar across the road from where the first municipal airport was later located. Up to this time the only aviation experience that Weber County had with flying was an occasional "flying circus" or "barnstorming" visit that came to the area as part of an aviation show.

In 1928 a progressive Ogden City Council and a number of citizens began to realize the importance of air transportation for the area. They established the old Ogden Municipal Airport near South Burch Creek at the southern end of the county. Three graveled runways were built on this site of about 200 acres. In that same year, National Parks Airways made mail and passenger stops in Ogden as part of its operation in the West. Two early aviation boosters, Dean R. Brimhall and Robert H. Hinckley, organized a commercial flying organization in 1928 known as Utah Pacific Airways. Hinckley later went on to become the director of the Federal Aviation Administration, which established many of the first national flying guidelines for commercial aviation. Utah Pacific Airways became the major force in the development of the Ogden Municipal Airport, including such airport improvements as runways, hangars, night lighting, and beacons to guide the planes.

At first, passengers were few. Initially, passengers sat in the front cockpit of an open bi-plane. Next came a four-passenger Boeing 40 B4 model; then Al Frank of National Parks Airways brought in several seven-passenger Fokker monoplanes. In 1933 the Boeing ten-passenger twin model 247 was used. Greater interest in flying developed with a Weber College flying program and a Civil Pilot program. Larger planes also required larger runways, and soon a larger field was needed. At that time, airport commissioner William J. Rackham and city engineer J. C. Brown recommended that the airport be located in an area between two state roads, U.S. Highway 91 and Utah Highway 39 in the southwest corner of Ogden's city limits. Ogden City purchased 748 acres in the recommended area at a cost of $80,000, and the federal government helped in the airport development. At that time, the name was changed from Hinckley Airport to Ogden Municipal Airport. A U.S. Weather Bureau station was established at the airport. Three concrete landing strips were built and an administration building and a control tower were added. Initial construction costs were approximately $671,000; other additions during the 1940s added another $200,000 to the cost. In 1943 Western Air Lines scheduled mail and passenger service to Ogden, and in 1946 United Airlines did the same. Both major airlines ended their service in 1960 when it was determined that the Salt Lake Airport was close enough to allow the discontinuation of the Ogden service. During these early years, two local companies did much to promote Ogden aviation operations—Charlesworth Flight and Utah Western Aviation.[39]

## *The Media in Weber County*

The twentieth century saw some major developments in the media. In 1920 the *Ogden Standard* and the *Ogden Examiner* were consolidated into the *Ogden Standard-Examiner.* The *Ogden Standard* was founded by Frank Cannon in 1888; and he was joined by William Glasmann in 1892. The *Morning Examiner* was first established by Glasmann family money with Frank Francis as editor; in 1911 it was sold to a group of Utah businessmen headed by J.U. Eldredge, Jr. Eldredge became the *Examiner's* general manager, and he ran the paper until 1920 when the two papers were consolidated. After the consolidation, which made Ogden a one newspaper town, Abraham Lincoln Glasmann operated the paper. The two papers had operated out of two downtown buildings; but, following the merger, they moved into the Kiesel Building. The paper later moved to its headquarters on 23rd Street, which was the old National Guard Armory building.

Another means of public communication in Weber County in the period was the development of the radio industry. Radio broadcasting started in Utah with the KZN (which later became KSL) station making its debut on 6 May 1922. Other stations soon followed in Salt Lake City and other cities in the state. Ogden's first stations were KDZL in 1922, KFPC in 1923, and KFUR and KFWA in 1924. Only KFUR survived the first "hectic decade," and in the early 1930s A.L. "Abe" Glasmann, owner of the *Ogden Standard-Examiner,* helped KFUR financially through the hard times and changed the call letters to KLO. Glasmann established the Interstate Broadcasting Corporation as the parent organization to KLO in 1934 and hired son-in-law George Hatch to manage the Ogden station in 1941. Other radio stations including KOPP and KVOG were established after World War II.

Several individuals born in Weber County had an impact on radio and television development. Earl J. Glade was a pioneer in building the KSL empire and was also elected mayor of Salt Lake City. Rolfe Peterson, one-time student body president at Weber College, became a broadcaster at KLO and participated in 1939 in the first television program of the college presented in Salt Lake City. Peterson later went on to become a radio announcer and television personality in the San Francisco area. Douglas Stringfellow worked as an announcer at KLO for a period of time before his involvement in politics. Utah radio and television personalities Roy Gibson and Paul James, both graduates of Ogden High School, had a great impact on Utah broadcasting. Len Allen has had perhaps the longest stint as an announcer at KLO, beginning his career in 1947 and continuing his career to the present.

Archibald G. Webb and his son John have had a major influence on media development in Weber County. Arch Webb served in the army during World War II, and following the war he established station KVOG in January 1947 in Ogden. In 1972 the Webbs applied for a 100,000-watt FM station; when their application was granted, they began operating station KZAN. Arch Webb also received from the

Federal Communications Commission the license for the only standard-band television channel (Channel 9) in Ogden. After operating the station for a year, Webb sold the station to the Ogden City School Board. John Webb is the current general manager of KLO and KZAN radio stations.[40]

## *Sports*

Sports activities have been important for the residents of Weber County both to watch and to participate in. Young men of the county participated in the Farm Bureau baseball leagues and families enjoyed being spectators. Perhaps the largest promoters of organized sports have been the high schools and Weber College. During the first half of the century, Ogden High School's students came from the city and Weber High School's students were from the rural areas of the county. Later, Ben Lomond High School was added in the city, and Bonneville, Roy, and Fremont high schools were added in the county. The rivalries have been intense between all of the high schools. In football Weber High fielded its first team in 1922 and lost that year to Ogden 24–6. Until 1955 Ogden generally dominated the county school, winning most games against Weber High and also against Ben Lomond High, which fielded its first team in 1953. Weber High had its first victory against Ogden in 1929; Ben Lomond won its first game against its city rival in its first year, by a score of 7–6.[41]

Weber College provided the county with great spectator opportunities, with many of the athletic teams being made up of local talent. In 1922–23 Weber Academy moved from high-school status to junior-college status. By 1925 Weber College became a part of the Intermountain Junior College Athletic League, playing several Utah and Idaho junior colleges. During the interwar period, Weber College was known primarily for its football teams, and from 1924 to 1931 the school won eight straight conference titles under the coaching of Merlin Stevenson. Sherman "Pete" Couch was one of the outstanding players of this time. A series of games was developed between Weber College and McKinley High School of Honolulu, Hawaii, that lasted from 1928 through 1947. Reed Swenson was hired as both coach and athletic director at the college in 1933. Robert Davis replaced Swenson as head football coach in 1937, though Swenson continued to coach basketball and direct athletics.

Reed Swenson coached the Weber College basketball team, which won the state AAU basketball tournaments in 1938 and 1939. They lost in the championship game of the National Junior College AAU in 1939. The war years generally reduced competitive sports, but in 1942 Weber College took the Intermountain Conference basketball championship. Wat Misaka was named the most valuable player of the tournament and he and Jay Hancey were selected as all-tourney team members.

Track had some outstanding performers including Willie Thomas, who hailed from Kansas City and was one of Weber's first African-American athletes. Thomas set a conference record in the high hurdles and also won events in the 100-yard dash and low hurdles. Ray Freeman and LaMar Green were outstanding track men in the early 1940s. Wrestling, boxing, fencing, golf, and swimming were other sports played at the college. Ralph Clark, Stan Benson, and Jim Sundquist were champions in tennis in the 1930s.

After World War II Weber College expanded its athletic programs. In 1947 the college joined the National Junior College Athletic Association while still competing in the Intermountain Conference. Reed Swenson served as vice-president of the National Junior College Athletic Association and Weber student (and later faculty member) Laurence Burton edited its official journal. Milt Mecham was Weber's football coach from 1946 to 1956. Weber College played its first football game in the new stadium on the upper campus in 1953. Wally Nalder began as Weber's football coach in 1956 and directed the football program through the end of the junior-college period into the first three years after Weber became a four-year college. Outstanding players during these years were Brent Hancock, Terry Van Vleet, Lynn Corbridge, and Lynn Smith as backfield players, and LeRoy Overstreet and Lynn Foley as linemen.

Weber College basketball teams took six league crowns—in 1950, 1958, 1959, 1960, 1961, and a shared title in 1962. They won the National Junior College Tournament in 1959. Among the nationally recognized First-Team Junior College All-American players during this era were Darrell Tucker in 1950, Allen Holmes in 1958 and 1959, and Gene Kunz in 1960. Other outstanding players were Kenny Berrett, Bob Subic, and Eddie Tillman.[42] Dick Motta and Phil Johnson coached Weber's basketball teams during the 1960s before both moved on to coach in the National Basketball Association (NBA).

Arnold Ferrin and Wat Misaka played basketball at Ogden High and went on to become members of the University of Utah cinderella team that won the National Collegiate Athletic Association championship in 1944. Arnie Ferrin was chosen as the outstanding player of the tournament, which was played in Madison Square Garden. In his senior year, Ferrin was also on the Utah team that won the National Invitational Tournament in 1947; he went on to play professional basketball for three years with the Minneapolis Lakers. Ferrin was on the Lakers teams that won the National Basketball Association crown in 1949 and 1950.

Elmer Singleton played baseball in the Farm Bureau leagues in Weber County, and he was signed by the Cincinnati Reds as a pitcher in 1939. He later played for the New York Yankees in their minor league program, and in 1945 he moved to the big leagues when he joined the Boston Braves. Singleton also played for the Pittsburgh Pirates, the Washington Senators, and the Chicago Cubs. He played until he was forty-three years old and then retired to Plain City in Weber County where he had begun to play baseball.[43]

A history of sports in Weber County would not be complete without some mention of Al Warden, who came to Ogden as a reporter for the *Ogden Standard* in 1919 and became the sports editor and columnist for the *Standard-Examiner* in 1926. Warden not only was a sports writer but he also promoted and organized several sports events and leagues until his death in 1968. Warden was a track star at West High School in Salt Lake City and a runner on a navy team in San Diego before World War I. In the years before public broadcasting, Al Warden, assisted by newspaper writer Glen Perrins, set up a board representing a baseball field on a small balcony on the north side of the Kiesel Building. He sent a runner to the nearby Western Union telegraph office, and the runner would carry telegrams describing the events of each inning of play in the World Series. Warden would then depict the events on the board, indicating the movement of batters and runners and the play-by-play account. This dramatization drew large crowds on 24th Street. Wrote one:

> Sometimes the crowd was so large that the street was blocked to traffic. However, the streetcars had to run on schedule with gongs clattering, a car crept slowly through the crowd. All the passengers could be seen on the south side of the car where they could get a glimpse of the inning scores Al and his associates had posted in plain view.[44]

Warden helped organize the Western America Winter Sports Association in Ogden in 1928, and this association sponsored ski jumping and dog races in the area. In 1930 he was a major force in the dedication of a jumping hill at Shanghai Flat in Ogden Canyon and the naming of it Becker Hill, after G.L. Becker, one of Weber County's prominent businessmen and sports boosters. Halvor Bjorngaard, Norwegian champion ski jumper, and the Engen brothers participated in jumping events at that site.[45]

During the 1930s there was a growing interest in skiing, and this led to the development of Wheeler Basin as a ski resort. Through the efforts of Weber County leaders and the Ogden Chamber of Commerce some badly deteriorated watershed lands in Wheeler Basin were restored and funds were raised to purchase this land. It was turned over to the U.S. Forest Service as a part of the Cache National Forest. A.G. Nord directed a program of rehabilitation which restored the watershed. In 1938 there was a great deal of interest to develop the basin into a winter sports area. On 2 August 1940, following a contest sponsored by the chamber of commerce to name the new area, the name Snow Basin was given to the site. In 1944, a lodge was built by the Forest Service in the basin, and the Forest Service, assisted by the CCC and the WPA, built a road into the basin. A chair lift was added in 1946. On 20 January 1946 dedication and naming ceremonies were held, with Gus Becker the major participant. In 1957, during Raymond Wright's administration as mayor, Ogden City sold Snow Basin to a private developer, S.S. Huntington of Colorado, who continued development of the resort.

Al Warden brought many athletic events to Weber County including professional football games and boxing matches such as the

Rex Layne-Ezzard Charles fight with Jack Dempsey as referee in 1952 and the televised fight of Archie Moore and Joey Maxim from Ogden Stadium in 1953. Harlem Globetrotters basketball teams and baseball figures such as Babe Ruth, Ty Cobb, Dizzy Dean, and Satchel Paige visited Ogden at Warden's invitation. He helped organize the Utah Baseball League in 1920, the Utah-Idaho League in 1926, and the Pioneer Baseball League in 1938. Some of the future major league baseball players who played for the Ogden Reds and the Ogden Dodgers farm teams in that league include Steve Garvey, Johnny Temple, Bill Buckner, Tom Paciorek, Frank Robinson, and manager Tommy Lasorda.[46] Ogden had always been a strong baseball town, and in the 1990s baseball came back to Ogden when the Ogden Raptors, formerly the Salt Lake Trappers, came as an independent team in the Pioneer League. In 1996 the Raptors became a farm team of the Milwaukee Brewer organization and, along with building a new baseball stadium, this seemed to herald the beginning of a new era for baseball in Weber County.

Hunting and fishing were favorite activities in Weber County down through the years, and the terrain and waterways provided good habitat for wild game animals. In the nineteenth and early twentieth centuries wild game and fish were hunted and fished locally to provide food for local restaurants and family tables. It has been observed that the abundance of game led to its wholesale slaughter by professional market hunters and its consumption by an eager public. This in part led in 1916 to international migratory bird treaties that put limits and controls on migratory bird hunting. By 1929 Utah protected some of the species that had been drastically diminished to the point that there were no open seasons on many of them, including quail, grouse, wood duck, sage hens, Hungarian partridge, elk, antelope, and mountain sheep. Alex Brewer recalled his experiences as a market hunter:

> When it was legal to buy and sell wild game I used to handle the kill from 25 hunters during the hunting season. I have shipped out as many as 500 dozen wild ducks in one shipment to Omaha, Kansas City and St. Louis. I used to supply all the railroad eating houses between here and Omaha. We used to buy and sell blue grouse. I recall one Jim Wangsgaard came to my store and asked if

> I could handle some grouse. I told him I would take all he could bring and he brought an entire wagonload! I sold them at $4.50 per dozen. John Browning, the gun inventor and myself used to drive out on the hills at the south end of town near where the Mountain View Cemetery is now located. We could often shoot 25 or 30 prairie chickens in an evening. . . . About 1894 some ranchers came in and offered to sell a box car load of deer. I contracted for the deer, big and little at $.50 per head. The men started out on the hills south of Huntsville and hunted across the big flats then down the head of Lost Creek. Wagons followed the hunters on horseback. I had the Union Pacific set out a car at Croyden and the hunters brought in wagon loads of deer and we hung them as closely as possible in that car and I shipped it to St. Louis. There were literally thousands of deer on the head of the Magpie in those days. Then after a time the deer disappeared and for 20 years one was rarely seen. Now the deer are coming back under proper protections and we often see them right along the road in South Fork. It is very encouraging to see wild game "come back."[47]

Many Weber County sportsmen participated in trap shooting, and among the most noted shooters in the 1930s were E.L. Ford, G.L. Becker, and A.P. Bigelow. Becker was named to the American Olympic trap-shooting team but was unable to go to the event at that time.[48]

Since 1950 Weber County schools have been very successful in athletic contests. Ogden High School won the state football championship in 1958 and 1966; Bonneville High won the championship in 1980; Roy High in 1981; and Weber High in 1985. In boys basketball, Weber County high school teams have won several state championships over the years. Ogden High School won the state championship in 1932 and 1940, and Mitch Wilcox coached the Ogden Tigers to two state championships in 1991 and 1992. Weber High won the basketball championship in 1910, 1913, 1919, 1948, and 1971. Bonneville High won the state basketball championship in 1985 and 1987, as did Ben Lomond High in 1986. In baseball, the county schools also produced state champions—Ogden High in 1948, 1951, 1953, 1954, 1958, and 1982; Weber High in 1961; and St.

Joseph's in 1980. In track and field competition, Weber County high schools have won state championships several times over the years.

High school girls in Weber County also have been very successful in athletics. Ogden High girls have won five state basketball titles, and Weber High girls have won seven state track titles. Weber High girls have also won six state volleyball titles, and Ogden High has won the volleyball title once. The most successful girls team in the county has been the Ogden High tennis team, which has won the state title fifteen times since 1979. St. Joseph's High School has won one tennis title. Ben Lomond High School girls have won two state soccer championships.

From these school programs came several athletes who went on to college or professional levels of competition. Among these were Ken Hunt (Ogden) and Glen Hubbard (Ben Lomond) in baseball; Jim McMahan (Roy), Glen Redd (Ogden), Rulon Jones (Weber), Shawn Miller (Weber), and Clyde Brock (Weber) in football; Tom Chambers (Weber) in basketball; Ed Eyestone (Bonneville) in track—five-time NCAA champion and Olympic participant in 1988 and 1992; Wade Bell (Weber) in track—NCAA champion and participant in the 1968 Olympics; Chris Jones (Ben Lomond) in track—three time All American; Darrin Williams (Bonneville) in track—All American in steeple chase; Mathew Godfrey (Weber) in track—All American in steeple chase; Teri Okelberry Spiers (Weber) in women's track—three time winner of NCAA javelin title. Charles "Chick" Hislop coached at Ben Lomond High and Weber State University, and was the distance coach for the United States Olympic Team in the 1996 Olympics in Atlanta, Georgia.[49]

In Weber County communities sports and recreation have continued as an important part of the lifestyle. For the past three decades, women sports have become an integral part of community and school life. By the 1960s Farm Bureau baseball had ended and been replaced by American Legion leagues, which continued summer baseball for the high-school-age players. Adult softball leagues were organized after World War II and continued through the following decades, with several parks developed for the community leagues. Affleck Park, Fourth Street Park, South Ogden Friendship Park, the Weber County Fairgrounds Park, and several other fields in the county communities have housed regular leagues in softball—both fast-pitch and slow-pitch versions. The Weber County Recreation Department ran young girls fast-pitch softball tournaments that averaged sixty teams in the 1980s; and this was only a portion of the many teams in the county plus all the teams that played in the various city leagues. Young men participated in the boys baseball program, which averaged fifty teams in the playoff tournaments in the 1980s—again only a portion of all the teams in the county.[50]

In the 1960s, 1970s, and 1980s the Little League Football program became established in most of the county communities. Basketball and soccer programs were organized and run by the various city recreation departments. By 1968 youth soccer programs had 2,000 participants in Weber County. It is estimated that in 1996 there are approximately 20,000 people involved in soccer programs in the Weber County–North Davis County region. In 1982 the first women soccer teams were organized in the area; and it is estimated that there are now 12,000 women playing soccer in the area. In 1982 soccer was recognized as an official men's sport in the high schools and at the college. The Weber State men's soccer team won the national collegiate soccer championship in 1992, 1994, and 1995, and took second place in 1993. The Weber State women's team won the national championship in 1994.

Golf was a sport which came to involve many Weber County people. The Schneiter family, with both Ernie Schneiter, Senior, and Junior, has been particularly prominent among golf professionals. Golf courses were developed throughout the county, including Wolf Creek and Nordic Valley in the upper valley and Ben Lomond, the Barn, Mt. Ogden, Mulligan's, El Monte, Royal Greens, Schneiter's Riverside, and the Ogden Country Club in the lower valley.

## *Cultural Societies, Fraternal Societies, and Civic Clubs*

Women's activity organizations in Weber County had their beginnings in the pioneer period. An important movement of the Presbyterian church was the organization of the Women's Home Mission Society in 1893, which in 1895 became a national society to help in special missions where poverty was a problem. In 1905 the Ogden Presbyterian church organized a social board which later became its women's association. This association carried out education programs for some of the Japanese people located in the county and during the war years gave much volunteer service. The Mormon church Relief Society was organized before its adherents came to Utah; and it continued in Weber County in the nineteenth and twentieth centuries. This organization was dedicated to compassionate service, and its functions included work for the Red Cross during both World War I and World War II. The Methodist church established the Grace French Wesleyan Service Group, named in honor of the wife of Reverend Walter French, founder of the organization in Weber County. The Elim Lutheran Church, through the efforts of Sister Hulda Hultquist, established the Elim Ladies' Aid Society in the early 1900s. During World War II this society supported the U.S.O. canteen in Ogden by providing cookies and other services. In that same period, the Lutheran Dorcas Society served breakfasts to the soldiers at the U.S.O., and the Luther League invited soldiers and new civilian families in the area to its meetings. The Catholic church demonstrated some of its humanitarian efforts through the service given at the Saint Benedict's Hospital, established in Ogden in 1946.[51]

The Child Culture Club has had a long tenure in the county. The club organized in 1897 to "co-operate with mothers . . . in meeting the problems which confront all mothers in the formative period of their childrens' lives." Annie Wright, Ellen Hamer, Martha Wright, Jane Ballantyne, Minnie Farr, and C. E. Driver helped organize this group. Yearbooks show that in addition to study of the child from infancy to adolescence, the club also studied economics, hygiene, art, U.S. history, and home economics. They raised money for a community swimming pool and performed service work for food conservation and the Red Cross during the wars. This organization continues to perform community work at the present time.

The Martha Society of Ogden started out as the Ogden Charity Society in 1908 when it was organized in the home of Mrs. Frank Cannon, who was the first president. Martha Cannon died shortly after the establishment of the society, and the name was changed in her honor to the Martha Society. Through the years, the society has done much community service, including the opening of a day nursery in 1913 for working mothers, which expanded to both day and night care later on and eventually took motherless children and placed them in homes or helped work out adoption of the children. In 1919 there were 122 children being cared for, of which twenty-one were motherless children. In 1920 a Martha Junior Society was formed to allow young women to support the programs of the Martha Society. In 1938 the Martha Society had to close the Martha Home Nursery, and in 1947 the Martha League disbanded and turned over its remaining funds ($10,000) to the Welfare League of Ogden.

The Welfare League of Ogden was organized on 27 March 1934, with Dolores Eccles as one of the founders and the first president. The Welfare League existed until 1953, when it became the Junior League of Ogden and was accepted into the National Association of Junior Leagues. Throughout the years, the Junior League has expanded its community involvement from social and health-oriented projects to cultural and educational programs, based on the needs of the community. These projects have included well baby clinics, establishment of the YWCA in Ogden, bringing the Utah Symphony Orchestra to Ogden for concerts, organizing a community arts council, and establishing the Bertha Eccles Art Center. The Junior League continues to support many important community programs.[52]

Besides the clubs and societies established by the women of Weber County, the men of the county have had their fraternal, social, and civic clubs. Some men's organizations were national organizations that had their origins in the nineteenth century. Among them in Weber County were the Grand Army of the Republic, the Knights of Columbus, the Chinese National League of America, the Intermountain Japanese Association, the Ancient Free and Accepted Masons, the Benevolent Protective Order of Elks, the Brotherhood of American Yeomen, the Fraternal Order of Eagles, the Independent Order of Odd Fellows, the Knights of Pythias, the Knights of the Maccabees, the Loyal Order of Moose, the Modern Woodmen of America, the Woodmen of the World, the Royal Neighbors of America, the Sons of Herman, the United Commercial Travelers, and the Neighbors of Woodcraft. After World War I, the American Legion became a major organization. Many of these organizations remained active in the county until mid-century, with Rotary International, Kiwanis International, Lions Club, and the Masons remaining the most active in contemporary civic affairs.[53]

It has been estimated that there are more that 200 different clubs functioning in Weber County. Some of the long-term organizations still functioning in 1996 include the Rotary Club, Kiwanis Club, Lions Club, American Legion, Junior League, Masons, Eagles Lodge, and Elks Lodge. Others are the General Federated Women's Club, which has two active organizations in Ogden; the Fine Arts Guild; and the World Affairs Club. Other clubs include the Altrusa Club, the Junior League of Women Voters, Daughters of Utah Pioneers, Daughters of the American Revolution, Toastmasters International, the Weber County Historical Society, Southern Pacific Oldtimers, Sons of Utah Pioneers, Sons of the American Revolution, and Veterans of Foreign Wars.[54]

Strongest of all the general service organizations outside of the established churches has been the YCC (Your Community Connection) organization. In 1995 this organization celebrated its fiftieth anniversary and looked back on that many years of community service. In 1945 the YCC was first formed as the Young Women's Christian Association (YWCA) for Ogden and Weber County. Mattie Wattis Harris was recognized a "founding mother" of that first society. The YMCA chapter in Ogden always tailored its programs to meet the needs of the local community. During the 1950s and 1960s, it concentrated on the needs of the youth, focusing on what it recognized as problems of youth in a "non-conformity rebellion" and an attempt by youth to "find" themselves. In the 1970s the YWCA organized such programs as the Rape Crisis Program, the Women's Crisis Center, the Crisis Hotline, and the Child Care Center. In the 1980s similar programs continued, and in 1982 several award programs were developed to bring recognition to community members who were doing outstanding service. Programs of educational counseling, parenting classes, and programs for families with violence and poverty problems were instituted. In 1987 the YWCA constructed a new 22,000-square-foot facility at 2261 Adams Avenue at a cost of $2,500,000, giving them better facilities to serve an ever-growing clientele.

In 1988 a major change in the organization was made. The YWCA membership at that time voted to open the association's membership to men and in that way become a full community-service agency which would better meet the needs of all of the people. By this action, the organization was disaffiliated from the national YWCA and took the new name of "Your Community Connection of Ogden/Northern Utah." This new status led to a more comprehensive approach to community service. Under this new concept, the Child Care Center was expanded in service, the Family Treatment Center provided many aids to help families in violence and abuse crises, and a literacy training program was added. In the 1990s many grants were obtained from government, church, and business organizations, which led to more extensive programs. It led to attorneys providing free legal advice, VISTA volunteers working with homeless families, the conversion of some apartments into a transitional housing program, a fast-track home buyer's program to help families to get into their first home, and a $900,000 project to build a youth center. The YCC has been a major player in the Weber County community with Gaye D. Littleton as executive director of the organization.[55]

## *Churches and Religious Activities*

Religious developments were another part of the cultural scene in the twentieth century. The Mormon church still remained the dominant religion in the county, but there was significant growth and additions of different faiths during the century. At the turn of the century, there was one Mormon stake—the Weber Stake—in the county. In 1920 there were three Mormon stakes in the county—the Ogden Stake, the North Ogden Stake, and the Weber Stake. By 1955 there were seven Mormon stakes in the county; and by 1996 there were thirty-two stakes in the county. Important Mormon church leaders during this period whose roots were in Weber County include David O. McKay, who was appointed president of the church in 1951 and served in that capacity until his death in 1970, and William J. Critchlow, Jr., who had served as a stake president in the Weber area before being appointed an assistant to the Quorum of the Twelve Apostles in 1958. The Mormon church erected a tabernacle on Washington Boulevard and 22nd Street as well as approximately seventy-five chapels, education buildings, and church welfare buildings in the Ogden area during the first half of the twentieth century.[56] The Ogden temple of the Church of Jesus Christ of Latter-day Saints was completed in 1972.

The David O. McKay Hospital was opened in Ogden in 1969, and the Thomas D. Dee Wing of the hospital was added in 1971. At that time, the name of the hospital was changed to the McKay-Dee Hospital and the old Dee Hospital on 24th Street was razed. The Mormon church had assumed ownership of the Dee Hospital in 1915 and continued to be involved in ownership of the McKay-Dee Hospital until 1976, at which time ownership was transferred to Intermountain Health Care.

The Catholic church has been very active in the Weber County area during the twentieth century, with its main parish located at St. Joseph's church at 24th Street and Adams Avenue. In addition to St. Joseph's, the church operated the Sacred Heart Academy, which was constructed at 25th Street and Quincy in 1879 and operated as a girls boarding school under the Sisters of the Holy Cross until it was discontinued and the buildings demolished in the early 1960s. Another important area in which the Catholic church made contributions in Weber County was the establishment of the St. Benedict Hospital, built in 1946 and located on the east bench of Ogden. The hospital was operated by the Sisters of St. Benedict, whose Mother House was in St. Joseph, Minnesota. Sister Mary Margaret was the first administrator of this hospital.[57] The hospital was moved from the Ogden bench to Washington Terrace on 6 March 1977, and the institution changed its name to the Ogden Regional Medical Center on 15 August 1994.

The First Presbyterian church sold its church and property on 24th Street and Adams Avenue in 1949 and built a new church at 28th and Quincy Avenue. By 1940 the Elim Lutheran church had outgrown its chapel on 23rd Street and plans were made to construct a new chapel; but the war years delayed that project until 1947 when construction commenced. The new church was completed in 1949 at 575 23rd Street. The Missouri Synod Lutheran church began its missionary efforts in Weber County in 1931 and was formally organized as a congregation in 1942 as St. Paul's Evangelical

Lutheran Church of Ogden. After meeting for many years in rented halls, the Missouri Synod built a church at 28th Street and Quincy Avenue in 1942; after a war-time increase in membership, the congregation constructed a more adequate building at 3329 Harrison Boulevard, which was dedicated in 1963. The Baptist church built its distinctive New England style church at 25th and Jefferson Avenue in 1926 after selling is properties and church near 24th and Grant Avenue to the Ogden Japanese Union church. The new building was constructed at a cost of $110,000. In 1924 the Methodist church sold its church located on 24th Street, and in 1925 it acquired the James Pingree home at 26th Street and Jefferson Avenue for $27,000 to serve as a temporary chapel and "Community House." Plans were soon made to construct a church on property adjacent to the Pingree home. On 28 April 1929 the new church was dedicated by Bishop Charles L. Mead, with Dr. Charles W. Hancher, district superintendent of the mission, and the Reverend Lester P. Fagen, pastor, assisting in the dedication. [58]

The Catholic church added another major church building in South Ogden with the building of the Holy Family Catholic Church in 1981. The Saint Joseph's church on 24th Street also received some major refurbishing to maintain its importance as a religious and historical edifice in the downtown area of Ogden. The needs of the people of the inner city were also served by the work done at St. Mary's church and St. Anne's Rescue Mission. The Episcopal Church of the Good Shepherd congregation was able to save its historic church at 24th and Grant Avenue from being torn down during the reconstruction of the city mall area, and it remains as a historical religious site. The Washington Heights Baptist church built a new meetinghouse on Highway 89 in South Ogden in 1989, and the Crossroads Christian Fellowship built a new church at 6545 Combe Road in 1992.

In all, there were some fifty-nine different religious denominations listed in the Weber County area in 1996. Almost all were Christian; but some, including Buddhist and Zen congregations, were of other religions. Some residents of Weber County chose not to affiliate with any religious organization.

## *The Growth of Ethnic Diversity*

Weber County was early recognized as a place where diverse cultures came into contact with the mainly Mormon culture which had dominated the area in Utah's territorial days. For many years the transcontinental railroad brought outside cultures into Utah, and Ogden was the gateway of entry.

The importance of the Native American culture that was in northern Utah as Anglo-American settlement came and how it was affected by the Mormons and others has been recounted earlier. Weber County Native Americans suffered the same fate that befell Utah Indians and American Indians generally after the settlement period and the end of the American Civil War. United States government policy was mainly responsible for any new policies in regard to Native Americans. In the 1860s the spread of settlement and travel in Indian lands in Utah led to widespread Indian unrest and a war known as the Black Hawk War. In 1860 the Shoshoni took offense at the white movement into northern Utah and, as a result, a band of Shoshoni raided farms near the South Weber (Kington Fort) area. At that same time, raids near Willard (Willow Creek) brought out the Weber County Militia to protect the area.[59]

In the late nineteenth century the federal government followed a policy generally approved by Utahns of moving Indians to reservations to train them in what the government called the "arts of civilization." Under President U.S. Grant the government developed plans to put many Indians in the West on various reservations. For northern Utah Indians, this meant that the Shoshonis were placed on the Fort Hall Reservation near Blackfoot, Idaho, and the Wind River Reservation in Wyoming. Some Northwestern Shoshoni took homesteads under Mormon church direction at Washakie in northern Utah. Ute Indians ended up at the Uintah and Ouray Reservation in the Uinta Basin. This policy essentially put all Native Americans on limited reservation lands without paying for or otherwise recognizing the tribal lands that they had occupied when the white settlers had come. In 1887 the government changed its policy by enacting the Dawes Severalty Act that designated that the reservation land should be broken up into farming allotments given to individual Indians, with the purpose of changing their old tribal lifestyle and integrating them into the white society as farmers, a lifestyle that Indians little understood or approved of. In 1905 the federal government opened many unclaimed Indian lands to white settlement, and a large amount of land in the Uintah-Ouray Reservation was taken over by white claimants.

The overall effect of these government policies on Weber County Native Americans was to remove most of the population of Shoshonis onto the Fort Hall Reservation or to the Washaki area. Virtually all the Weber County Shoshoni went there, and they did not subsequently live in or visit Weber County except when invited to participate in pioneer parades or celebrations to represent the early inhabitants of the county or when they were on food-gathering expeditions in the county area.

Reservation life was difficult and degrading in many ways under the allotment policy of the federal government. In 1934, through the work of John Collier of the Bureau of Indian Affairs, a new policy established under the Wheeler-Howard Indian Reorganization Act proposed that native peoples should be encouraged to maintain their native cultures and organize tribal councils to run and govern their reservations and tribal organizations.

Later, in the 1950s, things changed again when the U.S. government began a program which is described as the "Termination Program." It proposed that the federal government terminate the government's special relationship with the Indians—stop providing schooling, medical care, and roads—and let the Indians manage their own affairs. As a result of these policies, Native Americans were more free to move off the reservations and move about in society. In Weber County, many came to seek work in such employment as railroad workers, and some were engaged in the track crews that laid and maintained the railroad routes. Some school-age Native Americans came into the county through the Mormon church's Indian Placement Program, which placed young Native Americans in Mormon homes to be provided a home environment and an opportunity to attend county schools, with the idea that this would improve their skills and ability to function in the Anglo society in a way that was not provided on the reservation. Northwestern

Shoshoni historian Mae Parry suggests that a young man of the Washaki group was the first to be placed under this program. His Anglo name was James Brown, and he was named after the Brown family with whom he lived in Weber County. He later became an interpreter of the Shoshoni language for the federal government.

Native Americans thus began to filter back into Weber County. In the period of World War II many Native Americans served in the armed forces and others came to Weber County as workers in the war industries and as farm laborers. With this trend, many Native Americans became citizens integrated into the broader local society and in many ways left their tribal culture behind.

In recent years there has been a greater effort to preserve the native culture. One aspect of this was helped along by Ernest Wilkinson, who was raised and educated in Weber County and was student body president of Weber College from 1916 to 1918. Wilkinson became an attorney and represented the Ute Indian Tribe in a case against the United States, which, under a due-process claim that the government had taken original tribal lands from the Native Americans when they were moved to the limited reservations, awarded payment for that land taken. In 1950 this case awarded some $31.7 million to the Ute Tribe and started a whole movement of other tribes of the United States to get similar payments. Wilkinson also acted as attorney for the Northwestern Shoshoni, which had a direct effect on some of the Indians who lived in Weber County.

Another reason for Native Americans coming into Weber County was the organization of the Intermountain Indian School in Brigham City, which functioned from 1950 until it closed in 1984.[60] Many Native Americans employed there lived and socialized in Weber County; and many Native American programs such as powwows and other cultural events were brought to the county through that school. Weber State University was a major promoter of Native American students and their culture. Many Native American students attended and received degrees from the university, and a Native American counsellor was assigned to deal with special needs. A Native American club and Indian Week activities made university and community people more aware of the presence of the Native Americans and their culture. Enrollment of Native American students at Weber

State in the 1980s reached approximately 300; but it dropped to eighty-three in 1987 after the Intermountain Indian School was closed. In 1996, following a concerted effort by Weber State to bring more minority students to the campus, this number had increased to 109 Indian students representing several tribal groups throughout the United States.[61]

Among the important Native American leaders who have impacted Weber County is Mae Parry, who lives in Davis County and has done much to teach and develop recognition of the Indian history in the area. In 1984 Mae and her brother, Frank Timbimboo, were among several people who placed the Indian Trails Monument in North Ogden Pass; it outlined the main Indian trails of the area and the early history of the Indians in Weber County. Walter Ottergary, George P. Sam, Lee Deaman, and Wallace Zundel are other local area Indian leaders. One of the reasons that Native Americans have not had a great impact on the Weber County region is that in many ways they have chosen to integrate into the society and have not unified like some other ethnic groups to push for their particular interests. Thus the small Native American population in the county has not been a strong political force.[62]

African-Americans came into the area in the nineteenth century as railroad workers. This trend continued in the twentieth century, and in the war years others arrived to work as military personnel or defense workers. In 1900 there were 678 blacks living in the state, with 80 percent of them residing in Salt Lake and Uintah counties. Many were soldiers in the army on Indian reservation duty. Weber County in 1900 had fifty-one black people, 9 percent of the state's total black population. In 1978 it was estimated that there were 7,870 blacks in Utah, 81.7 percent of whom were in Salt Lake (3,300), Weber (2,400), and Davis (730) counties; and the preponderance of these people were living in the inner-city districts of Salt Lake City and Ogden. The 1990 census reported 2,533 African-Americans living in Weber County, 1.6 percent of the county population.[63]

Some blacks who came to Weber County early in this century found life lonely. Lloyd Cope arrived in Ogden in the 1930s from Kansas City to work as a railroad worker. He remembered, "Oh, it was terrible. I got here and snow was piled up all over the streets. I wanted to go back. There weren't any black people here." But Cope and others stayed and raised their families. James Turner remembered arriving in the 1930s and that he "didn't like it here at first . . . But then I started working on the road, going from one place to another and I started to like traveling. So I stayed."[64] Prior to World War II, most African-Americans in Ogden worked for the railroads, and their jobs were in service positions. Many worked as porters, waiters, and cooks, with a white supervisor overseeing their work. Some held jobs in the railroad shops or as boiler washers or engine wipers—hard and unskilled types of jobs, for the most part. During the highest period of employment there were twenty African-Americans who served as Redcaps at the Union Station. Many African-American women worked in domestic service, usually as housekeepers for private employers.

Most of the influx of African-Americans in 1938–39 came with the increase of federal defense agencies coming to the area; and the increases in the 1950s directly resulted from military-based industrial growth during and after World War II. It is clear that Ogden's African-American population grew from people coming in from the outside and not from an internal birth rate.[65]

For the most part, during the first half of the twentieth century, African-Americans in Weber County were segregated physically and socially from others in the community. This segregation forced African-Americans to live in an area of Ogden which was six blocks wide and stretched lengthwise north to south from 24th Street to 30th Street and between Grant and Wall avenues.[66] During the period from 1920 to 1950 there were some area African-Americans who managed or owned businesses. Harold Gray earned a living as a junk dealer in 1924; Temezia Gray owned a rooming house at 165 26th Street. Jesse Williams was a farmer in Farr West, Sam Smith was a bricklayer, and Elmer Hatton was a butcher in 1935.

Some African-American businesses had a high profile in the city; but most were transient in nature, not lasting for long periods of time. Most of these businesses were located in the area of 25th Street and along Wall Avenue because it was close to the area where African-Americans lived and worked. In about 1932 Eugene Howard opened a barber shop at 109 25th Street which lasted through the 1940s. The

White Front Cafe was at 115 25th Street; it later became the White Front Bar and Cafe, managed by Joe and Dora Williams. George Smith ran the Silver Dollar Pool Hall for a number of years at 169 25th; it also was where Post No. 66 of the American Legion of African-American members held its meetings. Velma McHenry and Helen Walker ran the Wonder Coffee Shop at 131 25th which lasted throughout the 1940s. Jerome Brawley had a billiards hall which later became Jerome's Breakfast Club. Leon King had the Shadow Land Club at 165 25th and the One Eleven Cafe at 111 25th Street. Ralph Price had a gas station on the corner of 25th Street and Lincoln until after World War II.

Businesses off 25th Street included Sloppy Joe's at 2702 Wall Avenue. The Cotton Club, run by Leager Davis, was located in the Davis Hotel at 2548 Wall Avenue. Davis owned the Davis Hotel and sold it after acquiring the Royal Hotel at 2522 Wall Avenue. Dewey's Record Store operated in the south lobby of the Davis Hotel. Tillie Jones owned Tillie's Cottage Beauty Shop at 133 27th Street. Scott Stewart, Jr., organized a model airplane club and opened a model airplane store on Washington Boulevard in 1948.[67]

The largest businesses run by African-Americans were the hotels—the Porters' and Waiters' Club, the Davis Hotel, and the Royal Hotel. The Davis Hotel was the first to offer rooms to all African-Americans in Ogden; the Porters' and Waiters' Club provided rooms only to railroad workers. In 1942 the federal government took over the Davis Hotel and converted it to government housing for military and defense workers, and it became essentially an all white hotel. It was at that time that Leager Davis bought the Royal Hotel and turned it into a hotel for African-Americans. Earlier it has been a hotel that advertised that it was the "Headquarters for Livestock and Sheepmen," and, in fact, it became a favorite place for Basque visitors to room. In a recent remodeling of the building, a large room was found which had served as a jai alai court for a game that was popular among Basque people, many of whom had come to the region as sheep herders. It became the only hotel for African-Americans in Ogden. It was the place where the Harlem Globetrotters roomed while playing in Ogden, even after integration had begun to take place.[68]

Ogden's 25th Street looking east from the Union Station in 1928. (Utah State Historical Society)

The Porters' and Waiters' Club became the most popular, the most familiar, and one of the longest established African-American businesses in Ogden. The Porters' and Waiters' Club started out in about 1916 as a hotel-like facility for black railroad employees who worked in the sleeping and dining cars of the transcontinental trains. Its first location was at 151 25th Street as the "Railroad Porters and Waiters Club," but it later relocated to 127 25th Street. It eventually became a ninety-three-bed dormitory-style hotel where black porters and waiters could lodge overnight or for several days in between their runs. It provided not only room and board but also a club atmosphere that made the clientele feel welcome. Whites frequented the club, but for a time they were denied access. The cost to the individual was 25 cents a night before World War II; later the rates reached $1.25 per night. The club was subsidized by the Union Pacific and Southern Pacific railroads and other companies using the Ogden terminal. The railroads paid yearly sums to help finance the club.

As early as 1909 efforts began to form such a club. Billy Weakley, through the help of the Weber Club, got things going with the location of a place to accommodate black railroad workers. The club was first managed by F. K. Turner, but later Billy Weakley became the club president. Weakley and Turner were considered to be two of the most prominent members of the local African-American community through the 1920s, 1930s, and 1940s. Weakley's wife, Anna Belle, also played a major role in making the club successful. She helped make certain the club was respectable and a symbol of "caring and a place of pride." A former Ogden police captain, Clifford Keeter, claimed that the police had little trouble with the Porters' and Waiters' Club. The club finally closed in 1960 and the building was torn down. Anna Belle Weakley ran a restaurant nearby until 1970. When the Ogden Hilton was built in the area, it honored her by naming one of the hotel restaurants "Annabelle's."[69]

African-Americans were not only segregated physically in Weber County during the first half of the twentieth century, they also were segregated socially and religiously. A recent study by Eric Stene concludes that local segregation was more of an indifference to the plight of the African-Americans than it was a vicious and malevolent racism that was shown in other parts of the country where larger African-American populations seemed to be threatening to others in the society. Stene quotes James Gillespie in regards to black-white relations in Utah: "In Mississippi [Gillespie's birthplace] they'll kill you, in Utah they just starve you to death." Gillespie went on to maintain that because many white Utahns have had little or no contact with African-Americans or their community, they believe Utah does not have a race problem. However, among African-Americans in Weber County there seemed to be plenty of race problems, and there was plenty of blame to go around.[70] Segregation occurred in movie theaters, for example, where whites only were allowed on the main floor while blacks and Asians were to sit in the balcony.

Since the middle of the nineteenth century, the Mormon church had not allowed black male members to hold the priesthood of the church, which limited their membership because they were not able to hold positions of leadership in the local congregations. This situation lasted until 1978, when the Mormon priesthood was opened to all "worthy" male members. This long tradition of denial gave many

African-Americans in the Weber County area little interest in becoming members of or close to the Mormon church. For many years African-Americans also felt that the local newspaper, the *Ogden Standard-Examiner*, played up their difficulties with the police, gave them undue attention and publicity, and used racist language in many of their stories.

During World War II, black troops passing through Ogden were directed to the segregated recreational center at 27th and Wall Avenue. They were not allowed to visit the other U.S.O. sites situated elsewhere in the city and available for other troops. At the end of the war, the center became the Wall Avenue Community Center to accommodate persons of every nationality.[71]

An incident in 1944 involving a young African-American man by the name of Clifford Worley, Jr., living in Washington Terrace led directly to the establishment of the National Association for the Advancement of Colored People (NAACP) in the county. The young man was killed during an altercation as he tried to board a bus in Ogden to report for induction into the army in Oklahoma. The bus driver thought Worley was drunk and refused to let him board the bus. After trying to board again, Worley was ejected and the police were called. In the confusion, the young man ran away and was shot in the back by a policeman. The shooting was ruled as justifiable homicide by a police board. The African-American community was particularly angered at this shooting and the board's ruling, and it resulted in the organization of a chapter of the NAACP in Ogden and Weber County.[72]

One of the most disturbing incidents of segregation came in 1958 when, during the planning and building of the Washington Terrace community, the governing body tried to segregate twenty-two black families to a particular part of the project. This was rejected by the families concerned, who took their case to the federal courts. After several meetings with the board of directors, they were allowed to move their project houses to a more acceptable site, and a court case was avoided.[73]

Because of the limitations placed on Weber County African-Americans by segregation, the African-American community created their own religious and social organizations. There were three main churches attended by African-American churchgoers. The Embry Chapel of the African Methodist Episcopal church was organized in 1908, with J. C. Owens as its first pastor. In 1913 they had their first chapel at 2817 Pingree Avenue, with a chapel capacity of 100 people. A second congregation was the Wall Avenue Baptist church, with A. J. Billingsley as the first pastor. It met in a red brick building located at 2701 Wall Avenue from which it took its name. In 1939 Reverend Donald Mosher organized a Pentecostal congregation located at 165 25th Street. It closed in 1944. In 1946 Reverend Brealy B. Mike organized another significant African-American church in Ogden, the Church of God in Christ. Female members, as in most Christian churches, made up the largest part of these congregations.[74]

Area African-Americans remained segregated in most social activities. The churches provided many activities, but there were men's social clubs such as the Colored Benevolent Protective Order of Elks of the World, the Esquire Club, the Calendar Club, and the Beau Brummel Club. For women, there was the Gardenia Girls Club, the Anytimers Club, the Elite Club, and the Ladies Inspirational Club. On occasion, these groups rented the Berthana Dance Hall or the Old Mill Club, which would be used for a dance and party. The American Legion Pioneer Post No. 66 functioned as a social organization for many black war veterans.

Sports also gave the black community some recreational involvement. In 1910 a baseball team of African-Americans started playing in Ogden as the Occidental Baseball Team. Al Langford and "Red" Toner were two of the outstanding pitchers for the team. In 1910 they won the championship of their league. There were also some local boxers from Ogden in the 1940s such as Buddy Washington, Paul Perkins, and Benny Flake. There were only a few African-American athletes on the public school teams at this time.

In 1930 there were forty-four African-Americans of school age in Weber County, and in 1940 there were forty-five. With these small numbers there was no segregation of the students, but it was often lonely and difficult for young people who were minority students. In 1941 Ethelda Kinsey became the first African-American student to receive a degree from Weber Junior College.[75] With the ruling by the Supreme Court of the United States in the *Brown v. Board of*

*Education* case in 1954 against segregation and with a more aggressive mood of eliminating discrimination arising throughout the country, many racial attitudes began to change after the mid-1950s.

In the past three decades leaders from the black community have been highly involved in Weber County affairs. They have included James and Bettye Gillespie, James Gillespie, Jr., Donald Carpenter, Forrest Crawford, Betty Sawyer, Selma Hutchinson, Willie and Betty Stewart Moore, Freddie Cooper, Dovie Goodwin, Mary Tolliver, Ann Brown, Marguerite Allen-Horton, Shirley Jones, Nathan Johnson, Bobby Allen, John Miller, Chandler Owens, and George Merritt. Some African-Americans have been involved in local government; they include Otis Walton, a member of the Ogden City Planning Commission; Robert Harris, a member of the Utah State Legislature; George Garwood, a member of the South Ogden City Council; H. C. Massey, executive director of the Ogden Area Community Action Agency; Ed Taylor, Utah Job Service; Donald Cope, Ombudsman for the State of Utah; and Velma Saunders, longtime receptionist for the Weber County Commission. The number of black athletes on teams at Weber State University has grown, and a number of these athletes have gone on to play for professional teams including Lee White, Henry Owens, Bob Wilson, Carter Campbell, Bruce Collins, Bob Davis, Stan Mayhew, and Willie Sojourner.

The first Asians to arrive in Weber County came as workers on the transcontinental railroad, and this influx continued into the twentieth century. The Chinese were particularly responsible for the success of the Central Pacific Railroad. Some Japanese people came to Utah in the 1880s to work as railroad track workers, replacing Chinese men who had left because of unfavorable treatment. Some Japanese immigrants also worked in the mines, sometimes being used as "scab" laborers when other workers went on strike; and many of them turned to farming as soon as they had the opportunity to do so, since many of them had been farmers in Japan. These Japanese farmers settled mainly in Box Elder, Weber, and Salt Lake counties and became known for their nationally distributed brands of "Sweetheart" and "Jumbo" celery and "Twentieth Century" strawberries.[76] Sugar beets, tomatoes, and onions were also important crops on these farms.

Some of the first Japanese farmers in Weber County were Genasku Miyagishima (generally know in the area as Jimmy Miya after his name was shortened by local use and judicial papers), the Yashimura family, the Kawaguichi family, the Kato family, the Yoshida family, and the Ushida family.[77] They proved to be excellent farmers, and they were also loyal American citizens, although they were not given that recognition during World War II. At that time, under the War Relocation Program of the United States, thousands of Japanese-Americans were sent to fifteen relocation camps in Rocky Mountain and Midwestern states. Utah had one camp, Topaz, located north of the city of Delta in Millard County. Most of the Japanese-American citizens of the far western United States were sent to these camps and kept as virtual prisoners of the government. As the war progressed, a movement to allow these Japanese-Americans to show their loyalty was organized by Mike Masaoka of Salt Lake City, who was working as a leader of the Japanese-American Citizens League. Masaoka and others were able to convince the government to allow the young men of the camps to serve in the army as a demonstration of their loyalty. As a result of this effort, a segregated army unit was organized—the 442 Regimental Combat Team—which served in the Italian Campaign in Europe and suffered the highest percentage of casualties of any unit in the war. Several Weber residents served in that unit, including Roy Yoshinaga, George Nakano, and Sam Yei.

Many Japanese-Americans who came to Weber County before the war were not affected by the relocation movement, but they still became victims of local prejudices. Many were called derogatory names in public, and some were denied service and business. Others were threatened with violence, and most had to live a rather restricted life in the community. There were some, however, who overcame this negative treatment. They included Wat Misaka, who played basketball at Ogden High and later was a starting player on the University of Utah basketball team that won the NCAA Tournament in 1944; Raymond Uno, who became a Utah State District court judge; and Robert Mukai, a professor of communication at Weber State College and died in an accident while returning from a debate trip.

After World War II, the Japanese citizens in Weber County were able to assume a greater role in the communities, and many families continued their farming. Some Japanese people organized businesses; they included Kay's Market, run by the Inouye family; the Eagles Cafe, run by the Kinomoto family; Kiesel Sales and Service, established by Mits Koga and run by his sons; Kay's Noodle, established by the Mukai family; the Bamboo Noodle run by Sam Yei; Star Noodle, run by George and Tom Ryujin; and Utah Noodle, established by Leo Iseki. Many of the younger generation of Japanese-Americans after the war went on further in education and achieved success in engineering, law, medicine, education, and other professions.

Many of the Japanese residents of Weber County affiliated with the Buddhist church or the Japanese Christian church; as time went on, others associated with other religious groups in the county. It is estimated that many, perhaps as high as 65 percent, of the marriages involving one Japanese partner involved a person of a different ethnic background. Such intermarriage had a great impact on the traditions and religious practices of the Japanese in the community. As a result, there has been a tendency among the Japanese to be associated with a movement known as "Kenjin Kai," or focus-group clubs, that associate with people on a broader basis than do the traditional religions. Two strong Kenjin Kai in Weber County are the Hiroshima-Ken and the Shiquoka-Ken.

The Chinese influence in the county which began in the nineteenth century has become more diversified in the twentieth century. Chinese restaurants dot the county, and several Chinese teachers and professionals have become involved in the community. Asian Indians, Iranians, Hawaiians, Tongans, Samoans, and immigrants from Southeast Asia have also made important contributions to the culture and economy of the county since World War II.

The Italian involvement in Weber County began in the nineteenth century. A large migration of Italians came to the county in the late nineteenth and early twentieth centuries when many Italian men came as railroad workers; many later became farmers. Among the Italian families that arrived at that time were the Favero, DeGiorgio, Punanzio, Martini, Ropelato, Delpais, Rauzi, D'Agnillo, Anselmi, and Colletti families, who settled in the outlying farm areas of the county. Their farms produced some of the usual truck garden crops and beef cattle, and Giovani Favero had a specialty of breeding and raising Perchon work horses.[78]

Another group of Italians included the Poce, Greco, Poppinga, Gentile, Genetti, Ligori, and Viscogliosi families. These families settled in the area of 21st and 22nd streets near Wall Avenue. This small community in Ogden were drawn together by the Santa Maria Mission of the Catholic church and remained together until the mid-1950s when they dispersed into the broader society. Another portion of the Weber County Italian community was associated with the World War II era when Italian prisoners of war were incarcerated at the Ogden General Depot. Following the war, some of these prisoners married local women and became residents of Weber County. In this group were Gene Miconi, Mario Alfonsi, Joseppe Giordano, and Giuseppe Batisti.[79]

Many of these Italian families are associated with Weber County business operations and some still remain in the agricultural business. Among the Italian business families at present are Tony Toscan, Rigo DeCarlo, and Ted Ligori in the restaurant business; the Durbanos in law and the metal business; and the Miconis in the tile business. Mike Panunzio and John Favero have remained in commercial farming.[80]

Many of the first Greeks in the county came in the early 1900s; for example, John Thiros came in 1906 and Alex Papageorge came in 1910. Others coming at that period were Nick Malkogianisis and Jim Nasiopoulos (Nass). The possibility of a better economic future drew many Greeks to America. Many new arrivals were helped by a kind of employment placement operation run by Harry Gavaris at the Arcade Hotel on 25th Street in Ogden. Gavaris helped many to find jobs in a variety of employments. As time went on, many Greeks became land owners and sheepmen. Alex Papageorge became a farmer and dairyman in the Taylor area; Herman and George Markos were farmers in the Plain City region; John Thiros, Nick Chournos, Jim Nass, and Nick Souravlis were all Weber County sheepmen working out of Huntsville and North Ogden. John Thiros used his ewe sheep for milk, which he made into sheep cheese and then used to supply a regional market; he was also involved in the lamb and wool business.

Some Greeks went into retail business in the county. Harry Pappas owned considerable property on 25th Street and ran a club there. Herman Markos had a wholesale candy business. John Dokos and John Bochus made candy, and Bochus ran a confectionery shop, the Sweet Shop, on 25th Street. The Cutrubus family first established themselves in Ogden as proprietors of a cigar store with a confectionery and soda fountain on 25th Street; they later became owners of automobile dealerships.

Early in the century, the Greek community was religiously oriented to the Greek Orthodox church in Salt Lake City; but in 1964 the Ogden congregation built the Greek Orthodox Church of the Transfiguration on 42nd Street in South Ogden. In addition to the religious services there, the church has become known for its annual Greek Food Festival, which draws people from all parts of the area to savor the Greek food specialties.[81]

Several Armenian families also came to Weber County. Many of the Armenians had been victims of Turkish persecution which forced them to migrate. Some of these people made their way to Utah and Weber County. The Hasratian, Plowgian, Aposian, and Arslanian families were among those who came to Weber County and made lasting impressions in the community. Sark Arslanian and his son David both have been football coaches at Weber State University.

The Jewish community in Weber County has always been small, and only Salt Lake County and Weber County were recognized as having any sort of organized Jewish minyan.[82] As late as 1970 there were only 2,500 Jews living in the state of Utah. Nevertheless the Jewish influence was felt in Weber County through the years because of the activities of such people as Abraham Kuhn, businessman, and Fred J. Kiesel, businessman and mayor of Ogden. Before 1920 there were several Jewish families in Ogden, and many of them had established small clothing stores on 25th Street. Some of the first merchants there were Joseph and William Benovitz, who came in 1907 and established a clothing business. By 1940 L.R. Samuels had established one of Ogden's most prestigious apparel stores.

For several years the Jewish community held their services in the IOOF Hall located on Grant Avenue between 24th and 25th streets. In 1921 Jewish residents organized officially the Congregation Brith

Sholem, which celebrated its seventy-fifth anniversary in 1996. They erected a synagogue in 1921 at 2750 Grant Avenue which still serves the local congregation. Important in keeping that community together through the years have been Rabbi Finkelstein, Rabbi Barris, and Lillian Rubin. Other associations established by the community were the B'nai Brith Lodge Number 1390 and the Ogden Jewish Welfare Fund, both of which were established in 1939.

Early area Jewish families included the Benowitz brothers, Gordon brothers, Kertz brothers, Kreines brothers, and the Rosenberg, Oppman, Lutzker, Rubin, Rubenstein, Smith, Medoway, Oliash, Herscovitz, Greenband, Lavin, Booth, and Sugar families. In the 1920s and 1930s other Jewish families arrived to settle in the county. They included the Saperstein, Bruckner, Swartz, Seidner, Pally, Diamond, and Morrison families. During World War II many Jewish families came to the area with the military or through war-associated activities. Among the war-time arrivals were the Cohn, Meents, Rubin, Levy, Brodstein, Mazer, Pelham, Kaufman, Tachman, Shaw, Havas, and Kuperman families.

Many Jewish families came to Ogden during the 1940s, 1950s, and 1960s to manage retail chain stores; but, over the years, the community also saw individuals engaging in a variety of professions—doctors, lawyers, engineers—as well as diverse businesses such as grocery stores, a chicken ranch, sporting goods stores, animal by-products, tailoring, salvage, hide and fur, jewelry stores, pawn shops, and a ski resort. Many also were engaged in the arts, education, politics, charities, and the chamber of commerce.[83] In 1916 Simon Bamberger was nominated at the state Democratic party convention in Ogden as the party's candidate for the governorship, and he went on to win the 1916 election, becoming Utah's only Jewish governor.

The migration of Mexican and other Hispanic people into the United States increased in the period following the turn of the century. The migration was stimulated by the possibility of employment, especially during World War I. According to the census of 1920, there were 1,666 Mexicans in Utah. The opportunity to work on the railroad brought other Mexicans into Weber County in the 1920s and 1930s. By 1930 the number of Mexicans in Utah had grown to over 4,000 inhabitants. The sugar beet industry also attracted many workers after World War I, and, as a major producer of beets, Weber County attracted many of those workers. These workers generally organized into their own ethnic communities, known as *colonias,* where they essentially remained apart from the surrounding communities.[84]

After 1930 the *colonias* disappeared because the nature of the Mexican labor situation changed. Instead of staying in one place as agricultural laborers, the workers began to move across the country following the various labor jobs as they developed at different times. A migrant labor force developed and the *colonias* declined. At this time, the effects of the Depression reduced railroad construction activities and the Mexican workforce was cut back. The size of the Spanish-speaking community in the state was actually reduced during the Depression years. According to the 1930 census, there were 4,012 Mexicans living in Utah; by the 1940 census the number had dropped to 1,069. It was not until World War II and the build-up of government military installations in the Weber County area that Mexican laborers came back into Weber County in significant numbers as agricultural and defense workers. The number of Hispanic people in Weber County in the 1990s is approximately 12,000, nearly 7 percent of the county population.

Since World War II, much has changed in the nature of the Hispanic community. Moving from the status of farm laborers or workers on railroad track gangs to fully accepted middle-class residents has been a slow process which is still ongoing, just as the Hispanic population of the county is still growing. To assist in this transformation, many Hispanic organizations have been established. Among them are local affiliates of the national Movemento Estudiantil Chicanos de Atzlan (MECHA) and La Raza. On the state level, there are the Utah Office of Hispanic Affairs with its Hispanic Advisory Council, the Utah Office of Education, the Utah Coalition for Advancement of Minorities in Higher Education, and the Image of Utah. In Weber County there are the Ogden City Cultural Diversity Program; the Ogden School District Task Force on Hispanic/Bi-Lingual Education; Colors of Success; Success by Six; the Ogden City Multicultural Advisory Committee; and Origenes, a writers group to promote Spanish literature.[85]

Many in the Hispanic community have become county leaders, including Alex Hurtado, Richard Ulibarri, John Ulibarri, Christopher Rivera, Jim Sandoval, Jesse Garcia, Art Martinez, Lee Martinez, Vicki Magana, Cal C. Ortiz, Margarita Guerra, Diana Cortez, John Medina, Eleanor Pulida, John Henry Ibarguen, Gloria Perez-Jensen, and Maria Parrilla-Vasquez.

In the 1920s the Ku Klux Klan raised its head in the community for a short period of time. There seemed to be some religious connection to a protestant church leader in the area, and there was a demonstration against the Catholic community by the burning of two crosses on a mountainside during the dedication ceremonies for St. Joseph's parochial school in Ogden. Much later, in the spring of 1980, three white-robed members of the Riverton, Utah, chapter of the Knights of the Ku Klux Klan appeared on the campus of Weber State College to recruit students to their organization. This recruitment effort came in part because of a confrontation between Iranian students and others on the campus relative to the hostage situation in Iran. The recruitment efforts of the Klan proved to be futile.

From its earliest days, Weber County has been a melting pot for immigrants, and the influences of the fur trade and the railroad are now continued by government installations and educational institutions. The ethnic culture of the county continues to grow and develop with a rich and vibrant mix of peoples.

## *The Vietnam War*

The Vietnam War was very divisive in American society. Yet, regardless of the arguments about it, the war greatly affected many American men and women. Many Weber County citizens were drafted or volunteered for service; 4,840 Weber County citizens were involved directly in the war. Others of draft age avoided the war through various deferments such as marriage or status of dependents, college, military deferment as a member of the National Guard or the Reserve forces (which units for the most part were not called into the war), and conscientious objection. Those who served in the military spent their tours of duty in various kinds of military duty, with some involved in the fighting in the war zone of Vietnam. Of those who served from Weber County, several were killed and an undetermined number were wounded; but the survivors all came home to an uncelebrated homecoming, something much different from any of America's previous wars. This unenthusiastic and divisive aspect of the war hurt the veterans deeply, as they expressed their feelings in several veteran demonstrations and marches throughout the country.

Terry Schow served in Vietnam in 1970 as a member of the 5th Special Forces, and after returning from the war he became active in veterans' affairs and was president of the Northern Utah Veterans Association. Ty Whelan left Weber County as an enlistee in the Marine Corps and served in Vietnam with the 1st Marine Division of the 7th Fleet. He spent a year in the war operating out of fire bases around the area of Da Nang, where he was wounded twice and received the Purple Heart. Clayton Christiansen served in the 101st Airborne Division in Vietnam and saw action at different bases. He was injured with a shell concussion. Robert Chugg, a marine, was badly wounded in combat, and the wounds subsequently made his life difficult. The same happened to Richard Whitehead, who was badly wounded in the stomach. Mike Naegle served two tours in Vietnam, for a total of eighteen months. He was a marine volunteer and served his first tour as an aircraft mechanic in the area of Da Nang. During a second tour, he was flying missions in a C-47. Lynn Ward was drafted into the army in 1966 and served in Vietnam with the 4th Infantry Division for ten months during 1968. He came back with no physical wounds, but he was very disturbed by the reception he received in the community; some seemed to blame him for the things that were happening in the war.

The community of Farr West erected a monument honoring veterans of the community who served in World War I, World War II, Korea, Vietnam, and the Gulf War. Marine first lieutenant Serge B. Simmons of Farr West was among those killed in Vietnam; he died leaving his wife, Jane, and three children.[86] Under the direction of teacher Dave Thomas, Lynn Elementary School children in Ogden researched Weber County soldiers who died in the Vietnam War. They found thirty-one; one other also has been added to the list of Weber County servicemen who were killed in that war.[87] Weber County residents also served in Operation Desert Storm in Kuwait and Iraq in 1991 in the Persian Gulf conflict, and many Weber County citizens continue to support the military expeditions of the United States.

## *Education*

Education has undergone tremendous changes through the years, and those shifts have become apparent especially since the 1930s. On 1 July 1933, as the United States and the rest of the world suffered the worst depression in history, Weber College became a state junior college. Three junior colleges in Utah—Weber, Dixie, and Snow—were begun and operated by the Mormon church; but, in 1932, Snow College became a part of the state system of higher education, and a year later, in 1933, both Weber and Dixie were transferred to the state. Weber's facilities at the time included the Moench Building, with twelve lecture rooms, eight laboratories, an auditorium which could seat 800 people, and a library. Some classes were held in the Weber gymnasium. President Aaron Tracy's salary was set at $2,600 annually, while the seven highest paid faculty members received an annual salary of $1,600 each. The Utah State Board of Education was responsible for state junior colleges.

Enrollments at Weber grew during the next decade; from 683 in 1933–34 to 875 in 1938–39 and 1,337 during 1940–41. The number of students declined during World War II but grew rapidly following the war (465 during 1944–45 and 1,808 during the 1946–47 year). The *Signpost* was first published in 1937 as the campus student newspaper. From 1940 to 1952 the old Weber County Courthouse was used as a college dormitory; in 1948 the Bertha Eccles home was given to the college to be used as a women's dormitory.

Aaron Tracy was president of the college for thirteen years—from 1922 to 1935. He assisted with the transition from church to state control and worked under some difficult financial situations. In 1966 Tracy received the second honorary doctorate awarded by the new Weber State College; David O. McKay had received the first a year earlier. Leland H. Creer served as college president for two years, from 1935 to 1937, and Henry Aldous Dixon laid the foundations for the move to four-year status for the college during his presidency from 1937 to 1953. During World War II, Weber received national recognition for its technical division and war-effort work. Dixon laid the groundwork for the move to the new Harrison Avenue campus which began in 1952. For several years the college operated with a split campus—the Jefferson Avenue campus and the Harrison Avenue campus.

During the fall of 1949, work had begun on the new campus. During 1952 Weber was given authorization to begin a practical nursing program, which was begun during the fall quarter. On 8 August 1953 President Henry Aldous Dixon was appointed as president of Utah State Agricultural College and, a month later, William P. Miller was appointed president of Weber College. Miller served as president of the college for nineteen years, from 1953 to 1971—the longest tenure of any of the college's chief executives. Miller guided the growth and development of the new campus as well as navigating the college from its junior-college status to becoming a four-year institution.

The efforts of Weber College in gaining a new campus and moving to become a four-year institution were supported particularly by the citizens of Weber, Davis, and Morgan counties. Buildings were constructed on the new campus, including the first four classroom and administrative buildings, a technical-education building, a gymnasium, a library, and a student union building. In 1959 the state legislature approved a bill authorizing Weber to become a four-year state college, with the first graduating class of seniors in 1964. At the 1 June 1964 commencement sixteen bachelor of arts degrees and 249 bachelor of sciences degrees were awarded.

Joseph L. Bishop was appointed Weber State College president from 1972 until 1978; he was followed by President Rodney H. Brady, who served from 1978 to 1985. Stephen D. Nadauld was Weber State College president from 1985 until 1990; and Paul Thompson has served as Weber State president since 1990. Weber State College became Weber State University on 1 January 1991, with important support from the community. During this period of time, enrollments grew along with academic programs.

Primary and secondary education in Weber County has experienced great growth in this century. The Ogden School District has been relatively stable in terms of growth during the period since

1940. Total enrollments for the Ogden District by decade include 1940, 10,608 students; 1950, 12,237 students; 1960, 18,077 students; 1970, 16,801 students; 1980, 11,587 students; 1990, 12,109 students; and 12,791 students in 1995. The Weber County School District had 3,511 students in 1940 and 6,326 in 1950. By 1960 the total district enrollment was 10,423; and 19,235 students attended Weber District schools in 1970. In 1980 total enrollment was 21,152, with 25,860 attending in 1990; and, in 1995, 27,951 students attended schools in the Weber District. Private schools, particularly St. Joseph's and St. Paul Lutheran schools, have also seen substantial growth and development during this era.

The post–World War II years saw a burst of growth in both districts, and then, beginning with the 1960s, the Weber School District has experienced a building boom and the ensuing growth in school enrollments. Boards of education and school administrations in both districts have struggled to keep ahead of growth and deal with the ever-present problems of funding. School superintendents have offered stability during the growth era; they include Ogden School District superintendents W. Karl Hopkins (1940–1948); T.O. Smith (1948–1969); William L. Garner (1969–1987); James L. West (1987–1996); and Michael F. Paskewicz, who was appointed as superintendent in 1996.

William P. Miller served as superintendent of the Weber School District from 1940 to 1943; he was followed by A. Parley Bates (1943–1957) and Terel H. Bell (1957–1962), who later became United States Commissioner of Education in the administration of President Ronald Reagan. William R. Boren became the Weber District superintendent in 1962 and served until 1973. He was followed by G. Leland Burningham (1973–1982), Jay B. Taggart (1982–1988), and William Reese (1988–1993). Steven R. Mecham has served as Weber District superintendent since 1993.

Construction of new buildings as well as the remodeling of older buildings has been a continuing process in both districts. In 1996 Ogden School District had three high schools—Ben Lomond, Ogden, and Washington—four middle schools, and fifteen elementary schools. Weber District had four senior high schools—Bonneville,

Fremont, Roy, and Weber—eight junior high schools, and twenty-six elementary schools.

The Ogden-Weber Area Vocational Center was established in 1971 as a vocational training school, known at the time as the Utah Skill Center North. The school was first located in the old Madison School in Ogden; but, after several changes in location and titles, in 1982 it became the Ogden-Weber Area Vocational Center and took up its present location at 200 North Washington Boulevard, the location of the old state reform school. Under the guidance of Superintendent C. Brent Wallis, the campus grew to ninety acres. The center graduates over 1,000 students a year, and it has been a major asset in providing a trained workforce for the county and region.[88] Other career-oriented schools in Weber County include branches of Stevens Henager College of Business and the University of Phoenix.

## *Weber County Looks to the Future*

Looking back at the past, Weber County reveals both continuity and change. In many ways, the natural features of the county—rivers, mountains, and the lake—have remained the same. The land surface has changed somewhat, as humans have moved about on the land and have settled it over the past centuries. Settlers have enjoyed successes and failures and have learned to work together for the common good. Weber County and its residents face a variety of problems as they move into the twenty-first century, including those related to the environment, growth, the economy, and ethnic diversity. The county has a solid record of achievements and cooperation on which to build for the future.

## ENDNOTES

1. Bernard DeVoto, "Ogden: The Underwriters of Salvation," in Duncan Aikman, *The Taming of the Frontier* (Freeport, NY: Books for Libraries Press, 1967).

2. Lyle J. Barnes, "Ogden's Notorious 'Two-Bit Street,' 1870–1954," M.A. thesis, Utah State University, 1969, 25–32, 66–67, 71–73; Ira Huggins, interview, at Ogden, Utah, 14 July 1980 with Patricia A. Buchanan, transcript in possession of the authors; Dyana Ruth Thatcher, "A Brief History of Organized Crime in Ogden, Utah," paper, Weber State College, 1975, 3–4, copy in authors' possession.

3. Barnes, "Ogden's Notorious 'Two-Bit Street,'" 58–59; W. Rulon White, interview, at Ogden, Utah, 9 April 1975 with Beverly Caton, transcript in possession of the authors; Thatcher, "A Brief History of Organized Crime," 4–5.

4. Barnes, "Ogden's Notorious 'Two-Bit Street,'" 55–56.

5. Ibid., 72–73.

6. *Ogden Standard-Examiner,* 10 April 1923, 1; 13 April 1923, 1; 26 April 1923, 1; 8 May 1923, 1; 10 May 1923, 1; 12 May 1923, 1; 24 July 1923, 3; 14 August 1923, 12; 7 November 1923, 10; 19 November 1923, 6; 23 November 1923, 6; 8 December 1923, 2.

7. *Salt Lake Tribune,* 1 July 1936, 1; *Ogden Standard-Examiner,* 30 June 1936, 1; 1 July 1936, 1; 2 July 1936; 4 July 1936, 1; 15 October 1936, 1; 16 October 1936, 1; 22 October 1936, 1; 9 November 1936, 2; 22 November 1936, A-7; 23 June 1942, 1B; 25 June 1942.

8. LaMar C. Kap, "File on John Kap, Sr.," office of LaMar C. Kap, Weber State University; *Ogden Standard-Examiner,* 20, 27, 28 May 1936; 2 June 1936; 7, 8, 10, 11 July 1936.

9. *Ogden Standard-Examiner,* 24 July 1943, 1; 16 August 1987, 4A.

10. Ibid., 16 August 1987, 4A.

11. Ibid., 1 January 1945, 1A; 2 January1945, 1–2B; Richard C. Roberts, "How Trains Helped Win a War," *Beehive History* 8 (1992): 4–5; Howard Wade, interview, Ogden, Utah, 29 May 1996.

12. *Ogden Standard-Examiner,* 15, 16, 17 October 1963.

13. Ibid., 10, 11, ,17, 18, 19, 20 24, 25, 28, 29 August 1987, and 5 September 1987.

14. See ibid., 5, 8, 30 June 1994, 2 November 1994, 1A; 14 December 1994, 1A; 3 February 1995, 1B; 24 December 1995, 1B; 18 March 1996, 1A; 21 April 1996, 1A; 26 April 1996, 1A.

15. Ibid., 9 July1993, 1A; 23 February 1994, 2B; 11 September 1994, 1B.

16. Ibid., 2 June 1992, C4; 27 March 1996, B1.

17. Ibid., 4 October 1994, 1A; 13 January 1995, 1A; Craig Dearden, interview, 3 October 1996, Ogden, Utah, with Richard Roberts, tape in possession of the authors.

18. Dearden, interview.

19. Ogden City Planning Department, "Ogden City Subdivisions," map, shows the location of each subdivision and date of subdivision approval; W. Allen Jackson, interview, Ogden, Utah, 19 April 1996, tape in possession of the authors; Roscoe Hunter, interview, Ogden, Utah, 2 March 1996, transcript in possession of the authors; Glade B. Nielsen, interview, Roy, Utah, 11 June 1996, transcript in possession of the authors.

20. Allen Roberts, "Historical Periods: Ogden City, Utah"; Weber County Heritage Foundation, "Annual House Tour: A Heritage of Styles Pamphlet"; Craig M. Call, "Ogden Historic Buildings Survey, March 1977, copy in possession of the authors.

21. Weber County Heritage Foundation, "Heritage House Tour," 26 May 1990; Weber County Heritage Foundation, "Calendar 1993, Marilyn Drive," with pictures of the work of S. Arthur Shreeve.

22. Teddy Fullmer, "Leslie Simmons Hodgson: Architect of Ogden," copy in possession of the authors; John L. Piers, "A Biographical Sketch of Eber F. Piers," Nebeker-Moore Collection, Weber State University Library; "Dedication of St. Benedict's Hospital, Ogden, Utah, 18 September 1946," pamphlet in possession of the authors.

23. Keith Wilcox, interview, 1 November 1996, Ogden, Utah, with Richard Roberts, tape in possession of the authors; Keith W. Wilcox, *An Architect and His Buildings* (n.p., n.d.).

24. Brett Richards, interview, 1 November 1996, Ogden, Utah, with Richard Roberts, tape in possession of the authors.

25. Alfred E. Stratford, "History of the Ogden Tabernacle Choir," 1969, Weber County Library; Marlin Ray Sorensen, "The Tabernacle Choir, Its History and Contributions to the Cultural History of Utah," thesis abstract, Brigham Young University, 1961, 1–7.

26. William Terry, *Weber County is Worth Knowing,* 246–47; Richard W. Sadler, ed., *Weber State College: A Centennial History* (Salt Lake City: Publishers Press, 1988), 24, 32, 44, 52, 356; Leo Walker, *The Wonderful Era of the Great Dance Bands* (Garden City, N.Y.: Doubleday, 1972), 19–27, 43, 69, 144, 160–61, 209, 228–33; *Standard-Examiner,* 28 April 1995, 8D.

27. Gordon T. Allred, "A Center of Cultural Excellence," in Sadler, *Weber State College: A Centennial History,* 187–88.

28. Ibid., 188–89; Souvenir Program, "All Faces West," July 1959, copy in possession of the authors; *Standard-Examiner,* 3 April 1996, 13A.

29. Fred J. Holton, *Mathew William Dalton, 1829–1918, a Biography* (Brigham City, Utah: 1917), 36–38.

30. *Standard-Examiner,* 21 March 1996, 1D; Spencer and Kathleen Klomp, interview, Ogden, Utah, 27 October 1995, with Richard C. Roberts, notes in possession of the authors.

31. Janice Dawson, "Chautauqua and the Utah Performing Arts," paper in possession of the authors; Terry, *Weber County is Worth Knowing,* 306–7.

32. Allred, "A Center of Cultural Excellence," 180–82; Terry, *Weber County is Worth Knowing,* 231–54; Elizabeth Tillotson, *A History of Ogden* (Ogden: J.O. Woody Printing Company, 1962), 108–11.

33. Vern G. Swanson, R. S. Olpin, and W. C. Seifrit, *Utah Art* (Layton, Utah: Gibbs Smith, 1991), 231–37.

34. *Standard-Examiner,* 11 July 1982, 16B; Terry, *Weber County is Worth Knowing,* 248–49.

35. "Welcome Home to Moroni Olsen," brochure in possession of the authors; "Robert Walker," in Ephraim Katz, *The Film Encyclopedia* (New York: Thomas Y. Crowell, 1970), 1203; Ann W. Engar, "Theater in Utah," in Kent Powell, ed., *Utah History Encyclopedia* (Salt Lake City: University of Utah Press, 1994), 553; Morgan, *Utah: A Guide to the State* (New York: Hastings House, 1945), 207.

36. Works on Bernard DeVoto are numerous, but for further reference see Catherine Bowen, Edith Mirrielees, Arthur M. Schlesinger, Jr., and Wallace Stegner, *Four Portraits and One Subject: Bernard DeVoto* (Boston: Houghton Mifflin, 1963); Wallace Stegner, *The Uneasy Chair* (Garden City, NY: Doubleday, 1974).

37. See Newell Bringhurst, "Fawn M. Brodie: Her Biographies as Autobiography," *Pacific Historical Review* 59 (May 1990): 203–29; Newell Bringhurst, ed., *Reconsidering No Man Knows My History, Fawn M. Brodie and Joseph Smith in Retrospect* (Logan: Utah State University Press, 1996).

38. Morgan, *Utah: A Guide to the State,* 207; Arthur Guy Empey, *Over the Top: By An American Soldier Who Went* (New York: G.P. Putnams Sons, 1917).

39. Tillotson, *A History of Ogden,* 41–45.

40. *Salt Lake Tribune,* 2 November 1995; Linda Thatcher, "Radio in Utah," in *Beehive History* 10: 21–27; Sadler, *Weber State College: A Centennial History,* 92; Tim Larson and Robert K. Avery, "Utah Broadcasting History," in Powell, *Utah History Encyclopedia,* 55–58; John Webb, interview, Ogden, Utah, 19 May 1996; Archibald Webb, unpublished autobiography in possession of the authors.

41. George B. Felt, *A Century of Utah High School Football* (Salt Lake City: Utah Sports Publications, Inc, 1993).

42. Sadler, *Weber State College,* 248–52.

43. Arnold Ferrin, interview, Salt Lake City, Utah, 20 May 1996, with Richard Roberts, notes in possession of the authors; Jim Ison, *Mormons in the Major Leagues* (Cincinnati: Action Sports, 1991), 170–75.

44. Terry, *Weber County is Worth Knowing,* 350–51.

45. "Highlights of Al Warden's Career," unpublished papers in possession of Mrs. Al Warden of Ogden; *Ogden Standard-Examiner,* 20 January 1930, 8.

46. "Highlights of Al Warden's Career"; Roberts and Sadler, *Ogden: Junction City,* 171.

47. Manuscript A1178, Utah State Historical Society.

48. *Ogden Standard-Examiner,* 31 August 1930.

49. Charles (Chick) Hislop, interview, 13 November 1996, Ogden, Utah, with Richard Roberts, notes in possession of the authors.

50. Archie Skeen, interview, 7 November 1996, Plain City, Utah, with Richard Roberts, tape in possession of the authors.

51. "Activities of Women in Weber County," unpublished manuscript located in Weber County Library; Lynn Miller, "A History of the First Presbyterian Church in Ogden, Utah," unpublished manuscript in possession of the authors; Henry Martin Merkel, *History of Methodism in Utah* (Colorado Springs: The Dentan Printing Co., 1938), 173–76; Ronnie L. Stellhorn, "A History of the Lutheran Church in Utah," M.A. thesis, Utah State University, 1975, 24–25.

52. "Activities of Women in Weber County"; *Junior League of Ogden Yearbook—1984,* copy in possession of the authors.

53. *Polk's Ogden (Weber County, Utah) City Directory* (Omaha: R. L. Polk and Co.), for the years 1920, 1930, 1940 and 1951.

54. Mary "Polly" Harrington, interview, 4 November 1996, Ogden, Utah, with Richard Roberts, tape in possession of the authors.

55. "1995 Annual Report of the YCC."

56. *Deseret News: 1991–1992 Church Almanac* (Salt Lake City: Deseret News, 1991), 176–222, 39, 55; Tillotson, *A History of Ogden,* 114–15.

57. Tillotson, *A History of Ogden,* 118–19.

58. Miller, "A History of the First Presbyterian Church," chap. 3; Stellhorn, *A History of the Lutheran Church in Utah,* 27–30, 100–3; Henry Martin Merkel, "History of Methodism in Utah," 176; "The First Century of the Methodist Church in Utah," article found in the Weber County Library with library number S 287 F527, 23–25.

59. Thomas G. Alexander, *Utah: The Right Place* (Salt Lake City: Gibbs Smith, 1995), 137.

60. Ibid., 120, 137, 145, 246–48, 381–83, 449–50.

61. *Standard-Examiner,* 24 July 1987, 1C; 15 January 1996, 1B.

62. Mae Parry, interview, 7 October 1996, Clearfield, Utah, with Richard Roberts, notes in possession of the authors.

63. *Standard-Examiner,* 17 February 1985, 1F.

64. Ibid.

65. Eric Stene, "The African American Community of Ogden, Utah: 1910–1950," M.A. thesis, Utah State University, 1994, 8–9, 42, 44–45.

66. Ibid., 8, 59.

67. Ibid., 14–17.

68. Ibid., 17–18; *Standard-Examiner,* 1 September 1995, 1A.

69. Stene, "The African American Community," 18–20; *Ogden Standard-Examiner,* 22 August 1982, 16C.

70. Ibid.

71. Tillotson, *A History of Ogden,* 16.

72. Stene, "The African American Community," 47–59.

73. Charles Orval Stott, *This is Washington Terrace* (n.p., 1958), 19.

74. Stene, "The African American Community," 22–25.

75. Ibid., 12–13, 25–29; Sadler, *Weber State Colleg,* 250–51.

76. Helen Z. Papanikolas and Alice Kasai, "Japanese Life in Utah," in Helen Z. Papanikolas, ed., *The Peoples of Utah* (Salt Lake City: Utah State Historical Society, 1976), 339.

77. Mildred Miya, interview, 5 December 1996, Ogden, Utah, with Richard Roberts, notes in possession of the authors; Mildred Miya, "G. J. (Jimmy) Miya, the First Japanese in Roy," in Emma Russell, *Footprints of Roy: 1873–1979* (Roy, Utah: Emma Russell Publisher, 1979), 139–40.

78. Dan Favero, interview, 10 November 1996, Ogden, Utah, with Richard Roberts, notes in possession of the authors.

79. Cleon Battisti, interview, 11 November 1996, Ogden, Utah, with Richard Roberts, notes in possession of the authors; Gene Miconi, interview, 11 November 1996, Ogden, Utah, with Richard Roberts, notes in possession of the authors.

80. Dominic Ligori, interview, 7 November 1996, Ogden, Utah, with Richard Roberts, notes in possession of the authors.

81. Mary Kagiannis, interview, 10 November 1996, Ogden, Utah, with Richard Roberts; Nick Thiros, interview, 10 November 1996, Ogden, Utah, with Richard Roberts; Veda Nass, interview, 11 November 1996, Ogden, Utah, with Richard Roberts, notes in possession of the authors; *Standard-Examiner,* 14 October 1984, 1C.

82. Jack Goodman, "Jews in Zion," in Papanikolas, *The Peoples of Utah,* 201.

83. Ralph Benowitz, "Congregation Brith Sholem History Project," copy in possession of the authors.

84. Vincente V. Mayer, "After Escalante: The Spanish-speaking People of Utah," in Papanikolas, *The Peoples of Utah,* 440–44, 447.

85. Gloria Perez-Jensen, interview, 7 November 1996, Ogden, Utah, with Richard Roberts, notes in possession of the authors.

86. Jane Chugg Simmons Stevenson, interview, 14 November 1996, Ogden, Utah, with Richard Roberts, notes in possession of the authors.

87. *Standard-Examiner,* 12 November 1996, 1B. The servicemen of Weber County killed in the Vietnam War were: Lilo Elmer Aldous, Lawrence F. Bond, Larry L. Brown, Dewey F. Butcher, John M Christensen, Leland S. Crowley, Jr., Robert E. Crowley, David P. Dunyon, Jack C. Everts, Richard M. Facer, Franklin J. Hiner, Robert K. Horspool, Lynn E. Hunter, Ronald L. Johnson, Verne DeWitt Johnson II, Val L. Lafon, Paul D. Myers, Boyd K. Newbold, Frederick Pinsonault, Darrel L. Price, Jim M. Rhead, Val C. Robinson, Serge B. Simmons, Blair H. Simpson, Gerald A. Smith, Mark S. Steiner, Lenny M. Tippets, Joseph G. Vogrinec, Brent F. Ward, Randolph B. Ward, Robin K. Wetzler, Gregary A. Wilks.

88. *Standard-Examiner,* 5 May 1985, supplement; *Standard-Examiner,* 28 July 28 1995.

*Appendix*

# Roster of Weber County Officers

### *Elected Magistrate of Weber River Precinct*

| | |
|---|---|
| 1849 | James Brown |

### *Chief Justice, Weber County Court*

| | |
|---|---|
| 1851 | Isaac Clark |

### *Associate Justices*

| | |
|---|---|
| 1851 | Erastus Bingham |
| | Daniel Birch |

### *Probate Judges*

| | |
|---|---|
| 1854–1857 | Jonathan Browning |
| 1857–1858 | Chauncey W. West |
| 1859–1860 | Aaron F. Farr |
| 1861–1863 | Francis A. Brown |
| 1864–1869 | Aaron F. Farr |
| 1869–1882 | Franklin D. Richards |
| 1883–1889 | Lewis W. Shurtliff |
| 1889–1894 | A. C. Bishop |
| 1894–1896 | Archilles Perrin |

### *Selectmen*

| | |
|---|---|
| 1852–1855 | Erastus Bingham |
| | Lewis Hardy |
| | Jonathan S. Wells |
| 1856–1860 | Abraham Palmer |
| | Erastus Bingham |
| | Ira N. Spaulding |
| 1860–1862 | Ira N. Spaulding |
| | Levi Wheeler |
| | Abraham Palmer |
| 1862 | Abraham Palmer |
| | Levi Wheeler |
| | James McGraw |

| | |
|---|---|
| 1862–1864 | Levi Wheeler |
| | Lester J. Herrick |
| | Richard Ballantyne |
| 1864–1866 | Levi Wheeler |
| | Lester Herrick |
| | John Spiers |
| 1866–1867 | John Spiers |
| | Lester J. Herrick |
| | Richard Ballantyne |
| 1867–1873 | Richard Ballantyne |
| | Lester J. Herrick |
| | Henry Holmes |
| 1873 | Gilbert Belnap |
| 1873–1874 | Gilbert Belnap |
| | Aaron F. Farr |
| 1874–1876 | Richard Ballantyne |
| | Gilbert Belnap |
| | Lester J. Herrick |
| 1876–1882 | P. G. Taylor |
| | Francis A. Hammond |
| | Lester J. Herrick |
| 1882–1883 | F. A. Hammon |
| | S. W. Shurtliff |
| | Thomas Wallace |
| 1883–1884 | Robert McQuarrie |
| | Ammon Green |
| | George Halls |
| 1885–1886 | Robert McQuarrie |
| | Ammon Green |
| | Thomas Wallace |
| 1886–1888 | Joseph Stanford |
| | Ammon Green |
| | Thomas Wallace |
| 1888–1889 | Thomas Wallace |
| | Joseph Stanford |
| | W. W. Child |
| 1889–1890 | W. W. Child |
| | Lewis W. Shurtliff |
| | John Pincock |
| 1890–1891 | John Pincock |
| | Lewis W. Shurtliff |
| | Frederick Foy |
| 1891–1892 | Lewis W. Shurtliff |
| | Frederick Foy |
| | R. W. Cross |
| 1893–1894 | O. J. Swanson |
| | J. C. Wangsgard |
| | E. W. Wade |
| 1895–1896 | W. G. Wilson |
| | J. C. Child |
| | E. W. Wade |

### *County Commissioners*

| | |
|---|---|
| 1896 | J. C. Child |
| | William G. Wilson |
| | Edward W. Wade |
| 1897–1898 | J. C. Armstrong |
| | L. B. Hammon |
| | John Seaman |
| 1899–1900 | Louis B. Adams |
| | William G. Smith |
| | Lyman Skeen |
| 1901–1902 | Lyman Skeen |
| | Joseph Stanford |
| | William G. Wilson |
| 1903–1905 | William G. Wilson |
| | Joseph Stanford |
| | Oscar B. Madsen |
| 1905–1906 | William G. Wilson |
| | Joseph Stanford |
| | Oscar B. Madsen |

| | |
|---|---|
| 1906–1908 | David McKay |
| | Oscar B. Madsen |
| | Frank Moore |
| 1909–1910 | Oscar B. Madsen |
| | Frank Moore |
| | John T. Bybee |
| 1911–1912 | Oscar B. Madsen |
| | Frank Moore |
| | John T. Bybee |
| 1913–1914 | William C. Hunter |
| | John T. Bybee |
| | Moroni Skeen |
| 1915–1916 | William C. Hunter |
| | Moroni Skeen |
| | Warren C. Child |
| 1917–1918 | Martin P. Brown |
| | D. H. Ensign |
| | Moroni Skeen |
| 1919–1920 | J. M. Child |
| | D. H. Ensign |
| | Martin P. Brown |
| 1921–1922 | Moroni Skeen |
| | E. S. Green |
| | J. M. Child |
| 1923–1924 | J. M. Child |
| | Moroni Skeen |
| | C. G. Pettegrew |
| 1925–1926 | J. M. Child |
| | C. G. Pettegrew |
| | F. W. Stratford |
| 1926–1928 | H. P. Randall |
| | A. M. Hammon |
| | F. W. Stratford |
| 1929–1930 | R. A. Norris |
| | H. P. Randall |
| | G. W. Stratford |
| 1931–1932 | F. W. Stratford |
| | H. P. Randall |
| | W. R. McEntire |
| 1932 | F. W. Stratford |
| | W. R. McEntire |
| | Charles Woods |
| 1933–1934 | Charles Halverson |
| | William R. McEntire |
| | F. W. Stratford |
| 1934 | Charles Halverson |
| | William R. McEntire |
| | George E. Stratford |
| 1934–1938 | William R. McEntire |
| | Charles Halverson |
| | George F. Simmons |
| 1939–1940 | George F. Simmons |
| | W. R. McEntire |
| | John W. Arrington |
| 1943–1946 | George F. Simmons |
| 1946–1956 | Lyman M. Hess |
| 1947–1948 | Charles Halverson |
| 1947–1964 | Arthur P. Brown |
| 1949–1966 | Elmer Carver |
| 1957–1962 | George T. Frost |
| 1963–1964 | Jen Patterson |
| 1965–1966 | Bud Favero |
| 1965–1963 | Maurice Richards |
| 1967–1970 | Albert Bott |
| 1967–1972 | William Moyes |
| 1969–1970 | Boyd K. Storey |
| 1971–1972 | Charles Storey |
| 1971–1972 | George T. Frost |
| 1973–1978 | Keith G. Jensen |
| 1973–1976 | Boyd K. Storey |
| 1973–1976 | Monte Bailey |
| 1977–1980 | Douglas I. Hunt |
| 1977–1978 | Ronald C. Sessions |

| | |
|---|---|
| 1979–1984 | Boyd K. Storey |
| 1979–1980 | Robert W. Bowen |
| 1981–1989 | Robert A. Hunter |
| 1981–1982 | Franklin Maughan |
| 1983–1986 | Roger F. Rawson |
| 1984–1990 | William A. Bailey |
| 1987–1992 | Lowell S. Peterson |
| 1989–1990 | A. Stephen Dirks |
| 1991–1995 | Joan Hellstrom |
| 1991–1995 | Randall Williford |
| 1992–1996 | Spencer F. Stokes |
| 1995– | Joe Ritchie |
| 1995– | Bruce Anderson |
| 1996– | Glen Burton |

### *Mayors of Ogden*

| | |
|---|---|
| 1851–1870 | Lorin Farr |
| 1871–1876 | Lester J. Herrick |
| 1877–1878 | Lorin Farr |
| 1879–1882 | Lester J. Herrick |
| 1883–1886 | David Harold Peery |
| 1887–1888 | David Eccles |
| 1889–1890 | Fred J. Kiesel |
| 1891–1892 | William H. Turner |
| 1893–1893 | Robert C. Lundy |
| 1896–1897 | Hiram H. Spencer |
| 1898–1899 | John A. Boyle |
| 1900–1901 | Matthew S. Browning |
| 1902–1905 | William Glasmann |
| 1906–1907 | Dr. E. Conroy |
| 1908–1909 | A. L. Brewer |
| 1910–1911 | William Glasmann |
| 1912–1915 | A. G. Fell |
| 1916–1917 | Abbot Rodney Heywood |
| 1918–1919 | Thomas S. Browning |
| 1920–1923 | Frank Francis |
| 1924–1925 | P. F. Kirkendall |
| 1926–1927 | George F. Browning |
| 1928–1929 | Frank Francis |
| 1930–1933 | Ora Bundy |
| 1934–1939 | Harman W. Peery |
| 1940–1941 | Fred M. Abbot |
| 1942–1943 | Harman W. Peery |
| 1944 | Kent S. Bramwell |
| 1944–1947 | David S. Romney |
| 1948–1949 | Harman W. Peery |
| 1950–1951 | W. Rulon White |
| 1952–1953 | George T. Frost |
| 1954–1959 | Raymon W. Wright |
| 1960–1961 | LeRoy B. Young |
| 1962–1965 | Dr. Merle E. Allen |
| 1966–1973 | Dr. Bart Wolthius |
| 1973–1983 | A. Stephen Dirks |
| 1983–1987 | Robert A. Madsen |
| 1987–1989 | L. Clifford Goff |
| 1989–1991 | Scott Sneddon |
| 1992– | Glenn J. Meacham |

# *Selected Bibliography*

Alexander, Thomas G. *Utah: The Right Place.* Salt Lake City: Gibbs Smith, 1995.

Arrington, Leonard J., and Thomas G. Alexander. *A Dependent Commonwealth: Utah's Economy from Statehood to the Great Depression.* Provo: Brigham Young University Press, 1974.

———. "Supply Hub of the West: Defense Depot Ogden, 1941–1964." *Utah State Historical Quarterly* 32 (Spring 1964): 99–121.

Arrington, Leonard J., and Anthony T. Cluff. *Federally-Financed Industrial Plants Constructed in Utah During World War II.* Logan: Utah State University Press, 1969.

Athearn, Robert G. *Union Pacific Country.* Lincoln: University of Nebraska Press, 1982.

Barker, Elwood I. "Pioneer Forts in Ogden, Utah: 1848–55, Brown's, Farr's, Bingham's, Mound Fort." Folder at Weber County Library, Ogden, Utah.

Barnes, Lyle J. "Ogden's Notorious 'Two-Bit' Street." M.A. thesis, Utah State University, 1969.

Blaylock, John Q. "History of North Ogden: An Economic and Social Study." M.A. thesis, University of Utah, 1922.

Bluth, John V., and Charles F. Middleton. "Early History and Reminiscences of Ogden City and Weber County." *Development and Houseeker's Souvenir, The Morning Examiner* (Ogden, Utah) 8 (April 1911).

Brodie, Fawn M. "Inflation Idyl: A Family Farm In Huntsville." *Utah Historical Quarterly* 40 (Spring 1972): 112–21.

Cannon, Connie Duncan. "Jane Snyder Richards: The Blue-White Diamond." In Vicky Burgess-Olson, ed., *Sister Saints.* Provo: Brigham Young University Press, 1978.

Cline, Gloria Griffen. *Peter Skene Ogden and the Hudson's Bay Company.* Norman: University of Oklahoma Press, 1974.

Doxey, Clifford B. "The History of the Ogden City Public Schools." M. A. thesis, University of Utah, 1944.

Farr, John. *My Yesterdays.* Salt Lake City: Granite Publishing Company, 1957.

Fawcett, William B., and Steven R. Simms. *Archaeological Test Excavations in the Great Salt Lake Wetlands and Associated Analyses, Weber and Box Elder Counties, Utah.* Utah State University Contributions to Anthropology, Number 14, 1993.

Frémont, John C. *The Exploring Expedition to the Rocky Mountains.* Reprint. Washington: Smithsonian Institution Press, 1988.

Gerlach, Larry R. "Ogden's Horrible Tragedy: The Lynching of George Segal." *Utah Historical Quarterly* 49 (Spring 1981): 157–72.

Glenn, Cora Lou. *Ogden Industrial Development Corporation: Projects, Partnerships, and Progress.* Ogden: Weber State University Continuing Education and Community Services, 1992.

Greer, Deon, ed. *Atlas of Utah.* Provo: Brigham Young University Press, 1981.

Griffiths, David B. "Far Western Populism: The Case of Utah, 1893–1900." *Utah Historical Quarterly* 37 (Fall 1969): 396–407.

Hipwell, Arvil C., and Ida Mae Deem Hipwell, comps. *The Big Bend of the Weber River: History of West Weber, 1859–1976.* Ogden: Empire Printing Co., 1976.

Historical Records Survey. *Preliminary Inventory of the County Archives of Utah, No. 29, Weber County.* Ogden: Works Progress Administration, 1939.

*The History of Medicine in Weber County from 1852 to 1980.* Compiled by Mrs. Louis R. Snider et al. Ogden: Weber County Medical Society, 1983.

Holton, Fred J. *Mathew William Dalton, 1829–1918: A Biography.* Brigham City, Utah: n.p., 1917.

Hunter, Milton R., ed. *Beneath Ben Lomond's Peak.* Salt Lake City: Publishers Press, 1966.

Jenkins, Ronald W. "A History of the Grand Opera House and Ogden's Golden Age of Theatre, 1890–1909." M.A. thesis., Utah State University, 1965.

Jones, Gordon Q. *Pioneer Forts in Ogden, Utah.* Ogden: Gordon Jones, 1996.

Kelly, Charles, and Maurice L. Howe. *Miles Goodyear, First Citizen of Utah.* Salt Lake City: Western Printing Company, 1937.

Knighton, James Barker, Lisa Knighton Delap, and J. Malan Heslop. *Malan Book of Remembrance; John Daniel Malan.* N.p., 1992.

Kotter, Richard E. "An Examination of Mormon and Non-Mormon Influences in Ogden City Politics, 1847–1896." M. A. thesis, Utah State University, 1967.

Launius, Roger D. "Crossroads of the West: Aviation Comes to Utah, 1910–1940." *Utah Historical Quarterly* 58 (Spring 1990): 108–30.

Lewis, David Rich, "La Plata, 1891–1893, Boom, Bust, and Controversy." *Utah Historical Quarterly* 50 (Spring 1990):4–21.

Madsen, Brigham D. *Corinne, The Gentile Capital of Utah.* Salt Lake City: Utah State Historical Society, 1980.

———. "The Northwestern Shoshoni in Cache Valley." In Douglas D. Alder, ed. *Cache Valley, Essays on Her Past and People.* Logan: Utah State University, 1976.

———. *The Shoshoni Frontier and the Bear River Massacre.* Salt Lake City: University of Utah Press, 1985.

Madsen, Brigham D., ed. *Exploring the Great Salt Lake, The Stansbury Expedition of 1849–1850.* Salt Lake City: University of Utah, 1989.

Middleton, Henry J. "The Life of Charles Franklin Middleton, a Man and his Times." M.A. thesis, Utah State University, 1965.

Miller, David E., ed. "A Great Adventure on Great Salt Lake—A True Story by Kate Y. Noble." *Utah Historical Quarterly* 33 (Summer 1965): 218–36.

Morgan, Dale L. *The Great Salt Lake.* New York: Bobbs-Merrill Co., 1947.

———. "Miles Goodyear and the Founding of Ogden." *Utah Historical Quarterly* 21 (1953): 195–218, 307–29.

———. *The State of Deseret.* Salt Lake City: Utah State Historical Society, 1940.

Morgan, Dale L., ed. *A History of Ogden.* Ogden: Ogden City Commission, 1940.

Newey, LaVerna Burnett. *Remember My Valley, A History of Ogden Canyon, Eden, Liberty, and Huntsville.* Salt Lake City: Hawkes Publishing Co., 1977.

Oaks, Harold R. "An Evaluation of the Beginnings, Purposes, and Influence of Drama in Ogden from 1840 to 1900." M.A. thesis, Brigham Young University, 1962.

Pardoe, T. Earl. *Lorin Farr, Pioneer.* Provo: Brigham Young University Press, 1953.

Pawar, Sheelwant Bapurao. "An Environmental Study of the Development of the Utah Labor Movement." Ph.D. diss., University of Utah, 1968.

Poulsen, Ezra J. *Happy Day, Life and Times of Edward I. Rich M.D., 1868–1969.* Salt Lake City: Utah Printing Company, 1970.

Roberts, Richard C. "The Utah National Guard in the Great War, 1917–1918." *Utah Historical Quarterly* 58 (Fall 1990): 312–33.

Roberts, Richard C., and Richard W. Sadler. *The History of the Weber County Watershed Protective Cooporation.* Ogden: Weber County Watershed Protection Association, 1989

———. *Ogden, Junction City.* Northridge, CA:Windsor Press, 1985.

Russell, Emma. *Footprints of Roy: 1873–1979.* Roy, UT: Emma Russell, 1979.

Sadler, Richard W. "Fair Ogden and Its Early Settlement." *Encyclia* 59 (1982): 4–20.

———. *Weber State College, A Centennial History.* Salt Lake City: Publishers Press, 1988.

Sadler, Richard W., and Richard C. Roberts. *The Weber River Basin: Grass Roots Democracy and Water Development.* Logan: Utah State University Press, 1994.

Sawatzki, Bob, ed. *The Word From Weber County: A Centennial Anthology of Our Best Writers.* Salt Lake City: Publishers Press, 1966.

Shurtleff, Luman Andros. *Luman Andros Shurtleff, His Personal History, 1807–1884.* Salt Lake City: Litho grafics Inc., n.d.

Simms, Steven R., with Mark E. Stuart, Sheila Beckstead, Eva Jensen and Suzanne Sarver. *Archaeological Reconnaissance in the Lower Bear River Marshes, Utah.* Utah State University Contributions to Anthropology, Number 13, 1991.

Taft, Mack S. "The Great Depression in Weber County, Utah." M.A. thesis, Utah State University, 1973.

Terry, William W. *Weber County is Worth Knowing.* Ogden: Weber County School District, 1987.

Venable, Wayne L. "Miles Goodyear." M.A. thesis, University of Utah, 1966.

White, Jean Bickmore. "The Right to be Different: Ogden and Weber County Politics, 1850–1924." *Utah Historical Quarterly* 47 (Summer 1979): 254–72.

Woodfield, Floyd, and Clara Woodfield, comps. *A History of North Ogden: Beginnings to 1985.* Ogden: Empire Printing, 1986.

# *Index*